RESTORATION DRAMA
Modern Essays in Criticism

Restoration D*rama*

MODERN ESSAYS IN CRITICISM

EDITED BY
JOHN LOFTIS

76036

A GALAXY BOOK

New York   OXFORD UNIVERSITY PRESS   1966

Contents

v

Introduction

If we may consider Dryden as the founder of English criticism, as "the writer who first taught us to determine upon principles the merit of composition," in Dr. Johnson's words, then we may conclude that Restoration drama produced the first important body of English criticism. For Dryden's earliest essay and most of his best essays are taken up with problems raised by that drama. *An Essay of Dramatic Poesy* was, Johnson said, "the first regular and valuable treatise on the art of writing." If not altogether fair to writers of the Renaissance, notably Sidney, Johnson's appraisal of the significance of that essay and of Dryden's subsequent criticism is broadly justifiable; and it conveys an impression of the importance of Restoration drama in shaping English criticism. Since Dryden's time criticism has represented a major branch of literature, and criticism of the drama has attracted its full share of talent.

During the later seventeenth and early eighteenth centuries, the drama indeed attracted rather more than its share of critical talent. The essays of Shadwell, Rymer, Dennis, Addison, Steele, Jeremy Collier, and the many writers, of all shades of opinion and ability, who joined in the prolonged review of the significance of Restoration drama that goes by the name of the Collier controversy, reveal a searching examination of first principles: of, in the phrase of John Dennis, "the usefulness of the stage." Enlightened and intelligent men, as well as zealots, expressed doubts about the usefulness of *The Country Wife, The Man of Mode,* and *Love for Love* as sources of insight into human relationships. If religious bigotry misled Collier into a pedantic literalness in his identification of immorality and profaneness, he saw clearly enough the reasons for the vulnerability of Restoration comedy to hostile criticism. The dramatists who answered him, however shrill, saw the import of his charges; and they wrote their rebuttals in his terms, not denying the relevance or gravity of his accusations but rather insisting that he had misinterpreted the plays, which were, they maintained, fundamentally responsible, if comic and satirical, reports on human behavior.

The issues raised in the Collier controversy are perennial in the criticism of Restoration comedy. Collier himself, prolix and pedantic as he is, has been little read in the last century, but his arguments appear in the writings of later critics, and in none more forcefully than in those of Macaulay, who early in Queen Victoria's reign used a review of an edition of the Restoration dramatists by Leigh Hunt as an occasion for a spirited indictment of them. Here is the source of many modern judgments on Restoration dramatic and theatrical history, in Macaulay's erudite and persuasive account of the dramatists and the times that produced them. In Macaulay's essay we encounter opinions that subsequently have become commonplaces of literary history. He may be too severe in his criticism, Macaulay acknowledges.

> And yet it is not easy to be too severe. For in truth this part of our literature is a disgrace to our language and our national character. It is clever, indeed, and very entertaining; but it is, in the most emphatic sense of the words, "earthly, sensual, devilish." Its indecency, though perpetually such as is condemned, not less by the rules of good taste than by those of morality, is not, in our opinion, so disgraceful a fault as its singularly inhuman spirit.

His most forceful objection is identical with Collier's: that the dramatists endow immoral and profane characters with wit and charm. "But morality is deeply interested in this—that what is immoral shall not be represented to the imagination of the young and susceptible in constant connection with what is attractive."

Macaulay objected, as he had reason to object, to a famous defense of Restoration comedy which had appeared a generation earlier: that by Charles Lamb in his essay "On the Artificial Comedy of the Last Century." Lamb had attempted to rationalize his fondness for it by denying the relevance of moral standards to it. In the "Utopia of gallantry" represented by Restoration comedy, he argued, the morality of everyday life has no place. The world of the comedy is a self-contained fantasy world with standards of its own, to be accepted on its terms and not on ours. An attractive argument, we may conclude, but an unsatisfactory defense, for it surrenders too much, surrenders indeed the claim of the comedy to be taken seriously as a commentary on human affairs, something the dramatists themselves never would have done. With Macaulay, "we must plainly say that his argument, though ingenious, is altogether sophistical." And yet echoes of it can occasionally be heard in modern criticism, in the determined aestheticism of those who would deny the relevance of moral criteria in the criticism of Restoration comedy. Lamb can in fact be seen as an exponent of a classic and recurrent attitude toward the comedy, just as Macaulay—or Collier—can be seen as an exponent of another.

The case against Restoration comedy has been most persuasively stated in our own time by L. C. Knights. It may not be unfair or misleading to suggest an analogy between his position in modern criticism and Collier's in that of the late seventeenth and early eighteenth centuries. In prose style, controversial method, and literary perceptiveness they are as far removed from one another as they are chronologically. Yet they are alike in formulating clearly and effectively arguments denying the "significance" of Restoration comedy; and they are alike as important for the replies they evoke as for the criticism they articulate. To Knights the central fault of the comedy is not so much moral as intellectual: "it has no significant relation with the best thought of the time." And hence "The criticism that defenders of Restoration comedy need to answer is not that the comedies are 'immoral,' but that they are trivial, gross and dull." It was difficult in Addison and Steele's time to write about Restoration comedy without taking Collier's charges of immorality into account; it has been difficult in the mid-twentieth century to write about it without taking sides for or against Knights. Although F. W. Bateson's is the only essay in this collection written specifically in rebuttal to him, almost all the essays are relevant to his argument, including those which were written earlier than his own. For just as Collier did not originate but merely gave persuasive statement to the moral indictment of the drama, so Knights merely amplifies and restates with distinction uncertainties about the intellectual accomplishment of Restoration comedy that had long been felt. Thus Guy Montgomery's essay, written before Knights's, attempts to answer just such questions as the latter raises concerning the comedy's relationship to the thought of its time.

In the twentieth no more than in the seventeenth century have critics confined themselves to problems of significance and morality. Some of the best essays of both centuries are explicative rather than evaluative in intent. The rhetorical analysis of drama has in fact emerged in our own time as one of the most profitable undertakings of criticism. With full awareness of what they are doing, critics have put by the impressionistic methods of the Romantics and turned to formal analysis of a kind for which there is precedent among the Neoclassicists. Dryden's *examen* of Jonson's *The Silent Woman* in *An Essay of Dramatic Poesy* may be seen as an anticipation of the close reading of plays we encounter in Norman N. Holland's analysis of *The Country Wife* and Dale Underwood's analysis of *The Man of Mode*. Fundamental differences there certainly are between critics separated by three centuries and the Romantic movement. The precepts of ancient theorists and the precedents of ancient dramatists no longer seem worth citing, and the conception of literary genre is no longer compelling. Yet the preoccupation with the nuances of the text itself, observable in the best modern rhetorical critics, has more than a superficial resemblance to a similar preoccupation in Dryden, Rymer, Dennis, and—curiously—many of the controversialists on both sides of the Collier controversy. It is thus not altogether fanciful to find in the most recent approach to Restoration drama a return, a very profitable return, to the earliest.

Much of the best modern writing about Restoration and eighteenth-century drama is taken up with the theater rather than with the plays: with the theatrical milieu which helped to shape the plays. And here also there is precedent in the Augustan age. The eighteenth century is the earliest period in English dramatic history for which comprehensive documentation is available—available because of the sudden and vigorous growth of journalism starting approximately at the beginning of the century. Richard Steele is the first important journalistic critic of the drama; and in *The Tatler* and *The Spectator* he wrote about the actors and the playhouses as well as about plays. The large body of commentary on the theaters and the actors by Steele and his fellow journalistic critics and also by theorists writing books and pamphlets makes possible such an essay in historical analysis as Alan S. Downer's, which describes the changing styles in acting. The century was one of great actors; indeed notoriously so, for—the accusation goes—actors replaced dramatists as the central figures in the dramatic enterprise. This may be true of the later part of the century. At any rate, as Downer demonstrates, acting in the eighteenth century was no mere empiric art but rather one supported by a systematic and coherent body of theory that has an intelligible relationship to larger patterns of literary history.

In a period of drama such as that of the Restoration and eighteenth century—an important but not a supreme one—much of the interest of the plays lies in their usefulness as documents in social, political, and intellectual history. Literature has many uses, and one of them is that of recording the mind of an era for later generations. As we read a handful of the best plays, we may confine our attention to aesthetic matters, but we may not profitably do so with a very large number of others; and yet they repay study as an abstract and chronicle of the times. The elucidation of the drama as a form of history is in fact a major accomplishment of several of the essays in this collection—those, for example, on the sentimental movement. Ernest Tuveson's essay (which, although its relevance to drama is obvious, has less specifically to do with plays or the theater than any of the others) explores the background of sentimentalism in intellectual history; Paul E. Parnell's essay attempts to provide a conceptual framework for our understanding of the nature of sentimentalism; John Harrington Smith's essay suggests relationships between sentimentalism, changes in the structure of comedy, and changes in society.

Some of the essays are historical; others are explicative; still others evaluative. I have made an effort to illustrate the variety of modern criticism of Restoration drama: the differences in approach as well as in conclusions reached. Thus H. F. B. Brett-Smith's essay on Etherege examines his accomplishment within the context of dramatic tradition; whereas Underwood's essay on Etherege follows the method of close reading (though the book in which the essay first appeared is a notable study of intellectual history). All the essays were written after the First World War, and they exhibit, I believe, the more stringent discipline, the more rigorous methodology, that was introduced into criticism in the early postwar years. Collectively they will suggest the current state of literary scholarship on the subject.

J. L.

Stanford, California
September 1965

RESTORATION DRAMA
Modern Essays in Criticism

L. C. KNIGHTS

✿

Restoration Comedy:
The Reality and the Myth

I

Henry James—whose "social comedy" may be allowed to provide a standard of maturity—once remarked that he found Congreve "insufferable,"[1] and perhaps the first thing to say of Restoration drama—tragedy as well as comedy—is that the bulk of it is insufferably dull. There are long stretches of boredom to be found in the lower ranges of Elizabethan drama, but there is nothing comparable to the unmitigated fatigue that awaits the reader of *Love in a Tub, Sir Martin Mar-all, Mr. Limberham, The Relapse,* or *The Mourning Bride.* And who returns to Dryden's heroic plays with renewed zest? The superiority of the common run of plays in the first period to that of the second is, at all events, a commonplace. It should be equally commonplace that the strength of the Elizabethan drama lies partly in the kind and scope—the quality and variety—of the interests that the playwrights were able to enlist, partly in the idiom that they had at their command: the drama drew on a vigorous non-dramatic literature, and literature in general was in close relation with non-literary interests and a rich common language. That is not the whole story, but it is an important part of it, and it seems profitable, in a discussion of Restoration comedy, to keep these facts in mind for comparison. Ever since Collier published *A Short View of the Profaneness and Immorality of the English Stage* opponents of Restoration com-

From *Explorations: Essays in Criticism Mainly on the Literature of the Seventeenth Century* (London: Chatto and Windus, 1946), pp. 131-49. Reprinted by permission of New York University Press and Chatto and Windus Ltd.

3

edy have conducted their case almost entirely in moral terms, and it
has been easy for recent critics, rightly discarding Lamb's obvious
subterfuge, to turn the moral argument upside down, to find freedom of manners where Macaulay found licentiousness. "Morals" are,
in the long run, decidedly relevant—but only in the long run: literary criticism has prior claims. If, to start with, we try to see the comedy of manners in relation to its contemporary non-dramatic literature—to take its bearings in the general culture of the time—we may
at least make possible a free and critical approach.

During the forty years that followed the Restoration, English literature, English culture, was "upper-class" to an extent that it had
never been before, and was not, after Addison, to be again. "Now if
they ask me," said Dryden, "whence it is that our conversation is so
much refined? I must freely and without flattery, ascribe it to the
court," and his insistence, as a writer, on "the benefit of converse"
with his courtly patrons was not merely dedicatory fulsomeness; the
influence of the current conception of "the gentleman" is shown
plainly enough by the urbane ease of his critical prefaces; and Dryden's non-dramatic prose is fairly representative of the new age.[2]

It is this that explains why, if one comes to Resoration literature
after some familiarity with the Elizabethans, the first impression made
by the language is likely to be a sense of what has been lost; the dis-
integration of the old cultural unity has plainly resulted in impover-
ishment. The speech of the educated is now remote from the speech
of the people (Bunyan's huge sales were, until the eighteenth century, outside "the circumference of wit"), and idiomatic vigour and
evocative power seem to have gone out of the literary medium. But
there was gain as well as loss. The common mode of Restoration
prose—for there is now a common mode, a norm—was not evolved
merely in the interests of good form and polite intercourse; it had
behind it a more serious pressure. When, in 1667, Sprat attacked "this
vicious abundance of phrase . . . this volubility of tongue, which
makes so great a noise in the world," he had in mind the needs of
scientific inquiry and rational discussion. "They have therefore," he
said of the Royal Society, "been most rigorous in putting in execution the only remedy that can be found for this *extravagance,* and
that has been a constant resolution to reject all amplifications, di-
gressions, and swellings of style; to return back to the primitive purity
and shortness, when men delivered so many *things* almost in an equal
number of *words.* They have exacted from all their members a close,

naked, natural way of speaking, positive expressions, clear senses, a native easiness, bringing all things as near the mathematical plainness as they can."[3] For the first time the English language was made—and to some extent made consciously—an instrument for rational dissection.

> When once the aversion to bear uneasiness taketh place in a man's mind, it doth so check all the passions, that they are dampt into a kind of indifference; they grow faint and languishing, and come to be subordinate to that fundamental maxim, of not purchasing any thing at the price of a difficulty. This made that he had as little eagerness to oblige, as he had to hurt men; the motive of his giving bounties was rather to make men less uneasy to him, than more easy to themselves; and yet no ill-nature all this while. He would slide from an asking face, and could guess very well. It was throwing a man off from his shoulders, that leaned upon them with his whole weight; so that the party was not gladder to receive, than he was to give.

This is from Halifax's *Character of Charles II,* and the even tone, the sinuous ease of movement and the clarity of the analysis mark the passage as unmistakably post-Restoration. Halifax, of course, is in some ways an unusually handsome representative of his age; he is racy (the apt adjective is supplied by his editor, H. C. Foxcroft) as well as polite. But the achievement represented by his style was far from being a merely individual achievement. The shrewd and subtle portrait of Charles II is unlike anything that had appeared in English before his time, and it could only have appeared when it did.

Now an upper-class culture that produced *Absalom and Achitophel, The Character of a Trimmer,* Dryden's critical prefaces and Locke's *Second Treatise of Government,* may have been limited, but it was not altogether decadent. If the drama is inferior it is not because it represents—by Elizabethan standards—a limited culture, but because it represents contemporary culture so inadequately; it has no significant relation with the best thought of the time. Heroic tragedy is decadent because it is factitious; it substitutes violent emotionalism for emotion, the purple patch for poetry, and its rhetoric, unlike Elizabethan dramatic rhetoric, has no connexion with the congenial non-dramatic modes of the age; it is artificial in a completely damaging sense, *and by contemporary standards.* If we look for an early illus-

tration of the bad mid-eighteenth-century conception of poetry as
something applied from the outside[4] we find it in Dryden's verse
plays, where he adopts canons of style that he would not have
dreamed of applying—apart from his Odes—in his non-dramatic verse.
Tragedy, he said, "is naturally pompous and magnificent." Nothing
in English literature is more surprising—if we stop to consider—than
the complete discrepancy between the sinewy ease of Dryden's satires
and the stiff opaqueness of his dramatic verse; and "the lofty style,"
since it cannot modulate, is always coming down with a bump.

> I'm pleased and pained, since first her eyes I saw,
> As I were stung with some tarantula.
> Arms, and the dusty field, I less admire,
> And soften strangely in some new desire;
> Honour burns in me not so fiercely bright,
> But pales as fires when mastered by the light:
> Even while I speak and look, I change yet more,
> And now am nothing that I was before.
> I'm numbed, and fixed, and scarce my eyeballs move;
> I fear it is the lethargy of love![5]

It is only in the easy strength of occasional lines ("A good, luxurious,
palatable faith") that we hear his natural voice. In the plays as a
whole—each made up of a succession of "great" moments and heroic
postures—the "nature" that is "wrought up to a higher pitch"[6] bears
little resemblance to the Nature that was to figure so largely in the
Augustan code.

This, or a similar account, would probably be accepted by all critics
of the Restoration heroic play. What is not commonly recognized (it
is, at all events, not said) is that the comedy of manners exhibits a
parallel attenuation and enfeeblement of what the age, taken as a
whole, had to offer. I am not, for the moment, referring to the moral
or social code expressed. The observation to start from is that the
prose in which Restoration comedy is written—select which dramatist
you like—is poor and inexpressive in comparison with the staple non-
dramatic prose.

Congreve is usually accepted as the most brilliant stylist of the five
or six comic dramatists who count. But place beside the extract quoted
from Halifax a passage or two from *Love for Love* or *The Way of the
World* (it makes no difference whether the speaker is Scandal or Mirabell), and Congreve's style shows as nerveless in the comparison:

A mender of reputations! ay, just as he is a keeper of secrets, another virtue that he sets up for in the same manner. For the rogue will speak aloud in the posture of a whisper; and deny a woman's name, while he gives you the marks of her person: he will forswear receiving a letter from her, and at the same time show you her hand in the superscription; and yet perhaps he has counterfeited the hand too, and sworn to a truth; but he hopes not to be believed; and refuses the reputation of a lady's favour, as a doctor says *No* to a bishopric, only that it may be granted him. In short, he is a public professor of secrecy, and makes proclamation that he holds private intelligence.

A. To give t' other his due, he has something of good nature, and does not always want wit.

B. Not always: but as often as his memory fails him, and his common-place of comparisons. He is a fool with a good memory, and some few scraps of other folks' wit. He is one whose conversation can never be approved, yet it is now and then to be endured. He has indeed one good quality, he is not exceptious; for he so passionately affects the reputation of understanding raillery, that he will construe an affront into a jest; and call downright rudeness and ill language, satire and fire.

This reminds me of Arnold's definition of Macaulayese, "the external characteristic being a hard metallic movement with nothing of the soft play of life, and the internal characteristic being a perpetual semblance of hitting the right nail on the head without the reality." Both construction and movement are so far from being expressive *of* anything in particular that the main function of some words is, it seems, to complete an antithesis or to display a riddling wit.[7] The verbal pattern appears at times to be completely unrelated to a mode of perceiving. The passages quoted have an air of preening themselves on their acute discriminations, but the antitheses are mechanical, and the pattern is monotonously repeated: "She has beauty enough to make any man think she has wit; and complaisance enough not to contradict him who should tell her so"—the common form soon loses the sting of surprise. Burnet can write in an antithetical style which also penetrates:

> And tho' he desired to become absolute, and to over-
> turn both our religion and our laws, yet he would neither
> run the risk, nor give himself the trouble, which so great
> a design required. He had an appearance of gentleness in
> his outward deportment: but he seemed to have no
> bowels nor tenderness in his nature: and in the end of
> his life he became cruel.[8]

The nearest approach to subtlety that Congreve's style allows is represented by such things as this:

> FAINALL. You are a gallant man, Mirabell; and though
> you may have cruelty enough not to satisfy a lady's
> longing, you have too much generosity not to be ten-
> der of her honour. Yet you speak with an indifference
> which seems to be affected, and confesses you are con-
> scious of a negligence.
> MIRABELL. You pursue the argument with a distrust that
> seems to be unaffected, and confess you are conscious
> of a concern for which the lady is more indebted to
> you than is your wife.

It isn't, really, very subtle. As for the "wit," when it isn't merely verbal
and obvious ("Fruitful, the head fruitful;—that bodes horns; the fruit
of the head is horns," etc.) it is hopelessly dependent on convention.

> She that marries a fool, Sir Sampson, forfeits the repu-
> tation of her honesty or understanding: and she that
> marries a very witty man is a slave to the severity and
> insolent conduct of her husband. I should like a man of
> wit for a lover, because I would have such a man in my
> power; but I would no more be his wife than his enemy.
> For his malice is not a more terrible consequence of his
> aversion than his jealousy is of his love.

An intelligent husband, you see, must be jealous; take away that entertaining assumption and the point is blunted. Halifax is a witty
writer, but his wit springs naturally from the situation he is concerned
with and illuminates it:—"A partner in government is so unnatural a
thing that it is a squint-eyed allegiance which must be paid to such a
double-bottomed monarchy."[9] Congreve's wit is entirely self-regarding.

  If there were space to discuss the manner of Wycherley, Etherege
and Vanbrugh, it is a similar account that would have to be given. I
am not suggesting that they write in a completely indistinguishable

common mode (though they all have passages that might come from any play); but in essentials—in the way in which they use their similes and antitheses, in the conception of "style" and "wit" that they exhibit—they all stand together. Not one of them has achieved a genuinely sensitive and individual mode of expression; and in each the pattern of the prose inhibits any but the narrowest—and the most devastatingly *expected*—response. That, I should claim, is the judgment to which an analysis of their prose inevitably leads. The trouble is not that the Restoration comic writers deal with a limited number of themes, but that they bring to bear a miserably limited set of attitudes. And these, in turn, are factitious to exactly the same degree as the prose is artificial and non-representative of the current non-dramatic medium.

II

Apart from the presentation of incidental and unrelated "wit" (which soon becomes as tiring as the epigrams of the "good talker"), Restoration comedy has two main interests—the behaviour of the polite and of pretenders to politeness, and some aspects of sexual relationships. Critics have made out a case for finding in one or other of these themes a unifying principle and a serious base for the comedy of manners. According to Miss Lynch, the "thoroughly conventionalized social mode" of the courtly circle "was discovered to have manifestly comic aspects, both when awkwardly misinterpreted, and when completely fulfilled through personalities to which, however, it could not give complete expression,"[10] and both these discrepancies were exploited by Etherege and his successors. Bonamy Dobrée, attributing to the comic dramatists "a deep curiosity, and a desire to try new ways of living," finds that "the distinguishing characteristic of Restoration comedy down to Congreve is that it is concerned with the attempt to rationalize sexual relationships. It is this that makes it different from any other comedy that has ever been written. . . . It said in effect, 'Here is life lived upon certain assumptions; see what it becomes.' It also dealt, as no other comedy has ever done, with a subject that arose directly out of this, namely sex-antagonism, a consequence of the experimental freedom allowed to women, which gave matter for some of its most brilliant scenes."[11]

These accounts, as developed, certainly look impressive, and if Restoration comedy really answered to them—if it had something fresh and penetrating to say on sex and social relations—there would be no need to complain, even if one found the "solutions" distasteful. But Miss Lynch's case, at all events, depends on a vigorous reading into the plays of values which are not there, values which could not possibly be expressed, in fact, in the prose of any of the dramatists. (The candid reader can turn up the passages selected by Miss Lynch in support of her argument, and see if they are not all in the factitious, superficial mode that I have described.)

We may consider, by way of illustration, Etherege's *The Man of Mode*. When the play opens, Dorimant ("the finest of all fine gentlemen in Restoration comedy") is trying to rid himself of an old mistress, Mrs. Loveit, before taking up with a new, Bellinda, whilst Young Bellair, in love with Emilia, is trying to find some way out of marrying Harriet, an heiress whom his father has brought to town for him. The entertainment is made up of these two sets of complications, together with an exhibition of the would-be modishness of Sir Fopling Flutter. Events move fast. After a night spent in various sociabilities Dorimant keeps an appointment with Bellinda at 5 a.m. Letting her out of his lodgings an hour or so later, and swearing to be discreet "By all the Joys I have had, and those you keep in store," he is surprised by his companions, and in the resulting confusion Bellinda finds herself paying an unwilling visit to Mrs. Loveit. Dorimant appears and is rated by the women before he "flings off." Meanwhile Young Bellair and Emilia have secretly married. Dorimant, his equanimity recovered, turns up for the exposure, followed by his mistresses. The lovers are forgiven, the mistresses are huddled off the stage, and it is decided that Dorimant, who, the previous day, had ingratiated himself with Harriet's mother, and whose "soul has quite given up her liberty," shall be allowed to pay court to the heiress.

It seems to me that what the play provides—apart from the briskly handled intrigue—is a demonstration of the physical stamina of Dorimant. But Miss Lynch sees further. For her, Dorimant is "the fine flowering of Restoration culture." Illustrating her theory of the double standard, she remarks: "We laugh at Sir Fopling Flutter because he so clumsily parodies social fashions which Dorimant interprets with unfailing grace and distinction. We laugh at Dorimant because his assumed affectation admits of so poor and incomplete an expression of an attractive and vigorous personality."[12] The "unfailing grace and distinction" are perhaps not much in evidence in Dorimant's spiteful treatment of Mrs. Loveit;[13] but even if we ignore those brutish scenes we are forced to ask, How do we know that there *is* this "attractive and vigorous personality" beneath the conventional forms? Dorimant's intrigues are of no more human significance than those of a barn-yard cock, and as for what Miss Lynch calls "his really serious affair with Harriet" (I feel this deserves a *sic*), it is purely theatrical, and the "pangs of love" are expressed in nothing but the conventional formulae: "She's gone, but she has left a pleasing Image of herself behind that wanders in my Soul." The answer to the question posed is that Miss Lynch's account is a mere assumption. Nothing that Dorimant actually *says* will warrant it—and nothing in the whole of Restoration comedy—in the words actually spoken—allows us a glimpse of those other "personalities" to which the conventional social modes "could not give complete expression." The "real values"[14] simply are not there.

A minor point can be made in passing. It is just possible to claim that Restoration comedy contains "social criticism" in its handling of "the vulgar." "Come Mr. Sharper," says Congreve's Belinda, "you and I will take a turn, and laugh at the vulgar; both the great vulgar and the small," and Etherege's Lady Townley expresses the common attitude of the polite towards the social nuisances: "We should love wit, but for variety be able to divert ourselves with the extravagancies of those who want it." The butts, unfortunately, are only shown as fools by the discrepancy between their ambitions and their achievements, not because their ambitions are puerile. The subject is hardly worth discussing, since it is obviously nothing but an easily satisfied sense of superiority that is diverted by the "variety" of a constant succession of Dapperwits, Froths and Fopling Flutters. "When a humour takes in London," Tom Brown remarked, "they ride it to death ere they leave it. The primitive Christians were not persecuted with half that variety as the poor unthinking beaus are tormented with upon the theatre . . . A huge great muff, and a gaudy ribbon hanging at a bully's backside, is an excellent jest, and new-invented curses, as, Stap my vitals, damn my diaphragm, slit my wind pipe, sink me ten thousand fathom deep, rig up a new beau, though in the main 'tis but the same everlasting coxcomb."[15]

III

In the matter of sexual relations Restoration comedy is entirely dominated by a narrow set of conventions. The objection that it is only certain characters, not the dramatists themselves, who accept them can be more freely encountered when the assumptions that are expressed most frequently have been briefly illustrated.

The first convention is, of course, that constancy in love, especially in marriage, is a bore. Vanbrugh, who was the most uneasy if not the most honest of the comic dramatists (I think that in *The Provok'd Wife* he shows as unusually honest), unambiguously attributes this attitude to Sir John Brute:

> What cloying meat is love—when matrimony's the sauce to it! Two years marriage has debauch'd my five senses. . . . No boy was ever so weary of his tutor, no girl of her bib, no nun of doing penance, or old maid of being chaste, as I am of being married. Sure there's a secret curse entail'd upon the very name of wife!
>
> The woman's well enough; she has no vice that I know of, but she's a wife, and—damn a wife![16]

What Vanbrugh saw as a fit sentiment for Sir John had by that time (1697) served the Restoration stage—without change—for thirty years. In *She Wou'd if She Cou'd* Etherege had exhibited Sir Oliver Cockwood in an identical vein: "A pox of this tying man and woman together, for better, for worse." "To have a mistress love thee entirely" is "a damn'd trouble." "There are sots that would think themselves happy in such a Lady; but to a true bred Gentleman all lawful solace is abomination."[17] If Sir Oliver is a fool it is only because he is a trifle gross in his expression. "If you did but know, Madam," says the polite Freeman, "what an odious thing it is to be thought to love a Wife in good Company."[18] And the convention is constantly turning up in Congreve. "There is no creature perfectly civil but a husband," explains Mrs. Frail, "for in a little time he grows only rude to his wife, and that is the highest good breeding, for it begets his civility to other people."[19] "Marry her! Marry her!" Fainall advises Mirabell, "Be half as well acquainted with her charms, as you are with her defects, and my life on't, you are your own man again."[20] And Witwoud: "A wit should no more be sincere than a woman constant; one argues a decay of parts, as t'other of beauty."[21] Appetite, it seems (and this is the second assumption), needs perpetually fresh stimulus. This is the faith of Rhodophil in *Marriage à la Mode* and of Constant in *The Provok'd Wife,* as well as of Wycherley's old procuress, Mrs. Joyner. "If our wives would suffer us but now and then to make excursions,"

Rhodophil explains to Palamede, "the benefit of our variety would be theirs; instead of one continued, lazy, tired love, they would, in their turns, have twenty vigorous, fresh, and active lovers."[22] "Would anything but a madman complain of uncertainty?" asks Congreve's Angelica, for "security is an insipid thing, and the overtaking and possessing of a wish, discovers the folly of the chase."[23] And Fainall, in *The Way of the World,* speaks for a large class when he hints at a liking for sauce—a little gentleman's relish—to his seductions: "I'd no more play with a man that slighted his ill fortune than I'd make love to a woman who under-valued the loss of her reputation."[24] Fainall, of course, is what he is, but the attitude that makes sexual pleasure "the bliss," that makes woman "delicious"—something to be savoured—as well as "damned" and "destructive," demands, for its support, "the pleasure of a chase."[25]

> Would you long preserve your lover?
> Would you still his goddess reign?
> Never let him all discover,
> Never let him much obtain.[26]

Restoration comedy used to be considered outrageously outspoken, but such stuff as this, far from being "outspoken," hovers on the outskirts of sexual relations, and sees nothing but the titillation of appetite (" 'Tis not the success," Collier observed, "but the manner of gaining it which is all in all") .[27] Sex is a hook baited with tempting morsels;[28] it is a thirst quencher;[29] it is a cordial;[30] it is a dish to feed on;[31] it is a bunch of grapes;[32] it is anything but sex. (This, of course, explains why some people can combine a delighted approval of Restoration comedy with an unbalanced repugnance for such modern literature as deals sincerely and realistically with sexual relationships.)

Now the objection referred to above was that sentiments such as these are not offered for straightforward acceptance. Many of them are attributed to characters plainly marked as Wicked (Maskwell, for example, is the black-a-vised villain of melodrama) , or, more frequently, as trivial, and the dramatist can therefore dissociate himself. He may even be engaged in showing his audience the explicit, logical consequences of the half-unconscious premises on which they base their own lives, saying, as Mr. Dobrée has it, "Here is life lived upon certain assumptions; see what it becomes." To this there are several answers. The first is that reflexions of the kind that I have quoted are indistinguishable in tone and style from the general epigrammatic stock-in-trade (the audience was not altogether to be blamed if, as Congreve complained, they could not at first "distinguish betwixt the character of a Witwoud and a Lovewit") ; and they are largely "exhibited," just as all the self-conscious witticisms are exhibited, for the sake of their immediate "comic" effect. One has only to note the laughter of a contemporary audience at a revival, and the places where the splutters occur, to realize how much of the fun provides a rather gross example of tendency wit.[33] The same attitudes, moreover, are manipulated again and again, turning up with the stale monotony of jokes on postcards, and the play that is made with them demands only the easiest, the most superficial, response. But it is, after all, useless to argue about the degree of detachment, the angle at which these attitudes and assumptions are presented. As soon as one selects a particular comedy for that exercise one realizes that all is equally grist to the mill and that the dramatist (there is no need, here, to make distinctions) has no coherent attitude of his own. A consistent artistic purpose would not be content to express itself in a style that allows so limited, so local an effect.

But it is the triviality that one comes back to. In Dryden's *Marriage à la Mode* the characters accept the usual conventions: constancy is dull, and love only thrives on variety.

> PALAMEDE. O, now I have found it! you dislike her for no other reason but because she's your wife.
> RHODOPHIL. And is not that enough? All that I know of her perfections now, is only by memory . . . At last we arrived at that point, that there was nothing left in us to make us new to one another . .
> PALAMEDE. The truth is, your disease is very desperate; but, though you cannot be cured, you may be patched up a little: you must get you a mistress, Rhodophil. That, indeed, is living upon cordials; but, as fast as one fails, you must supply it with another.

The mistress that Rhodophil selects is Melantha, whom Palamede is to marry; Palamede falls in love with Doralice, Rhodophil's wife, and the ensuing complications provide sufficient entertainment (the grotto scene, III, ii, is really funny). Mr. Dobrée, however, regards the play as a witty exposure of the impossibility of rationalizing sex relations, as Palamede and Rhodophil attempt to rationalize them. Dryden "laughs morality back into its rightful place, as the scheme which ultimately makes life most comfortable."[34] But what Dryden actually does is to *use* the conventions for the amusement they afford, not to examine them. The level at which the play works is fairly indicated by the opening song:

> Why should a foolish marriage vow,
>   Which long ago was made,
> Oblige us to each other now,
>   When passion is decayed?
> We loved, and we loved, as long as we could,
>   'Till our love was loved out in us both;
> But our marriage is dead, when the pleasure is fled:
>   'Twas pleasure first made it an oath.
>
> If I have pleasures for a friend,
>   And further love in store,
> What wrong has he, whose joys did end,
>   And who could give no more?
> 'Tis a madness that he should be jealous of me,
>   Or that I should bar him of another:
> For all we can gain, is to give ourselves pain,
>   When neither can hinder the other.

The lovers make no attempt to "rationalize sex" for the simple reason that genuine sexual feelings no more enter into the play as a whole than feelings of any kind enter into the song. (The obviously faked emotions of the heroic plot are, after all, relevant—and betraying.) And according to Mr. Dobrée, "In one sense the whole idea of Restoration comedy is summed up in the opening song of *Marriage à la Mode.*"[35]

In a sense, too, Mr. Dobrée is right. Restoration comedy nowhere provides us with much more of the essential stuff of human experience than we have there. Even Congreve, by common account the best of the comic writers, is no exception. I have said that his verbal pattern often seems to be quite unrelated to an individual mode of perceiving. At best it registers a very limited mode. Restoration prose is all "social" in its tone, implications and general tenor, but Congreve's observation is *merely* of the public surface. And Congreve, too, relies on the conventional assumptions. In *The Way of the World,* it is true, they are mainly given to the bad and the foolish to express: it is Fainall who discourses on the pleasures of disliking one's wife, and Witwoud who maintains that only old age and ugliness ensure constancy. And Mirabell, who is explicitly opposed to some aspects of contemporary manners, goes through the common forms in a tone of rather weary aloofness: "I wonder, Fainall, that you who are married, and of consequence should be discreet, will suffer your wife to be of such a party." But Congreve himself is not above raising a cheap snigger;[36] and, above all, the characters with some life in them have nothing to fall back on—nothing, that is, except the conventional, and conventionally limited, pleasures of sex. Millamant, who says she loathes the country and hates the town, expects to draw vitality from the excitement of incessant solicitation:

> I'll be solicited to the very last, nay, and afterwards
> . . . I should think I was poor and had nothing to be-
> stow, if I were reduced to an inglorious ease, and freed
> from the agreeable fatigues of solicitation. . . . Oh, I
> hate a lover than can dare to think he draws a moment's
> air, independent of the bounty of his mistress. There is
> not so impudent a thing in nature, as the saucy look of
> an assured man, confident of success. The pedantic arro-
> gance of a very husband has not so pragmatical an air.

Everyone seems to have found Millamant intelligent and attractive, but her attitude is not far removed from that expressed in

> Would you long preserve your lover?
> Would you still his goddess reign?

and she shares with characters who are decidedly not attractive a disproportionate belief in "the pleasure of a chase." Which is not surprising in view of her other occupations and resources; visiting, writing and receiving letters, tea-parties and small talk make up a round that is never for a moment enlivened by the play of genuine intelligence.[37] And although Congreve recognizes, at times, the triviality of his characters,[38] it is to the world whose confines were the Court, the drawing-room, the play-house and the park—a world completely lacking the real sophistication and self-knowledge that might, in some measure, have redeemed it—that he limits his appeal.

It is, indeed, hard to resist the conclusion that "society"—the smart town society that sought entertainment at the theatres—was fundamentally bored.[39] In *The Man of Mode* Emilia remarks of Medley, "I love to hear him talk o' the intrigues, let 'em be never so dull in themselves, he'll make 'em pleasant i' the relation," and the idiotic conversation that follows (II, i), affording us a glimpse of what Miss Lynch calls "the most brilliant society which Restoration comedy has to offer,"[40] suggests in more than one way how badly society *needed* to

be entertained. It is the boredom—the constant need for titillation—
that helps to explain not only the heroic "heightening" of emotion,
but the various scenic effects, the devices of staging and costume that
became popular at this period. (Charles II "almost died of laughing"
at Nell Gwynn's enormous hat.) The conventions—of sexual pursuit,
and so on—were an attempt to make life interesting—an impossible job
for those who were aware of so limited a range of human potentialities.

The dominating mood of Restoration comedy is, by common account, a cynical one. But one cannot even say that there is here, in
contrast to naïve Romantic fervours, the tough strength of disillusion.
If—recognizing that there is a place in the educational process for, say,
La Rochefoucauld—one finds the "cynicism" of the plays distasteful, it
is because it is easy and superficial; the attitudes that we are presented
with are based on so meagre an amount of observation and experience.
Thus, "Elle retrouvait dans l'adultère toutes les platitudes du mariage"
has, superficially, much the same meaning as, "I find now, by sad experience, that a mistress is much more chargeable than a wife, and
after a little time too, grows full as dull and insignificant." But whereas
the first sentence has behind it the whole of *Madame Bovary*, the second comes from *Sir Martin Mar-all*, which (although Dryden shares
the honours with the Duke of Newcastle) is perhaps the stupidest play
I have ever read, and the context is imbecility.

But the superficiality is betrayed at every turn—by the obvious
rhythms of the interspersed songs, as well as by the artificial elegance
of the prose. And the cynicism is closely allied with—merges into—
sentimentality. One thinks of the sentimentally conceived Fidelia in
the resolutely "tough" *Plain Dealer;* and there is no doubt that the
audience was meant to respond sympathetically when, at the end of
Love for Love, Angelica declared her love for Valentine: "Had I the
world to give you, it could not make me worthy of so generous a passion; here's my hand, my heart was always yours, and struggled very
hard to make this utmost trial of your virtue." There is, of course, a
good deal of loose emotion in the heroic plays, written—it is useful to
remember—for the same audience:

> I'm numbed, and fixed, and scarce my eyeballs move;
> I fear it is the lethargy of love!
> 'Tis he; I feel him now in every part:
> Like a new lord he vaunts about my heart;
> Surveys, in state, each corner of my breast,
> While poor fierce I, that was, am dispossessed.[41]

> A secret pleasure trickles through my veins:
> It works about the inlets of my soul,
> To feel thy touch, and pity tempts the pass:
> But the tough metal of my heart resists;
> 'Tis warmed with the soft fire, not melted down.[42]

"Feeling," in Dryden's serious plays, is fairly represented by such passages as these, and Dryden, we know, was not alone in admiring the Fletcherian "pathos." But it is the lyric verse of the period that provides the strongest confirmatory evidence of the kind of bad taste that is in question. It is not merely that in Etherege, Sedley and Dorset the feeling comes from much nearer the surface than in the Metaphysicals and the Caroline poets, intellectual "wit" no longer strengthens and controls the feeling. Conventional attitudes are rigged out in a conventional vocabulary and conventional images. (The stock outfit—the "fair eyes" that "wound," the "pleasing pains," the "sighs and tears," the "bleeding hearts" and "flaming darts"—can be studied in any anthology.[43]) There is, in consequence, a pervasive strain of sentimental vulgarity.

> Farewell, ungrateful traitor!
>   Farewell, my perjured swain!
> Let never injured creature
>   Believe a man again.
> The pleasure of possessing
> Surpasses all expressing,
> But 'tis too short a blessing,
>   And love too long a pain.
>
>   .   .   .   .   .
>
> The passion you pretended,
>   Was only to obtain;
> But when the charm is ended,
>   The charmer you disdain.
> Your love by ours we measure
> Till we have lost our treasure,
> But dying is a pleasure
>   When living is a pain.

This piece of music-hall sentiment comes from Dryden's *The Spanish Friar*, and it does not stand alone. The mode that was to produce, among other things of equal merit, "When lovely woman stoops to folly," had its origin in the lyrics of the Restoration period. Most of these were written by the group connected with the theatres, and they serve to underline the essential criticism of the plays. The criticism that defenders of Restoration comedy need to answer is not that the comedies are "immoral," but that they are trivial, gross and dull.

NOTES

1. *Letters*, Vol. I, p. 140.
2. On "the last and greatest advantage of our writing, which proceeds from *conversation*," see in particular the *Defence of the Epilogue*. And the dialogue form in which Dryden cast the *Essay of Dramatic Poesy* was not unrecognizably far from actuality.
3. *The History of the Royal Society of London*: Spingarn, *Critical Essays of the Seventeenth Century*, Vol. II, pp. 112ff.
4. ". . . enriching every subject (otherwise dry and barren) with a pomp of diction and luxuriant harmony of numbers."—Gray's note to *The Progress of Poesy*, 1754.
5. *The Conquest of Granada*, Part I, III, i.
6. ". . . the nature of a serious play; this last is indeed the representation of nature, but 'tis wrought up to a higher pitch."—*Of Dramatic Poesy*. The final paragraph of the Preface to *Religio Laici* has some interesting remarks in this connexion; e.g. "The florid, elevated, and figurative way is for the passions."
7. *The Old Bachelor* shows the riddles in the process of manufacture. *Bellmour:* He is the drum to his own praise—the only implement of a soldier he resembles; like that, being full of blustering noise and emptiness. *Sharper:* And like that, of no use but to be beaten, etc.
8. I quote from Professor Nichol Smith's excellent anthology, *Characters from the Histories and Memoirs of the Seventeenth Century* (Clarendon Press) , p. 222.
9. Also from *The Character of a Trimmer*:—". . . the indecent courtship of some silken divines, who, one would think, did practise to bow at the altar, only to learn to make the better legs at Court."
10. K. M. Lynch, *The Social Mode of Restoration Comedy*, p. 216.
11. Bonamy Dobrée, *Restoration Comedy*, pp. 22-23.
12. *The Social Mode of Restoration Comedy*, p. 181.
13. See II, ii and V, i, where Dorimant, trying to force a quarrel with Mrs. Loveit, attributes to her a fondness for Sir Fopling. The first of these scenes was too much for Etherege, and he makes Bellinda say:

> He's given me the proof which I desired of his love,
> But 'tis a proof of his ill nature too.
> I wish I had not seen him use her so.

But this is soon forgotten, and we are not, of course, called on to register an unfavourable judgment of Dorimant.

14. "The love affairs of Courtal and Ariana, Freeman and Gatty [in *She Wou'd if She Cou'd*] are similarly embarrassed by social convention. . . . The conduct of these polite lovers acquires comic vitality through

the continually suggested opposition of artificial and real values."—*Op. cit.*, p. 152.

15. Tom Brown, *Works*, Vol. III, *Amusements Comical and Serious*, "At the Playhouse," p. 39.
16. *The Provok'd Wife*, I, i; II, i.
17. *She Wou'd if She Cou'd*, I, i; III, iii.
18. *Ibid.*, III, iii.
19. *Love for Love*, I, ii.
20. *The Way of the World*, I, ii.
21. *Ibid.*
22. *Marriage à la Mode*, II, i. Cf. *The Provok'd Wife*, III, i: *Constant*, "There's a poor sordid slavery in marriage, that turns the flowing tide of honour, and sinks us to the lowest ebb of infamy. 'Tis a corrupted soil: Ill-nature, sloth, cowardice, and dirt, are all its product."
23. *Love for Love*, IV, iii.
24. *The Way of the World*, I, i.
25. *The Old Bachelor*, I, i; III, ii ("O thou delicious, damned, dear, destructive woman!") ; IV, ii.
26. *Ibid.*, II, ii.
27. *A Short View of the Profaneness and Immorality of the English Stage*, Fifth Edition, 1738, p. 116.
28. " 'Tis true you are so eager in pursuit of the temptation, that you save the devil the trouble of leading you into it: nor is it out of discretion that you don't swallow the very hook yourselves have baited, but . . . what you meant for a whet turns the edge of your puny stomachs."—*The Old Bachelor*, I, i. "Strike Heartwell home, before the bait's worn off the hook. Age will come. He nibbled fairly yesterday, and no doubt will be eager enough to-day to swallow the temptation."—*Ibid.*, III, i.
29. "What was my pleasure is become my duty: and I have as little stomach to her now as if I were her husband. . . . Pox on't! that a man can't drink without quenching his thirst."—*The Double-Dealer*, III, i.
30. "You must get you a mistress, Rhodophil. That indeed, is living upon cordials; but as fast as one fails, you must supply it with another." *Marriage à la Mode*, I, i.
31. "Because our husbands cannot feed on one dish, therefore we must be starved."—*Ibid.*, III, i.
32. "The only way to keep us new to one another, is never to enjoy, as they keep grapes, by hanging them upon a line; they must touch nothing, if you would preserve them fresh."—*Ibid.*, V, i.
33. The Freudian "censor" is at times projected in the form of the stage puritan. The plays written soon after the Commonwealth period appealed to Royalist prejudice by satirizing the "seemingly precise"; and even later, when "the bonfires of devotion," "the bellows of zeal," were forgotten, a good deal of the self-conscious swagger of indecency seems to have been directed against "our protestant husbands," city merchants, aldermen and the like; the "daring" effect was intensified by postulating a shockable audience somewhere—not necessarily in the theatre. Not that the really obscene jokes were merely bravado: Collier quite rightly re-

marked that "the modern poets seem to use smut as the old ones did Machines, to relieve a fainting situation."—*A Short View*, Fifth Edition, p. 4.

34. *Restoration Comedy*, p. 133.
35. *Ibid.*, p. 106.
36. Ay there's my grief; that's the sad change of life,
   To lose my title, and yet keep my wife.
           The Way of the World, II, ii.
37. As Lady Brute remarks, "After all, a woman's life would be a dull business, if it were not for the men . . . We shou'd never blame Fate for the shortness of our days; our time would hang wretchedly upon our hands."—*The Provok'd Wife*, III, iii.
38. *Mirabell:* You had the leisure to entertain a herd of fools; things who visit you from their excessive idleness; bestowing on your easiness that time which is the encumbrance of their lives. How can you find delight in such society?—*The Way of the World*, II, i.
39. The constitution, habits and demands of the theatre audience are admirably illustrated by Alexandre Beljame in that neglected classic of scholarship, *Le Public et les Hommes de Lettres en Angleterre au Dix-Huitième Siècle*, 1660-1740. See also C. V. Deane, *Dramatic Theory and the Rhymed Heroic Play,* Chapter I, Section 6.
40. *The Social Mode of Restoration Comedy*, p. 177.
41. *The Conquest of Granada*, Part I, III, i.
42. *Don Sebastian*, III, i.
43. See, for example, Aphra Behn's "Love in fantastic triumph sate," Buckingham's *To his Mistress* ("Phyllis, though your all powerful charms") , Dryden's "Ask not the cause why sullen spring," and "Ah, how sweet it is to love," and Sedley's *To Chloris*—all in *The Oxford Book of English Verse*, or Ault's *Seventeenth Century Lyrics*.

F. W. BATESON

✿

L. C. Knights and Restoration Comedy

"Restoration Comedy: the Reality and the Myth" is one of Professor Knight's *Explorations* (1946), a collection that is described in its sub-title as "Essays in Criticism mainly on the Literature of the Seventeenth Century." Like most of the rest of the volume—one as a whole of great critical and literary distinction—the essay originally appeared in *Scrutiny,* in the number for September 1937, of which Mr. Knights was then an active co-editor. In many ways, indeed, it is a characteristic *Scrutiny* product—the revaluation of a conventional assessment concluding in a drastic depreciation. But, unlike some similar critical exercises, this deflation is extraordinarily persuasive. The tone of voice, the selection and presentation of the evidence, the tactful elaboration of the argument are all—or at any rate give the appearance of being— nicely detached, scholarly and conclusive. The essay, not unnaturally, has been acclaimed one of the show-pieces of the Cambridge school. In their useful omnibus anthology *Criticism* (1948) Mark Schorer, Josephine Miles and Gordon McKenzie reprinted it to the exclusion of anything by Dr. Leavis—an outrageous preference, of course, but one that is at least comprehensible. And in 1937 certainly, as a counter-blast to the elegant or sophisticated nonsenses represented at their best by Bonamy Dobrée's *Restoration Comedy* (1924) and Kathleen M. Lynch's *Social Mode of Restoration Comedy* (1927), Mr. Knights's icy distaste came as a healthy critical shock. "The criticism that defenders

From *Essays in Criticism,* VII (1957), 56-67. Reprinted by permission of the publishers.

of Restoration comedy need to answer is not that the comedies are 'immoral,' but that they are trivial, gross and dull," is the way he ends. Even Wycherley and Congreve's most hysterical disparagers, even Jeremy Collier, Macaulay, Thackeray and Meredith (for whom *The Way of the World* is only an exception that proves the barbarous rule) had not gone quite as far as that.

But 1937 is twenty years ago. The phrase-making and aestheticism and naughtinesses of the 1920s, the whole post-1914-18 philosophy of life for which Lytton Strachey is a convenient symbol, are now as dead as donkeys. The danger today, as I see it, is that, because of the brilliance with which its then necessary half-truths were brandished, Mr. Knights's essay may come to be mistaken for the definitive judgment on Restoration comedy. I was probably not the only reader of this journal who was dismayed to read in our October issue John Wain's almost unqualified acceptance of Mr. Knights's general position. The time, it seems, has come when it is necessary to say, politely but firmly, that the Knights line—and *a fortiori* Mr. Wain's amusing and ingenious variations on it—misses the essential critical point about Restoration comedy. Etherege, Wycherley, Congreve and Vanbrugh (with Dryden, the only ones that really matter) are not, of course, among the world's great dramatists. At times, even in their best plays, they *are* trivial, gross and dull. But in the best scenes of *The Man of Mode*, *The Country Wife* and *The Way of the World*, the three masterpieces of the *genre*—and perhaps in some scenes of Etherege's *She Would if she Could*, Congreve's *Love for Love*, and two of Vanbrugh's plays— most of the grossness and all the triviality disappears. At their best these dramatists are *serious*—in a way that Goldsmith, Sheridan or Wilde never are—though naturally it is in the paradoxical modes of seriousness appropriate to comedy. Something important is being said.

Mr. Knights denies any seriousness to the plays. While recognizing that "there is a place in the educational process for, say, La Rochefoucauld," he cannot detect in Restoration comedy a similar "tough strength of disillusion" (p. 17). The plays seem to him to be confined to "a miserably limited set of attitudes" (p. 9). Dorimant's intrigues in *The Man of Mode* are, he asserts, "of no more human significance than those of a barn-yard cock" (p. 11); and Restoration comedy as a whole lacks "the essential stuff of human experience" (p. 15). Moreover, the plays have "no significant relation with the best thought of the time" (p. 5), and the unreal sexual conventions that they appeal to—that constancy is a bore, "the pleasure of the chase," etc.—contrast unfavourably with "such modern literature as deals sincerely and realistically with sexual relationships" (pp. 12-13).

Most of these objections seem to me to derive from a misunderstanding of what comedy can or should attempt. There is a concealed premise in Mr. Knights's assumptions as to what constitutes non-trivial literature, which comes out when he says, in the essay's first sentence, "Henry James—whose 'social comedy' may be allowed to provide a standard of maturity—once remarked that he found Congreve 'insufferable.'" James's judgment, a casual comment apparently in one of his letters, is intended to carry more force than it very well can. Naturally James thought Congreve insufferable. Congreve would have thought James insufferable. And why should James's "social comedy" provide a standard of the comically serious? How would Shakespeare's or Molière's comedies fare if they were judged by such a criterion? Underlying Mr. Knights's more specific objections to Restoration comedy there is always the lurking implication that Wycherley and Congreve *ought* to have written like James or D. H. Lawrence, or at any rate (Mr. Knights was writing while the seventeenth-century Dissociation of Consciousness was still booming) like an Elizabethan or Jacobean dramatist.

Ought they? It is the crucial issue. Or is literature necessarily limited and directed by the processes of history to different dramatic forms at different times? Now if Eliot's dictum is accepted, as I suppose it must be (it is an unconcealed premise in Mr. Knights's own *Drama and Society in the Age of Jonson*), that a "radical change in poetic form" is almost always the "symptom of some very much deeper change in society and in the individual" (*The Use of Poetry and the Use of Criticism*), it surely follows that any deep change in society and in the individual's relation to society will be reflected or expressed in a radical change in the dominant literary form. The depth of the social and individual changes brought about by the Civil War will not be disputed. The first question, then, to be asked of Restoration comedy, in order to determine a properly relevant approach to it, is not whether it is like James or Shakespeare, but in what respects it is the appropriate dramatic expression of the social revolution of the mid-seventeenth century. Until this question has been answered the strictly literary issues do not arise at all. Mr. Knights begs it when he contrasts the "rich common language" available to an Elizabethan dramatist with the "mechanical" antitheses of Congreve. Rich in what currency? And the same fallacy seems to be present in Mr. Knights's comparison

of Halifax's *Character of Charles II*—and later of some sentences from
Burnet—with passages from *Love for Love* and *The Way of the World*.
Can dramatic prose *ever* be usefully compared with that appropriate
to historical or political commentary? It is no criticism of chalk that
it isn't cheese. The question is whether it is good or bad chalk.

I have not the learning, nor is this the place, to attempt a comprehensive critical account of the Restoration comedy of manners. All that
I can hope to do is to suggest a perhaps more relevant approach to
these plays. The sexual impropriety is still, of course, the real bone
of contention. The seventheenth century distinguished between low
comedy, which was merely meant to make an audience laugh, and
high or "genteel" comedy, which used the laugh as a form of social
comment—*ridendo corrigere mores*. A defence of Restoration comedy
must demonstrate that its sex jokes have a serious social function. I
think it can be shown that they have and that the plays, at their best,
need fear no comparison even in Mr. Knights's eyes, with "such modern literature as deals sincerely and realistically with sexual relationships." But if the demonstration is to be effective it will be necessary
to analyse the Restoration treatment of sex in some detail.

Here, then, as an elementary test-case, is part of a seduction scene
between two minor characters in *Love for Love*—Tattle, who is described in the list of *dramatis personae* as a "half-witted beau," and
Miss Prue, "a silly awkward country girl." Tattle has just explained to
Prue that, if she is to be thought well-bred, she must learn how to lie;
her words must contradict her thoughts, though her actions should also
contradict her words.

> PRUE. O Lord, I swear this is pure!—I like it better than
> our old-fashioned country way of speaking one's mind;
> —and must not you lie too?
> TAT. Hum!—Yes; but you must believe I speak truth.
> PRUE. O Gemini! well, I always had a great mind to tell
> lies: but they frightened me, and said it was a sin.
> TAT. Well, my pretty creature; will you make me happy
> by giving me a kiss?
> PRUE. No, indeed; I'm angry at you.
>   *[Runs and kisses him.*
> TAT. Hold, hold, that's pretty well;—but you should not
> have given it me, but have suffered me to have taken it.
> PRUE. Well, we'll do't again.
> TAT. With all my heart.—Now then, my little angel!
>   *[Kisses her.*

PRUE. Pish!

TAT. That's right—again, my charmer!

[*Kisses again.*

PRUE. O fy! nay, now I can't abide you.

TAT. Admirable! that was as well as if you had been born
and bred in Covent Garden. And won't you show me,
pretty miss, where your bed-chamber is?

PRUE. No, indeed, won't I; but I'll run there and hide
myself from you behind the curtains.

TAT. I'll follow you.

PRUE. Ah, but I'll hold the door with both hands, and be
angry;—and you shall push me down before you come
in.

TAT. No, I'll come in first, and push you down afterwards.

The episode is not one of Congreve's high spots, but its theatrical
potentialities should be obvious. In the hands of a competent actor
and actress the scene can be very funny indeed. In what, however,
does the fun consist? First of all, I suppose, in the reversal—painless and
in a way satisfying—of the auditor's normal rational expectations. On
the stage are two human beings—looking, in spite of the beau's oddities
and girl's country ways, very much like you and me—and a sort of
lesson is apparently in progress. Tattle, the would-be seducer, is in-
structing Prue in the way a well-bred woman will receive the advances
of a young man like himself. Part of the reversal of our expectations
is, of course, the unusualness of the subject for a lesson, part of it is
the contrast between Prue's uncouth speech and manners with her
unerring knowledge of what she wants, but the big surprise, I suppose,
is the girl's innocently enthusiastic progress, under her teacher's approving eyes, from kisses to copulation. So the human beings are not
so human after all! But Prue is enjoying herself so much that the
audience finds itself involuntarily sharing in the sudden topsy-turvy
values. Nevertheless the scene is not, as Lamb tried to argue in the
Elia essay "On the Artificial Comedy of the Last Century," an excur-
sion into an amoral fairyland, the land of cuckoldry, a Utopia of gallantry. For the effectiveness of the dramatic paradoxes depends upon
the audience's continuous awareness that it is *not* in fairyland. Prue
is an adolescent girl, and if she goes on as she seems determined to do
she will soon find herself "in trouble." As the seduction proceeds to
its final physical conclusion the tension between reality and what had
at first seemed just a *façon de parler,* a mere make-believe parody of
an ordinary lesson, mounts and mounts until the audience's laughter

is replaced by an incredulous gasp. Is it all just an elaborate joke, or is Congreve going to take Prue at her word? The Nurse's interruption a moment later comes with the effect of a reprieve. We can laugh now; we are back in the world of the theatre; the realism to which we seemed committed, the ugliness of an actual seduction, has been waived. But it was a near thing, and with the relaxation of the tension the audience giggles happily in nervous relief.

At this point a tentative definition of comedy will have to be attempted. The agreeable reversal of an expectation that will itself be reversed must imply two separated planes of reality which the dramatist can assume in his audience: one that of everyday commonsense, and parallel and contiguous to it the fairyland plane of Lamb's essay, "where pleasure is duty, and the manners perfect freedom." It is obviously in the auditor's sudden transition from the objective plane of everyday rational reality, which must always be the point of comic departure, to the subjective plane of dream-fantasy or irrational dream-fulfilment that the ridiculous is born. Its most elementary form is the top-hatted gentleman who skids on a banana-skin. In terms of the dramatic structure of a Restoration comedy it is the continuous collision of the plays' heroes (including the heroines), that is, the "men of sense," with their grotesque opposites—Sir Fopling Flutter, the Widow Blackacre, Foresight, Lady Wishfort and their like—each of whom is imprisoned in his own fantasy. The refinements all fall within this general pattern. Thus Tattle, who is a grotesque, "a half-witted beau," in the scenes he shares with Valentine and Scandal, is the realist in the Miss Prue episode. To her the seduction is clearly just a new game, a variant of hide-and-seek ("you shall push me down before you come in"), whereas Tattle means business ("No, I'll come in first and push you down afterwards"). And there is a similar metamorphosis of Prue's own role later in the play, when she confronts Ben, the even more fantastic sailor-fiancé.

The possibilities of serious social comment within the comic framework seem to depend upon the degree to which either or both of the opposed planes of meaning are conceptualized. The clash in that case, instead of being between casual examples of human life to which the auditor reacts realistically or fantastically, is now between *representative* examples, that is, figures or attitudes that he recognizes as either typical (on the plane of common sense) or symbolic (on the plane of fantasy).

A historical approach will make it easier to appreciate the "serious" role of sex in a Restoration comedy of manners. To the Puritans "immorality" had virtually reduced itself to sexual irregularity, with drunkenness and blasphemy as poor seconds, a man's other sins being considered a private matter between him and God. (By the 1650 Act "for suppressing the detestable sins of Incest, Adultery and Fornication" incest and adultery became capital crimes without benefit of clergy, as did fornication on the second offence, first offenders getting three months' imprisonment.) On the other hand, to the restored Royalists by a natural reaction sexual licence—and drunkenness and blasphemous oaths—almost became a political duty. "Joy ruled the day and love the night," as Dryden summed up Charles II's reign in *The Secular Masque*. The two attitudes were the points of maximum social divergence between the two parties into which England remained divided. As in politics a compromise was eventually worked out, for which Addison and Steele usually get most of the credit. But the relative sexual respectability of *The Tatler* and *The Spectator* was the end-product of a long process that was closely connected with political developments. If the political problem *par excellence* in the second half of the seventeenth century was to avoid the recurrence of a second Civil War, its social parallel, essentially, was to rationalize the sex instinct. Until such a rationalization had been achieved genuine communication between Whigs and Tories was hardly possible. Intermarriage, the final solution, was unthinkable. It is now a matter of history that a kind of sexual rationalization was achieved, perhaps over-achieved (it is a curious fact that hardly any of the eighteenth-century poets married). From one point of view, in the mode of allegory proper to high comedy, the Restoration drama records the strains that accompanied the achievement.

The term "Restoration comedy" is really a misnomer. The first completely successful comedy of manners, Wycherley's *The Country Wife*, was not written until 1674—fourteen years after the Restoration itself. By that time the rationalization of sex had already made some progress. The two extremes had come to be identified on the stage with (1) younger members of the landed gentry (Tory), who spent their winter months in London applying to the pursuit of love the methods of the chase, which was their principal occupation on their country estates, and (2) London merchants (Whig), who treated their wives as pieces of property to be even more jealously guarded than their gold. The earlier dramatists were all ex-Cavaliers and inevitably their heroes had been the gentlemanly rakes. In Wycherley's Horner, how-

ever, the rake-hero undergoes a sexual transformation, which prepared
the way for Dorimant's surrender to Harriet in *The Man of Mode*
and the complete rationalization of sex by Mirabell and Millamant
in the fourth act of *The Way of the World*.

With these considerations in mind a re-appraisal may now be attempted of the *double entendres* in the notorious "china scene" in
The Country Wife. The criterion can now be the specifically literary
one on which Mr. Knights rightly insists. But an inquiry into the nature of comedy, hurried though it was, and a summary of the play's
historical context should ensure that the literary questions which are
asked are the relevant questions. It will be remembered that Lady
Fidget, the hypocritical urban opposite of the innocently instinctive
Country Wife (Mrs. Pinchwife), has told her husband that she is going
to the China House. In fact, however, she goes to Horner's lodgings, as
she has discovered that Horner, who has tricked her friend Mrs.
Squeamish and the others into believing him impotent, is not really
impotent at all. Horner and Lady Fidget disappear, and when they
return it is to find Mrs. Squeamish, who is just as vicious as Lady
Fidget but is not yet in the secret, busily inquiring for him. Lady
Fidget has a piece of Horner's china in her hand.

> LADY FIDGET. . . . I have been toiling and moiling for
> the prettiest piece of china, my dear.
> HORNER. Nay, she has been too hard for me, do what I
> could.
> MRS. SQUEAMISH. Oh, lord, I'll have some china too. Good
> Mr Horner, don't think to give other people china and
> me none; come in with me too.
> HORNER. Upon my honour, I have none left now.
> MRS. SQUEAMISH. Nay, nay, I have known you deny your
> china before now, but you shan't put me off so. Come.
> HORNER. This lady had the last there.
> LADY FIDGET. Yes, indeed, madam, to my certain knowl-
> edge he has none left.
> MRS. SQUEAMISH. Oh, but it may be he may have some
> you could not find.
> LADY FIDGET. What, d'ye think if he had had any left, I
> would not have had it too? For we women of quality
> never think we have china enough.
> HORNER. Do not take it ill, I cannot make china for you
> all, but I will have a roll-wagon [= wheel-barrow] for
> you too another time.

The episode is usually presented as a mere fireworks-display of clever *double entendres*. In fact, its insolent power—which no-one has denied, though it has often been deplored—seems to derive from the openness of the innuendoes and the almost equal openness of Mrs. Squeamish's apparently innocent complaints. Can Mrs. Squeamish have possibly failed to realize what Horner and Lady Fidget had been up to? But such issues of psychological realism should not be allowed to arise. The *double entendres* obtain their shock-effects from the fantasy world they create to oppose to and, temporarily, to supersede the world of realistic probabilities. At this fantasy level we approach an allegory of sex. Lady Fidget and Mrs. Squeamish, appetite satisfied and appetite still clamorous, are essentially both embodiments of the same possessive feminine lust. And the china—instead of being, as it is at the literal level, either a device to conceal a disreputable act (Lady Fidget) or a precious object desired for its own sake (Mrs. Squeamish)—is now a drawing-room phallic symbol. In the general transmutation of values Horner, the would-be aggressively masculine woman-hunter, disappears—displaced by the symbolic china.

Under analysis the scene's sardonic force proves to derive from the insistent repetitions. The word "china" is used six times. Mrs. Squeamish asks what is really the same question twice if not three times. Lady Fidget and Horner keep on repeating the same dirty joke. Wycherley will not let his audience off. The post-Civil War anti-Puritan convention had grown up that this sort of thing was funny. Well, they shall have their fun—over and over again. The audience, disgusted but fascinated, is quite unable to break away. The tension—it is a spectacle, within the auditor's mind, of fellow-human beings persistently reverting into objects or machines—is disturbing. I may seem to exaggerate if I compare it with that aroused in the reader by Swift's account of the Yahoos, but a critical parallel can, I think, be worked out. At any rate it is a measure of the implicit seriousness of *The Country Wife*—on the whole, I think, in spite of its local imperfections, the best of all the Restoration plays—that such a comparison can be suggested.

For the values to which Wycherley appeals are not wholly negative or satiric. In antithesis to Horner, the professional of the love-game, and his urban concubines, there is the Country Wife herself—the "freehold," as he describes her, of her jealous London husband—whose innocent amateur escapades put sex into its proper proportions. Margery Pinchwife is hilariously positive. In the end, therefore, in terms of the symbolic impression the play leaves behind, its ultimate "meaning," it is Horner, the sophisticated Man of Sense, who emerges as a Grotesque or mere mechanism, and Margery, the primitive country girl, who stands for the ordinary human decencies. The Tories were, of course, the Country Party.

No doubt, to carry complete conviction, a defence of Restoration comedy in the terms I have suggested would need to be greatly elaborated. My sketch is only a sketch. It will have served its purpose, however, if it has shown that a different and more sympathetic critical approach is possible, to Wycherley and Congreve at any rate, from Mr. Knights's. And Mr. Wain has already spoken up for Etherege.* Critical justice still waits to be done to the comic scenes in Dryden's tragi-comedies, especially perhaps *Secret Love,* which prepared the way for the others, and also, I think, to Vanbrugh, a hit-or-miss dramatist whose best scenes have to be disentangled from much perfunctory stuff. I agree with Mr. Wain, if with certain reservations, that the academic commentators have not been very helpful. I have read a good many more of them than he has, and critically Horace Walpole's "Thoughts on Comedy," a most intelligent essay that everybody (including both Mr. Knights and Mr. Wain) seems to have forgotten, is worth all of them put together. As for Mr. Knights's "Reality and the Myth," well, it takes its place, I suppose, in the roll of sparkling charge and sprightly countercharge that has constituted hitherto the critical history of Restoration comedy. Jeremy Collier, John Dennis, Lamb and Hazlitt, Macaulay and Thackeray, Mr. Dobrée, Mr. Knights—all lively and all wrong! On Mr. Wain it will be only fair to reserve judgment. The article in the last number of *Essays in Criticism* was only the first half of a long essay that we shall soon be able to read in its entirety in a collection of his critical excursions which is to be published, I understand, in the very near future.

* John Wain, "Restoration Comedy and Its Modern Critics," *Essays in Criticism,* VI (1956), 367-85 [Editor's note].

GUY MONTGOMERY

❀

The Challenge of Restoration Comedy

Restoration Comedy has always, I think, needed protection. It was simply offensive to Jeremy Collier and his kind in the seventeenth century; Addison suffered it, but was pained at its indelicacy; Lamb with characteristic gentleness provided it with a dream-veil that carried it into a realm beyond the actual. Thackeray and Macaulay merely branded it as an illegitimate offspring of the French and summarily excluded it from the respectable British dramatic hearthstone. Certainly the Comedy has been unfortunate in its critics of later days. They have too quickly regarded it as the product of an age that had abandoned all moral standards. Thus it has had to bear sins perhaps not entirely its own. It may be the Comedy's misfortune to reflect too faithfully the society that encouraged its development. At any rate, critics who have not been able to damn it on its own account have easily found the age responsible for its iniquities. This latter procedure of criticism is sometimes hopefully modified by a slight concession to the claims of dramatic art. Allardyce Nicoll describes Restoration society in terms as lurid as those of Jeremy Collier, but finds in the end that "despite and sometimes because of these limitations, this drama . . . gave to art something which could not have been achieved either in the theatre of Athens, with its thirty thousand spectators, or in the theatre of Elizabeth, with its mixed audiences of apprentices and peers." Nicoll tries to be fair, but there lurks in his criticism the toxin

From *University of California Publications in English*, I (University of California Press, 1929) , 133-51. Reprinted by permission of the publishers.

that weakens all judgments of this comedy. This poison is generated whenever moral and esthetic standards are mixed. To describe the comedy is safe; to judge it is hazardous, because it inevitably leads to the circular reasoning that characterizes the Collier-Congreve controversy. Collier might accuse the dramatists of corrupting the manners of the age; Congreve could retort that the manners of the age had corrupted the dramatists, and could add that if the parsons would do their duty they might reform the manners, and thereby the dramatists too. The same matter with less art than Congreve had at his disposal takes the form of the judgment that

> such a comedy bore a natural resemblance to the society which gave it birth. That society manifested no profound interest in the momentous issues that hung upon the political strength of the period. Its only tribute to religion was a persistent effort to escape all the restraints which any form of morality might impose. All its energies were consequently absorbed in leading the dance through a profligate carnival of the senses. It was therefore incapable of the generous romantic interests of Elizabethan England or of the golden age of Spain. It was totally averse to reflecting on the mystery of life or the problems of destiny. It was interested only in itself and its own superficial amusements.

The critic who is responsible for the foregoing observes that "since virtue and chivalry no longer molded men's thoughts or influenced their actions, what could playwrights do but fashion the scenes about them into a long succession of *Relapses* and *Plain Dealers?*" Would that this observation were true! If it were, what might we not say about Restoration drama as a whole? We are obliged to remind the critic that there was only one *Relapse,* and as well only one *Plain Dealer.*

So suggestive a critic as Dobrée seems to stumble into the traditional trap. "If we are disgusted at the impurities which," he says,

> are the material of much of this comedy, are they handled with sufficient skill to make us indifferent to the subject matter? Or is there, in spite of much that disgusts us, enough beauty and intelligence to overbalance our revulsion in favour of delight? Or can we simply accept the life of the times; and without associating it with ourselves, derive interest and pleasure from the observation

and understanding of men whose outlook on life died
with their erring ladies some two centuries ago? Surely
this seems the reasonable attitude.

Mr. Dobrée has indulged in a neat bit of rationalization. To obscure
the subject matter by means of the method of treating it is much like
trying to visualize a painting by Hogarth by reading his essay on the
technique of drawing. To overbalance the disgust by means of delight
is to attempt to reconcile the irreconcilable. Neither a dyed-in-the-wool
literalist nor a hard-minded scientist will pay much attention to the
suave arguments of the well-fed trimmer. And to dissociate the "life
of the times" from ourselves is to take to ourselves a superiority that
the facts of human nature do not warrant our doing. I am willing to
assume the position that to the influence of the period we owe the
kind of drama that has been a scandal to the moralists and an offense
to the artists. I venture to think, however, that not those forces traditionally regarded as responsible for the scandalous comedy are the
primary influences that determined its nature. I should like to know
whether there were not beneath those *manners,* a system of ideas, of
which the manners, and incidentally, the comedy, were not a "realization." It seems proper to believe that the outward and visible conduct
of a society is controlled by springs of action that are much more
significant than the conduct itself.

There were more things in London during the last forty years of the
seventeenth century, than cuckolding and wenching.

> But now since the king's return the blindness of the
> former Ages and the miseries of this last, are vanish'd
> away: now men are generally weary of the Relicks of An-
> tiquity, and satiated with Religious disputes: now not
> only the eyes of men, but their hands are open, and pre-
> par'd to labour: Now is there universal desire, and appe-
> tite after knowledge, after the peaceable, the fruitful, the
> nourishing knowledge: and not after that of antient Sects
> which yielded hard indigestible arguments or sharp con-
> tentions instead of food, which when the minds of men
> required bread, gave them only a stone and for fish a
> serpent.

In these words does Dr. Thomas Sprat, biographer of the infant Royal
Society, strike a note that during the next two centuries is to grow into
a swelling theme. This call to the scientists was not sounded to a
narrow "sect" but to a body of performers drawn from all sorts, condi-

tions, and professions of men, from royalty in Westminster to the trader in the city, from the doctor in the university to the navigator on the high seas. It is true that the comic writers played fast and loose with the collectors of the stings of wasps, the searchers of perpetual motion, and their enthusiastic brethren; but "one is led to guess shrewdly that the superficiality of the scientist in comedy is due largely to the superficial knowledge on the part of the play writers. To them it was a humor and nothing more." It may be true that the satiric arrows of the playwrights darkened the scientific sun; it is, however, significant that those men assumed that their audiences were well enough informed to know what the battle was about. I cannot help detecting in the over-boldness of men and women in their relationships and in the frankness of their conduct, instead of an abandonment of all moral standards, an approach to conduct, if not technically scientific, yet genuinely experimental. It was not yet time for setting up hypotheses; scientists were engaged in collecting curious facts. They were doing what ethnologists twenty years ago were doing, making reports. Any one who will take the trouble to read the *Transactions* of the Royal Society during the early years of its activity will smile, no doubt, at the naïveté; but the one who thinks for a moment will stop to admire the earnest sincerity. Shadwell's *Virtuoso* is an amusing burlesque of a scientific "projector." Whether or not he was a quack neither Shadwell nor his audience knew. The latter were not in a position to judge that matter. The general impression made by the comedy upon me was that Shadwell is much more severe upon the lack of knowledge on the part of the beaux and the wits than upon the misdirected enthusiasm of the Virtuoso himself. I might argue that Shadwell, whose character both as dramatist and man has been darkened by Dryden, had a lurking suspicion that there was more in these curiosities of Gresham College than his age realized. I'll not do that now. I am suggesting only that the materials of experimental science were so much a part of the thinking of the period that their use by dramatists was almost a guaranty of a successful play. The moment when these materials so familiar to all could be made to contribute to the comfort or the welfare of society, that moment, I say, would change the whole course of human thought and conduct.[1] I am suggesting further that these materials and these methods of science were significantly affecting thought and conduct. They were bringing about a questioning that has been judged as flippant, cynical, disillusioned. With all the admitted ugliness of the Comedy which is a striking representation of this questioning attitude, there marches a distinct desire to know how to *live* in a suddenly altered external world.

Of course, it may not be so simple as I have suggested. I may have over-emphasized the influence of the newly awakened scientific spirit upon the daily conduct of society. When the story of seventeenth-century thought is finally told in a popular version the facts will doubtless become clear. One aspect of Restoration Comedy that has led to its deepest damnation assumes, however, a different cast when viewed in the light of my contention. I refer to wenching and one of its attendant sports, cuckolding. Now both these amusements we have always with us. Swift once pointed out in a brilliant essay that vocabulary alone, not human nature, changes. One may hold the opinion that words are the signs of ideas. This opinion is not necessarily sound; for words may be only the faintest of shadows of ideas. Some words are only taboos parading in the disguise of a sophisticated society. It will be remembered that the institution of the civil marriage ceremony was one of Oliver Cromwell's most revolutionary acts. To be sure, it fell into disuse after the Restoration; true also, that it was but the Independent's challenge to one of the sacred mysteries of Catholicism, Anglican as well as Roman. These facts are incidental to the importance of the act. It is the opinion of those whose study of the subject has been far more extensive than mine, that the institution of the civil ceremony meant more to the thinking of seventeenth-century England than its sponsor could know at the time of its introduction as a valid foundation for matrimonial bliss. It became a challenge to another "relick of antiquity," it struck at one of those vocabulary taboos that frequently enough give way before experiment, and, good or ill, the effect must have been to set currents of thought overflowing into channels but poorly adapted to the strength of the new streams. Puritanism had failed as a political machine; and as a moral instrument it proved a kind of boomerang. It had struck off the fetters of theological authority, but in a most unexpected quarter. That is, although the Church regained her primacy in matrimony, yet the number of Fleet marriages must have encouraged the growing sense of individual responsibility in matters of conduct.

I am well aware of the soundness of the position that too much individual responsibility is merely another name for license. It may not be that a social order reaches its solidarity when it places the individual's satisfaction of impulse above his willingness to share with others the responsibility of maintaining the law. It is questionable,

however, whether a social order will survive if it does not from time
to time subject its foundations to a search for weak spots. It is probably a fact that an honest social order never was; there have been
times when society was in the process of *becoming* honest. Thanks to
Restoration Comedy, I think we have preserved for us a fairly faithful
picture of a society at one of these "becoming" times. The attention
directed to experiment in scientific matters helped to create an atmosphere which affected moral conduct. The shifting of theological
ground created a necessity for social adjustment. Perhaps this adjustment is most strikingly illustrated by the position woman took toward her rights and responsibilities. Briefly to exemplify this position
is not easy. Let me quote, however, from three plays that fairly well
represent the comedy of the period:

> EUGENIA: I do so [love the man of whom she is speaking
> to her maid], Jane, ah! were my husband such a man,
> how happy a creature should I be? but I was forced to
> marry him to please my parents.
> JANE: 'Tis then your turn to please yourself now with a
> gallant, to supply the defects of a husband; when a
> man will press a woman to marry against her inclina-
> tions, he lays the foundation himself of being a Cuck-
> old after.[2]

again,

> GATTY: How I envy that Sex: Well! we cannot plague
> 'em enough, when we have it in our Power, for those
> Privileges which Custom has allow'd 'em above us.
> ARIANA: The Truth is, they can run and ramble here
> And there, and everywhere, and we, poor Fools,
> Rather think the better of 'em.[3]

and again,

> LUCINDA: Why let it [the world] think; this fear of the
> World destroys all the satisfaction of a woman's life:
> Hang the World, a woman that minds what the World
> thinks or says, had better never have been in the
> World.[4]

Women begin to doubt the soundness of the tradition that they are
but goods and chattels, and that the ceremony of holy matrimony is
necessarily a guaranty of conjugal bliss or of marital equality. And so
women experiment and rediscover the ancient privileges and powers

established and bequeathed to them in Eden. True daughters of Eve are they. Thus it is that the interesting characters of *Restoration* Comedy are women, and without question the most fascinating of these is that apotheosis of *Restoration* women, Millamant.

This frankness and unconventionality has often been turned to the disadvantage of the moral tone of *Restoration* Comedy. If it were not that I have proceeded to justify that Comedy by a theory that considers changing values or ideas, I should have recourse to another set of facts. These I can only touch upon. Criticism up to the present time has rarely made enough of the changes that visibly took place in the methods of *Restoration* Comedy from its beginning—the reopening of the theaters in 1660—to the end of the century. It is because of the faint recognition of these changes that misconceptions of the nature of the Comedy have become general. If one follows, year by year, the appearance of the comedies on the stage or in print, one observes that it was not until late in the century that the true type—that wicked, insinuating, abandoned, and godless comedy began to assume a form. During the first ten years of Charles's reign, Brome, Shirley, Massinger, Beaumont, Fletcher, Jonson served both playwright and manager to keep the audiences of the two theaters amused. Dryden struck into a form suited to his public's taste anything—English, French, or Spanish—that came to his hand. Shadwell clung close to his idol Ben. "Humors" ran strong in the blood that was heated with wine and infected with the pox. Of such stuff was *Restoration* Comedy made, a traditional comic mold into which any material at hand was run. In 1676 Etherege's *Sir Fopling Flutter* was produced. Charles II suggested to Crowne the composition of *Sir Courtly Nice*. The play appeared in 1684, the year Charles died. From the eighties on, the art of comedy was following two ways, and though the ways may have crossed each other now and again, yet they led to separate and distinct destinations. It would be interesting to trace the "humors" comedy to that type of farce which gains its effects by means of the "eccentric" character. It is much more to the point at this time to suggest that, on that second highway of change, comedy was moving unhesitatingly toward the comedy of wit, that type in which the characters, though representatives of types, achieve their place not so much by an exaggeration of conventional—"humorous"—eccentricities as by an exhibition of those traits that are normal in the society of which the character is a member. The ideal of the men and women of this society is conformity to a definite pattern of conduct, that of wit and breeding. It may be true that a reputation for virtue is more highly prized than virtue itself. I am not so sure that this is the case. It should be noticed that the characters who place reputation higher than honesty itself are the objects of the dramatist's severest satire. They are the persons whose conformity to a social code shows a lack not only of taste but of breeding. Of such are Lady Cockwood, Mrs. Loveit, Lady Wishfort. The men who covet the reputation for wit without possessing the quality itself are, without question, delightful creations of dramatic comedy. They are, however, those at whom the shafts of satire from their fellow-players as well as from the dramatist are hurled most often. Their refusal to conform, springing from that egotism of which I spoke earlier, lacks not only good taste but also wit.

These comedies, which have emerged from the dramatic chaos and puritanical night, show us a society struggling for adjustment in a newly discovered world. That new world proposed to men and women an equality scarcely known before to English society. In doing so it proposed new bases for marriage and family life. But love in a cottage was hardly practicable, nor was it desirable to a man who had known the pleasures of the palaces. Love in the city with a rich though impotent old merchant may not have been pleasant, but it was more prudent for a woman who knew that brisk though poor young gallants could be found at the other end of the town. Society intellectually leaped far ahead of the economic restraints, which, it must be known, have an annoying way of refusing to be moved by the romantic notions of young heads. The new world of the late seventeenth century offered to society still other proposals. The king who returned to the throne had lost some of his divinity. This monarch, Charles Stuart, second of the name, made up for that loss by his excessive humanity, if the term may be applied to those weaknesses which have since the beginning of the Christian era been regarded as specially the property of the human species.

It is significant, too, that these comedies are dramas of youth triumphant, youth flaming, perhaps, but forever triumphant. It is not surprising that the vigor, the strenuousness of the great company of young men who flung themselves impudently through the gay whirl of life represented by the drama should be singled out as the crowning expression of shamelessness. The modern and conventional moral code was formulated in the seventeenth century with the murder of the first Charles. And coeval with that code is the critic with a "moral" standard. Judge Falstaff, Hal, Romeo, Benedick, Malvolio, Autolycus,

Iago, Macbeth, Antony, Angelo, by the same standard and the characters are likely to become positively wicked. But no one but an egregious moralist will apply the standard to the conduct of these persons! I submit that for the Restoration young men, as well as for the Renaissance young men, the world was full of a number of things. Youth does not change; the face of things alters its make-up. The characters remain the same; the scene shifts, and the most engaging of all comedies, that of living, goes on. The observer—critic in this case— who fails to see this should give up the practice of theater-going. Better still, he should continue attendance at any conventicle, where he may to his heart's peace hear denounced without variation the perennial lewdness of fallen humanity.

The methods of the Comedy were, too, those of lively youth in the face of suspected doctrines. Here the moral critic points out that Restoration Comedy in general, and the Comedy of Manners in particular (with more gracefulness and so with deadlier cynicism), denies to love more than the physical attraction between the sexes; denies to marriage its sacramental nature; denies to friendship any generous impulse to sacrifice for another; denies to patriotism disinterested zeal for one's country; denies to religion the awfulness that surrounds its mysteries. Denial is the word. Denial of the values that have been regarded as the foundation of individual happiness and social stability. Denial because of disillusionment. Disillusionment because it had been found that romantic love was a dream of fantastic poets, because it had been discovered that marriage was hire and salary; that in times of trial men had been known to betray friends for a handful of gold; that patriotism was an empty catchword of factions; and that religion was but the pious cant of those who would cover sharp and secret practices. Were these the discoveries at the bottom of that disillusionment that has been seen as the mark of the beast upon Restoration Comedy? In a sense, yes; at least a certain fact had been rediscovered; namely, that theories of conduct did not square with the facts of conduct. Might one not hazard a guess that all Restoration Comedy, in varying degrees of artistic excellence, was a reaffirmation of the individual's inalienable privilege to live naturally in a world whose limits were rapidly becoming circumscribed, on the one hand by a popular conventional moral code, and on the other were being extended by scientific and social experiment and research as they had not been extended by the discoveries of the sixteenth century? In other words, may not this

Comedy be regarded as one faint premonitory glow of the summer sun of the enlightenment that was to follow hard upon Newton, Locke, and the Royal Society? The apology for Restoration manners in terms of a reaction against the Puritan prohibitions is in my opinion a weak one. It is negative; and signifies, I think, an evasion. Restoration manners were positive, downright, plain-dealing. Behind them was an affirmation of the individual battling for existence in a world that threatened and promised at the same time.

> Born to myself, I like myself alone;
> And must conclude my Judgment good, or none:
> For cou'd my Sense be nought, how should I know
> Whether another Man's were good or no.
>
> If then I'm happy, what does it advance
> Whether to Merit due, or Arrogance?
> Oh, but the World will take Offence thereby!
> Why then the World shall suffer for't, not I.

These lines attributed to John Wilmot, Earl of Rochester, perhaps the epitome of Restoration manners, encourage my theory of the Restoration period that gives its Comedy reason for existing.

From the point of view of the moral critic, the Comedy of Manners disappeared because it was unsound. "It was out of sympathy with the opinions and the sentiments of the people at large," declares one judge. This is all too true, but it is not necessarily a tribute to popular taste or to popular morality. After all, however, only the poor bodily frame of the Comedy of Manners met a tragic end. Its spirit lived on. It found but another house swept and garnished. Chastened, perhaps, it hovered over the pen of Bickerstaff; with much of its native impudence it stirred Matt Prior, and awakened the torpid Gay. I suspect that it had its share in lacerating the heart of Jonathan Swift; surely in devil's shape it led men to their ruin in speculation and stock-jobbing. It was found and ever will be found where youth, curiosity, impudence, courage dwell in the heart of a sensitive individual. The form peculiar to the seventeenth century withered, for several reasons. Back of them all was business and morality—the crowd. Colley Cibber was partly to blame. I omit Jeremy Collier because he was right as far as he went. Cibber, however, with one eye on the box office and the other on the pulpit, brought his comedies to the double focus of both eyes. He compromised. It was not art, but it satisfied the conventionally moral. That was the end; the divine right of kings to play the part of tyrants was mortally wounded by the ax that fell upon the neck of Charles I; the biological right of the individual male to cuckold doddering miserly husbands, or of every individual female to outwit her stupid sisters was mortally wounded when the pious demon rose in all its mediocrity.

What Cibber began, Steele finished. I need only to quote two passages, separated by thirty years to illustrate the point. In the opening scene of the *Man of Mode,* Dorimant says, as he looks upon a note he has addressed to Mrs. Loveit:

> What a dull insipid thing is a Billet-doux written in
> Cold Blood, after the heat of the business is over?
> It is a tax upon good Nature which I have
> Here been labouring to pay, and have done it,
> But with as much regret, as ever Fanatick paid
> The Royal acid, or Church Duties; 'T will
> Have the same Fate, I know, that all my Notes
> To her have had of late. 'T will not be thought
> Kind enough. Faith, women are in th' right
> When they jealously examine our Letters, for in them
> We always first discover our decay of Passion.

In scene ii of Act I of *The Conscious Lovers,* Bevil, Junior, is "discovered" reading. He murmurs:

> These moral writers practise virtue after death. This charming vision of Mirza! Such an author consulted in a morning sets the spirit for the vicissitudes of the day better than a glass does a man's person. But what a day have I to go through! to put on an easy look with an aching heart! If this lady my father urges me to marry should not refuse me, my dilemma is insupportable. But why should I fear it? Is she not in equal distress with me? Has not the letter I have sent her this morning confessed my inclination to another? Nay, have I not moral assurances of her engagements, too, to my friend Myrtle? It's impossible but she must give in to it; for, sure, to be denied is a favour any may pretend to. It must be so—Well, then, with the assurance of being rejected, I think I may confidently say to my father, I am ready to marry her. Then let me resolve upon, what I am not very good at, though it is an honest dissimulation.

The divine right of tyranny has been transplanted. There is no longer individuality, there are only society, law, order. Others have usurped the right, and to others the individual bows his head in submission. Doing so he presses his body and his mind into the mold of the group, and the comedy that represents him thus distorted dwindles to a moral tract. The impudent and graceless values of Restoration Comedy foresaw the rising tide of cant, I suspect. They rebelled, but it was too late, for the current against them was over strong. In the end they followed the examples of the originals from which they were drawn. His Grace the Duke of Buckingham retired to the country, where Etherege sought him out with a bantering letter; Sir Charles Sedley settled down to humdrum respectability; John Wilmot, Earl of Rochester, repented in his last hours. Society in the end gained, no doubt, by the reformation of these gentlemen and by the purification of its manners and its comedy. That art was the gainer, I am not so willing to grant. That neither proposition is to the point I trust is clear. Too often this Comedy is treated as a temporary aberration of English comic drama, an abnormality induced by the extraordinary nervous strain of Puritan domination. There may be some truth in this contention; but its conclusion is to make this Comedy an anomaly. As such it has but the significance of a curiosity; whereas it has human significance which is to be found in its representation of one of those recurring efforts of individuality to maintain its integrity in a world threatened by the confining limitations of law.

NOTES

1. I must quote these sentences from Sprat to indicate the change that is approaching:
    "It is true, that terrible evil [the plague] has hitherto in all countries, been generally too strong, for the former remedies of Art. But why should we think that it will continue so forever? Why may we not believe, that in all the vast compass of Natural virtues of things yet conceal'd there is still reserved an Antidote that shall be equal to this poison? If in such cases we only accuse the Anger of Providence, or the cruelty of Nature: we lay the blame where it is not justly to be laid. It ought rather to be attributed to the negligence of men themselves that such difficult cures are without the bounds of their reason's power." (p. 123.)
2. *London Cuckolds*, Act II, sc. i.
3. *She Would if She Could*, Act I.
4. *She Gallants*, Act I.

H. F. B. BRETT-SMITH

⚘

Sir George Etherege

The praise may seem high, and yet—if to found a new type of comedy
be sufficient title—a great master Etherege certainly was. Wycherley
soon surpassed him in strength; Congreve was to beat him on his own
ground; but he had taught them both, and his claim to novelty was
admitted by his age. In the Prologue to his first piece, he had begged
the judges to forget those "Records of Wit," the plays of Fletcher and
Jonson,

> And only think upon the modern way
> Of writing, whilst y'are censuring his Play,

but in the modern way his comedies showed possibilities hitherto only
vaguely shadowed, and Rochester was right, when he spoke of the
excellence of Shakespeare and Jonson, to add

> Whom refin'd E . . . , coppy's not at all,
> But is himself a sheer Original.[1]

It was the novelty of Etherege's characters and methods that struck
his contemporaries. Shadwell, whose idea of comedy seldom rose beyond the creation of fresh "humours," realised that even on this basis

> *Frolick,* and *Cockwood* yet were good and new,[2]

and Dryden, throughout the Epilogue to *The Man of Mode,* is careful
to praise Sir Fopling as a compound of the latest fashionable whims.[3]

From the Introduction to *The Works of Sir George Etherege* (Oxford: Basil
Blackwell, 1927) , pp. lxix-lxxxiii. Reprinted by permission of the publishers.

Less favorable criticism is more illuminating; Captain Alexander Rad-
cliffe, in his *News from Hell,* represents Etherege as damned

> for writing superfine,
> With words correct in every Line:
> And one that does presume to say,
> A Plot's too gross for any Play:
> Comedy should be clean and neat,
> As Gentlemen do talk and eat.
> So what he writes is but Translation,
> From Dog and Pa[r]tridge[4] conversation.[5]

In other words, Etherege was more concerned to give an exact picture
of fashionable life, with the added polish that comedy demands, than
to elaborate the plots of his plays, which have some of the easy negligence of the social world they depict. The criticism is equally true of
Congreve.

But it was the picture of life that was new—for we must forget the
host of Etherege's successors in the type of comedy he founded, and
recall the condition of the English stage in 1664.[6] Since the Restoration, play-writing had begun again, but the theatres were still dependent on pieces produced before the civil war, and among the
older comedies those of Jonson and Fletcher were favourites, Shakespeare's being too full of poetry and romance to suit the modern taste.
Jonson and Fletcher, however, had in them qualities which maintained
their appeal up to the close of the century; the "humours" of Jonson
were still welcome, and Fletcher had the courtly air and the liveli-
ness which Restoration audiences loved. Yet both of them were manifestly out of date, and there were elements in Jonson's comedy—his
didacticism, his learning, the heavy-handed treatment of his women—
that were no longer congenial. The Town was waiting for something
that should represent its own image; and neither Cowley's juvenile
extravagances,[7] nor Sir Samuel Tuke's Spanish intrigues,[8] nor Dryden's
cumbersome improbabilities[9] had hit that mark. *The Comical Revenge* was the first of the new plays to hold the mirror up to Covent
Garden and the Mall.[10]

The defects of the piece are obvious enough, and were not overlooked at the time, though its merits carried them off triumphantly.
The heroic rhymed drama of Davenant and Lord Orrery could not
reasonably be yoked with realistic comedy and farce,[11] and it was inevitable that the prose and verse scenes should assert their independence. The comic part of the play is itself a medley; the tub scenes

are farcical, Cully and the sharpers recall the knaves and dupes of the Elizabethan stage,[12] and Sir Frederick and the Widow are finished creations of the comedy of manners. But the non-heroic scenes are unified by the ease and truth of their dialogue; the prose was such as no English theatre had yet heard, and the people were alive. Audiences which had suffered, only a year ago, from the lumbering unreality of Dryden's *Wild Gallant*,[13] were suddenly confronted with the world they knew. A gentleman of fashion has amused himself overnight in an escapade; valets discuss him, coachmen and link-boys come to claim their hire, fidlers must be satisfied for broken heads, and Jenny brings an indignant message from her mistress: he has made such an uproar in the street that they must be forced to change their lodging. "And thou art come to tell me whither;—Kind heart!" says the irrepressible knight. This was the easy, impudent wit that might be heard any day in St. James's Street and the New Exchange. It is true that Sir Frederick is a first sketch, and although he has the nonchalance of the man of fashion, and the skill in rejoinder that is never at a loss, he is not yet so finished a rake as Courtall or Dorimant; his nocturnal window-breakings are too crude,[14] and his raillery of Mrs. Rich is sometimes boorish. But this would be accepted in an age when widows were a mark for the broadest jests;[15] and speeches, otherwise intolerable, may be condoned when there is a good understanding between the persons. Sir Frederick and the Widow are very nearly certain of one another; they have made up their minds, though the knight affects to boggle at the loss of liberty, and follows the maxim of the Restoration stage that no man commits matrimony, even with a known Fortune, without first assuring himself that she is not to be won upon easier terms.[16] This necessary point being decided, Sir Frederick, like Courtall and Dorimant, submits to his fetters willingly enough. And his sparring matches with the Widow—an opponent as formidable as she is charming—were to set a model in the thrust and parry of comedy for the next half century.[17]

Etherege did not fail to realise where his strength lay, and in *She wou'd if she cou'd* he renounced heroics, farce, and the cheats of the town, and devoted himself to the life around him. "Well, Franck," says Courtall in the third speech of the comedy, "what is to be done to day?," and the answer comes readily enough:—"Faith, I think we must e'ne follow the old trade; eat well, and prepare our selves with a Bottle or two of good *Burgundy*, that our old acquaintance may look lovely in our Eyes; for, for ought as I see, there is no hopes of new."

An idle man's life; an idle man's play; but the life was that of the writer and his friends, "men of great imployment," that were "every moment ratling from the Eating-Houses to the Play-Houses, from the Play-Houses to the Mulberry-Garden,"[18] and taking, as lightly as it came to them, "the harmless lust of the Town."[19] In consequence there is obvious reality in the portraits of Courtall and Freeman, Ariana and Gatty, Mrs. Gazet and Mrs. Trinckit and Mr. Rake-hell; and vigorous life also in Lady Cockwood and the two country knights, though here the modish townsman's contempt for the country gives a touch of satire to the brush, and Lady Cockwood is as near as Etherege ever comes to a Jonsonian "humour" or a type character of Molière. Sir Edmund Gosse has even called her "a female Tartuffe,"[20] and has not been alone in the belief.[21] But the claims of French comedy may be urged too far.[22] It is true that Etherege had probably seen Molière's early plays, *L'Étourdi, Le Dépit Amoureux, and Les Précieuses Ridicules,* before 1664, and he certainly made use of the latter in his portrait of Sir Fopling. He is likely enough to have seen *Le Tartuffe* before 1668. But the comedy of Molière, with its corrective satire, its type-characters, and its trick of exaggeration, is as plainly a different growth from the English comedy of manners as Jonson's moral lessons and satirical "humours" had been. The one thing that the Restoration could learn from Molière was ease of dialogue, and this was probably studied more from London life than from Parisian rhymed couplets, though the English court may have owed something to French society in this matter of wit and conversation. In plot and incident, of course, Molière was pillaged right and left from 1660 to the end of the century, but the very openness of the theft[23] shows how little he was regarded as a master; his plays were simply a public treasury, like the Spanish comedies, from which useful scenes and situations might be abstracted, to be worked up into something more nearly approaching the English taste for detailed observation of life, unhampered by generalising tendencies. The characters of Etherege are not types in the sense that those of Jonson, of Plautus, of Molière are types; they are contemporary portraits of persons who fall, of course, into some classification or other, but are painted in their own colours. Tartuffe is abstract hypocrisy clothed in flesh; Lady Cockwood is the flesh making use of hypocrisy as a cloak for a single failing. It is true that she is a satiric portrait; her insistence on her "honour"[24] anticipates, at times, Wycherley's savage exposure of Mr. Horner's visitors. But it is not her hypocrisy that makes her distasteful to Courtall; it is the fact that she is a woman of one idea, who reverses the proper relation of hunter and quarry, and has never had the benefit of the instructions which Tattle was to impart, some quarter of a century later, to Miss Prue.

Throughout this play, the author shows an easy familiarity with the pursuits and conversation of society, and a nice observance of its distinctions; Sir Oliver and Sir Joslin, rustic in their manners and excesses, are objects of the slightly contemptuous tolerance of Courtall and Freeman, who do not even acknowledge the existence of Mr. Rake-hell till he obsequiously brings himself to the notice of each in turn.[25] But everything leads up to the joyous courtship of Ariana and Gatty; in their dialogues with the two honest Gentlemen of the Town —eclipsing those of Sir Frederick and the Widow—the new comedy of manners has come to its own. The clever fencing between two pairs of opponents, whose hearts are just enough touched to give zest to the combat, is as delightful as it is brilliant, and the rapid turns and shifts of situation and intrigue[26] make an effective substitute for a more solid plot.

In *The Man of Mode,* plot is still secondary to life, that easy life of society, when all the world meets in the Park at high Mall, the most entertaining time of the evening, and the fops criticise passing beauties, and the ladies grumble at the intrusion of the rabble of the Town: "See what a sort of nasty Fellows are coming," says Loveit as the "four ill-fashion'd Fellows" enter singing *'Tis not for kisses alone.*[27] Etherege, who "perfectly understood the World,"[28] makes these scenes as vivid as the reminiscences of London in his letters from Ratisbon, but the care for detail led to no neglect in structure, and it was a clever touch to defer Sir Fopling's entrance till the Third Act.[29] Sir Fopling, however, is not the chief attraction in the play, though his "great acquir'd Follies" make him its most conspicuous person. He is in some respects the goodliest fop of fops since born, for Etherege has handled him lovingly, humouring his extravagances, and tempering the breath of satire, so that he has an ingenuousness absent in his progeny, Sir Courtly Nice[30] and Lord Foppington,[31] as it had been in his predecessors, Mr. Frenchlove[32] and Monsieur de Paris.[33] He is an admirable piece of emptiness, but the core of the play is Dorimant, whose duels with Harriet are the final example of Etherege's chief contribution to English comedy. As in *She wou'd if she cou'd,* the scenes gain depth and charm from the undercurrent of seriousness they conceal so well; neither Dorimant nor Harriet will risk the exposure of real feeling, and when he seeks favour in so many words, she evades him with practised skill: "Let us walk," she says to Bellair, " 'tis time to leave him, men grow dull when they begin to be particular."[34] It is the height of polished coquetry; Etherege's women are fully a match for the men in any trial of wits; the sexes are on that equal footing which Meredith held essential for true comedy. But though the characters follow the social code that conceals all feeling under epigram and carelessness, Harriet is given enough heart to make her lovable, and enough head to win our respect; it is a wise woman who banishes Dorimant till his love is grown strong enough to make him bear being laughed at,[35] and yet will consent to his visits if he cares to endure even the country—that bugbear of all gallants[36]—for her sake. Her invitation is half a warning; it is "to a great rambling lone house, that looks as it were not inhabited, the family's so small; there you'l find my Mother, an old lame Aunt, and my self, Sir, perch'd up on Chairs at a distance in a large parlour; sitting moping like three or four Melancholy Birds in a spacious vollary—Does not this stagger your Resolution?"[37] Etherege is sparing indeed in the use of tenderness, but his restraint is justified in those rare moments when he allows himself such an effect as this. Millamant and Mirabel were not the first of their race.[38]

As for Dorimant, his head is unquestionably better than his heart, and the modern reader must resign himself to a world which held that its Loveits and Bellindas could not eat their cake and have it too. An amour is pleasant, but when it ceases to be pleasant, it is broken off as a matter of course; Etherege had written in his own person some years earlier,

> It is not, *Celia,* in our power
> To say how long our love will last,
> It may be we within this hour
> May lose those joys we now do taste;
> The Blessed, that immortal be,
> From change in love are only free.[39]

Consequently, if either party has grown tired of the connection, it is unreasonable for the other to object. Such objections even justify a little rigour in the handling of the separation, though it must be contrived with wit, and a man of fashion remains calm and resourceful under any provocation. Dorimant is weary of Mrs. Loveit, and has taken another lady to the playhouse; when next they meet, Loveit attacks him hotly: "Faithless, inhuman, barbarous man——" ("Good," says Dorimant interrupting, "now the Alarm strikes") "without sense of love, of honour, or of gratitude, tell me, for I will know, what Devil masked she was, you were with at the Play yesterday?"[40] Dorimant has no intention of answering this, and he has the perfect parry in readiness: "Faith," he says, "I resolved as much as you, but the Devil was obstinate, and would not tell me." He is imperturbable throughout the scene, and one of its neatest exchanges occupies, in attack and defence, the space of four words; Loveit grows more and more furious, and at last exclaims "False man!" Dorimant's reply is simply "True woman!"

The amours of Dorimant raise at once all those questions of conduct and taste which have been hotly debated ever since 1698. It is largely a question of disposition and training; there will always be angry moralists to side with Jeremy Collier, Steele, Macaulay, and William Archer; there will always be sane and not less intelligent persons who hold the view of Dennis and Hazlitt and Mr. John Palmer; and there will always be the half-hearted, who enjoy Restoration comedy, are afraid of the moralists, and perch uneasily on the fence provided by Charles Lamb. It may perhaps be suggested, however, that in this matter the *sæva indignatio* of Steele is out of place. The question is one, not of morals, but of history: "Blame 'em not," says Wycherley's Dorilant of the dramatists of his time, "they must follow their Copy, the Age."[41] Macaulay's judgment of Wycherley is notorious; his "indecency is protected against the critics as a skunk is protected against the hunters. It is safe, because it is too filthy to handle, and too noisome even to approach." Yet Dryden, a contemporary witness, acquainted with the manners of the day, says that "the author of the *Plain Dealer,* whom I am proud to call my friend, has obliged all honest and virtuous men"[42] by that satirical piece.

In more recent years, Macaulay's unsavoury comparison has been revived by William Archer, who says of Restoration comedy in general, "We hold our noses as we read. It is all very interesting from a 'historical' point of view, as illustrating the coarse insensitiveness of our ancestors' nerves. But, æsthetically, a stench is a stench, even if it is wafted to us from the seventeenth century."[43] Of course, every one knows that the reader of these plays must expect the freedom of language used by their authors and audiences, and if he cannot stand it, he will not read. But let us examine an instance. "Dorimant (supposed to represent Lord Rochester)," says Archer, "addresses the orange-woman with gratuitous and foul-mouthed ruffianism." Not a bit of it

—though if his critic had used such language at a twentieth-century fruit-stall, there would have been some excuse for the adjectives. Dennis—a contemporary witness—does not call Dorimant's language foul-mouthed or ruffianly; he calls it Rochester's "agreeable Manner of his chiding his Servants."[44] But the victim herself is the best evidence of all; she had been greeted as "double Tripe," a "Cart-load of Scandal," and even "an insignificant Brandy Bottle"; but what does she know of the virtuous indignation of to-day? She takes the language as it is meant, without turning a hair, knowing perfectly well that Dorimant and Medley think none the worse of her for their fertility of epithet; but the moment they send for the Shoomaker, who is like to call her names in good earnest, she speaks her mind, and the mind of the orange-woman of all time: "Good Mr. *Dorimant,* pay me; Gad, I had rather give you my Fruit than stay to be abus'd by that foul-mouth'd Rogue; what you Gentlemen say it matters not much, but such a dirty Fellow does one more disgrace."[45]

It is the same with the amours of Mrs. Loveit and Bellinda; we must adopt the point of view of the age, and not blame the author for picturing what he saw. Bellinda had made herself too cheap, and Loveit had added to this error the folly of expecting the impossible. The verdict of experience and the world is spoken by Harriet: "Mr. *Dorimant* has been your God Almighty long enough, 'tis time to think of another."[46] Dorimant himself, earlier in the play, complains of Loveit that women are commonly as unreasonable in love as they are at Play, since "without the Advantage be on your side, a man can never quietly give over when he's weary."[47] No one will deny that for the modern reader he is too cold-blooded in this matter, and we are apt, like Sir Richard Steele, to censure his "falsehood to Mrs. Loveit, and the barbarity of triumphing over her anguish for losing him." Steele, however, went further than this; he called Dorimant not only a knave but a clown, and complained that though "the received character of this play is, that it is the pattern of genteel comedy," yet the "whole celebrated piece is a perfect contradiction to good manners, good sense, and common honesty. . . . At the same time I allow it to be nature, but it is nature in its utmost corruption and degeneracy."[48]

The answer is simple: *tempora mutantur. The Man of Mode* is not the idealising sentimental comedy that Steele created, but a genteel comedy it certainly is, for it drew the polite manners of its day, and showed nature as nature was to be seen in the London of 1676. The final word is that of John Dennis, who was acquainted with Etherege, and survived to refute Steele. Dorimant, says Dennis, "is an admirable Picture of a Courtier in the Court of King *Charles* the Second. But if *Dorimont* [*sic*] was design'd for a fine Gentleman by the Author, he was oblig'd to accommodate himself to that Notion of a fine Gentleman, which the Court and the Town both had at the Time of the writing of this Comedy. 'Tis reasonable to believe, that he did so, and we see that he succeeded accordingly. For *Dorimont* not only pass'd for a fine Gentleman with the Court of King *Charles* the Second, but he has pass'd for such with all the World, for Fifty Years together. And what indeed can any one mean, when he speaks of a fine Gentleman, but one who is qualify'd in Conversation, to please the best Company of either Sex."[49]

Sir George Etherege, himself an ornament of a court "the most polite that ever *England* saw," would have asked, perhaps, no greater praise than that.

NOTES

1. *An Allusion to Horace. The* 10th *Satyr of the* 1st *Book.* (Rochester's *Poems*, 1685, p. 36.) The Antwerpen edition (*circa* 1680) reads "a meer Original."
2. Prologue to *Bury-Fair*, 1689.
3. Dryden goes out of his way to praise Etherege in his attack on Shadwell some years later:—

    > Let Gentle *George* with Triumph Tread the Stage,
    > Make *Dorimant* betray, and *Loveit* rage,
    > Let *Cully, Cockwood, Fopling* charm the Pit,
    > And in their folly show the Writers Wit.
    >   *Mac Flecknoe*, ll. 151-4.

4. The *Dog* (or *Setting-Dog*) *and Partridge* was a fashionable tavern, frequented by Etherege and Sedley; Charles Montague called the latter its "Darling Son" (Add. MS. 28644, f. 57 b.) , and Etherege wrote home to Jephson, "I expect to see my Lord Carlingford in his way to Vienna, then you may be sure all the remains of the Dog & Partridge will be remembred." (27 Feb./8 Mar. '87/8: f. 170.) References to it may be found in *The Country Wife*, I. i, and *The Sullen Lovers*, II. iii.
5. *The Ramble*, 1682, p. 5. Etherege's name is added in a footnote to the text of the poem printed in Dryden's *Miscellany Poems*, 1716.
6. Oldys attributes the applause given to Etherege's plays by his contemporaries to "our Author's changing the study after old copies, and chimerical draughts from ungrounded speculation, which is but painting with dead colours, for those, taken directly from the freshest practise and experience in original life. He drew his characters from what they called

the *Beau monde;* from the manners and modes then prevailing with the
gay and voluptuous part of the world; which has made them appear the
more natural, tho' we cannot say the more innocent. He has also spirited
his dialogues, especially in the courtship of the fair sex, for which he is
distinguished by Mr. Dryden and others, with a sparkling gaiety which
had but little appeared before upon the stage, in parts pretending to the
character of modish Gallants." *Biographia Britannica,* Vol. III., 1750, p.
1842.

7. *Cutter of Coleman Street,* 1661.
8. *The Adventures of Five Hours,* 1663.
9. *The Wild Gallant,* 1663.
10. Its better known sub-title, *Love in a Tub,* was imitated in countless later
    pieces—*Love in a Wood, Love in a Maze, Love in a Sack, Love in a Rid-
    dle, Love in a Hollow Tree, etc.*
11. Etherege's general practice in the play is simple. The comic scenes are
    in prose; the heroic scenes are in heroic couplet, varied sometimes by a
    few lines of blank verse where he found couplets inconvenient (*e.g.* 17.
    19-31, 18. 36, 21. 150-2, 22. 177-80, 40. 3-4, 41. 20-1, *etc.*). But he also
    tends to mark any passage among the prose scenes, where deep feeling is
    introduced, by the use of blank verse. Even in his latest play this device
    is occasionally found; Emilia's speech to Young Bellair on the frailty of
    love and life (205. 30-2) has a marked blank verse rhythm, and so have
    the short passage between Dorimant and Harriet in the Mall (235. 63-5),
    her answers to him after the dance (248. 114-120), the farewell of
    Bellinda and Dorimant (259. 42-4), and a few of Loveit's more passionate
    lines (267. 87, and 271. 225). But in *The Comical Revenge,* with its rapid
    transitions from heroic play to riotous comedy, there is naturally more
    scope for such variation. In its second scene, Sir Frederick and Beaufort
    talk easily in prose until the knight inquires after Beaufort's fortunes in
    love, whereupon the heroic lover takes to blank verse (7. 172-206), while
    his light-hearted cousin does not. Etherege seems to regard blank verse
    as a half-way house between the rhyming couplet of heroics and the
    prose of comedy; it is so used by bearers of ill tidings, too agitated, per-
    haps, to speak correct couplets, but bringing news too serious for prose.
    Thus Lord Bevill and the Mourner use blank verse to announce the
    supposed deaths of Bruce (56. 11-7) and Sir Frederick (60. 1-19). Again
    in Act IV, sc. iv, Etherege marks the difference between the heroic duel-
    list and the masked villains by confining the use of the couplet to the
    former, but at the same time there is something emotional and tragic
    about the villains which lifts them a little above prose, and their ring-
    leader opens with two lines of unmistakable blank verse, while later
    speeches (52. 3-17), though they will not fall into decasyllables, have
    some obvious blank verse rhythms. Similarly one comic scene, the third
    of Act I, begins with prose, but at line 10 Palmer embarks upon some
    serious meditations upon his career, which are held to justify fifteen lines
    of extremely rough blank verse, the return to prose being made as soon
    as the theory of knavery gives place to the practical prospect of bubbling
    Cully.

As an example of their highly artificial kind, the verse scenes of *The Comical Revenge* are less open to objection than those of most heroic plays; Etherege allowed the servant to speak in prose (40. 14-5), was chary of the dangers of double rhyme, and only once sank into downright bathos—when

> Noble *Beaufort,* one unlucky day,
> A Visit to our Family did pay. (43. 90-1.)

Two of the more gnomic couplets (77. 42-3 and 12. 21-2) were honoured by inclusion in *Thesaurus Dramaticus,* 1724.

12. Here, however, as so often in Restoration comedies, it is necessary to remember that the most extravagant events might be modelled on plain fact. To the modern reader Cully's duel is chiefly suggestive of the more famous experiences of Bob Acres. But Roger North, in his *Life of the Lord Keeper Guilford,* describes how young Charles Crompton "not only diverted, but instructed his lordship in all the rakery and intrigues of the lewd town; and his own follies were his chief subject to rally upon, as he did with most lively description and wit: particularly his being cheated of his best horses brought up to him from the North, and bubbled into a duel, which came off with an acquittance signed upon the cheat's back in the field, and was the very action which Mr. Etheredge describes in his play of 'Love in a Tub.'" (*Lives of the Norths,* 1826, II. 233.)

13. "This mottley garniture of Fool and Farce," Dryden himself calls it in the Epilogue he wrote for its revival.

14. Such feats were common enough (*e.g.* Rochester's *Maim'd Debauchee,* st. 9), but they laid him open, even then, to several shrewd thrusts from the Widow (33. 4-5 and 70. 103-8).

15. Tom Killigrew's Mr. Jolly (An Humerous Gentleman, and a Courtier) speaks in the same tone to Lady Wild:—"Farewell, Widow, mayst thou live unmarryed till thou run'st away with thyself." (*The Parsons Wedding,* 1663, I. i.)

16. The test is not unnecessary in a society which includes Loveit and Bellinda as well as Harriet and the Widow, and the ladies themselves are aware that they must show their colours; see Ariana's speeches, 173. 454-7 and 174. 474-7.

17. For instance, III, iii. 1-32 (pp. 33-4).

18. 108. 140-3.

19. Etherege to Jephson, 27 Feb./8 March '87/8: Letter Book f. 169 b.

20. *Seventeenth Century Studies,* p. 243.

21. "Après une étude approfondie, on reconnait en Lady Cockwood une soeur de Tartufe." (*Molière en Angleterre* 1660-1670, par J.-E. Gillet, 1913, p. 70.) Dr. Gillet finds Etherege to be the "adaptateur le plus intelligent et le plus personnel" of Molière; but Dr. D. H. Miles, though he recognizes "the profound influence of Molière on Etheredge," points out many important points of contrast between them, and admits, in his final chapter, "that the Restoration would have produced a comedy not much different from the actual product, even had Molière never lived."

(The Influence of Molière on Restoration Comedy, by D. H. Miles, 1910, pp. 180, 66-8 and 220.)

22. It is perhaps worth noting that several phrases in *She wou'd if she cou'd* suggest a recent reading of the two parts of *Henry IV.* Freeman hopes (108. 132) that Ariana and Gatty "have more charity, than to believe us of the number of the wicked" (*cf.* Falstaff, Part I, I. ii. 106); Sir Joslin (127. 23) promises Sir Oliver "a whole Bevy of Damsels in Sky, and Pink, and Flame-colour'd Taffeta's" (the latter as worn by the blessed sun himself, Part I, I ii. 10-11); and Courtall (154. 183) thinks 'twere pity the ladies should have their "Curtains drawn in the dead of night" (like Priam's; Part II, I. i. 72). And the waiter's name is Francis.

23. "Moliere is quite rifled, then how should I write?" Song (satirising Shadwell) in Durfey's *Sir Barnaby Whigg,* 1681, p. 28.

24. In this point she had herself been anticipated by Tom Killigrew's Lady Love-all in *The Parsons Wedding,* III. v. This play is not very likely, however, to have been previously known to Etherege, as it was not acted until October 1664 (the year of its publication); though it may very possibly have been written before 1642, and a manuscript copy of another of Killigrew's plays still exists.

25. 134. 186; 136. 224.

26. These make the play peculiarly rich in dramatic irony; *e.g.* 102. 103, and 126. 260-1.

27. 240. 227-9.

28. Dennis, *A Defense of Sir Fopling Flutter,* 1722, p. 1.

29. Molière had employed the artifice in *Le Tartuffe.* It is interesting to compare Sir Fopling's dress, and his song, with those of Mascarille in the ninth scene of *Les Précieuses Ridicules,* which Etherege had in mind.

30. John Crowne, *Sir Courtly Nice,* 1685.

31. Sir John Vanbrugh, *The Relapse,* 1697.

32. The Hon. James Howard, *The English Monsieur,* 1674 (acted 1666).

33. William Wycherley, *The Gentleman Dancing Master,* 1673.

34. 236. 90-1. Shadwell, who consistently steals from Etherege, copied and spoilt this in *A True Widow.* "If you make love, you'll grow dull," says Theodosia to Carlos in Act II.

35. 249. 181-2.

36. And of all ladies too; witness Gatty (102. 129-30), and the adventure of Bellinda (265. 28-44) which Congreve imitated in the still more famous experience of her namesake in *The Old Bachelor* (IV. iv.).

37. 287. 421-6.

38.   In Him all Beauties of this Age we see;
            Etherege his Courtship, *Southern*'s Purity.
    Dryden, *To my Dear Friend Mr. Congreve, On His Comedy, call'd, The Double-Dealer.*

39. *To a Lady, asking him how long he would love her.* Kemp's *Collection of Poems,* 1672.

40. 214. 153-7.

41. *The Country Wife,* 1675, III. ii.

42. *Apology for Heroic Poetry*, 1677.

43. *The Old Drama and the New*, 1923, p. 174.

44. *A Defence of Sir Fopling Flutter*, 1722, p. 19.

45. 194. 163-7.

46. 286. 388-9.

47. 228. 107-8.

48. *Spectator*, No. 65. A very sensible examination of Steele's objections, by Oldys, will be found in *Biographia Britannica* Vol. III, 1750, pp. 1843-4.

49. *A Defence of Sir Fopling Flutter*, 1722, pp. 8-9.

DALE UNDERWOOD

❀

The Comic Values—*The Man of Mode*

Etherege's third and last play, *The Man of Mode, or Sir Fopling Flutter,* is one of the acknowledged masterpieces of Restoration drama. Properly understood it is also, I believe, one of the master-pieces of English comedy. In both contexts it gives a certain definitive and final form to lines of interest which had gathered through the course of seventeenth-century dramatic practice and which in eight-eenth-century drama were either abandoned or transformed into new values and assumptions.[1] At the same time, though it was produced eight years after Etherege's second comedy, its immediate lines of de-velopment stem from his previous works.[2] The outlines of *She Would If She Could* are clearly discernible in it; but they have been enlarged and realigned in comic meaning. And in this process the third comedy looks back in some significant ways to the first. While our interest, then, in moving from the first to the second play was to see how a given set of concerns developed into a more fully integrated and distinctive expression, we shall want now to see how aspects of both works become part of an enlarged and modified comic view. We shall want also to see how this development gives a more comprehensive and, from its particular point of view, a consummate definition to those questions of reality and value which constitute the essential interest of Restoration comedy of manners.

From *Etherege and the Seventeenth-Century Comedy of Manners* (New Haven: Yale University Press, 1957), pp. 72-93. Reprinted by permission of the publishers.

For each of these considerations we may best begin once more with the "hero." By the end of the expository first act we have learned that Dorimant—who "has more mistresses now depending than the most eminent lawyer in England has causes" (208)—has before the play seduced one member of its comic world, is about to succeed in seducing another, has laid plans for the immediate seduction of a third, has encouraged the marriage of a friend in the hope that he may thereafter more easily seduce the wife, and, finally, has been the dubious "ruin" of one who is dismissed as merely a "true-bred whore."[3] While there is much in this notable activity which is characteristic of the earlier comedies, there are also fundamental shifts in emphasis. The markedly more numerous and involved undertakings of the hero are no longer primarily the expression of libertine freedom, variety, and "epicurean" pleasure. These are allegedly doctrinal terms of value for him still. But his activities are now explicitly and predominantly the expression of what in the earlier plays was largely implied and secondary—a Hobbesian aggressiveness, competitiveness, and drive for power and "glory"; a Machiavellian dissembling and cunning; a satanic pride, vanity, and malice; and, drawing upon each of these frames of meaning, an egoistic assertion of self through the control of others.[4]

These shifts of emphasis in the hero correspond to further changes of form and meaning in the play. The use of a double plot shows lines of relationship with *The Comical Revenge*. Yet the total action of the play is now "heroically" single after the fashion of *She Would If She Could*. It is still concerned with the comedy of the fall. But it is pre-eminently a comedy of power in a wider and more sobering sense than in either of the earlier works. Specifically it involves the hero's conflict with and ultimate conquest of several contrasting "worlds" within the total world of the play. This comedy of power and conquest remains in part one of appearance versus reality, though its implications in these latter terms also acquire new meaning. The hero is now acclaimed at the end of the play as a very "civil" gentleman although he has behaved throughout very much like a villain. But this development, in turn, is part of the larger comedy of values. While the hero is repeatedly viewed by the various worlds of the play as "devil," he also "has something of the angel yet undefaced in him" (210). The vitality and meaning of the play derive primarily from the problems which this duality creates not only for those conquered by the hero but possibly by the end of the play for the hero himself. And the issues at stake include further terms of value. They reflect, for example, a corresponding duality in Art and Nature. If by nature the hero seems in some respects a devil, he is one with superior intelligence and great physical attraction. And these gifts of Nature are further enhanced by his art—his impeccable dress, the consummate "good breeding" of his manners (when, of course, he wishes to have them such), the skill and polish of his wit, the restraint, self-control, and order which all these accomplishments require. Yet if his art serves thus to enhance his nature, it also serves to conceal it. In the language of the play, the hero is the supreme "dissembler" of his comic world. He is at the same time the full embodiment of those interrelated but disparate assumptions and values which we have reviewed in the second chapter of this study. And while in all these respects he is the Restoration "man of mode," he is also the embodiment of archetypal problems and values in the life of man.[5]

Here again the characteristics of the hero's role are broadly generic for Etheregean comedy. What distinguishes them from the earlier works is not only the shifts in emphasis among them but the wider, more varied, and more fully defined context in which they operate. Each of the several worlds conquered by the hero has its particular set of values which in some way qualifies his. But he, in turn, in some way qualifies theirs. The relationships involved, however, are not static. They have their own distinctively comic development through the action of the play. By inspecting that development we derive an account of the play's own values, including a final definition for Etheregean comedy of Nature and Reason. And here, though the carefully guarded surfaces of *The Man of Mode* continue to reflect the pervasive ambiguity of the earlier plays, they are more committed in their treatment of the libertine-Machiavel "honest man." With this commitment go further changes in concern. The question remains as to what Nature in reality is. But the several discrete worlds stress more fully now the fact of Nature's diversity. The question accordingly is not only what apparent aspects of Nature are real but which of them in terms of value are to be most approved. Dorimant wins, if not like Edmund in *King Lear* his "land," then at least his supremacy in the worlds he conquers by his gifts from Nature and his exercise of an amoral wit, passion, and art. Yet while he is thus the comic conqueror, he is also in less ambiguous and qualified senses than his predecessors the comic villain. In this respect, indeed, *The Man of Mode* presents a special problem in the Restoration comedy of manners and an exception to its general practice. Its treatment of the problem, however, reflects those values which are typical of its genre.[6]

The two interlocking plots of *The Man of Mode* mark the division
of the play into two basic though again interlocking worlds of value.
Each has further divisions or "worlds" within it. But the characters of
the minor plot are distinguished from those in the major, which centers upon the hero, by being neither libertine nor Machiavellian.
Their values may for the moment be labeled merely "traditional" or
"conventional," and include concepts of genuine honor which contrast with the libertine-Machiavel "mode" exemplified by the hero.
This bipartite division in the play is thus reminiscent of the similar
division in *The Comical Revenge*. Meanwhile the major plot provides
in its totality much the same general pattern of action for the hero as in
each of the earlier plays. Though he now engages simultaneously in
three principal "intrigues" as compared with two in the second play and
one in the first, the total course of his action ostensibly moves in much
the same fashion from undertaking to fall. Here too, however, there
are fundamental modifications.[7]

The lines of both continuity and change are especially evident and
meaningful in Dorimant's undertaking with the first of his female
dupes, Loveit. Though she has been seduced by the hero before the
action of the play, Loveit continues in many ways the role of Lady
Cockwood. She too is the embodiment of "passion," and she has many
of the courtly assumptions concerning love which characterize her
predecessor. As a result she seems initially to stand at the opposite
extreme from the libertine appetite and values of her seducer. And
his alleged desire to escape from her passion seems again to prepare for
the comedy of his being caught in his own as he engages in subsequent
battle with the heroine. Yet like Lady Cockwood, Loveit seems in
other ways to maintain the distinction in "degree" between dupe and
hero: She is unwittingly used in the latter's further undertakings; and
she fails in her counterintrigue against him. Here her role as dupe
seems chiefly defined by the inferiority of her "wit" and by her lack
of self-control.

Despite these similarities, the role of Loveit has essential differences from that of Lady Cockwood. She has none of the grossly ridiculous excesses and incongruities of the earlier dupe and her more
characteristic descendants in Restoration comedy. Her passionate love
is simply that, not concupiscence in courtly disguise.[8] It is her seducer
who now assumes this mode of hypocrisy in the comic world of the
play. Nor does the dupe now expect honor from others while practic-
ing dishonor herself. She is no longer, in other words, the embodiment
of that extreme discrepancy between appearance and reality which

Lady Cockwood represented in the earlier work and which is now vested primarily in the hero. She is instead chiefly the dupe because she is helplessly the victim of a passionate love and nature which prevent dissembling in a world where the nature and art of the hero make dissembling a requisite for survival. What principally distinguishes Loveit, then, from the non-libertine world in the minor plot is her excessive and uncontrollable passion. She has been drawn into the orbit of the hero by that passion, but within the major plot she represents a variant world of her own. And if as such she continues in some respects the role of Lady Cockwood, she continues in others the values of the courtly world in *The Comical Revenge*.[9] The three plays of Etherege thus treat in three different but related ways and contexts what may be called the "problem of passion" in Restoration comedy of manners.

The problem has further ramifications in the Dorimant-Loveit relationship. Though the hero's sexual appetite stands initially at the farthest remove from Loveit's courtly passion, it is the dupe's uncontrolled passion of love which is the fullest object of torment by Dorimant's superficially controlled but in reality equally unbounded passion for conquest, power, and the exercise of malice.[10] As this conflict progresses, the dupe's open passion increasingly reflects those emotions which covertly characterize the hero's—"jealousy, indignation, spite, and thirst of revenge" (213) —while in Dorimant's conflict with the heroine, his passion and his appetite may possibly be converted to love. These developments in passion merge with a similar comedy in wit. Loveit's original belief in honor, faith, constancy, devotion are clearly not the beliefs of the libertine-Machiavel, as the initial encounter of hero and dupe makes clear.

> DOR. Love gilds us over and makes us show fine things to
>   one another for a time, but soon the gold wears off,
>   and then again the native brass appears.
> LOV. Think on your oaths, your vows and protestations,
>   perjured man.
> DOR. I made 'em when I was in love.
> LOV. And therefore ought they not to bind? Oh, impious!
> DOR. What we swear at such a time may be a certain proof
>   of a present passion; but, to say truth, in love there is
>   no security to be given for the future.   (216)

The question of "binding," of course, goes back to the provisos concerning "honor" and "virtue" in the resolution of the previous plays. But at the moment the hero's wit seems to establish the superiority of his views despite the fact that his art, even in such apparent candor, still conceals his real nature and convictions. His "oaths," as the play has already made clear and will presently make clearer in the seduction of Belinda, are not at all a "certain proof of a present passion" so far as love is concerned. They are instead part of the hero's disguise for his libertine appetite.[11] But in either case the assumptions involved are antithetical to those of the dupe. And they prepare for the questions to be raised in the play's denouement, when the hero's oaths will again be sworn to the heroine.

But by the time of the denouement, the dupe's belief reveals a change of view: "There's nothing but falsehood and impertinence in the world, all men are villains or fools" (286). Her conviction now echoes the disenchanted assumptions of the libertine-Machiavel, while the hero in the act of his "conversion" may possibly be approaching the initial position of the dupe. At beginning and end, however, the professed convictions of both call each other into question. In the total structure of the play they are mutually suspect because they are mutually oversimple. Neither of them gives an adequate account of Nature—either in its diversity as demonstrated by the differing worlds of the play or in its paradoxical potentials as demonstrated by the developments within those worlds. Yet the precise extent of falseness in the wit of either hero or dupe is part of the ambiguity in the resolution of the play. Loveit's concluding conviction that all men are villains or fools has as its immediate provocation the two "men of mode," Dorimant and Sir Fopling. She has just suffered the final "villainy" of the one in being exposed to the "impertinence" of the other. To this extent her conviction seems justified. Beyond that she has just witnessed the general acceptance of the hero as a very "civil" gentleman though he has in many and perhaps in all ways continued to the last to play the villain. In this respect her statement is justified by the total world of the play. Concerning the hero they have all—with the possible exception of the heroine—played the fool.

Nevertheless it is Loveit who does so last and most spectacularly. In calling Fopling a fool she has unwittingly fulfilled the intrigue of the hero against her and thus added the final stroke to the triumph of the "villain." Her wit has been at once wiser and more foolish than she knew, at once true and false. And its final if still equivocal obliquity derives chiefly from the fact that she remains to the last too passionate still. In this respect she assumes her closing relationship to the hero. Her conviction is juxtaposed with his avowal to the heroine:

"But now my passion knows no bounds" (279). Whether this unbounded passion is in reality one still of conquest and power or now of love is, however, part of the concluding question.

The question has meanwhile been enlarged and more precisely defined by the further intrigues of the hero. His seduction of Belinda, as the second line of action in the major plot, establishes her as a second comic dupe. In doing so it enlarges the comedy of values. Unlike Loveit, Belinda is not the embodiment of passion or of courtly assumptions. Essentially she belongs to what we shall presently see is the traditional honest-man group of the minor plot. Her seduction becomes one aspect of Dorimant's power over and control of that world. But unlike the other members of it, she is drawn into the libertine-Machiavel orbit of the hero by her love. Knowing the folly of her actions, she not only succumbs to the hero but joins him in playing the Machiavel, thereby further contributing to her own undoing.[12] Her comedy in both respects lies in the triumph of her passion over her reason. Her principal weakness in terms of value, however, is not the excess of passion but the capacity of her love to corrupt her understanding. While in these terms she has still a relationship to Loveit, she also prepares for the hero's third intrique, his undertaking to seduce the heroine, Harriet.

In the hands of the heroine, Dorimant too undergoes the conflict between passion and reason which has been the characteristic lot of the comic hero—though the reason here, of course, is that of the libertine-Machiavel. But he is here again to be distinguished from his predecessors and from the customary Restoration practice. He has not, as we have seen, played the Machiavel primarily at the prompting of his reason—as a deliberate badge of his revolt from conventional morality or as a necessity for survival or even as a calculated device for libertine appetite. He has, like his dupe, Belinda, played the role chiefly at the prompting of his passion, though in his case the passion has been one less of "love" than of self-love. While his attraction to the heroine, then, involves a conflict between passion and reason, it is more fundamentally a conflict in passions—of love on one hand and power and control on the other.[13] Consequently the most immediate question at the end of *The Man of Mode* is not, as in the previous comedies, whether the hero's love will eventually prove to be only libertine appetite or something more. The question is still present, but it depends on the precedent consideration as to whether in his professed passion of love Dorimant is still playing the Machiavel. This, of course, is to ask whether his desire for conquest is still stronger than his desire for love. But it is also to ask what, for the hero, the nature of love itself involves—how much of its passion is assertion of self and how much is self-submission. As a result, while the course of his final intrigue calls into doubt the value of his previous convictions, it also questions the nature and value of his passion. In these terms the play, despite the special aspects of its treatment, continues a central interest in the Restoration comedy of manners.[14] And to this interest the heroine makes a significant contribution.

In itself the role of the heroine in *The Man of Mode* shows the least change from preceding practice of any character in the work, though it acquires fuller meaning through its expanded context. Like her predecessors, Harriet is the heroine chiefly because she has sufficient wit and self-control to withstand the assaults of the hero and to hold out, at least through the end of the play, for marriage. In contrast to the dupes, she has kept her virtue by refusing to be drawn into either the libertine or Machiavellian elements of Dorimant's world. In these respects and in others she belongs to the traditional honest-man group of the minor plot. She thereby not only remains the final and crucial point of resistance in the hero's conquests but threatens to draw him into the world of honor from which he has seduced the dupes. Yet she is not herself entirely a member of the traditional honest-man world. She has much of the combativeness which characterizes the hero; she is almost as fond of and quite as skilled at dissembling as he; and she is far from immune to the pleasure of conquest and power. She has, that is, some of the nature and most of the art of the hero. And she shares in the "problem of passion" that runs through the characters and actions of the major plot. She has something of Loveit's intensity but with a greater self-control. And she has something of the dupe's courtly desires but with sufficient wit to understand their necessary limitations given the problematic nature of man and particularly the hero.[15] Finally, while she has something of Dorimant's pride and self-assertion, she has a greater willingness to submit herself to the "bonds" of love. She combines, in sum, distinctive attributes from the two basic worlds or plots of the play. At the close of the comedy, therefore, one possibility for hero and heroine is that they may combine the best of the two contrasting worlds—the passionate vitality of one and the stability, order, and honor of the other. But there is also the possibility, as further inspection will reveal more clearly, either of stalemate arising from a deadlock of opposing

powers or of a continued war of conflicting aims in which one of the
adversaries will finally become the conquered "victim" of the other.
The element of passion involved in each of these eventualities remains for *The Man of Mode* as for Restoration comedy of manners at
large the most pervasive source of doubt. Meanwhile its place in the
play's scheme of values is further defined by the characters and actions
of the minor plot.

The minor plot of *The Man of Mode* is divided into two groups of
characters. In one is what we have called the traditional honest-man
world—Young Bellair, Emilia, whom he unqualifiedly wishes to marry,
and Lady Townley, whose house becomes the principal setting in
which the several worlds of the play commingle. In the other are the
two parents, Old Bellair and Lady Woodvil. As members of an older
generation, and one should perhaps add of the landed gentry, the
parents are opposed by all the other worlds of the play not only because they represent the "former age" but because they also represent the broadly prevailing world of established institutions and customs which has not heretofore been projected in the dramatis personæ of Etherege's comedies but against which the world of the hero
has from the first been in revolt. As members of this older world the
parents are further distinguished by lacking the temper, understanding, and manners of the honest man. Yet they possess a set of moral
attitudes which puts them in a world of genuine honor. And in this
respect they are like the honest-man group of the minor plot but
strikingly unlike the libertine-Machiavel world of the hero. In the
play's comedy of values the parents represent one extreme for which
the "mode" of the hero provides the opposite. The traditional honest-
man group stands between the two as a mean and, in terms of the
play's own values, the nearest approach to an ideal. Consequently,
while the deficiencies of the parents are to be measured chiefly by
their lack of true honest-man attributes, they serve also to qualify
the characteristics of the hero.

In the parents there is no discrepancy between appearance and reality. Yet their inability to distinguish between the two and between
art and nature in the worlds about them consistently makes them the
comic dupes. They readily mistake the outward forms for the reality
of love in the mock courtship of their children (222-4). And Lady
Woodvil is as readily fooled by the dissembling of Dorimant in his
assumed role, calculated to win her favor, of "Mr. Courtage," a pro-

fessed admirer of "the forms and civility of the last age" (193). But
while the parents are here the dupes through the deficiences of their
particular world, they emphasize the fact that the more fashionable
worlds which reject them are also fooled by appearance and art
through a concern with different values. In their disregard for the
manners of the honest man, the parents are the only ones not taken in
by the modish surfaces of the hero. This situation of give-and-take
between the old world and the new works, however, in different ways.
One aspect of the elder Bellair's attitute toward love and marriage is
summed up in his request, "Please you, sir, to commission a young
couple to go to bed together a God's name?" (280) "A God's name"
sufficiently distinguishes the world of the parents from that of the
hero. But the assumptions involved concerning the desires of love
are not very different from the appetitive convictions of the libertine.
For the problems posed by *The Man of Mode,* both are inadequate.

Again the play gives an easy sanction to the revolt of its "young
couples" against the custom of parentally arranged and economically
motivated marriage. Old Bellair's "The rogues ha' got an ill habit of
preferring beauty" (223) states one aspect of the revolt. And he himself comically exposes the inconsistency in his world between custom
and nature as he also prefers beauty in becoming enamoured of Emilia. At the same time his "undertaking" with her, a parallel to the
activities of the hero, is pointedly honorable. He not only wishes to
marry her but, for all his farcical lack of honest-man polish and restraint, possesses a genuine good will and good nature which contrasts with the very different character of the hero's undertakings.

Nevertheless the lack of the honest man's restraint and balance of
temper remains a major deficiency in the parents' world of values.
Old Bellair's ebullient good nature, in itself an essential requisite for
the honest man, is entirely without the equally requisite self-control.
It converts in an instant into impetuous fits of anger which relate
him, despite the more ludicrous elements of his behavior, to the passionate excesses of Loveit (207). And his excesses in good nature itself make him the comic dupe. At the end of the play his ready acquiescence in being outwitted by his son's secret marriage contrasts
with Dorimant's ill-natured revenge on Loveit for temporarily out-
witting him. Yet by the same impetuous good nature with which he
accepts his son's marriage, he also indiscriminately accepts both the
hero and his modish companion, Medley: "Mr. Medley, my sister tells
me you are an honest man, and, adod, I love you" (257). Medley, of

course, is indeed an "honest man," but not in the sense in which Old Bellair through the values of his own world accepts him. Like the hero, Medley is one kind of honest man while Old Bellair is another. But in terms of traditional honest-man values and those of the play they are mutually aberrant.

Among these obliquities, the world of Young Bellair, Emilia, and Lady Townley stands in most respects as the true perpendicular.[16] That they are to be distinguished from the hero is repeatedly made clear in the opening scene. To Dorimant, Young Bellair is "handsome, well-bred, and by much the most tolerable of all the young men that do not abound in wit" (201). The alleged deficiency in wit lies partly, of course, in Bellair's desire to marry:

> BELL. You wish me in heaven, but you believe me on my
> journey to hell.
> MED. You have a good strong faith, and that may contrib-
> ute much towards your salvation. I confess I am but
> of an untoward constitution, apt to have doubts and
> scruples, and in love they are no less distracting than
> in religion; were I so near marriage, I should cry out
> by fits as I ride in my coach, *Cuckhold, Cuckold,* with
> no less fury than the mad fanatic does *Glory* in Bed-
> lam.
> BELL. Because religion makes some run mad, must I live
> an atheist?   (199)

Though the wit of Medley, like that of the hero, seems to have more "art," Bellair's wit in the view of the play is the more nearly "true." It is not only a "happy mean"; it takes cognizance of Nature's diversity as neither Dorimant's libertine assumptions nor, at an opposing extreme, Loveit's courtly expectations do. And in the face of this diversity, the significant word is "faith." Dorimant initially has no faith. Like Medley, he is an "atheist." Loveit originally has too much and none at the end.

This same common-sense moderation continues to distinguish the world of the traditional honest man from that of the libertine-Machiavel. Thus when Young Bellair offers to "vow" his constancy—as the hero is throughout the play doing—he is prevented by Emilia:

> EMIL. Do not vow—Our love is frail as is our life, and full
> as little in our power; and are you sure you shall out-
> live this day?

> BELL. I am not, but when we are in perfect health 'twere
> an idle thing to fright ourselves with the thoughts of
> sudden death.   (205-6)

In light of the play's own values, Emilia's awareness is an essential
one. It constitutes a principal source of dubiety in the problems of
love as viewed by the Restoration comedy of manners. It also bears an
obvious relationship to the convictions of the libertine.[17] But Bellair's
reply provides the common-sense complement. And here love is
"health," not as for the hero a "fit" or, in the case of the prolonged
seizure, a "disease." As a result, while the "passion" of the honest-man
lovers is markedly less intense than in the other worlds of the play, it
is far more stable and secure. Except for parental interference, Emilia
and Young Bellair remain a point of calm in the midst of more violent extremes around them. While Dorimant and Loveit bitterly argue the relative merits of modish "wits" and "fools" as lovers, the
honest-man world establishes the merits of lovers who are neither of
these. And while Dorimant and Harriet exchange barbed accusations
and establish elaborate conditions for "proof of passion," Emilia and
Bellair quietly accept their faith in each other.

In other areas of professed value, however, the world of the traditional honest man and of the hero appear to be and to an extent are
one. Young Bellair is "ever well-dressed, always complaisant, and seldom impertinent." Emilia "has beauty enough to provoke detraction;
her carriage is unaffected, her discourse modest, not at all censorious
nor pretending, like the counterfeits of the age" (202). These praises
come from the "honest-man" world of Dorimant and Medley—with
what comic inconsistency will be apparent. Together with a long list
of ethico-social characteristics such as "good humour," "kindness,"
"obligingness," they represent values subscribed to by both worlds,
though in the world of the hero they are consistently corrupted by disparate assumptions and practices. They are values for the play only
when, as in Emilia and Young Bellair, they establish a harmony between appearance and reality rather than a discrepancy. And in these
terms they also serve to establish a harmony among Nature, Reason,
and Art. They are part of the play's assumption not only that Nature's "degrees" must be kept by the restraint of Reason but that the
"natural" balance and harmony of those degrees within the body social is also a matter of art. "Good breeding" in the face of Nature's
diversity is an essential if social intercourse is to be "natural and easy."
The code of manners for the honest-man values of the play, accord-

ingly, is "Nature still, but Nature methodised." Terms like "unaffected" and "impertinence" look to the need of keeping degree. Others like "complaisance," "civility," "good nature," and lack of censoriousness reflect the need of tolerance in a natural harmony that encompasses diversity. In all these respects the world of Emilia and Young Bellair provides for *The Man of Mode* a norm in manners, wit, passion, and control which helps to define contrasting divergencies in the several worlds about them. They continue this role in the comedy which develops between the play's two "men of mode," Dorimant and Sir Fopling. But here they reveal also the fact that their world does not escape the perspective which sees them too as in certain ways defective.

In the hero and the dupe, the wit and the fool, the gentleman and the fop, Nature's diversity seems to exist at its most obvious extremes, though the extremes again reflect the play's shifts in concern. The ludicrous excesses of Sir Fopling look more to the manners and values of the honest man than to the libertine. The grossly libidinous predilections of the country knight are replaced by the sterility of the city fop in his overrefined devotion to the surfaces of clothes and social ritual.[18] These alterations have still a place, however, in the comedy of love. As the universally acclaimed "fool" in the total world of *The Man of Mode*, Sir Fopling involves a thematic term which works in many directions. But among them is the fact that he plays the fool in love. His attempted "intrigue" with Loveit—prompted by the hero as part of his own undertaking—ends, as we expect from the hero's dupe, in fiasco. Apart from his evident witlessness, he has played the fool because his only real desire in his undertaking was to conform to the ritual of the "mode." He is incapable of either "heroic" appetite or love. Yet his lack of both keeps him from playing the fool in other ways—as it has been played by Loveit and Belinda and is perhaps being played by Harriet or, from the libertine point of view, as it is possibly being played at the end by the hero.[19] Since he is incapable of "passion," he is also incapable of "the fall." When Loveit rebuffs his advances at the close of the play by calling him a fool, he happily decides that "An intrigue now would be but a temptation to me to throw away that vigour on one which I mean shall shortly make my court to the whole sex in a *ballet*" (285).

By his freedom from passion, Sir Fopling as fool acquires further implications. Critics have long commented upon his "delightfulness." "He is in himself a delight, presented from pure joy of him, and is not

set up merely as a target for the raillery of wiser fools."[20] But it would
seem to be very much as a target for wiser fools that he is "set up." A
chief source of his delightfulness is that of all the characters in the
play he is the most fully and naturally good humored. His open pride
and vanity, unlike these covert traits in the hero, are both innocuous
and free of guile. In his nature there is no drive for power and no
Machiavellian cunning. Yet he is repeatedly rejected by the wiser
fools as they acclaim the hero, whose surface good humor conceals his
natural malice.[21] The irony is heightened by the hero himself. Concerning the fool he suggests to an approving audience that "Nature
has her cheats, stums a brain, and puts sophisticate dulness often on
the tasteless multitude for true wit and good humour" (232). But it is
clear at the moment and throughout the play that Nature has her
cheats in sophisticate charm as well as dullness.

The comedy of values takes accordingly still another turn. Sir Fopling's chief offense in terms of his relations to others is his "impertinence." He fails in his lack of restraint to keep decorum or degree. But
beneath the hero's surface control lies, of course, the most extreme
"impertinence." The fool and the hero are the only two characters in
the play who are persistently guilty of aggression—the one open, bump-
tious, and repelled, the other covert, mannered, and successful. We are
reminded thereby that for the hero the essential purpose of his restraint is not moderation but indulgence, not the keeping of order but
its violation. And while the fact enhances the comedy of appearance
and reality, it also extends the comedy of values in which the hero
conquers the worlds of honor in the minor plot.

The lines of conquest involved are established in the opening scene
of the play. Emilia's marriage to Young Bellair is to be encouraged by
Dorimant in the hope that thereafter he may more easily seduce her
(202). In the meantime Young Bellair's friendship is being cultivated
for an additional reason.

> MED. You and he are grown very intimate, I see.
> DOR. It is our mutual interest to be so: it makes the
> women think the better of his understanding and
> judge more favourably of my reputation; it makes him
> pass upon some for a man of very good sense and I
> upon others for a very civil person.   (202)

Meanwhile in the world of the parents there remains to be won over
Harriet's mother who, as a member of "the last age," shares the opin-

ion of those in the present that Dorimant is "an arrant devil" (193).
As the hero's three undertakings—with Loveit, Belinda, and Harriet—
develop in the major action of the play, his undertakings with the two
groups of the minor plot develop also. After Belinda, as part of her
own intrigue with Dorimant, has witnessed his first "cruel" treatment
of Loveit, she engages in the following conversation at Lady Townley's:

> BEL. Well, that Dorimant is certainly the worst man
>   breathing.
> EMIL. I once thought so.
> BEL. And do you not think so still?
> EMIL. No. indeed!
> BEL. Oh, Jesu!
> EMIL. The town does him a great deal of injury, and I
>   will never believe what it says of a man I do not know
>   again, for his sake.
> BEL. You make me wonder!
> L. TOWN. He's a very well-bred man.
> BEL. But strangely ill-natured.
> EMIL. Then he's a very witty man.
> BEL. But a man of no principles.
> MED. Your man of principles is a very fine thing indeed!
> BEL. To be preferred to men of parts by women who
>   have regard to their reputation and quiet. Well, were
>   I minded to play the fool, he should be the last man
>   I'd think of.   (225-6)

The situation for Belinda is clear. It involves both her struggle between passion and reason and the comedy in which the character of
the hero is rendered more equivocal by the dissembling of his critic.
The most potent comedy, however, lies in his being defended by Emilia, though this situation too remains in part ambiguous. The eventual success of Dorimant's designs upon Emilia is left in question at
the end of the play. That he has found a "little hope" was indicated
in the opening scene. And Emilia's change of mind concerning him
presumably provides a basis of the hope. Yet by his own grudging admission he has found her "a discreet maid" (202). And the play makes
clear not only that she is that and much more but that she is altogether in love with Young Bellair, whom she marries. Nevertheless,
since one of the realities in the play which remains fundamentally
elusive is the ultimate nature of love, Emilia's marriage raises rather

than settles the question of Dorimant's eventual success. He had himself promoted the marriage with the conviction that "nothing can corrupt her but a husband. . . . I have known many women make a difficulty of losing a maidenhead who have afterwards made none of making a cuckold" (202). But whatever the eventuality in this regard, Emilia's defense of Dorimant here promotes his conquests and expands the comedy of appearance and reality.

At the same time it sharpens the comedy of values. Emilia and Lady Townley have lost perspective among the various values of the honest man. To Belinda's charge that the hero is both "ill-natured" and "a man of no principles"—which he, of course, is—they offer no direct refutation. Nor do they to Medley's "Your man of principles is a very fine thing indeed!" They only suggest instead that Dorimant is, nevertheless, "a very well-bred man" and "a very witty man." For this world of the honest man, the importance of manners has obscured the importance of morals, even though that world itself is essentially moral in its actions and convictions.

Immediately following the scene in which Emilia has defended Dorimant, Young Bellair does the same. He is in the Mall with Harriet. She is about to meet Dorimant for the first time, but she has already seen and been captivated by him. He is here the subject of conversation:

> HAR. I never saw anything in him that was frightful.
> Y. BELL. On the contrary, have you not observed something extreme delightful in his wit and person?
> HAR. He's agreeable and pleasant I must own, but he does so much affect being so, he displeases me.
> Y. BELL. Lord, madam, all he does and says is so easy and so natural.
> HAR. Some men's verses seem so to the unskilful, but labour i' the one and affectation in the other to the judicious plainly appear.
> Y. BELL. I never heard him accused of affectation before.
> (Enter Dorimant and stares upon her)
> HAR. It passes on the easy town, who are favourably pleased in him to call it humour.   (234)

Harriet's criticisms, like Belinda's, are accurate though complicated by her own dissembling and affectation. But here it is Bellair who, like Emilia in the scene before, is the center of the comedy, not only in being fooled by Dorimant's friendship and in being the instrument for sustaining his reputation, but in the superbly equivocal and thematically central irony of his phrase "so easy and so natural." These are fundamental terms in the traditional criteria of the honest man. But what is easy and natural for Dorimant is to play the hypocrite in appearing to have an "agreeableness" and "pleasantness" which in reality are far from natural for him. The phrase places him and his particular "honest-man" mode in critical juxtaposition with true honest-man values. It also makes clear, as the previous scene had done for Emilia and Lady Townley, the essential confusion and debility of Bellair's own honest-man sense of values which permit him and his world to be conquered by the hero.

The discussion between Bellair and Harriet serves as preface for Dorimant's third and last undertaking, the attempted seduction of the heroine. While the development of that action follows Etherege's customary pattern, its resolution is merged with and modified by the larger denouement in which the hero's several conquests are completed. In the last scene of the play, Dorimant's entrance and the final conditions of acceptance between hero and heroine have as prelude a song written by the hero himself. In part it reads:

> None ever had so strange an art
> His passion to convey
> Into a listening virgin's heart,
> And steal her soul away.   (277)

The "satanic" posture embedded in the verses' synthetic pastoralism ("As Amoret with Phyllis sat") catches many of the play's comic tensions.[22] But it specifically prepares for the denouement that follows. With an art not totally strange to the reader of Etherege's earlier plays but now more consummate and deeply ironic, Dorimant conveys his "passion" into the listening heart of the virgin heroine as he vows his surrender and reform: "By all the hope I have in you, the inimitable colour in your cheeks is not more free from art than are the sighs I offer." And again "I will renounce all the joys I have in friendship and in wine, sacrifice to you all the interest I have in other women—" (278).

When this undertaking is interrupted by the untimely arrival of both Loveit and Belinda, all Dorimant's intrigues are simultaneously threatened with exposure and he, like the earlier heroes, is threatened with reduction to the status of a dupe. For Dorimant too, however, his wit saves his reputation and restores his heroic status.

DOR. (to Lov.). I had trusted you with this secret, but that I knew the violence of your nature would ruin my fortune, as now unluckily it has. I thank you, madam.

LOV. She's an heiress, I know, and very rich.

DOR. To satisfy you I must give up my interest wholly to my love; had you been a reasonable woman, I might have secured 'em both and been happy.

LOV. You might have trusted me with anything of this kind, you know you might. Why did you go under a wrong name?

DOR. The story is too long to tell you now—be satisfied, this is the business, this is the mask has kept me from you.

BEL. (aside). He's tender of my honour, though he's cruel to my love.

LOV. Was it no idle mistress then?

DOR. Believe me, a wife, to repair the ruins of my estate that needs it.

LOV. The knowledge of this makes my grief hang lighter on my soul; but I shall never more be happy.

DOR. Belinda!

BEL. Do not think of clearing yourself with me, it is impossible. Do all men break their words thus?

DOR. Th' extravagant words they speak in love; 'tis as unreasonable to expect we should perform all we promise then, as do all we threaten when we are angry. When I see you next—

BEL. Take no notice of me, and I shall not hate you.

· · · · ·

DOR. We must meet again.

BEL. Never.

DOR. Never?

BEL. When we do, may I be as infamous as you are false. [The aside conversation with Belinda ends here.]

L. TOWN. Men of Mr. Dorimant's character always suffer in the general opinion of the world.

MED. You can make no judgment of a witty man from common fame, considering the prevailing faction, madam.

O. BELL. Adod, he's in the right.

MED. Besides, 'tis a common error among women to believe too well of them they know and too ill of them they don't.

O. BELL. Adod, he observes well.

> L. TOWN. Believe me, madam, you will find Mr. Dorimant
>   as civil a gentleman as you thought Mr. Courtage.
> HAR. If you would but know him better—   (282-4)

The comedy here, of course, is rampant. The lie to Loveit saves Dorimant's reputation in two ways: She no longer believes he has "bar-
barously" abandoned her; and she accordingly rebuffs the advances of
Sir Fopling, thus completing the hero's control and conquest of the
dupes. Medley's consequent, "Dorimant! I pronounce thy reputation
clear, and henceforward when I would know anything of woman, I
will consult no other oracle" (286), furthers the hero's triumphs by
reinstating his supremacy within his own world. Medley's praise, in
turn, would indicate that he, who should best know, does not take the
professed "conversion" as more than continued stratagem. Were Dorimant about to fall into marriage, Medley, as an "atheist" in such matters, would hardly consider his reputation clear. Next, Belinda's "He's
tender of my honour" continues the comedy. It was his own "honor"
and vanity of which he was tender, but an essential part of his reputation and conquest is thus salvaged from the affair with Belinda. Again,
Dorimant's reminder to Belinda concerning the "extravagant words"
men speak in love casts its light upon the words he has just spoken to
Harriet in avowing his passion. Finally, while Belinda's realization
that Dorimant is "false" is immediately followed by the general assertion that he is "civil," the comedy in the hero's successes is climaxed
by Harriet's "If you would but know him better—." Unconsciously the
heroine herself thus underscores the comedy of Medley's own "malicious" wit concerning the "common error among women." But the
result of all this is that the hero conquers his last enemy, Lady Woodvil. And the way is prepared for the closing lines:

> L. WOOD. If his occasions bring him that way, I have now
>   so good an opinion of him he shall be welcome.
> HAR. To a great rambling lone house that looks as it
>   were not inhabited, the family's so small; there you'll
>   find my mother, an old lame aunt, and myself, sir,
>   perched up on chairs at a distance in a large parlour,
>   sitting moping like three or four melancholy birds in a
>   spacious volery. Does not this stagger your resolution?
> DOR. Not at all, madam. The first time I saw you you left
>   me with the pangs of love upon me, and this day my
>   soul has quite given up her liberty.
> HAR. This is more dismal than the country!   (287)

It is part of the comedy of the hero and of the play that neither we nor perhaps the hero himself can be entirely certain as to what his real intentions have by this time come to be. But Harriet's dissembling to the last, while it may seem to augur well for her success, works another way. Dorimant's pangs of love and his soul's surrendering its liberty are dismal in more ways than Harriet in her final affectation can be aware. One recalls that with the "pangs of love" for the heroine upon him, the hero successfully pursued his seduction of Belinda;[23] that the "forty days" which he had vowed at his first meeting with Harriet would be "well lost to gain your favour" (236) have only just begun; that for one whose soul has quite given up her liberty, the behavior with Belinda immediately preceding that avowal was something more than curious; and that in general the dubious nature of Dorimant's soul qualifies the possibilities of future action implied in the resolutions of Etherege's previous comedies. The play in its totality and particularly in the closing scene suggests that if the hero troubles at all to undergo his "trial"—a temporary endurance of the country— he will do so more for conquest than for love and that the country accordingly is more likely to become the setting for a "ruin" than a romance. Yet if the hero's protestations should prove sincere, the basic dubiety of the play still exists concerning the ultimate nature of love. Harriet's "dismal" echoes the reticences of Etherege's previous heroines; and her affectation in this respect looks forward to the same affectation in Congreve's Millamant, to the explicit problem of *The Relapse,* and to the continuity of interest for Restoration comedy of manners as a whole.

In this regard one further point remains which distinguishes *The Man of Mode* from Etherege's previous works. In the context of the play, Harriet's "melancholy" picture of the "country" becomes in certain ways a possible and paradoxical "symbol of fertility." If Dorimant is finally drawn into the country by love, his passion will at least to some extent have transcended the element of sterility and triviality which characterizes the total "city" milieu of the play. It is surely wrong to assume that Etherege was not aware of this sterility.[24] In the first two plays the libertine worlds were fully conscious of their own frivolity. It was an aspect of their assertion to themselves and to the conventional world from which they revolted that the traditional ideals which they rejected had been invalidated by the realities of man. But in *The Man of Mode* Lovett can banish "poor Mr. Lackwit but for taking up another lady's fan" without seeing anything comical in the situation (210), a state of affairs foreign even to the befuddled Lady Cockwood. The condition of the hero is not greatly different from the dupe's. Though he may take up the lady's fan, his greater "pleasure" is in provoking her to break it.[25] And while he has, unlike the dupe, some sense of the absurdity involved, there is nevertheless beneath his posturing a compulsive malice and vanity which, given their milieu, are more deeply absurd than the hero is aware. The demonic passions of a Don Juan are now comic in part because they so willingly vent themselves in the trivialities of the drawing room and the Mall.

The world of Emilia, Young Bellair, and Lady Townley, in turn, is, for all its value as a "happy mean," unworthy of being conquered by any but a comic hero. Lady Townley's house is, as she herself states, "the common refuge of all the young idle people" (228). But the idleness of this middle world is not a conscious or comic revolt against anything. There is simply nothing better to do. For Lady Townley, Medley is a "very necessary man." He knows "all the little news o' the town" (207). Emilia "loves" to hear him "talk o' the intrigues; let 'em be never so dull in themselves, he'll make 'em pleasant i' the relation" (207). The comedy of love, of nature and art, of wit, passion, and control is everywhere conditioned by this comedy of manners. The comedy has, of course, those other facets which we have inspected—in the hero, the libertine-Machiavel beneath the manners of the honest man; in the world of Lady Townley, the capacity of manners to corrupt their own value and the value of a sanctioned morality which they in other ways express. But the final comedy of both concerns is that the society of the play, whether it pursues pleasure or power, does so in an endless and sterile round of play houses, parks, drawing rooms, and "all the little news o' the town."

This comedy, however, is again ambiguous, though now in a somewhat different sense. If the play insists upon the frivolity of its society, it suggests no adequate set of values by which that frivolity may be judged. A temporary endurance of the country is at best a partial and tentative antidote.[26] As envoy to Ratisbon, particularly during the final months of crisis in James' reign, Etherege was to take up the cause of something besides pleasure with a devotion, skill, and even passion which easily give the lie to much that has been said and written about him as a man.[27] But for all that, his own and man's real worth remained a matter of doubt. The comic dramatist certainly did not at any time return simply to "traditional" orthodoxy. If he saw the sterility of an idle leisure class devoted to pleasure and politesse, he also saw, even as he worked valiantly in the midst of it, the sterility —the hypocrisy, cunning, pettiness, and amorality—in the traditionally worthier realms of man's endeavor and aspiration. Indeed, in the maze of political intrigue and malice which surrounded him at Ratisbon he could perceive a comedy of power, of Machiavellian ruthlessness garbed in politesse, of nature versus reason, and of man in the dark which was not fundamentally very different from the comedy of the leisure society in his plays. And there is no reason to suppose that he found the one world more noble and worthy and less comic than the other. He himself served them both, but without, one can be sure, believing fully in either. Thus the fact that his plays offer no adequate alternative to the frivolity which they expose would seem to indicate for their author the final comedy of man.

NOTES

Page references in parentheses are to H. F. B. Brett-Smith, *The Works of Sir George Etherege*, the Percy Reprints No. 6, Oxford: Oxford University Press, 1927, but Mr. Underwood has used the modernized spelling and punctuation of the edition by A. Wilson Verity, *The Works of Sir George Etherege*, London: John C. Nimmo, 1928. [Editor's note]

1. The practice of grouping Restoration drama with that of the 18th century is open, I believe, to question. The last part of the 17th century is in many profound respects a period of transition. But its drama, and particularly its comedy of manners, is in more ways the end of an era than the beginning of a new one. The principal traditions which produce Restoration comedy have their final voice in Pope, Swift, and Gay. Goldsmith and Sheridan, for all their alleged revolt from "sentimental" comedy, are essentially of a different world, and one much closer to Steele and Cumberland than to Etherege, Wycherley, and Congreve.

2. *The Man of Mode* was first produced in March 1676, after all but one (*The Plain Dealer*) of Wycherley's plays had appeared. But it does not seem likely that the changes which we are about to note in Etherege's final comedy can be attributed to direct influence from the preceding works of his contemporary.

3. The "whore's" illiterate "billet-doux" at the end of the act (204) provides a significant climax to the "undertakings" of the hero which have been the major concern of the exposition.

4. See *Leviathan*, p. 35: "Joy, arising from imagination of a man's own power and ability, is that exultation of the mind which is called *Glorying*." Also p. 64: "So that in the first place, I put for a general inclination of all mankind, a perpetual and restless desire of power after power, that closeth only in death. . . . Competition of riches, honour, command, or

other power, inclineth to contention, enmity, and war: because the way of one competitor, to the attaining his desire, is to kill, subdue, supplant, or repel the other."

5. In this regard the similarities between Dorimant and the Don Juan of 17th-century drama seem especially noteworthy. The libertinism, the seeming rationality, the wit and general polish of manner, the physical attractiveness, the "Machiavellianism," the Satanic egoism, pride, and malice are among the specific characteristics which they share. The similarity is especially apparent in the Don Juans of Molière, Rosimond, and Shadwell—the versions with which Etherege and the Restoration were most familiar. (Shadwell's *The Libertine* was produced in June 1675, nine months before Etherege's play.) At the same time it seems apparent that the 17th-century concerns reflected in Dorimant and Don Juan are to be related to those which produced the "Machiavellian villain" of pre-Restoration English drama. The Jacobean and Caroline comedy discussed in the final portion of this study shows further aspects of this relationship.

6. Critics have frequently likened Dorimant to Horner in Wycherley's *The Country Wife*. But apart from their busy sex lives, the two characters are fundamentally different. Horner is the sheer sensualist whom Dorimant has too often been thought to represent. He has little concern with power and self-assertion as such. In the Machiavellian aspects of his role, Dorimant is more fully related to Congreve's villains, Maskwell in *The Double-Dealer* and Fainall in *The Way of the World*. Congreve's comic heroes, to the extent that they play the Machiavel, do so primarily as a necessity for survival in their world.

7. This progression in the number of the hero's intrigues or undertakings is not an incidental one. It corresponds to the increasing complexity and articulation of the successive plays.

8. Loveit's name, particularly in the general context of Restoration practice, is, in fact, misleading. In her passion Loveit as comic dupe is more like Mrs. Marwood in *The Way of the World* than she is like Lady Fidget in *The Country Wife* or Lady Wishfort in *The Way of the World*, who are more fully in the line of descent from Lady Cockwood. Unlike Mrs. Marwood, however, Loveit's passion does not involve her in playing the "Machiavel." These distinctions, like those noted above in the "heroes" and "villains," suggest the variety of mutations by which the characteristic concerns of Restoration comedy of manners are expressed.

9. The specialized involvements in "honor" which distinguish the heroic-courtly world of *The Comical Revenge* have in Loveit, as in the minor plot of *The Man of Mode*, been largely normalized. Consequently Loveit's courtly assumptions concerning honor merge in most respects with those of the traditional honest man and of Christian-classical orthodoxy. But in seeking fulfillment outside marriage, Loveit's passion invokes also the courtly honor of secrecy and thus merges with the code of expedient "honor" which operates in the world of the libertine hero.

10. See Loveit's awareness: "You, who have more pleasure in the ruin of a woman's reputation than in the endearments of her love" (270). Com-

pare Belinda's similar understanding that "he is never well but when he triumphs, nay, glories to a woman's face in his villainies" (273). Compare also Dorimant's "He guesses the secret of my heart!" (242), when Medley reminds him that some men "fall into dangerous relapses when they have found a woman inclining to another" (242). The "secret" of Dorimant's "heart" becomes at the end of the play the principal comic question, as we shall see in more detail.

11. Thus, following his seduction of Belinda:

> MED. You have had an irregular fit, Dorimant?
>
> DOR. I have.
>
> Y. BELL. And is it off already?
>
> DOR. Nature has done her part, gentlemen; when she falls kindly
> to work, great cures are effected in little time, you know.   (260)

12. For the comedy of power between the hero and his dupe, see III.2, p. 227. For the comedy of the dupe as Machiavel, see II.2, particularly Belinda's closing lines in the scene (218) and her earlier aside: "Now to carry on my plot; nothing but love could make me capable of so much falsehood" (212).

13. See his asides after each of his first two encounters with her—III.3, p. 237, and IV.1, p. 249.

14. For this interest, as for most of the others which characterize the genre, *The Way of the World* provides a culminating perfection of expression.

15. Thus in answer to Dorimant's vows of reform: "In men who have been long hardened in sin we have reason to mistrust the first signs of repentance" (278). And again, "Though I wish you devout I would not have you turn fanatic" (278-9).

16. Dobrée, *Restoration Comedy*, p. 75, has seen that Young Bellair (presumably Emilia and Lady Townley would also be included) presents "the happy mean, or an indication of the most comfortable way to live." But this aspect of their role is not explored; and the interpretation offered for the play as a whole is very different from the one here proposed.

17. The problem, of course, was also a subject of constant debate in the traditions of courtly love. This point is discussed in our subsequent inspection of pre-Restoration comedy.

18. Both types of dupe had, of course, been conspicuous features of Restoration comedy from its beginning, and are among the most obvious aspects of the traditions inherited from Jacobean and Caroline drama.

19. Thus Belinda's "Well, were I minded to play the fool, he [Dorimant] should be the last man I'd think of" (226); Loveit's "He [Dorimant] shall not find me the loving fool he has done" (239); and Fopling's "Women are the prettiest things we can fool away our time with" (252) bring the play's women, hero, and fop together in the enveloping comedy.

20. Dobrée, *Restoration Comedy*, p. 73.

21. One of the obvious points of comedy here is that Fopling affects "maliciousness" in an attempt to comply with the "mode" of the hero (see III.3, p. 243). But as the naturally good-humored fool, he is incapable of it.

22. It catches also many of the "comic tensions" in the society of Etherege's time. The song is typical of the period's "courtly" love lyrics.

23. See IV.1, p. 254: "The hour is almost come I appointed Belinda, and I am not so foppishly in love here to forget: I am flesh and blood yet."

24. This is the assumption made in L. C. Knights's essay, "Restoration Comedy: The Reality and the Myth," *Explorations* (London, Chatto & Windus, 1946), pp. 131-49, which cites as a characteristic deficiency of Restoration comedy rather than its society several of the points mentioned in the following paragraphs.

25. "There has been such a calm in my affairs of late I have not had the pleasure of making a woman so much as break her fan, to be sullen, or forswear herself these three days" (195).

26. The proviso scene in *The Way of the World* is in this respect also a point of culmination for Restoration comedy of manners. It involves the explicit attempt of hero and heroine to come to some kind of meaningful terms with the trivial "ways" of their "world."

27. From Ratisbon in November of 1688, Etherege wrote, "At such a time as this a man is not to wait for instructions, but to hazard all to save his King and Country. I should be glad of a word now and then to encourage me [he had virtually none in the closing confusion of James' reign] but the want of that shall never coole the passion I have to perform my duty." The passion was not "dissembled." On his own initiative Etherege tirelessly urged his fellow diplomats at other posts in central Europe to exert "every effort" to save their "King and Country." (The quotations and the information come from a manuscript of Etherege's correspondence which the Houghton Library at Harvard University has permitted me to inspect.)

NORMAN N. HOLLAND

❀

The Country Wife

With his third play, Wycherley hit the jackpot. The King's company produced at Drury Lane in January 1675 *The Country Wife,* the first of the great Restoration comedies. Many critics think it *the* best; certainly it is one of the great comedies of all time. With it, Restoration comedy came of age. The play is often criticized, often adapted (i.e., expurgated), and is probably the most often revived of all the Restoration comedies. Too often, however, critics and directors fail to realize that *The Country Wife,* like *The Gentleman Dancing-Master,* is a right-way–wrong-way play. That is, the significance of the play lies in the contrast and interaction of three closely woven lines of intrigue. Two of these intrigues define a "wrong way," a limited, half-successful way of life. The third intrigue defines a "right way" that contrasts with the limitations of the other two.

The intrigue of the title makes up one of the wrong ways. Pinchwife, an aging, conceited rake, has married a naïve, simple country girl in hopes that her ignorance (and hence, he says, her innocence) will keep her faithful to him, but things don't work out that way. Pinchwife's constant references to cuckolding plant the idea in his rakish friends' minds. Moreover, every step that Pinchwife takes to prevent being cuckolded seems to bring him closer to it—with a little help from Margery, his wife, and Horner, the rake he is most worried

From *The First Modern Comedies* (Cambridge, Mass.: Harvard University Press, 1959), pp. 73-85, notes on p. 250. Reprinted by permission of the publishers. Copyright ©, 1959, by the President and Fellows of Harvard College.

about. Pinchwife diguises Margery as a boy; this makes Horner think he is concealing a wench, i.e., fair game, and he flirts with her and kisses her. Pinchwife forces Margery to write a letter rebuffing Horner; she cleverly substitutes a love letter. Finally, Pinchwife decides to use his sister Alithea to bribe Horner into leaving his wife alone; Margery disguises herself as Alithea, and Pinchwife literally puts his wife in Horner's arms. Margery, of course, is the most delightful character of the play. *"Mrs. Margery Pinchwife,"* wrote Hazlitt, "is a character that will last for ever, I should hope; and even when the original is no more, if that should ever be, while self-will, curiosity, art, and ignorance are to be found in the same person, it will be just as good and just as intelligible as ever in the description."[1]

Pinchwife is not by any means as charming, and most critics say so. Though one finds the seduction of Margery "grim tragedy,"[2] most feel that Pinchwife, for the sake of social justice, ought to be cuckolded.[3] Even Steele, probably the most insistently moral of Wycherley's early critics, dismisses Pinchwife as "one of those debauchees who run through the vices of the town, and believe, when they think fit, they can marry and settle at their ease."[4] Other critics find in the Pinchwife plot a narrow, tidy little moral. *The Country Wife,"* writes Henry Ten Eyck Perry, "is built around the idea that jealousy is petty, mean, absurd, and ultimately fatal to its own ends."[5] *"The Country Wife,"* says L. J. Potts, "has a moral, and a sound one: that the husband who mistrusts his wife and tries to keep her from other men will merely stimulate her desires and teach her to deceive him, however ill-equipped she is with natural cunning. This is in accord with the rationalism of the period."[6] It is true, of course, that each step Pinchwife takes to prevent his being cuckolded brings him closer to it, but Wycherley, I think, is dealing with matters much more basic.

Pinchwife boasts constantly, "I understand the town, Sir" (20ff.),[7] but he actually knows only enough to hate and fear the liberty the Town offers a woman. His speech is riddled with quasi-heroic images of hostility. For example:

Good Wives, and private Souldiers shou'd be Ignorant. (19)

There is no being too hard for Women at their own weapon, lying, therefore I'll quit the Field. (29)

Damn'd Love——Well——I must strangle that little Monster, whilest I can deal with him. (55)

> If we do not cheat women, they'll cheat us; and fraud
> may be justly used with secret enemies, of which a Wife
> is the most dangerous; and he that has a handsome one
> to keep, and a Frontier Town, must provide against
> treachery, rather than open Force. (59)

Pinchwife threatens with his sword twice in the play (66, 84); he
threatens Margery in the famous letter-writing scene (IV.ii): "Write
as I bid you, or I will write Whore with this Penknife in your Face"
(56). Wycherley, of course, had not read Freud: we cannot expect that
he was aware of the overtones of swords and knives. Nevertheless, his
insight here is brilliant. Pinchwife—his name is significant—fears and
distrusts women; these fears create a hostility that tends to make him
an inadequate lover: unconsciously, he satisfies his aggressive instincts by frustrating and disappointing women he makes love to.[8] Disappointing women, in turn, creates further situations that increase his
fears. Thus he falls into the typical self-defeating spiral of neurosis. As
Pinchwife himself puts it, free of the cumbersome jargon of psychology, "The Jades wou'd jilt me, I cou'd never keep a Whore to my
self" (20).

Set off against the defeat of Pinchwife are the successes of Horner,
successes achieved by a fabulous device that Wycherley probably took
from Terence's *Eunuchus*. Horner has announced to the town that he
is a eunuch, that, after a recent visit to France, the pox emasculated
him. His strategy is to find out by their abhorrence the ladies "that
love the sport" and then, by letting them in on the secret, to guarantee
the safety of their reputations. His ruse brings Sir Jaspar Fidget, delighted to have found a safe "playfellow" for his wife. That lady, delighted that she can keep her "honour" (i.e., reputation) intact,
promptly and joyfully becomes the first victim. Later, however, when
she shares the secret with her girl friends, she learns, much to her annoyance, that Horner has also shared "the dear secret" with them. In
the final scene, Sir Jaspar and Pinchwife begin to worry when they
find their wives in Horner's apartment, but all turns out well: the
ladies force Margery to lie and say Horner is impotent, and the husbands go away satisfied.

At least some critics see Horner as a villain: Mr. Bonamy Dobrée
compares him to Tartuffe and calls them both "grim, nightmare figures, dominating the helpless, hopeless apes who call themselves civilized men."[9] Is he a villain, though? He is undeniably a bad man who
does bad things, but he is not a villain in the sense that, say, Iago is,
for he does not prey on innocents. The people Horner victimizes, his

cuckolds and mistresses, are either far worse than he, or, like Margery, do not feel that they have been harmed. Horner is meaningful in other ways. His pretense that he is a eunuch, for example, is nicely symbolic—one might call it an anti-phallic symbol. Insofar as it is a pretense, it satirizes the importance of pretense in the town, particularly the conventional and convenient pretense on society's part that sexual desires do not exist. Horner is simply carrying into actuality the conventions of *Reader's Digest* morality. Insofar as his ruse is a maiming, it suggests the psychological and moral impotency of Sir Jaspar, Lady Fidget, her entourage, and Pinchwife; it parallels also the stultifying effects on Margery of her confinement to the country. Most important, it suggests Horner's own maiming; part of him has died. There are few things in his world above the belt-line, none higher than eye-level. His world never rises above the natural, and for him, the natural never rises above the animal: "A Quack is as fit for a Pimp, as a Midwife for a Bawd; they are still but in their way, both helpers of Nature" (11), he says as the curtain rises; and his metaphors never get much higher.

These two lines of intrigue, the Horner plot and the Pinchwife plot, define the play's "wrong way"—deception. It may be Horner's deceiving others or Pinchwife's deceiving himself, but the generic idea is that of forcing an appearance on a contrary nature. Insofar as the two plots contrast with each other, they set off town against country. Thus, Pinchwife's emphasis on appearance leads him to believe a country wife will be different. "I have marry'd no *London* wife," he says proudly. "We are a little surer of the breed there [in the country], know what her keeping has been, whether foyl'd or unsound," to which Horner drily replies, "Come, come, I have known a clap gotten in *Wales*" (19). Town and country are, of course, different; their difference is the contrast between Lady Fidget on one hand, and Margery on the other. "The Country is as terrible," laughs a ladies' maid, "to our young English Ladies, as a Monastery to those abroad" (52). "A Country Gentlewomans pleasure," says Alithea of walking, "is the drudgery of a foot-post" (22). The country is a place of bad manners (27) and restrictions. "The Town," however, is a place of pleasures, "Plays, Visits, fine Coaches, fine Cloaths, Fiddles, Balls, Treats"; it is no wonder that Margery, who begins by preferring the country, soon learns to like the town (23). It can be a place of "innocent liberty" (22), or "free education" (72): to poor, silly Margery a *"London* woman" is the very standard of cleverness (58).

But these are superficial differences—real, but appearances neverthe-

less. Underneath, human nature is the same in town or country. "I'm
sure if you and I were in the Countrey at Cards together," writes
Margery to Horner, "I cou'd not help treading on your Toe under
the Table" (58). When Pinchwife brags how different women in the
country are, Horner comments simply, "There are Cozens, Justices
Clerks, and Chaplains in the Country, I won't say Coachmen" (19).
This, then, is the irony of Pinchwife's repeated assertions, "I understand the Town, Sir (20ff.) He understands the town only enough to
know that he might be cuckolded—not enough to know that the human nature underneath the social appearance is what matters, that a
woman's state of mind is the index to the physical fact of her chastity,
not *vice versa*. Even Sparkish, the fop of the play, can call Pinchwife
"a silly wise Rogue" that "wou'd make one laugh more than a stark
Fool" (26). "If her constitution incline her to't, she'll have it sooner or
latter" (70).

The only underlying difference between town and country is the
amount of pretense each involves. It is worth noting, for example, that
while Horner's ruse is necessary for his seduction of Lady Fidget, it
plays no part whatsoever in his seduction of Margery Pinchwife. The
Country Wife knows what she wants—Horner. And says so: "Don't I
see every day at *London* here, Women leave their first Husbands, and
go, and live with other Men as their Wives?" she asks Horner. "You
shall be my Husband now" (82). The town wife, on the other hand,
Lady Fidget, goes through elaborate subterfuges and pretenses. She
pretends to hate the pretended eunuch, she rants about her "honour,"
and she speaks in the most elaborate periphrases, for example, the
famous "china scene" (61–63).

Lady Fidget is interrupted in Horner's closet and enters the room
apologizing: "I have been toyling and moyling, for the pretty'st piece
of China, my Dear." The lady who interrupted (and who is in on "the
dear secret") asks if she can have some china, too, and Horner replies: "This lady had the last there," and so on. The word "china" is
used six times in the scene and much of the sardonic, Swift-like force
of the episode, as Professor Bateson points out,[10] derives from these
insistent repetitions. The *double-entendre* is funny itself, but, at the
same time, a simile of extraordinary complexity. "China," as a vessel
for food, makes one more of the many conversions of love (or sex)
down to mere appetite. China, furthermore, is an object of surface
aspects. Originally mere clay, it has become worked and decorated to
the point where its appearance now completely hides its earthy origin.

So sex for Horner and Lady Fidget and their kind has become almost fantastic and allegorical, it is so separated from any of its original emotional or biological purposes. Moreover, as Wycherley handles the dialogue, not only is Horner's virility compared to china; also relatively right and wrong ways of relating them are contrasted. At first, the comparison of Horner's sexual energy to china simply conceals his relation with Lady Fidget; china stands for virility by way of appetite and fancy earthiness. As the conversation continues, that more or less reasonable relation is contrasted with the idea of Horner as a universal donor of china—and virility. "I cannot make China for you all," he tells Lady Fidget's friend, "but I will have a Rol-waggon for you too, another time" (63). The comparison of china to virility ultimately compares a monogamous appetite with a promiscuous one. Horner, as Professor Bateson puts it, becomes "a Grotesque or mere mechanism."[11]

Contrasted both to the concealed, elaborated earthiness of the town wife and the direct earthiness of the Country Wife, there is the "right way" of the lovers, Harcourt and Alithea. In this, the third line of intrigue, Alithea, an intelligent and sophisticated girl, is about to marry the fop Sparkish, whom she has accepted only because he shows no jealousy, even when Harcourt, the lover-hero, and Horner's friend, declares his love and urges her to drop Sparkish and marry him. Actually, of course, Sparkish can afford to be indifferent because he only wants to marry her estate. In the complications coming from Margery's disguise as Alithea, Sparkish accuses her of having given herself to Horner, so that Alithea drops the fop and marries Harcourt who still believes in her. The action of this third line of intrigue is the education of Alithea. She has to learn two things. First, she must learn not to substitute a mere appearance (Sparkish's lack of jealousy) for inner nature (Harcourt's merits), as she does when she says of Sparkish: "I own he wants the wit of *Harcourt*, which I will dispense withal, for another want he has, which is want of jealousie, which men of wit seldom want. . . . 'Tis *Sparkish's* confidence in my truth that obliges me to be so faithful to him" (51). In effect, she must learn not to let her knowledge of the deceptions of the town make her "over-wise"; thus, in her moment of revelation, she cries:

> I wish, that if there be any over-wise woman of the
> Town, who like me would marry a Fool, for fortune,
> liberty, or title; first, that her husband may love Play,
> and be a Cully to all the Town, but her, and suffer none

> but fortune to be mistress of his purse; then if for liberty,
> that he may send her into the Country, under the con-
> duct of some housewifely mother-in-law; and if for title,
> may the World give 'em none but that of Cuckold. (77)

Second, she must learn a wisdom of ends, a faith in love, a willingness
to prefer love as an end to "fortune, liberty, or title."

Alithea and Harcourt reflect this concern with ultimate ends in
their speech, which is starred with conversions upward, celestial, even
religious images. Harcourt loves Alithea, the "Divine, Heavenly Creature," the "Seraphick Lady" (53), "the most estimable and most glorious Creature in the World" (42); he loves her "with the best, and
truest love in the world" (44) "above the World or the most Glorious
part of it, her whole Sex" (25), a love that "can no more be equall'd
in the world, than that Heavenly form of yours" (44), and so on. It
is symbolic that Harcourt disguises himself as a priest to court her.
Alithea herself talks the same way. She twits her admirer: "You look
upon a Friend married, as one gone into a Monastery, that is dead to
the World." " 'Tis indeed, because you marry him," replies Harcourt
(25). So, too, Alithea converts Pinchwife's "greasie" comparison of a
masked woman to a covered dish to: "A Beauty mask'd, like the Sun
in Eclipse, gathers together more gazers, than if it shin'd out" (37).

The persons of the wrong way, like Lady Fidget, cannot grasp this
kind of simile:

> LADY FIDGET. But first, my dear Sir, you must promise to
>   have a care of my dear Honour.
> HORNER. If you talk a word more of your Honour, you'll
>   make me incapable to wrong it; to talk of Honour in
>   the mysteries of Love, is like talking of Heaven, or the
>   Deity in an operation of Witchcraft, just when you
>   are employing the Devil, it makes the charm impotent.
> LA. F. Nay, fie, let us not be smooty; but you talk of mys-
>   teries, and bewitching to me, I don't understand you.
>   (60)

And Horner dutifully converts the image to one of money: "I tell you,
Madam, the word money in a Mistresses mouth, at such a nick of
time, is not a more disheartening sound to a younger Brother, than
that of Honour to an eager Lover like my self." "They fear the eye of
the world, more than the eye of Heaven" (59).

Practical reality dominates the metaphors of all but Harcourt and
Alithea. Thus, to Pinchwife, as to the pompous Sir Jaspar, a woman is

a possession, like money. "Our Sisters and Daughters," says Pinchwife, "like Usurers money, are safest, when put out; but our Wives, like their Writings, never safe, but in our Closets under Lock and Key" (75). "To squire women about for other folks," sneers Sir Jaspar, "is as ungrateful an employment as to tell money for other folks" (61). Both these gentlemen look down on what they suppose to be the frivolities of Horner and his friends. "Business," counsels Sir Jaspar, "must be preferr'd always before Love and Ceremony with the wise Mr. *Horner*." "And the impotent Sir *Jaspar,*" laughs the supposed eunuch (13). "I have business, Sir, and must mind it," says Pinchwife, "your business is pleasure, therefore you and I must go different ways" (45). Pinchwife's and Sir Jaspar's concern with a supposedly practical reality contrasts with and highlights Harcourt and Alithea's achievement of an impractical reality, romantic love.

In the pretenses of the "low" plots, love, honor, and all abstractions are converted downward to physical facts. Thus, honor is a collateral or security (34), or, to Alithea's maid, "a disease in the head, like the Megrim, or Falling-sickness" (51). Love is something one can be cheated of, just as money is "the common Mistriss" (38). Marriage, Pinchwife describes as giving "Sparkish to morrow five thousand pound to lye with my Sister" (19). Love is most often compared to food (45): thus the town offers "such variety of dainties" rather than the "course, constant, swinging stomachs in the Country" (19). Lady Fidget, for example, is puzzled to know why gallants prefer to eat in an ordinary, "where every man is snatching for the best bit" rather than "be the only guest at a good Table" (80). "A woman mask'd," says Pinchwife, "like a cover'd Dish, gives a Man curiosity, and appetite, when, it may be, uncover'd, 'twou'd turn his stomach" (37). "A Rival," says Sparkish, is "as good sawce for a married Man to a Wife, as an Orange to Veale" (68). Even Mrs. Margery, walking about London, cries with outrageous innocence, "I han't half my belly full of sights yet" (41). Disease, too, is a word for love: "the *London* disease" (68). "Wife and Sister," complains Pinchwife, "are names which make us expect Love and Duty, Pleasure and Comfort, but we find 'em plagues and torments" (72–73). Horner's supposed maiming impliedly contrasts the old heroic idea of the "wound of love" with the venereal diseases or "that worse Distemper, love" (11), just as Dufoy's disease in *The Comical Revenge* did.

These two last conversions downward suggest the other important kind of metaphor: what we have called in *The Gentleman Dancing-*

Master, the right-way–wrong-way simile. Wife and sister can mean love and duty or plagues and torments. One can have Horner's "wound of love" or Harcourt's. Thus, Lady Fidget says, "Our Virtue is like the State-man's Religion, the Quaker's Word, the Gamester's Oath, and the Great Man's Honour," and so far the comparison is more or less innocuous, "but to cheat those that trust us" (80). The hearer is left to compare in his mind the society Lady Fidget describes in which these things are related by their falsity to a better society in which they would be related by their truth. The "given" of the play raises the same kind of question. Horner's pretending to be a eunuch not only compares—rather graphically—love as an ideal to love as a vene-real fact; it also contrasts the ways in which society will react to him. As long as he is thought a eunuch, he is received with joy by the hus-bands and contempt by the ladies; once they know his secret, however, the ladies receive him with delight. In a different society, he might as a supposedly real eunuch be received with sympathy; as a pretended eunuch—one simply marvels at Restoration mores. The opening scene of the comedy develops exactly these right and wrong ways, thereby setting the tone. Horner's doctor puzzles at the effect of the ruse; Sir Jaspar crows over the eunuch; Horner affects to be surprised the ladies have not more sympathy for him (11-15).

Not just the language, but the whole action of the play and all of its characters develop this right-way–wrong-way comparison. The wrong way is symbolized by Horner, the maimed man. In his way of life, limited to the world, the flesh, and the devil, things are never what they seem to be. Two kinds of deception, deceiving others and deceiv-ing oneself, shape the absurdities of human life. One deceives others by pretending to a character one does not have. "A Pox on . . . all that force Nature, and wou'd be still what she forbids 'em," cries Horner. "Affectation is her greatest Monster" (16). He is himself, of course, his own worst offender. He pretends to be a "shadow" (15), a "sign of a Man" (17) to hide his sexual intrigues. Knowing that no one would believe he had reformed, he pretends to virtue by assuring the town he has been forced into it. Lady Fidget affects more ob-viously; she pretends to honor "as criticks to wit, only by censuring others" (31). "Your Virtue is your greatest Affectation, Madam," Hor-ner calmly assures her (13). Lady Fidget adopts the outward appearance of a precise woman of honor, to hide her inner, lecherous nature. Sparkish also pretends—he is a remarkably complex instance of the type-character of the fop. He pretends to conversational wit: that is his foppishness. But his foppishness is itself a pretense to cover up his small, scheming nature. Under both these pretenses, Sparkish seems rather well endowed with a self-serving wit. Just as Horner uses his well-known lechery to create an appearance of virtue, so Sparkish rather cleverly uses his own disinterest in Alithea. It enables him to be unjealous, and that lack of jealousy persuades Alithea he has a real faith in her and very nearly enables him to marry her estate.

As with Etherege, pretending to a nature one does not have brings two results. First, by long usage, it corrupts both one's pretended outer appearance and also one's inner nature. The pretense and the self become so ludicrously confused that the pretense can never really be put away. Thus, Lady Fidget, even at the moment she is about to give herself to Horner, is saying: "You must have a great care of your conduct; for my acquaintances are so censorious, (oh, 'tis a wicked censorious world, Mr. *Horner*,) I say, are so censorious, and detracting, that perhaps they'll talk to the prejudice of my Honour, though you shou'd not let them know the dear secret" (60). Secondarily, however, continued pretense also gives the deceiver a certain cynical wisdom about human nature: an awareness that since one's own appearance does not reveal one's own nature, the same thing is probably true of the rest of mankind. "Most men," says Harcourt, who knows his way about the town, "are the contraries to that they wou'd seem" (17). Horner bases his whole plot on this kind of shrewd knowledge of social pretense:

> I can be sure, she that shews an aversion to me loves the sport. . . . And then the next thing, is your Women of Honour, as you call 'em, are only chary of their reputations, not their Persons, and 'tis scandal they wou'd avoid, not Men: Now may I have, by the reputation of an Eunuch, the Privileges of One; and be seen in a Ladies Chamber in a morning as early as her Husband. (14)

Even Sparkish is clever in this way: to Pinchwife, he says, "Let me tell you Brother, we men of wit have amongst us a saying, that Cukolding like the small Pox comes with a fear, and you may keep your Wife as much as you will out of danger of infection, but if her constitution inclines her to't, she'll have it sooner or latter" (70).

At the same time, however, one can be otherwise, as Alithea is at the beginning of the play. One can deceive oneself by substituting appearances for a real satisfaction of "natural" desires. Sir Jaspar, for example, wants his wife to have the appearance of having a gallant, he forces Horner on her—and is cuckolded. All of Pinchwife's ruses, disguises, and other pretenses represent appearances designed to frustrate Margery's innocently lecherous desires and they end only in Pinchwife's cuckolding. Similarly, Alithea substitutes (at first) Sparkish's lack of jealousy for Harcourt's naturalness. All of these people are "overwise," in that they substitute appearances for nature.

Opposed to the wise and overwise is Harcourt, who seems by contrast bumbling and ineffective. His schemes consistently misfire. He is ridiculed by the fools of the play, Sparkish and Pinchwife. Sincerity is the essence of his apparent folly. Everyone laughs at his sincere declarations of love, and they get him nowhere until Alithea finally learns the difference between the superficial appearance of faith and real faith. Harcourt's pretending to be a parson is symbolic enough, but only accidentally useful in the plot. The real key with which he unlocks the situation is his offer to marry Alithea even when she has apparently given herself to Horner. He succeeds only when he shows he is willing to make a fool of himself for her. In the end, though, his is the greater achievement. He brings about a real union with the woman he loves; Horner settles for fleeting affairs. Harcourt wins reality; Horner wins pretense.

Wycherley contrasts the women, too. Margery, the naïvely direct country wife, is set off against Alithea, the sophisticated London girl. Here, sophistication wins. Whereas in Harcourt's case, a bumbling sincerity succeeded, Alithea's strength comes from her knowledge of town ways. Wycherley is not being inconsistent. He is comparing two kinds of wisdom, a wisdom of means and a wisdom of ends. To select one's ends rightly is a matter of faith, and this wisdom sets Harcourt and Alithea off from the rest of the people. To achieve these ends, however, one must have the wisdom of means, the "free education" of the town. Even Lady Fidget's silly friends know "women are least mask'd, when they have the Velvet Vizard on" (80). Margery, however, while she can by flashes of ingenuity cut through the social barriers Pinchwife puts up, cannot sustain her effort and, ultimately, fails. Margery knows she wants love, and though her aim is the same as Alithea's, she cannot get it. Margery's intuitions are right, but she lacks the social acumen to carry them out. In other words, she has an intuitional wisdom about ends, but intuition will not give her a knowledge of means. She cannot translate her love for Horner into an enduring social form.

This, then, is the measure of success in the play—the extent to which the characters can free themselves from pretense by *openly* translating their "natural" desires into visible, enduring social forms. Horner's world, for example, is closed, defined by his pretense. It initiates the action, and, in the end, the husbands can be persuaded of their wives' fidelity only when Margery is forced to lie and keep up the pretense of Horner's impotency. Margery's love for Horner is open and honest, but she cannot translate it into the outward fact of marriage, even though she calls Horner her "husband." Lady Fidget openly reveals her relationship with Horner (V.iv) to her girl friends; her openness leads only to a community of lies, both by and to the ladies. They now know that all of them have been pretending and must continue to do so. Another open act is Horner's sympathy for Harcourt's love: "Thy wedding!" he says to Sparkish. "I'm sorry for't. . . . 'Tis for her sake, not yours, and another man's sake that might have hoped, I thought— (Aside) Poor Harcourt, I am sorry thou hast mist her" (67). Yet Horner's sympathy must remain untranslated into action. When Harcourt demands that Horner clear Alithea's honor by assuring the company he has not slept with her, he cannot comply. Despite his willingness, he has become so enmeshed in his own pretenses that he cannot help his friend (83-84). Sir Jaspar and Pinchwife, at the end, resign themselves to further pretense, taking a cold, epistemological comfort: "For my own sake fain I wou'd all believe./ Cuckolds like Lovers shou'd themselves deceive" (87). The only open, unpretended impulse that can be translated into permanent social form is Harcourt's love for Alithea. Only these two are completely successful, first, because they know how to achieve their aims in the social framework of pretense and, second, because they each realize the importance of an aim that goes beyond the merely social and answers one's inner nature. Each of the others is confined to the social box he has helped make, forced to continue a pretense that must finally corrupt the concealed inner nature. Only Horner is corrupt enough and wise enough to use social pretenses for his own purposes, to master them instead of being mastered. He, however, wins only a limited success. He is, in effect, maimed, cut off from the real and permanent happiness represented by the exuberant union of Harcourt and Alithea, and for which Horner expresses a half-regretful longing: "I alas, can't be [a husband]" (87). This is Wycherley's sense of the two ways: one accepts limited social aims; the other transcends them.

The play, however, does not deal simply with one right way *versus* one wrong way; it deals complexly with a gradation of "ways." The basic division is between Harcourt and Alithea on the one hand and all the rest of the characters on the other. Harcourt and Alithea are the most successful and the most right ethically; they seem foolish but turn out to be wiser than all the rest. Among the other characters, there is another right way, Horner's, more limited than Harcourt's and hardly ethical, but successful in a narrow sense on its own terms. We could diagram the action of the play as in the accompanying chart (using the semanticists' trick of subscripts to denote the two senses of "right" involved, $right_1$ meaning successful and $right_2$ meaning ethically right). Margery, and perhaps this is why she is the title character, stands at the center: her country naïveté links her to the sincerity of Harcourt and Alithea, but she lacks the social acumen they have to make her sincere aims survive. The action of the play brings Harcourt and Alithea out of the social whirl into a private world. The happy ending, as so often in comedy, affirms the idea of poetic justice: $right_2$ equals $right_1$; the good succeed, and the bad fail—unless they are Horner. For it is he and the complexity associated with him that keep *The Country Wife* from having simply a "happy ending."

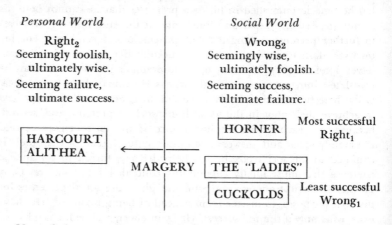

Nevertheless, we can see that the right-way–wrong-way structure has undergone a change in Wycherley's mind. *The Country Wife* represents a development beyond *The Gentleman Dancing-Master* toward the final, magnificent *The Plain-Dealer*. *The Gentleman Dancing-Master* was also a right-way–wrong-way play, but most of the dramatic interest was concentrated in the wrong way, the antics of Don Diego and Monsieur. The right way, moreover, was thoroughly realistic: Gerrard was a typical Restoration gallant and Hippolita a flirtatious

Restoration coquette. In *The Country Wife,* the dramatic interest is still focused on the wrong way, the doings of Horner, Margery, and Lady Fidget; but the right way has become more idealized in the person of Harcourt whose ineffectual schemes are definitely not typical of the hero of a Restoration comedy. *The Plain-Dealer* will carry the trend even further—the dramatic interest in that play centers on the misanthrope of the title who represents an almost supernatural, totally unreal "right way." The Plain Dealer, moreover, is perfectly opposite to the typical Restoration hero, and so is the girl he finally becomes engaged to. The right way of *The Country Wife* represented by Harcourt and Alithea, becomes in *The Plain-Dealer,* a colorless, half-successful center position.

The chronology of this trend in Wycherley's work is deceptive. Restoration comedy is, so far as the three major writers are concerned, nearing its apex. The antitheroic phase has ended, and the first of their five great comedies has appeared. Yet what is usually thought the first full-fledged "comedy of manners," *The Man of Mode,* has not yet been produced. And even in that supposedly heartless play this double sense of Wycherley's appears, though Etherege portrays the ideal far more ironically than Wycherley does in Harcourt. These later plays—including *The Country Wife*—constitute a second phase after the purely antitheroic comedies like *The Comical Revenge.* Though the heroics have dwindled to a faint overtone (Horner's castration can be thought of as a heroic "wound of love" like Dufoy's venereal disease), the dual structure persists. The two alternatives, however, are not heroic and antiheroic, but right way and wrong way, in the sense of successful and unsuccessful, but also in the sense of good and evil.

These comedies have far more meaning than the term "comedy of manners" suggests. The presence in one play both of an ideal and of activities like Horner's creates a very complex meaning indeed. The ideal developed by this pattern is not all the imposing of a code of manners on the self; it is just the opposite—adapting social forms to the expression of "natural" desires. But the ideal is nonetheless an ideal, and the presence of an ideal in a realistic situation signals the beginning of what we think of as eighteenth-century sentimentalism. The dreary "weeping comedy" of the "reformed" eighteenth-century stage was simply that—the presentation of an ideal in a realistic setting. The strength, then, of this second phase of plays (which includes all five of the "great" Restoration comedies) stems from a trace of that sentimentalism which literary historians almost unanimously relegate to the eighteenth century. *The Country Wife,* by showing an ideal in a realistic context, shows both the beginning of the great period of Restoration comedy and its decay.

NOTES

1. William Hazlitt, "On Wycherley, Congreve, Vanbrugh, and Farquhar" (1819), *Works,* ed. P. P. Howe, Centenary Edition, 21 vols. (London: Dent, 1930-1934), VI, 76.
2. George Nettleton, *English Drama of the Restoration and Eighteenth Century* (New York: Macmillan, 1914), p. 80.
3. Kathleen M. Lynch, *The Social Mode of Restoration Comedy,* University of Michigan Publications in Language and Literature, vol. III (New York: Macmillan, 1926), pp. 169-170, is one example.
4. Sir Richard Steele, *The Tatler,* no. 3 (April 16, 1709).
5. Henry Ten Eyck Perry, *The Comic Spirit in Restoration Drama* (New Haven: Yale University Press, 1925), p. 43.
6. L. J. Potts, *Comedy* (London: Hutchinson's University Library, 1948), p. 55.
7. My references are to pages in *The Complete Works of William Wycherley,* ed. Montague Summers, 4 vols. (London: Nonesuch Press, 1924), II, 1-88. They may be related to other editions by means of the following table:

    Act I, sc. i: 11-21.

    Act II, sc. i: 22-34.

    Act III, sc. i: 35-37; sc. ii: 37-50.

    Act IV, sc. i: 50-54; sc. ii: 54-59; sc. iii: 59-68; sc. iv: 68-70.

    Act V, sc. i: 70-73; sc. ii: 73-75; sc. iii: 75-77; sc. iv: 78-87.
8. Robert W. White, *The Abnormal Personality* (New York: Ronald Press, 1948), p. 278.
9. Bonamy Dobrée, *Restoration Comedy: 1660-1720* (Oxford: Clarendon Press, 1924), p. 94.
10. F. W. Bateson, "Second Thoughts: II. L. C. Knights and Restoration Comedy," *Essays in Criticism,* VII (April 1957), 65.
11. *Ibid.*

BONAMY DOBRÉE

❁

Congreve

Born 1670.
The Old Bachelor, 1693.
The Double Dealer, 1693.
Love for Love, 1695.
The Way of the World, 1700.
Died, 1729.

There can hardly be another instance to put beside Congreve of a man who sprang so immediately to the pinnacle of literary fame, and, if we make due allowance for the natural exaggeration of his contemporaries, has ever since maintained his position so inalienably. It is true that no one to-day would attempt to rank him with Shakespeare, as Dryden did in the well-known lines:

> Heaven, that but once was prodigal before,
> To Shakespeare gave as much; she could not give him more,

but compared with others, who have been likened to our eternal poet, Congreve has held his place with reasonable stability. The critics of the early nineteenth century were loud in his praises; Lamb gave him his full due, and even Macaulay could not withhold his admiration. Only Leigh Hunt tempered his enthusiasm, perhaps merely to balance Hazlitt's fine tribute. *The Way of the World*, the latter wrote, "is an essence almost too fine, and the sense of pleasure evaporates in an aspiration after something that seems too exquisite ever to have been realized." This is the true note, struck by Hazlitt with his faculty of seeing more clearly than any of his contemporaries, and of seeing things separately. He was the first, apart from the men of Congreve's day, to realize him as a poet, with a poet's longing for beauty. Other critics have failed to see that the masterly style accomplishes something

From *Restoration Comedy* (Oxford: Oxford University Press, 1924), pp. 121-50. Reprinted by permission of the Clarendon Press, Oxford.

other than a clear exposition of manners. So Coleridge wrote, "Wickedness is no subject for comedy. This was Congreve's great error and peculiar to him. The dramatic personalities of Dryden, Wycherley, and others are often viciously indecent, but not like Congreve's, wicked." Again, Leigh Hunt remarked, "We see nothing but a set of heartless fine ladies and gentlemen coming in and going out, saying witty things at each other, and buzzing in some maze of intrigue." To Mr. Gosse, the exquisite wording reveals no more than satire, and a "careless superiority." Congreve's brilliance, indeed, is so dazzling, that admiration nearly always stops short at praising it, and fails to perceive the real force of the man, the solid personality, and the knowledge of human beings. So Macaulay of his epigram: "In this sort of jewelry he attained to a mastery unprecedented and inimitable," and Henley—"He is saved from oblivion by the sheer strength of style." Meredith's famous passage is in the same vein: "He hits the mean of a fine style and a natural in dialogue. He is at once precise and voluble. . . . In this he is a classic, and is worthy of treading a measure with Molière." Mr. Whibley praises him for economy, as "a stern castigator of prose." "In point and concision, his style is still unmatched in the literature of England. There is never a word too much, or an epithet that is superfluous."

These praises are abundantly warranted, but too great an attention to style in this sense is apt to obscure the broader vision. A brilliant technique, of which verbal style is a part, is developed through the impulsion to express something, and it is in relation to this that style must be considered. If we read Congreve sympathetically we must admit that a comedy for him was not a mere game, but like every other good piece of writing, "the precious life blood of a master spirit embalmed and treasured up on purpose to a life beyond life." Congreve, indeed, had rather more to say than the mode he chose for speech would allow him; and one may suspect that it was the realization of this, combined with the failure of *The Way of the World*, that made him abandon the stage at the age of thirty.

Born ten years after the Restoration, he came to maturity after the Revolution. Times were becoming more stable, and men could look back upon the life of the last thirty years with something of detachment. The attempt to rationalize sexual relations had by now definitely failed, as may be judged by the outbursts against women, such as Rochester's *Satyr against Marriage,* and Gould's *Satyrs against Women and against Wooing,* all of which were published at the time

Congreve was writing. Collier was raising his voice; the age of reason, of Steele and Addison, was at hand. Congreve stands midway between the ages, with a temper as balanced as the couplets of Pope.

"Two kinds of ambition early took possession of his mind," Macaulay observed, "and often pulled it in opposite directions. . . . He longed to be a great writer. He longed to be a man of fashion. . . . The history of his life is the history of a conflict between these two impulses." But, at bottom, the impulse was the same. A man of undoubted sensibility, he was always seeking the finest quality in everything, in life as well as in writing. It is this which constitutes him a poet. His well-known remark to Voltaire that he wished to be visited "upon no other foot than that of a gentleman who led a life of plainness and simplicity," was no idle affectation. In any case one could pardon his irritation against a lion-hunting little Frenchman who had as yet written nothing very important, and who came to see him, not for what he was, but for what he had been more than twenty years before! But besides that he really did think it more worthy to be a gentleman than a wit, seeing that to be a wit involved so great a degradation of humanity. ["Those characters which are meant to be ridiculed in most of our comedies," he wrote, in the dedication of *The Way of the World*, "are of fools so gross, that in my humble opinion, they should rather disturb than divert the well-natured and reflecting part of an audience; they are rather objects of charity than contempt; and instead of moving our mirth, they ought very often to excite our compassion."] A bitter confession from a comic writer who, moreover, preferred, as he wrote to Keally, to "feel very sensibly and silently for those whom I love," and who said in a letter to Dennis, "I profess myself an enemy to detraction. . . . I never care for seeing things that force me to entertain low thoughts of my nature. . . . I could never look long upon a monkey without very mortifying reflections." Finally, he was one of the three "most honest hearted, real good men, of the poetical members of the Kit-Cat Club."

So, as one reads his first three comedies, one feels all the time that he is at war with himself. He has the technical brilliance of style, the rapier wit, the lively antithesis that no one can surpass, but not always that real style which is the complete fusion of manner and words with the artist's "sense of fact." For perfect expression the artist must be expressing himself, and this, one feels, Congreve was not always doing. Perhaps only Etherege could in this kind, and he never wearied as Congreve sometimes seems to do. The light-hearted atmosphere was

not really natural to him, for he had something of Jonson and Wycherley about him. Yet he was Wycherley with a difference, a Wycherley
who did not hate the people about whom he wrote so much as pity
them. If he despised some of them, he only showed it to the extent that
a gentle nature would permit. Etherege in a sense sings, Wycherley is
all imprecation, but Congreve is a constructive thinker. If he had too
much culture for the brutality of Wycherley and too much sympathy
for the irony of Jonson, he had too much knowledge for the airy light-
heartedness of Etherege. All the time, behind the coldly critical surface, there is much of the poet, of the man hungry for beauty. There is
often a caressing touch, and Millamant he must really have loved.
There are even moments when one wonders if he is not going to crash
his comic structure to pieces with some passionate outburst. He might
be saying with Stendhal, "Je fais tous les efforts possibles pour être sec.
. . . Je tremble toujours de n'avoir écrit qu'un soupir, quand je crois
avoir noté une vérité."

From the opening lines of *The Old Bachelor* we are in the realm of
ideas, and realize that we are in contact with a thinker.

> BELLMOUR. Business!—and so must time, my friend, be
> close pursued, or lost. Business is the rub of life, per-
> verts our aim, casts off the bias, and leaves us wide and
> short of the intended mark.
> VAINLOVE. Pleasure, I guess, you mean.
> BEL. Ay, what else has meaning?
> VAIN. Oh, the wise will tell you—
> BEL. More than they believe—or understand.
> VAIN. How, how, Ned, a wise man say more than he un-
> derstands?
> BEL. Ay, ay; wisdom's nothing but a pretending to know
> and believe more than we really do. You read but of
> one wise man, and all that he knew was, that he knew
> nothing.

The thought is not very profound—who would expect Bellmour to be
profound? "leave wisdom to fools, they have need of it," he says—but
it shows well enough that Congreve's "humours" were to be intellectual rather than bodily.

Heartwell, the old bachelor himself, is animated by a real comic
idea. He is a man who, in spite of all his efforts, is drawn to women,
hating and despising himself for it, but unable to fight against the
impulse. We find him in front of the lodging of Silvia, who attracts

him so much, that he finds, to his great disgust, that he is willing to
marry her. He soliloquizes:

> Why whither in the devil's name am I a-going now?
> Hum—let me think—is not this Silvia's house, the cave of
> that enchantress, and which consequently I ought to
> shun as I would infection? To enter here, is to put on
> the envenomed shirt, to run into the embraces of a fever,
> and in some raving fit, be led to plunge myself into that
> more consuming fire, a woman's arms. Ha! well recol-
> lected, I will recover my reason and begone. . . . Well,
> why do you not move? Feet do your office—not one inch;
> no, foregad I'm caught!—There stands my North, and
> thither my needle points.—Now could I curse myself, yet
> cannot repent. O thou delicious, damn'd, dear, destruc-
> tive woman!

This variant of Launcelot Gobbo is not only ludicrous in the extreme,
it is profound. It strikes at the deepest disharmonies in man's nature,
and touches that bedrock of discordant impulses, in the face of which,
if we cannot ignore, we must either laugh or perish.

There is already something of Congreve's final excellence in Bellmour and Belinda, precursors of Mirabell and Millamant. Here we
have sex antagonism in full blast, the realism touched with just the
necessary lightness and delicacy:

> BELINDA. (*Interrupting* BELLMOUR.) Prithee, hold thy
>   tongue—Lard, he has so pestered me with flames and
>   stuff—I think I shan't endure the sight of a fire this
>   twelvemonth.
> BELLMOUR. Yet all can't melt that cruel frozen heart.
> BELINDA. O gad, I hate your hideous fancy—you said that
>   once before—If you must talk impertinently, for
>   heaven's sake let it be with variety; don't come always,
>   like the devil, wrapped in flames—I'll not hear a sen-
>   tence more, that begins with an "I burn"—or an "I
>   beseech you, madam."

On the other hand, the Heartwell-Silvia scenes have none of this
charming fencing; frank statement takes its place. "If you love me you
must marry me," gives the true picture of Silvia's directness.

The Fondlewife scenes, which are irrelevant to the plot, fall from
the height of comedy to erotics and buffoonery, although Fondlewife
himself has a hint of Jonson's Kitely; like him he fears to go to busi-

ness lest he should be cuckolded in his absence. The pimping valet
Setter has some of the earthy philosophy Calderon, Regnard and
Beaumarchais knew how to give their servants, and this Congreve
probably derived from Terence. But the bawdy scenes are simply dull
comedy of intrigue, and the Nykin-Cocky dialogues reach a level of
realism which make them almost as humiliating as the Nicky-Nacky
scenes in *Venice Preserved,* though there is none of the degrading filth
of the masochistic Antonio.

Congreve's skill as a manipulator of pure frolic is immediately seen;
he could handle farce as well as anybody. The timid Sir Joseph Wittol,
with his cowardly protector, Captain Bluffe, provides unceasing amusement. We are clearly in the realm of Elizabethan comedy, and Bluffe,
the braggadocio, has a long ancestry through Bobadil and Parolles to
Thraso. The scenes where he appears are admirably rounded off in
real fun, with the point driven well home. It is no wonder that Dryden
called this the best first play he had ever read.

The next play, *The Double Dealer,* is in many respects puzzling. "I
designed the moral first," Congreve wrote, "and to that moral I invented the fable," and he prefixed to the comedy a line from Horace
to the effect that "sometimes even comedy exalts her voice." There is
no doubt about the admirable lucidity of the plot and the ingenuity
of the construction. "I made the plot as strong as I could, because it
was single," we are told. So far all is clear, but the difficulty is to
arrive at that very subtle and elusive thing, the "idea" of the play, the
dominating mood that led to its creation. This may be conveyed by
the action, the delineation of character, or by the atmosphere, which
is the resultant of these combined with the wording. And it is in regard to the atmosphere that the curious thing happens. Congreve tried
to mingle two distinct and separate worlds, the Charles Lamb world
of airy make-believe, and the familiar world of everyday life. Lady
Touchwood, indeed, displays passions of which a heroine of Ford
need not have been ashamed. "O I have excuses, thousands for my
faults; fire in my temper, passions in my soul, apt to every provocation; oppressed at once with love, and with despair"; and in a later
act, "Oh! that I were fire indeed, that I might burn the vile traitor.
What shall I do? how shall I think? I cannot think." Maskwell also is
of this tempestuous world; there is something tremendous about him.
He has a cold completeness, an absolute detachment from good, that
is masterly. "For wisdom and honesty, give me cunning and hypocrisy;
oh, 'tis such a pleasure, to angle for fair-faced fools," he says, and his

ingenious ingenuousness is as daring in conception as it is convincing in the execution. True, he is not very subtle, like all type figures he is not seen in the round, and one cannot conceive him as anything but a villain; he is villainy itself.

And mingling with this harsh world which enables us to understand Leigh Hunt's comment that "there is a severity of rascality . . . in some of his comedies that produces upon many of their readers far too grave an impression," we have the world of the Froths, the Plyants, and Brisk. This is the very culmination of social tomfoolery. Listen to Brisk making love to Lady Froth:

> LADY F. O be merry by all means—Prince Volscius, in love! ha! ha! ha!
>
> BRISK. O barbarous, to turn me into ridicule! Yet, ha! ha! ha!—the deuce take me, I can't help laughing myself, ha! ha! ha!—yet by heavens! I have a violent passion for your ladyship, seriously.
>
> LADY F. Seriously? ha! ha! ha!
>
> BRISK. Seriously, ha! ha! ha! Gad, I have, for all I laugh.
>
> LADY F. Ha! ha! ha!—what d'ye think I laugh at! Ha! ha! ha!
>
> BRISK. Me, egad, ha! ha!
>
> LADY F. No, the deuce take me if I don't laugh at myself; for, hang me! if I have not a violent passion for Mr. Brisk, ha! ha! ha!
>
> BRISK. Seriously?
>
> LADY F. Seriously, ha! ha! ha!
>
> BRISK. That's well enough; let me perish, ha! ha! ha! O miraculous! what a happy discovery; ah, my dear, charming Lady Froth!
>
> LADY F. O my adored Mr. Brisk!   (*They embrace.*)

all in deliberate contrast with the furies of Lady Touchwood or the sensibility of Cynthia.

Congreve himself does not seem to have been quite satisfied with this play, as he confessed in the Epistle Dedicatory; and he must have realized why it was not that pure comedy he had attempted to create. Omit the three lines spoken at the end by Brisk and Lady Froth, and the play would altogether cease to be critical comedy, and would become something much more dynamic; it would almost be melodrama. Those remarks, however, bring it back to the static, and make us realize that nothing had really happened. We have Maskwell unmasked, thwarted, consumed by a cold irony; Touchwood in a violent rage casting his wife out of the house; Lady Touchwood in an agony of despair, so that one cannot help being carried away by the dramatic movement. More than the intellectual apparatus is touched, one is borne along by the onrush of life; then suddenly, Brisk—"This is all very surprising, let me perish!" It is like an icy douche, everything is brought to a standstill, and we are once more in the realm of that comedy where none of the emotions are important. It is almost too sudden and drastic; the human spirit is hardly capable of adjusting itself so rapidly. Yet it succeeds on the stage, justification enough for such magnificently daring technique.

It is difficult to see how the Mellefont-Maskwell intrigue can be called comedy. Towards Maskwell and Lady Touchwood Congreve has not the attitude of the comedy writer, nor of the satirist; he is the cold and virtuous wielder of the chastening rod. Neither are Touchwood, Mellefont, or Cynthia figures of critical comedy; their appeal is to our sympathy. They are admirably honest, simple, likeable people, and Cynthia is altogether charming. They do, however, fulfil the purposes of critical comedy in so far as they provide models of the golden mean.

Congreve's wit is not at its deepest in this play, but if it descends too often to the cheap level of the Witwouds rather than aims at that of the Truewits, it is always light and spinning. It is worthy of Brisk, but not of Mellefont or Careless. One may, it is true, answer a fool according to his folly, but only if there is the likelihood of his being wise in his own conceit. And this is a little too facile:

> BRISK. Careless . . . you're always spoiling company by leaving it.
>
> CARE. And thou art always spoiling company by coming into 't.
>
> BRISK. Pooh! . . . Pshaw, man! When I say you spoil company by leaving it, I mean you leave nobody for the company to laugh at.

Yet the dialogue is nearly always magnificently neat and blade-like, the delineation of fops highly entertaining. Lady Plyant is perfect. She is to be met with in real life, but here she is raised to the power of comedy. She is, perhaps, most wonderful in the scene where she makes advances to the puzzled Mellefont, who cares nothing for her, but is eager to marry her daughter.

LADY P. And nobody knows how circumstances may happen together—To my thinking, now I could resist the
strongest temptation. But yet I know, 'tis impossible
for me to know whether I could or not; there's no certainty in the things of this life.

MEL. Madam, pray give me leave to ask you one question.

LADY P. O Lord, ask me the question! I'll swear I'll refuse
it! I swear I'll deny it!—therefore don't ask me; nay,
you shan't ask me; I swear I'll deny it. O Gemini, you
have brought all the blood into my face! I warrant I'm
as red as a turkeycock; O fie, cousin Mellefont.

MEL. Nay, madam, hear me; I mean——

LADY P. Hear you! No, no. I'll deny you first, and hear
you afterwards. For one does not know how one's mind
may change upon hearing. Hearing is one of the senses,
and the senses are fallible; I won't trust my honour, I
assure you, my honour is infallible and uncomatable.

MEL. For Heaven's sake, madam——

LADY P. O name it no more—Bless me, how can you talk
of Heaven! and have so much wickedness in your
heart? Maybe you don't think it a sin.—They say some
of you gentlemen don't think it a sin.—Or . . . Maybe
it is no sin to them that don't think it so; indeed, if I
did not think it a sin.—but still my honour, if it were
no sin.—But then, to marry my daughter, for the con-
veniency of frequent opportunities, I'll never consent
to that; as sure as can be, I'll break the match.

Here we reach levels Wycherley could barely guess at. It is indeed
being voluble as well as precise, and is really comic if comedy is concerned with the antics of the human being caught in the social net.
Moreover, the characterization is clearly drawn in the dialogue. Each
character speaks with his or her own authentic voice, and has an outside existence.

Work which aims at the quality after which Congreve was striving
is not to be produced hurriedly, and his next work, *Love for Love*,
shows traces of carelessness. It is often considered to be Congreve's
best play, and was very popular when first acted. But Congreve's best
was not for the vulgar, and we can imagine it was the return to a
certain Jonsonian obviousness that made *Love for Love* so palatable
to the playgoers. It is possible that the treatment of the humours, here
so evident, was suggested by the popularity of Wilson's *The Cheats*,
which had reached a fourth edition in 1693. Certain passages indicate

that the character of Foresight may have been taken from the astrologer Mopus, with this difference, however, that Mopus was a self-
professed charlatan, whereas Foresight deluded himself. Again, there
are many moments in the play where we think of Wycherley rather
than of Congreve. For instance, when Valentine feigning madness
says to Tattle, "My friend, what to do? I am no married man, and
thou canst not lie with my wife; I am very poor, and thou canst not
borrow money of me; then what employment have I for a friend?," it
might be Manly resuscitated.

Congreve seems to have felt that the comic stage was losing some
of its force, and that this needed reviving. In this connexion a portion
of the prologue is worth quotation:

> We've something too, to gratify ill-nature,
> (If there be any here) and that is satire.
> Though satire scarce does grin, 'tis grown so mild;
> And only shows its teeth, as if it smiled.
> As asses thistles, poets mumble wit,
> And dare not bite, for fear of being bit.
> They hold their pens, as swords are held by fools,
> And are afraid to use their own edge-tools.
> Since the Plain-Dealer's scenes of Manly rage
> No one has dared to lash this crying age.
> This time, the poet owns the bold essay. . . .

a sufficient indication of his purpose, and perhaps of his inspiration.
The position of the poet too, seems to have occupied Congreve's mind,
more, probably, from the need for effusive and insincere dedications,
than from such incidents as Otway's pitiful death from starvation. Says
Scandal:

> Turn pimp, flatterer, quack, lawyer, parson, be chaplain
> to an atheist, or stallion to an old woman, anything but
> a poet; a modern poet is worse, more servile, timorous
> and fawning, than any I have named; without you could
> retrieve the ancient honours of the name, recall the
> stage of Athens, and be allowed the force of open, honest
> satire.

Thus the general tone and the form of this play can be accounted
for. Indeed, Congreve from the first had not been altogether averse
from satire, and could make excellent thrusts, but his hand was too
light for a whole "essay" in this kind, and in comparison with his

best work, he here becomes a little tedious, and even repetitive. It
follows that many passages, though they are good Wycherley, are poor
Congreve. We may take as an example Scandal's account of Tattle:

> A mender of reputations! ay, just as he is a keeper of
> secrets, another virtue that he sets up for in the same
> manner. For the rogue will speak aloud in the posture
> of a whisper; and deny a woman's name, while he gives
> you the marks of her person; he will forswear receiving
> a letter from her, and at the same time show you her
> hand in the superscription: and yet perhaps he has coun-
> terfeited the hand too, and sworn to a truth; but he
> hopes not to be believed; and he refuses the reputation
> of a lady's favour, as a doctor says No to a bishopric, only
> that it may be granted him.—In short, he is a public pro-
> fessor of secrecy, and makes proclamation that he holds
> private intelligence.

This is overweighty, and not only are we forthwith given a scene
where, to illustrate the above, Tattle is easily trapped into indiscre-
tions, but the same is repeated in a later act.

The satiric lash is again apparent in the famous Tattle-Prue scene,
so different from the same kind of scene as treated by Etherege, quoted
in a previous chapter. Prue, we must remember, is an *ingénue* from
the country.

> PRUE. Well; and how will you make love to me? Come,
>   I long to have you begin. Must I make love too? You
>   must tell me how.
> TAT. You must let me speak, miss, you must not speak
>   first; I must ask you questions, and you must answer.
> PRUE. What, is it like the catechism?—Come then, ask me.
> TAT. D'ye think you can love me?
> PRUE. Yes.
> TAT. Pooh! Pox! you must not say yes already; I shan't
>   care a farthing for you then in a twinkling.
> PRUE. What must I say then?
> TAT. Why, you must say no, or you believe not, or you
>   can't tell—
> PRUE. Why, must I tell a lie then?
> TAT. Yes, if you'd be well-bred. All well-bred persons lie.
>   Besides, you are a woman, you must never speak what
>   you think; your words must contradict your thoughts:
>   but your actions may contradict your words. So, when

I ask you, if you can love me, you must say no, but you
must love me too. If I tell you you are handsome, you
must deny it, and say I flatter you. But you must think
yourself more charming than I speak you; and like me
for the beauty which I say you have, as much as if I
had it myself. If I ask you to kiss me, you must be
angry, but you must not refuse me. If I ask you for
more, you must be more angry—but more complying;
and as soon as ever I make you say you'll cry out, you
must be sure to hold your tongue.

PRUE. O Lord, I swear this is pure!—I like it better than
our old-fashioned country way of speaking one's mind;
and must not you lie too?

TAT. Hm!—yes, but you must believe I speak truth.

PRUE. O Gemini! Well, I always had a great mind to tell
lies; but they frighted me, and said it was a sin.

TAT. Well, my pretty creature; will you make me happy
by giving me a kiss?

PRUE. No, indeed, I'm angry at you. (*Runs and kisses
him.*)

TAT. Hold, hold, that's pretty well—but you should not
have given it me, but have suffered me to have taken it.

PRUE. Well, we'll do it again.

TAT. With all my heart.—Now then, my little angel.

(*Kisses her.*)

PRUE. Pish!

TAT. That's right—again my charmer! (*Kisses her again.*)

PRUE. O fy! nay, now I can't abide you.

TAT. Admirable! That's as well as if you had been born
and bred in Covent Garden.

What follows is as well as if she had been born and bred in some
Oriental *wazir*. Yet the whole is certainly trenchant satire, verging
upon the venomous, and conformable to the general opinion of
women in that age. But it lacks the exquisiteness one has learned to
expect from Congreve. He had abandoned the rapier for the bludgeon,
as he had abandoned the comedy of manners for the comedy of humours. The equally famous scene between Mrs. Foresight and Mrs.
Frail is at a better level.

MRS. FO. I suppose you would not go alone to the World's
End? [This was a somewhat disreputable tavern.]

MRS. FR. The world's end! What! do you mean to banter
me?

MRS. FO. Poor innocent! you don't know that there's a
place called the World's End? I'll swear you can keep
your countenance purely, you'd make an admirable
player.

MRS. FR. I'll swear you have a great deal of confidence,
and in my mind too much for the stage.

MRS. FO. Very well, that will appear who has most; you
were never at the World's End?

MRS. FR. No.

MRS. FO. You deny it positively to my face?

MRS. FR. Your face! What's your face?

MRS. FO. No matter for that, it's as good a face as yours.

MRS. FR. Not by a dozen years' wearing. But I do deny it
positively to your face then.

MRS. FO. I'll allow you now to find fault with my face;—
for I'll swear your impudence has put me out of countenance;—but look you here now—where did you lose
this gold bodkin? O sister, sister! . . .

MRS. FR. Well, if you go to that, where did you find this
bodkin? O sister, sister!—sister every way.

Such a disclosure serves but to make the sisters friends, for "ours are
but slight flesh wounds, and if we keep 'em from air, not at all dangerous." A neat statement of a social philosophy not unknown at the
present day, while the repartee throughout is as good as the characters
demand.

But in this play, in spite of its rather ponderous satire, and the
humours of Foresight and Sir Sampson Legend—the latter at times
reminiscent of Old Bellair—something of Congreve appears that is
peculiarly his own, an expression of longing to find the world finer
than it really is, a poetic fastidiousness and a depth of feeling that
make him more than any other Englishman akin to Molière. It is already adumbrated in *The Double Dealer:*

MELLEFONT. You're thoughtful, Cynthia?

CYNTHIA. I'm thinking, though marriage makes a man
and wife one flesh, it leaves 'em still two fools: and
they become more conspicuous by setting off one another.

MEL. That's only when two fools meet, and their follies
are opposed.

CYN. Nay, I have known two wits meet, and by the opposition of their wit, render themselves as ridiculous as

> fools. 'Tis an odd game we are going to play at; what
> think you of drawing stakes, and giving over in time?

The fear of lost illusion seems to haunt him. Like Valentine in *Love for Love*, Congreve is melancholy at the thought of spoiled ideals and spoiled beauty. A passionate ardour for the finer side of life breathes constantly from his pages. Valentine for instance says:

> You're a woman—one to whom Heaven gave beauty,
> when it grafted roses on a briar. You are the reflection of
> heaven in a pond, and he that leaps at you is sunk. You
> are all white, a sheet of lovely spotless paper, when you
> first are born; but you are to be scrawled and blotted by
> every goose's quill. I know you; for I loved a woman, and
> loved her so long, that I found out a strange thing; I
> found out what a woman was good for,

and this was "to keep a secret; for though she should tell, yet she is not to be believed." This is one of Congreve's "heartless" men; and now for one of his "heartless" women. Angelica speaks:

> Would any-thing but a madman complain of uncer-
> tainty? Uncertainty and expectation are the joys of life.
> Security is an insipid thing, and the overtaking and pos-
> sessing of a wish, discovers the folly of the chase. Never let
> us know one another better; for the pleasure of a mas-
> querade is done, when we come to show our faces.

This is not the observation of a jilt, of a baggage without sensibility, but of a woman who has known and suffered, who has been disappointed in her early estimate of things. It is the weary cry of the knower who realizes that happiness may not be sought for or grasped, and that joy must be snatched as it flies. These were not mere puppets, but breathing, living, desiring men and women.

Love for Love, indeed, ends on the wistful note, with Angelica's tender, sad argument, which is a plea for mutual trust, an almost despairing outburst against the injustice done her sex:—

> You tax us with injustice, only to cover your own want
> of merit. You would all have the reward of love; but few
> have the constancy to stay till it becomes your due. Men
> are generally hypocrites and infidels, they pretend to wor-
> ship, but have neither zeal nor faith.

The thread of sadness and disillusion runs through these plays, and live passions break through the veil of cynicism wherewith the critical comedy clothes itself. We pierce through the social world to the realm of our underlying motives, to our ardours and desires, for beauty as well as for grosser satisfactions; and Congreve reveals himself as a poet pleading for finer living.

If *Love for Love* is Congreve's best *stage* play, *The Way of the World* is his masterpiece of literary art, as well as his final vindication of mankind. In it glows the true Congreve, the Congreve to whom detraction was wearisome, and who aspired after that very fragile thing, beauty itself.

In reading his dedication and his prologue we are reminded of a Frenchman, not of Molière, however, nor of any one of that century, but of—Flaubert. The aspiration is the same, the dislike of human folly is the same; there is the identical feeling that the highest achievement is the creation of beauty through the quality and texture of words. Congreve does not explicitly mention his aim, but it is implicit in his paragraphs in which he speaks again and again of "purity of style," and "perfection of dialogue." This was his great aim, the creation of beauty by plastic means. "Je me souviens," Flaubert says, "d'avoir eu des battements de coeur, d'avoir ressenti un plaisir violent en contemplant un mur de l'Acropole, un mur tout nu . . . Eh bien! Je me demande si un livre, indépendamment de ce qu'il dit, ne peut pas produire le même effet." Surely Congreve too asked himself that question. Like Flaubert, he wrote, not for the mob, but for the *few* (the italics are his own), qualified to distinguish those who write "with care and pains." "That it succeeded on the stage, was almost beyond my expectation," and he might have gone on, "car j'écris (Je parle d'un auteur qui se respecte) non pour le lecteur d'aujourd'hui, mais pour tous les lecteurs qui pourront se présenter, tant que la langue vivra." Like Flaubert, again, he would not meddle between the audience and his presentation of life. He would

> Give you one instance of a passive poet
> Who to your judgements yields all resignation,

for, "Quant à laisser voir mon opinion personnelle sur les gens que je mets en scène; non, non, mille fois non!" It is this attitude that has led to the popular view of "the great and splendid Mr. Congreve," the man of "unruffled temper," the gentleman of "perfect urbanity." As though good art ever came out of perfect urbanity!

Thus his poetry, his art, the essential stuff he alone could give, is to be found not so much in the "fable," or in satire, as in the wording. He was not really interested in his material, and in his dedication envied Terence for having had his subject prepared for him by Menander, so that he could devote his energies to correctness of speech. It is to be remembered that Dryden hailed Congreve as his successor, and that Dryden's great aim was to perfect the language. "To please, this time, has been his sole pretence," to "give delight," in Corneille's and Dryden's sense of the words, with all the beauty of phrase of which he was capable, and thus to express his aspiration after the elusive beauty of humanity. Even on such a commonplace theme as that of sending English fools on the Grand Tour, Congreve could write, " 'Tis better to trade with a little loss, than to be quite eaten up with being overstocked." That is a perfect phrase, concise, but without the least suspicion of a rattle—and marvellous in balance. The vowel-sounds are carefully selected, so that those in the second part of the sentence echo, yet vary without ever repeating, those of the first. That is how poetry is written. A trifling detail, a commonplace remark, it may be said. Possibly: but think of the concentration of artistic purpose that can expend itself on a thing so humble. Certainly this play was not "prepared for that general taste which seems now to be predominant in the palates of our audience."

He puts into the mouth of his fool Witwoud a remark Etherege or another might have given to a *jeune premier:* "A wit should no more be sincere than a woman constant; one argues a decay of parts, as t'other of beauty," for Congreve hated all this false tomfoolery, this pretence of liking the hateful. But small wonder that the audience was puzzled, and that it was three days before some of the "hasty judges could find the leisure to distinguish between the character of a Witwoud and a Truewit." Even Pope, we remember, asked, "Tell me if Congreve's fools are fools indeed?"

The Way of the World naturally failed at its first appearance on the stage, as it has ever since, except for a short period of partial favour, some thirty years after its birth, when Peg Woffington played Millamant.* Downs said that "It had not the success the company expected because it was too keen a satire," but in reality, it was too civilized for an age that revelled in the scribblings of Mrs. Pix, and applauded the burlesque of Farquhar's *Love and a Bottle.* But there was

* This was written before its success in 1924. Do we grow civilized?

also the fact that in many passages Congreve had ceased to write the
ordinary comedy. While his secondary characters in his previous plays,
his Lord and Lady Froth and his Lady Plyant, are made of that
flimsy material which could enable Lamb to call them creatures of a
sportive fancy, this is not so with Mrs. Marwood and the Fainalls in
this play. Fainall is a repulsive villain, but Mrs. Fainall, whom Mirabell had once loved, is more sinned against than sinning. She remains
loyal to Mirabell, and even helps him in his advances to Millamant
(what profound psychology is here!), but at the same time her heart
aches at not being loved by her husband. "He will willingly dispense
with the hearing of one scandalous story, to avoid giving an occasion
to make another by being seen to walk with his wife," she says with an
affectation of lightness. But how bitter it is! How full of unnecessary
pain is the way of the world!

   She and Mrs. Marwood are figures of an intense realism, driven by
that insane jealousy which is often more bitter and nearer to the surface in illicit love than in the marriage tie. Mrs. Marwood is Fainall's
mistress; but she also loves Mirabell, so that Mrs. Fainall has double
reason to be jealous of her; yet it is rather on account of Mirabell she
is jealous, and this also is true to life. Fainall, again, is jealous of
Mirabell, and goads Mrs. Marwood into a very frenzy of despair, and
though all the time he is wounding himself, he cannot resist the impulsion. Never for a moment does the comic penetrate into this tense
scene:

> FAINALL. Will you yet be reconciled to truth and me?
> MRS. MARWOOD. Impossible. Truth and you are incon-
>   sistent: I hate you, and shall for ever.
> FAIN. For loving you?
> MRS. M. I loathe the name of love after such usage; and
>   next to the guilt with which you would asperse me, I
>   scorn you most. Farewell.
> FAIN. Nay, we must not part thus.
> MRS. M. Let me go.
> FAIN. Come, I'm sorry.
> MRS. M. I care not—let me go—break my hands, do—I'd
>   leave 'em to get loose.
> FAIN. I would not hurt you for the world. Have I no
>   other hold to keep you here?
> MRS. M. Well, I have deserved it all.
> FAIN. You know I love you.
> MRS. M. Poor dissembling!—O that—well, it is not yet——

FAIN. What? what is it not? what is not yet? It is not yet
   too late.—
MRS. M. No, it is not yet too late;—I have that comfort.
FAIN. It is, to love another.
MRS. M. But not to loathe, detest, abhor, mankind, myself, and the whole treacherous world.
FAIN. Nay, this is extravagance—Come, I ask your pardon
   —no tears—I was to blame, I could not love you, and
   be easy in my doubts. Pray forbear—I believe you; I'm
   convinced I've done you wrong; and any way, every
   way, make amends. I'll hate my wife, yet more, damn
   her! I'll part with her, rob her of all she's worth, and
   we'll retire somewhere, anywhere, to another world. I'll
   marry thee. Be pacified. 'Sdeath, they come, hide your
   face, your tears;—you have a mask, wear it a moment.
   This way, this way—be persuaded.

To say that these are puppets animated by no real passions is to mis-
understand Congreve; one might as well say the same of Richardson's
women.

   But he could still be comic when he wished; take this little inset:

MIRABELL. Excellent Foible! Matrimony has made you
   eloquent in love.
WAITWELL. I think she has profited, sir. I think so.

Delicious ridicule! O complacency of the satisfied male!

   But in spite of such passages, in spite of the drunken scenes of Sir
Wilful Witwoud and Petulant, and the masquerading of Waitwell as
Sir Rowland, which are calculated to appeal to the most stupid elements in an audience, the whole play needs close following sentence
by sentence. It is this which makes it everlasting literature. But even
that glorious farcical scene between Lady Wishfort and "Sir Rowland" (IV. xii) is too fine for immediate appreciation. When Lady
Wishfort hopes Sir Rowland will not "impute her complacency to any
lethargy of continence," nor think her "prone to any iteration of
nuptials," or believe that "the least scruple of carnality is an in-
gredient," he assures her, "Dear Madam, no. You are all camphire and
frankincense, all chastity and odour." On the stage? No, one must
repeat it, laughing, to oneself—"all camphire and frankincense, all
chastity and odour." Like good poetry, it speaks to the inward ear.

   Although much of this play is the pure presentation of the artist to
whom all life is material, and whose attitude towards it must be

guessed through the quality of the words rather than by their surface meaning, in the main personages we feel Congreve coming to more direct grips with his inmost self. And the theme in which this is apparent is, inevitably in that age, the theme of love. Millamant, "Think of her, think of a whirlwind!" From the first we know that she and Mirabell really love each other. Mirabell thinks it was for herself she blushed when he blundered into the "cabal night"; but it was for him, at seeing the man she loved make a fool of himself in company vastly inferior to him. For the first time in his life he is jealous for a woman, "not of her person, but of her understanding," and he feels that for a "discerning man" he is "somewhat too passionate a lover; for I like her with all her faults; nay, like her for her faults." And when they meet, how exquisite they are together, how tenderly she chaffs him:

> MIRABELL. You are no longer handsome when you've lost your lover; your beauty dies upon the instant: for beauty is the lover's gift; 'tis he bestows your charms—your glass is all a cheat. . . .
>
> MILLAMANT. O the vanity of these men! . . . Beauty the lover's gift! Lord! what is a lover, that it can give? Why, one makes lovers as fast as one pleases, and they live as long as one pleases, and they die as soon as one pleases; and then, if one pleases, one makes more.

Mirabell is too serious a lover to take her remarks as fun, or as affectionate teasing; he is goaded into gibes, and although Millamant gets bored with them, she sees the love behind. But she wants light and air, the freshness of spring and a clear gaiety—charming, lovable Millamant, no wonder the young men in the pit would gladly marry her in spite of Macaulay's sneer—she is the incarnation of happiness, or at least of the desire for it. "Sententious Mirabell!—Prithee don't look with that violent and inflexible wise face, like Solomon at the dividing of the child in an old tapestry hanging." Life is serious, but let us at least be gay while we can.

The culmination, of course, is the famous bargaining scene already referred to. It is Congreve's contribution to the philosophy of love.

> MIL. Ah! don't be impertinent. My dear liberty, shall I leave thee? My faithful solitude, my darling contemplation, must I bid you then adieu? Ay-h adieu—my morning thoughts, agreeable wakings, indolent slumbers, all ye *douceurs, ye someils du matin*, adieu?—I can't do't, 'tis more than impossible—positively Mira-

bell, I'll lie abed in a morning as long as I please.

MIR. Then I'll get up in a morning as early as I please.

MIL. Oh! idle creature, get up when you will—and d'ye hear, I won't be called names after I'm married: positively I won't be called names.

MIR. Names!

MIL. Ay, as wife, spouse, my dear, joy, jewel, love, sweetheart, and the rest of that nauseous cant, in which men and their wives are so fulsomely familiar—I shall never bear that—good Mirabell, don't let us be familiar or fond, nor kiss before folks, like my Lady Fadler and Sir Francis; nor go to Hyde Park together the first Sunday in a new chariot, to provoke eyes and whispers; and then never to be seen there together again; as if we were proud of one another the first week, and ashamed of one another ever after. Let us never visit together, nor go to a play together; but let us be as strange as if we had been married a great while; and as well bred as if we were not married at all.

MIR. Have you any more conditions to offer? Hitherto your demands are pretty reasonable.

MIL. Trifles!—As liberty to pay and receive visits to and from whom I please; to write and receive letters without interrogatories or wry faces on your part; to wear what I please; and choose conversation with regard only to my own taste; to have no obligation upon me to converse with wits that I don't like, because they are your acquaintance; or to be intimate with fools because they may be your relations. Come to dinner when I please, dine in my dressing room when I'm out of humour, without giving a reason. To have my closet inviolate; to be the sole empress of my tea-table, which you must never presume to approach without first asking leave. And lastly, wherever I am, you shall always knock at the door before you come in. These articles subscribed, if I continue to endure you a little longer, I may by degrees dwindle into a wife.

MIR. Your bill of fare is something advanced in this latter account. Well, have I liberty to offer conditions—that when you are dwindled into a wife, I may not be beyond measure enlarged into a husband?

MIL. You have free leave; propose your utmost, speak and spare not.

MIR. I thank you. *Imprimis* then, I covenant that your acquaintance be general; that you admit no sworn confidant, or intimate of your own sex; no she friend to screen her affairs under your countenance, and tempt you to make a trial of a mutual secrecy. No decoy-duck to wheedle you a *fop-scrambling* to the play in a mask —then bring you home in a pretended fright, when you think you shall be found out—and rail at me for missing the play, and disappointing the frolic which you had to pick me up and prove my constancy.

MIL. Detestable *imprimis!* I go to the play in a mask!

MIR. *Item,* I article, that you continue to like your own face, as long as I shall: and while it passes current with me, that you endeavour not to new-coin it. To which end, together with all vizards for the day, I prohibit all masks for the night, made of oiled-skins, and I know not what—hog's bones, hares' gall, pig-water, and the marrow of a roasted cat. In short, I forbid all commerce with the gentlewoman in *what d'ye call it* court. *Item,* I shut my doors against all bawds with baskets, and pennyworths of muslin, china, fans, atlasses etc.—*Item,* when you shall be breeding—

MIL. Ah! name it not.

MIR. Which may be presumed with a blessing on our endeavours—

MIL. Odious endeavours!

MIR. I denounce against all strait lacing, squeezing for a shape, till you mould my boy's head like a sugar-loaf, and instead of a man child, make me father to a crooked billet. Lastly, to the dominion of the tea-table I submit—but with *proviso,* that you exceed not in your province; but restrain yourself to native and simple tea-table drinks, as tea, chocolate and coffee; as likewise to genuine and authorized tea-table talk—such as mending of fashions, spoiling reputations, railing at absent friends, and so forth—but that on no account you encroach upon the men's prerogative, and presume to drink healths, or toast fellows; for prevention of which I banish all foreign forces, all auxiliaries to the tea-table, as orange brandy, all aniseed, cinnamon, citron, and Barbadoes waters, together with ratafia, and the most noble spirit of clary—but for cowslip wine, poppy water, and all dormitives, those I allow. These *provisos* admitted, in other things I may prove a tractable and complying husband.

MIL. O horrid *provisos!* filthy strong waters! I toast fellows! odious men! I hate your odious *provisos!*

And this is commonly considered the behaviour of an arrant coquette!
In reality it is a vision of the conflict in all marriage, of the desire to
maintain one's own personality fighting vainly with the desire to love
whole-heartedly. Her appeal has all the earnestness of real life about
it; it is vocal of all the hopes and fears of lovers when they see the
bright face of happiness tarnished with the shadow of possible disillusion. It *must* not happen that they are very proud of one another the
first week, and ashamed of one another ever after. Each of them has
seen the rocks which bring most marriages to ruin, and will strive to
avoid them. And this to Thackeray was "a weary feast, that banquet
of wit where no love is!"

Not to see this passionate side of Congreve is to lose the best in him;
it is like reading Shakespeare to find that he does not conform to
classical rules. For Millamant is a woman; she has the inestimable
power of giving, but she is rightly jealous of herself, and is not to be
undervalued. She is alive and breathing, hiding a real personality behind the only too necessary artifices of her sex. Once assured of Mirabell's love, she divests herself of her armour, and shows a perfect frankness. Meredith, in giving Congreve praise for the portraiture, does not
do her justice; she is only a "flashing portrait, and a type of the superior ladies who do not think, not of those who do." Millamant not
think! when on the face of it she has thought a great deal, and thought
very clearly, about the living of her own life. She needed to be certain
of Mirabell before taking the plunge and dwindling into a wife, for
she had all the fastidiousness of a woman of experience. "If Mirabell
should not make a good husband, I am a lost thing."

The only other figure at all comparable to Millamant is Lady Wishfort, but she is not in the round, and her presentation too nearly approaches satire. "Her flow of boudoir Billingsgate," says Meredith, "is
unmatched for the vigour and pointedness of the tongue. It spins
along with a final ring, like the voice of Nature in a fury, and is indeed
the racy eloquence of the educated fishwife."

> LADY WISHFORT. No news of Foible yet?
> PEG. No, madam.
> LADY W. I have no more patience.—If I have not fretted
>   myself till I am pale again, there's no veracity in me!
>   Fetch me the red—the red, do you hear, sweetheart?
>   An arrant ash colour, as I'm a person! Why dost thou
>   not fetch me a little red? Didst thou not hear me,
>   Mopus?

> PEG. The red ratafia does your ladyship mean, or the
> cherry brandy?
> LADY W. Ratafia, fool! no, fool. Not the ratafia, fool—
> grant me patience! I mean the Spanish paper, idiot—
> complexion, darling. Paint, paint, paint, dost thou
> understand that, changling, dangling thy hands like
> bobbins before thee? Why does thou not stir, puppet?
> thou wooden thing upon wires!

Her *De Arte Amandi* passage ripples along with unthinkable skill.
After scolding Mirabell, "Frippery! Superannuated frippery! I'll frippery the villain!" she turns to a more agreeable subject.

> LADY W. But art thou sure Sir Rowland will not fail to
> come? or will he not fail when he does come? Will he
> be importunate, Foible, and push? For if he should not
> be importunate,—I shall never break decorums—I shall
> die with confusion, if I am forced to advance!—I shall
> swoon if he should expect advances. No, I hope Sir
> Rowland is better bred, than to put a lady to the
> necessity of breaking her forms. I won't be too coy,
> neither—I won't give him despair—but a little disdain
> is not amiss; a little scorn is alluring.
> FOIBLE. A little scorn becomes your ladyship.
> LADY W. Yes, but tenderness becomes me best—a sort of
> dyingness—you see that picture has a sort of a—ha,
> Foible! a swimmingness in the eyes—yes, I'll look so—
> my niece affects it; but she wants features. Is Sir Row-
> land handsome? Let my toilet be removed—I'll dress
> above. I'll receive Sir Rowland here. Is he handsome?
> Don't answer me. I won't know: I'll be surprised. I'll
> be taken by surprise.
> FOIBLE. By storm, madam, Sir Rowland's a brisk man.
> LADY W. Is he! O then he'll importune, if he's a brisk
> man. I shall save decorums if Sir Rowland importunes.
> I have a mortal terror at the apprehension of offending
> against decorums.

Yet such a current of sympathy seems to flow from Congreve even into
this subject, that she becomes almost pathetic, and one feels a touch
of the tragic mingled with the comic vision.

The *dénouement* is forced, a mere trumped up affair, but it does
not matter, any more than it matters with Tartuffe. With the exposure

of Fainall, and the emotional torture of Mrs. Marwood, the atmosphere seems almost irretrievably ruined; but then we have,

> MILLAMANT. Why does not the man take me? Would you
>   have me give myself to you over again?
> MIRABELL. Ay, and over and over again,

so that the whole torrential scene dissolves before us into grace, and clear, straightforward feeling. When the first rush has gone, one can only gasp at the incomparable art.

Congreve had much of the classical writer of comedy about him; he preached the happy mean. His "wicked" *jeunes premiers,* and to a less degree his *premières,* are gentlemen and ladies. Bellmour, Mellefont, Valentine, and Mirabell, if their manners are not quite ours—but indeed they are little removed—are never underhand or malicious, and have generosity. Cynthia, Angelica, and Millamant are charming women, warm-hearted, companionable, and direct. These are not scandal-mongers and sharpers, nor would-be wits and heartless jades. They show up in solid relief against the dizzy world of Restoration comedy. It is true that the men are not righteous overmuch; they represent the common-sense attitude current even in Victorian days, they sowed their wild oats. But once they have come to marriage, they show the utmost sincerity. Congreve, however, never saw beyond this. It would never occur to him that an Alceste might, after all, be right. One does not feel with him, as one does with Molière, that the ideal of the *honnéte homme* is perhaps not the final philosophy of every-day life. At the same time one sees that his standard would be far above the average in sensibility.

If to refine upon existence was Congreve's dominant desire, as it would appear, there was no more for him to do in the world of comedy. He had tried to invest it with the delicacy of drawing-room poetry, and had failed. The medium of critical comedy was not suitable, and his appeal was to a circle more exquisite than an audience. He was tired of portraying fools and rascals, and the bodily lusts of men and women; and, indeed, the garb of the comic writer never set altogether easily upon his sensitive shoulders. Thus, in spite of his excelling qualities, one must confess failure, if we judge by the greatest standards. His criticism never won through to a broader vision; his disillusion conquered him. Too much a poet to accept the surface of life, he was too little a poet to find beauty in the bare facts of existence; and one cannot help regarding him a little as a tragic figure. If, as he believed, it was the duty of the comic poet to lash the vices and follies of human-kind, in view of the nature of man it hardly seemed worth while. And as for the creation of beauty, when, after great travail it was achieved, it went unrecognized, and all that the critics could say of it was to call it "too keen a satire." Was it not better to sport in the shade with the Amaryllis of social wit, or—with the tangles of a Bracegirdle's hair?

CLIFFORD LEECH

❀

Congreve and the Century's End

When Dryden returned to the theatre after the Revolution, it was with a sense that the glory had departed. The comedies of Etherege and Wycherley had all been written before 1680; the careers of Otway and Lee were done; the only notable dramatist to begin work in the 1680's was Southerne, and he had yet shown no signs of unusual worth. So, when *Don Sebastian, King of Portugal* was published in 1690, Dryden wrote in a melancholy strain on the exhausted condition of the Restoration theatre and drama:

> Having been longer acquainted with the Stage, than any Poet now living, and having observed how difficult it was to please; that the Humours of Comedy were almost spent, that Love and Honor (the mistaken Topicks of Tragedy) were quite worn out, that the Theatres could not support their Charges, that the Audience forsook them, that young Men without Learning set up for Judges, and that they talk'd loudest, who understood the least: All these Discouragements had not only wean'd me from the Stage, but had also given me a Loathing of it. But enough of this: the Difficulties continue; they encrease, and I am still condemn'd to dig in those exhausted Mines.[1]

What variations were possible on the Restoration comic formula, what could bring to serious drama something more than the setting-forth of

From *Philological Quarterly,* XLI (1962) , 275-93. Reprinted by permission of the publishers.

stereotyped attitudes? Gone was the excitement of Puritan-baiting under the protection of Charles's court, gone the feeling of release and adventure that came with the returning monarchy, gone even the dream of magnanimity that informed the heroic play. To Dryden after the Revolution the theatre was a source of livelihood, and he could yet work at it with skill, but in 1690 he could see no contemporary drama-tist worthy of much respect and no sign of a new development that would bring the spirit of William's reign into dramatic focus. This state of things needs to be remembered when we look at the com-mendatory verses published with Congreve's *The Old Bachelor* (1693) and *The Double Dealer* (1694). Southerne and Bevil Higgons, intro-ducing the earlier play, hailed the writer as Dryden's successor, and in well-known lines Southerne drew attention to the prevailing dearth of talent. Of Dryden's contemporaries he writes:

> His eldest *Wicherly,* in wise Retreat,
> Thought it not worth his Quiet to be Great.
> Loose, wandring, *Etherege,* in wild Pleasures tost,
> And foreign Int'rests, to his Hopes long lost:
> Poor *Lee* and *Otway* dead!

Dryden himself introduced *The Double Dealer,* claiming that the new playwright united the best qualities of Restoration comic writing:

> *In Him all Beauties of this Age we see;*
> Etherege *his Courtship,* Southern's *Purity;*
> *The Satire, Wit, and Strength of Manly* Wicherly.

In dramatic genius, Dryden averred, Congreve was Shakespeare's peer, and the tribute ends with a formal bequeathing of Dryden's own laurels.

We are not likely to go so far as Dryden in all he says here, but he may give us a clue to the understanding of Congreve when he says:

> *In Him all Beauties of this Age we see.*

Congreve brings the diverse and often conflicting elements of Restora-tion comedy into a unity. Even in *The Old Bachelor* we find nothing of that disharmony that marked Etherege's beginning in *The Comical Revenge* or Wycherley's in *Love in a Wood.* In regarding the earlier writers, moreover, it is possible, though often difficult, to divide up their work into such classes as the "comedy of manners," the "comedy of humours," the "comedy of intrigue":[2] this has no validity at all for

Congreve. He tells us in his letter to John Dennis, "Concerning Humour in Comedy," that good comic writing depends on the exposure of individual eccentricity and that this needs to be combined with the exposure of fashionable affectations; he uses plot-devices from the intrigue-comedies, and this is indeed suggested in the prologue to *The Way of the World* when he makes Betterton claim on the poet's behalf: *"Some Plot we think he has."* His characters belong for the most part to the stock-types of the age—men and women of wit and fashion; harmless eccentrics like Foresight and Heartwell; men and women amorously inclined despite their years, like Sir Sampson Legend and Lady Wishfort; unpolished intruders into London society, like Ben and Sir Wilfull Witwoud; women of light virtue; fops and would-be wits—but he so contrives his plays that the characters are not isolated targets but are seen in relation to one another and to their society as a whole. His manner is generally light and courtly, as Etherege's was at its best, but there is a deliberateness in his utterance that could remind Dryden of Wycherley. He makes great play with the passion for similitudes which the wits indulged; his own fineness of phrasing depends largely on the current antithetic sentence-structure and on repetitions of word or phrase in the Wycherley mode; but his writing is flexible, warm, and rich in copious, startling, and strangely happy flights of fancy. In *The Way of the World* we find almost every character speaking in character and yet sharing in the fineness and amplitude of Congreve's language. Here is Mirabel, when Millamant has left him with the behest "think of me":

> I have something more—Gone—Think of you! To think of a Whirlwind, tho' 'twere in a Whirlwind, were a Case of more steady Contemplation; a very Tranquility of Mind and Mansion. A Fellow that lives in a Windmill, has a more whimsical dwelling than the Heart of a Man that is lodg'd in a Woman. There is no Point of the Compass to which they cannot turn, and by which they are not turn'd; and by one as well as another; for Motion not Method is their Occupation. To know this, and yet continue to be in Love, is to be made wise from the Dictates of Reason, and yet persevere to play the Fool by the force of Instinct. (II.vi) [3]

This, for all its fancy, has a sobriety of tone, a faculty for sage yet witty generalisation, that marks out Mirabel as distinctive among lovers. And here is Mrs. Marwood speaking in soliloquy, when she has just

learned that Mrs. Fainall has been Mirabel's mistress and that her own
disappointed love for Mirabel is known to Foible the servant:

> Indeed, Mrs. Engine, is it thus with you? Are you be-
> come a go-between of this Importance? Yes, I shall watch
> you. Why this Wench is the *Pass-par-toute,* a very Mas-
> ter-Key to every Body's strong Box. My Friend *Fainall,*
> have you carry'd it so swimmingly? I thought there was
> something in it; but it seems it's over with you. Your
> Loathing is not from a want of Appetite then, but from
> a Surfeit. Else you could never be so cool to fall from a
> Principal to be an Assistant; to procure for him! A Pat-
> tern of Generosity, that I confess. Well, Mr. *Fainall,* you
> have met with your Match.—O Man, Man! Woman,
> Woman! The Devil's an Ass: If I were a Painter, I would
> draw him like an Idiot, a Driveler with a Bib and Bells.
> Man shou'd have his Head and Horns, and Woman the
> rest of him. Poor simple Fiend! Madam *Marwood* has a
> Month's mind, but he can't abide her—'Twere better
> for him you had not been his Confessor in that Affair;
> without you could have kept his Counsel closer. I shall
> not prove another Pattern of Generosity—he has not
> oblig'd me to that with those Excesses of himself; and
> now I'll have none of him. Here comes the good Lady,
> panting ripe; with a Heart full of Hope, and a Head full
> of Care, like any Chymist upon the Day of Projection.
> (III.vii)

There is a strain of suppressed hysteria in this, with its exclamations
and its quick turns of thought, yet there is delicacy in the very railing
and a kind of joy in the fanciful comparison of Lady Wishfort, as she
thinks of an amorous encounter, to an alchemist on the brink of riches.
Even in Congreve's first plays there is an evenness, a sureness, a delight
in the flow of word and image, and at the same time a feeling of tension. Here is the middle-aged Heartwell in *The Old Bachelor,* as he
finds himself against his will falling in love with Sylvia: he approaches
her door and longs, and fears, to enter:

> Why whither in the Devil's Name am I a going now?
> Hum—let me think—Is not this *Sylvia's* House, the Cave
> of that Enchantress, and which consequently I ought to
> shun as I would Infection? To enter here, is to put on
> the envenom'd Shirt, to run into the Embraces of a
> Fever, and in some raving Fit, be led to plunge my self

into that more consuming Fire, a Woman's Arms. Ha!
well recollected, I will recover my Reason, and be gone.
. . . Well, why do you not move? Feet do your Office—
not one Inch; no, foregad I'm caught—There stands my
North, and thither my Needle points—Now could I curse
my self, yet cannot repent. O thou delicious, damn'd,
dear, destructive Woman! S'death how the young Fellows
will hoot me! I shall be the Jest of the Town: Nay in two
Days, I expect to be Chronicled in Ditty, and sung in
woeful Ballad, to the Tune of the superannuated Maidens Comfort, or the Batchelors Fall; and upon the third,
I shall be hang'd in Effigie, pasted up for the exemplary
Ornament of necessary Houses, and Coblers Stalls—
Death, I can't think on't—I'll run into the Danger to lose
the Apprehension. (III.ii)

Thus in the general fabric, the characterisation and the prose style
of his plays, Congreve's fellow-poets could see an organised expression
of the Restoration aim, a fusion of judgment and delight, with a
greater range and a sharper sensitivity than English drama had known
since the Civil War.

Yet the special quality of Congreve's work does not depend only on
his bringing into a unity elements that can be found in drama of the
early Restoration years. He was writing in the reign of William III,
between the Revolution of 1688 and the accession of Anne. It was a
time that saw the birth of new tendencies in the drama and in the
society of London. In comedy, in particular, the last decade of the
century was a time of important change. Colley Cibber presented his
first play, *Love's Last Shift, or The Fool in Fashion,* in 1696, and the
popularity of this led to the appearance a few months later of
Woman's Wit, or The Lady in Fashion. Neither play can claim much
of our respect, but there is no doubt that the earlier of the two ministered luckily to the taste of its time. The main action shows how
Loveless, who deserted his wife Amanda after six months of marriage
and fled abroad, returns to London penniless and is won back by
Amanda through her device of pretending to be a stranger, conducting
an intrigue with him and then appealing to his better nature. In his
epilogue Cibber apologises for his hero's reformation, and says it has
been contrived to please the ladies in the audience: the gentlemen
should after all remember that "He's lewd for above four acts." But
the popularity of the play showed the apology to be hardly needed.
The people of the playhouse in the 1690's could still enjoy the bawdy

phrase or situation, but they could evidently enjoy too the sententious
utterance, the adaptation of the play's fable to the orthodox notion of
how life should be lived. It is wrong to think of *Love's Last Shift* as
merely consisting of four acts of commonplace Restoration intrigue
followed by one act of sentiment: though Cibber enjoys the salacious
aspect of Loveless's intrigue with his own wife, there is throughout the
play a cultivation of the moral idea. Thus Young Worthy reproaches
his brother's fiancée Hillaria for encouraging the attentions of the fop
Sir Novelty Fashion:

> HIL. The fool diverted me, and I gave him my hand, as I
> would lend my money, fan, or handkerchief, to a leger-
> demain, that I might see him play all his tricks over.
> Y. WOR. O, madam, no jugler is so deceitful as a fop; for
> while you look his folly in the face, he steals away
> your reputation with more ease than the other picks
> your pocket.
> HIL. Some fools indeed are dangerous.
> Y. WOR. I grant you, your design is only to laugh at him;
> but that's more than he finds out: therefore you must
> expect he will tell the world another story; and 'tis ten
> to one but the consequence makes you repent your
> curiosity.
> HIL. You speak like an oracle: I tremble at the thoughts
> on't.
> Y. WOR. Here's one shall reconcile your fears—Brother, I
> have done your business: *Hillaria* is convinc'd of her
> indiscretion, and has a pardon ready, for your asking
> it.
> EL. WOR. She's the criminal; I have no occasion for it.
> Y. WOR. See, she comes towards you; give her a civil word
> at least.
> HIL. Mr. *Worthy,* I'll not be behind-hand in the acknowl-
> edgment I owe you: I freely confess my folly, and for-
> give your harsh construction of it: nay, I'll not con-
> demn your want of good-nature, in not endeavouring
> (as your brother has done) by mild arguments to con-
> vince me of my error.
> EL. WOR. Now you vanquish me! I blush to be outdone in
> generous love! I am your slave, dispose of me as you
> please.
> HIL. No more; from this hour be you the master of my ac-
> tions and my heart. (II.i) [4]

We should bear this passage in mind when we turn to Act II of *The Way of the World* and find Mirabel similarly reproaching Millamant for rejecting his company for that of Witwoud and Petulant:

> MIR. . . . You had the leisure to entertain a Herd of Fools; Things who visit you from their excessive Idleness; bestowing on your Easiness that Time, which is the Incumbrance of their Lives. How can you find Delight in such Society? It is impossible they shou'd admire you, they are not capable: Or if they were, it shou'd be to you as a Mortification; for sure to please a Fool is some degree of Folly.
>
> MILLA. I please my self—Besides, sometimes to converse with Fools is for my Health.
>
> MIRA. Your Health! Is there a worse Disease than the Conversation of Fools?
>
> MILLA. Yes, the Vapours; Fools are Physick for it, next to *Assa-foetida.*
>
> MIRA. You are not in a Course of Fools?
>
> MILLA. *Mirabell,* if you persist in this offensive Freedom— you'll displease me—I think I must resolve after all, not to have you—We shan't agree. (II.v)

Of course, Congreve gives Millamant the victory of the last word, but Mirabel's complaint is firmly made. Young Worthy talked pompously of "reputation"; Mirabel shows impatience at a lack of aesthetic discrimination. Nevertheless, here *The Way of the World* includes within itself the sententious strain of the newer comedy, yet with no breaking of the play's fabric. Part of the secret is in Congreve's keying-down of the sentiments and passions of his dramatis personae. Just as the thwarted love of Mrs. Marwood is never a source of danger to the play's harmony, as that of Mrs. Loveit is in Etherege's *The Man of Mode,* so here Mirabel's seriousness makes its effect but Millamant's gaiety can prevent his tone from becoming dominant. Mirabel indeed must generalise at his peril when she is with him, as a moment later in the same scene:

> MIRA. I say that a Man may as soon make a Friend by his Wit, or a Fortune by his Honesty, as win a Woman with Plain-dealing and Sincerity.
>
> MILLA. Sententious *Mirabell!* Prithee don't look with that violent and inflexible wise Face, like *Solomon* at the dividing of the Child in an old Tapestry Hanging. (II.v)

Paul and Miriam Mueschke have suggested that Cibber's "vulgarity, casuistry, and irresponsible juggling with values" may have strengthened Congreve's wish to write in a more genuinely serious fashion.[5] That could well be true, even if at the same time his comic range included something of the newer mode. Cibber, moreover, in his flashy way could learn something from Congreve. In his *The Careless Husband* (1704) he produced one of the most popular plays in the sentimental style, but he included in it the figure of Lady Betty Modish, a gay creature who only slowly and reluctantly yields to man and marriage. Like Hillaria in *Love's Last Shift*, she is charged with giving her time to fools rather than to men of sense, but Lady Betty is kept free from the solemnity with which the repentant Hillaria is exhibited. Sir Charles Easy, who reproaches her on behalf of his friend, presents a more vivacious picture than Young Worthy could manage:

> L. BET. . . . pray, sir, wherein can you charge me with breach of promise to my Lord?
>
> SIR. CHAR. Death, you won't deny it? How often, to piece up a quarrel, have you appointed him to visit you alone; and tho' you have promis'd to see no other company the whole day, when he was come, he has found you among the laugh of noisy fops, coquets, and coxcombs, dissolutely gay, while your full eyes ran o'er with transport of their flattery, and your own vain power of pleasing? How often, I say, have you been known to throw away, at least, four hours of your good-humour upon such wretches? and the minute they were gone, grew only dull to him, sunk into a distasteful spleen, complain'd you had talk'd yourself into the head-ach, and then indulg'd upon the dear delight of seeing him in pain: and by that time you had stretch'd, and gap'd him heartily out of patience, of a sudden most importantly remember you had outsat your appointment with my Lady *Fiddle-faddle;* and immediately order your coach to the Park? (V.vii)

In his *Apology* Cibber says that he put the play aside after writing the first two acts, being "in despair of having Justice done to the Character of Lady *Betty Modish,* by any one Woman, then among us," since Mrs. Verbruggen was in a declining state of health and Mrs. Bracegirdle was "out of my Reach, and engag'd in another Company."[6] He took it up again when he realised that Mrs. Oldfield had the skill and the temperament for the part. That he thought of Mrs. Bracegirdle in this matter suggests that Millamant was in his mind, and indeed the impress of that character is strongly on Lady Betty. The relation of Congreve to the emerging new drama thus becomes more apparent in the linking of *Love's Last Shift*, *The Way of the World* and *The Careless Husband*. He viewed Cibber's success with disdain, describing *The Careless Husband* as a play "which the ridiculous Town for the most part likes, but there are some that know better":[7] his opinion may have been sharpened by a measure of realisation that one element was common to Cibber's work and his own complex comedy.

Congreve's subdued seriousness of tone first becomes apparent in his second play, *The Double Dealer*. It is accompanied there by the appearance of two characters who scheme to overthrow the fortunes of the lovers Mellefont and Cynthia, as in *The Way of the World* Fainall and Mrs. Marwood scheme against Mirabel and Millamant. In the list of dramatis personae preceding *The Double Dealer* we find Maskwell labelled bluntly "A Villain," and his actions and those of Lady Touchwood are presented, not comically, but as a manifestation of human evil. In this play Congreve's characteristic harmony is impaired: the villains and the lovers seem to belong to a different world from the Froths and the Plyants whose follies are displayed. It is noticeable too that Mellefont and Cynthia have not the wit and resiliency with which Congreve usually endows his lovers: he makes them more dependent on the gifts of Providence than on their own readiness to manipulate the skein of event. In *The Way of the World,* however, Fainall and Mrs. Marwood, at least in the first four acts, are admirably in tune: they are no mere villains, but people nourishing envy and a sense of wrong yet keeping it strictly under control. Here for example is Fainall speaking in prose with a strong nervous tension but with humour too, when he has learned that his wife has been Mirabel's mistress:

> MRS. MAR. Well, how do you stand affected towards your Lady?
> FAIN. Why faith I'm thinking of it.—Let me see—I am Marry'd already; so that's over—My Wife has plaid the Jade with me—Well, that's over too—I never lov'd her, or if I had, why that wou'd have been over too by this time—Jealous of her I cannot be, for I am certain; so there's an end of Jealousie. Weary of her, I am and shall be—No, there's no end of that; No, no, that were too much to hope. Thus far concerning my Repose.

> Now for my Reputation,—As to my own, I Marry'd
> not for it; so that's out of the Question.—And as to my
> Part in my Wife's—Why she had parted with hers
> before; so bringing none to me, she can take none
> from me; 'tis against all rule of Play, that I should lose
> to one, who has not wherewithal to stake. (III.xviii)

Only in the fifth act does *The Way of the World* fail to absorb this
villainous element into its harmony. There indeed Fainall and Mrs.
Marwood become melodramatic figures, and it requires all Congreve's
skill to make us accept the final stages of the action when the thwarted
villains have gone.

Now in Cibber's second play, *Woman's Wit, or The Lady in Fashion,* we can see this element of villainy in the newer comedy. There
Leonora, a light-minded lady, is exposed in her true colours by Longville, and in revenge she tries to ruin his friendship with Lord Love-
more and his love for Olivia. Her devices are many, and are successful
till the very end of Act V. When things go wrong for her, she cries
"Confusion!" like any villain of melodrama, and indeed like Fainall in
the last act of *The Way of the World* when his wife's deed of gift is
produced. In the final speech of Cibber's play, the virtuous Longville
notes: "we may observe that virtue ever is the secret care of Providence"—just as *The Double Dealer* ended with the assertion that mischief will always destroy the villain that gives it birth. There is no
question here of one dramatist influencing another: *The Double
Dealer* appeared three years before *Woman's Wit,* and neither play
was successful with the public: each appears to be making its separate
anticipation of the optimistic concern with hard-pressed virtue that
became prominent in eighteenth-century comedy. But it was Congreve's achievement that his comedy at its best—that is, in the first four
acts of *The Way of the World*—could include the villainy of a Fainall
along with the wit of Millamant and the ludicrous exposure of Lady
Wishfort, and through all these things combined could suggest an attitude of calm appraisal, made gentle through sympathy yet never irrational.

This attitude of Congreve is one fitting the end and summation of
an age. He includes, we have seen, elements from the comic drama of
forty years, deriving much from Etherege but something too from the
newest comedy of his time. While not being old-fashioned, not a mere
resurrectionist, he brings together all that is good, all that is truly
exploratory, in Restoration comic writing. In the commendatory verses

printed before *The Double Dealer,* as we have noted, Dryden praised
him for having *"The Satire, Wit and Strength of Manly* Wicherly,"
and in his dedication of the play Congreve referred to his "Satire" on
Maskwell and Lady Touchwood. But most often he lacks the animus
of the satirist. There is an affection in his presentation of Heartwell
and Fondlewife in *The Old Bachelor,* of the Froths and the Plyants in
The Double Dealer, of Tattle and Mrs. Frail in *Love for Love,* of Witwoud and Lady Wishfort in *The Way of the World.* The prologue to
Love for Love, the most vigorous of his plays, comments on the decay
of satire since Wycherley's time and adds that, though Congreve will
here wield the lash, he *"hopes there's no Ill-manners in his Play."*
When he came to write *The Way of the World,* he could say in his
prologue:

> *Satire, he thinks, you ought not to expect;*
> *For so Reform'd a Town, who dares Correct?*

Though this of course is a jibe at Collier, the lashing of abuses was,
in fact, never much Congreve's concern: he recognises villainy and
folly and will expose them, but apart from *The Double Dealer* the
final impression each play gives is that the way of the Restoration
world is amusing to watch and on the whole good enough. He holds
up the mirror, composing his picture from what he sees reflected, and
finds it pleasant. There is appraisal in his mind, but acceptance too.
There is wit, and consideration. He had powerful links with the earliest years of Restoration drama—Dryden was his friend—but he came
late enough to see the Restoration manners in perspective, to look at
them with just a sufficient trace of the newer seriousness. Ten years
later his comedy might have been sentimental and boneless. Coming
when he does, he combines the wit and strength of earlier years with
a stronger sympathy than Etherege and Wycherley knew. It was not
merely that his satire was better-mannered than theirs: rather, he
could mock at folly and pretension, yet realised the implications of
human vulnerability.

In another respect, too, his position in time was fortunate. Earlier
Restoration drama, though it had advanced a little towards the picture-frame stage, was still a frankly theatrical affair. The frequent use
of rhyme in tragedy, surviving long after the short vogue of the wholly
rhymed play, the elaborate conceits which Dryden and his contemporaries found natural to the dramatic style, the patterned speeches and
situations in both tragedy and comedy, the love of fantastic incident

and spectacular display, all marked off the traffic of the stage as belonging to a world apart. In the eighteenth century, however, the manner of drama become generally more homespun, less given to boldness
of speech and spectacle in tragedy, less marked by the obvious con-
trivances of wit in comedy. Before Congreve's time the mode is high-
pitched in tragedy, brittle in comedy; afterwards it generally became
stolid and flat in both. Congreve has sufficient of the older manner to
give his expression distinction and an air of authority, but he is close
enough to the new manner for his scenes and characters to seem
nearer to us, and therefore of more obvious concern, than those of
Dryden, Etherege or Wycherley. This is not merely a matter of his
prose style, though that too combines the virtues of fluency and study:
it relates to the whole planning of the work. In the dedication of *The
Double Dealer* Congreve was anxious to defend the play against the
charge of implausibility: such characters as Maskwell and Lady Touchwood did exist, he averred, and it was common enough for a Mellefont
to trust an untrustworthy friend. Moreover, apparently exception had
been taken to Maskwell's revelation of his villainy in soliloquies. In
view of the long-established use of the soliloquy in English drama, it
is indeed significant that such a complaint was made. Congreve in his
defence claims that, not the soliloquy, but the ill-advised use of it is
to be blamed. It is better, he implies, that a dramatist should employ
soliloquy than that he should implausibly introduce a confidant. A
villain like Maskwell will not confide his villainy: if, therefore, we the
audience are to know it, there must be soliloquy. Its use should, however, be hedged round with restrictions: the actor must be alone on
the stage, or think himself so, and must on no account suggest an
awareness of an audience:

> In such a Case therefore the Audience must observe,
> whether the Person upon the Stage takes any notice of
> them at all, or no. For if he supposes any one to be by,
> when he talks to himself, it is monstrous and ridiculous
> to the last degree. Nay, not only in this Case, but in any
> Part of a Play, if there is expressed any Knowledge of an
> Audience, it is insufferable.

We may question this as a theatrical principle, yet we can recognise
that the element of naturalism in Congreve does contribute towards
his special quality. He makes less use of the aside than we can find,
for example, in Wycherley: after *The Old Bachelor,* in fact, he em-

ploys it rarely, and he has no scenes like that in *The Country Wife* where Alithea provides continual comments on Pinchwife's ill-advised warnings to Margery against the daughters of the town. The result in Congreve is that the scenes and characters, while exciting our interest and sympathy, seem yet to belong to a self-contained world, one that is sufficiently like our own to have plausibility but is at the same time disconnected, free. This sense of a combined plausibility and separateness gives to Congreve's dramatic scheme of things both fragility and wholeness. We are spectators of it only, but more fascinated spectators than if the plain manner of our world were mirrored there.

The very structure of the stage helped in this. There was a large front platform, with two permanent doors on either side, and behind it there was painted scenery. Most of the action, most of the entries and exits, took place on the apron. Thus an antithesis was set up between a three-dimensional world in which the actors moved and a two-dimensional background which represented the world they were imagined as living in. Congreve's drama at its best depends on the tension between the individual figures and the society which imposes conventions, expectations, circumscription. Mirabel and Millamant, Mellefont and Cynthia, Valentine and Angelica, can assert themselves and win a measure of triumph; but that triumph must be fugitive, for the world remains fixed, unchangeable. The form of the Restoration stage, in its contrast of acting-area and pictorial scene, excellently objectified the basic element in Congreve's thought. It was not a theatre suitable for a great range of drama (Wycherley was perhaps never at home there), but Congreve's plays belong intimately to it. That its virtues were in part recognised can be seen from a passage in Cibber's *Apology*, where he compares it with the eighteenth-century stage:

> It must be observ'd then, that the Area, or Platform of the old Stage, projected about four Foot forwarder, in a Semi-oval Figure, parallel to the Benches of the Pit; and that the former, lower Doors of Entrance for the Actors were brought down between the two foremost (and then only) Pilasters; in the Place of which Doors, now the two Stage-Boxes are fixt. That where the Doors of Entrance now are, there formerly stood two additional Side-Wings, in front to a full Set of Scenes, which had then almost a double Effect, in their Loftiness, and Magnificence.
>
> By this Original Form, the usual Station of the Actors, in almost every Scene, was advanc'd at least ten Foot

> nearer to the Audience, than they now can be; because, not only from the Stage's being shorten'd, in front, but likewise from the additional Interposition of those Stage-Boxes, the Actors (in respect to the Spectators, that fill them) are kept so much more backward from the main Audience, than they us'd to be: But when the Actors were in Possession of that forwarder Space, to advance upon, the Voice was then more in the Centre of the House, so that the most distant Ear had scarce the least Doubt, or Difficulty in hearing what fell from the weakest Utterance: All Objects were thus drawn nearer to the Sense; every painted Scene was stronger; every grand Scene and Dance more extended; every rich, or fine-coloured Habit had a more lively Lustre.[8]

Cibber praised the older stage for the greater ease of seeing and hearing that it offered, but he gives us a sense of what that stage must have meant for Congreve. Neither the homogeneous world of the early-seventeenth-century theatre nor the approach to the picture-frame that came in the eighteenth century could have constituted so remarkable an analogue to the tensions of his writing. In discussing the way in which Restoration comedy should be performed to-day, Norman N. Holland has urged a re-creation of the stage-dichotomy of its time:

> The set for a Restoration comedy ought to give a sense of the complex dialectic between the outer layer of sense-impressions and the "solid" underlying core of personal and private life. The designer should give us a sense of the flatness of appearances and the roundness and depth of nature. One way of doing this—and I am sure there are many others—is to rely most heavily on flats and backdrops for the set. Only when absolutely necessary should a three-dimensional structure be permitted on the stage, for it will detract from the solidity that in Restoration comedy belongs only to the characters.[9]

It was supremely in Congreve that the characters achieved a recognisable solidity and, simultaneously, a full awareness of the thinness and rigidity of their environment.

Whatever the merits of his three earlier comedies—merits high above the general level of Restoration achievement—one is inevitably inclined to see them as preliminary sketches for *The Way of the World*. Yet, if they are preliminary sketches, each prepares the way in its own fashion. We have noted that *The Old Bachelor,* written when Congreve was twenty-three, has a harmony of atmosphere lacking in Etherege's and Wycherley's first plays. It is remarkable, moreover, for the variety within its structure. There is the Etheregean quartet of lovers; there is the old bachelor of the title, with his love for Sylvia, the cast mistress; there is the cuckolding of the citizen Fondlewife; and there is the exposure of the blustering Sir Joseph Wittol. All is light and good-humoured, though of course not all is of an equal quality. Sir Joseph and his bully, Captain Bluffe, are crude, Shadwell-like figures, and the kicking of them by Sharper in Act III reminds us of the horseplay of the early Restoration years, seen for example in Dryden's *The Wild Gallant* (1663), where the rakish hero kicks the bawd and her companions because they have revealed their character to his admired Constance. The use of the forged letter, which makes Vainlove believe his Araminta more complying than he would have her, is a tiresome device, and indeed Congreve's plots are often marred by contrivance of this kind. On the other hand, the playwright shows an unusual perception of human frailty when he makes Vainlove unwilling to go through with either an intrigue or matrimony itself as soon as he finds the lady willing, and at the end of the play his future with Araminta is appropriately left unsettled. The scenes between Heartwell and Sylvia and between Fondlewife, his wife Laetitia and her quickly adroit lover Bellmore are in their way excellent: they go racily, with skill in the unexpected phrase and in the continuous action. In comparison with them, the scenes between the quartet of lovers are immature. The lovers can speak pleasantly and with a consistent grace, but they have not the precision of Etherege's lovers, and none of the four, even Vainlove, who is psychologically interesting, is sufficiently individualised: they stand mid-way between the Etheregean abstraction and the rounded character. The play's general atmosphere is suggested in Araminta's words:

> Nay come, I find we are growing serious, and then we are in great Danger of being dull. (II.vii)

Here seriousness and dullness are securely kept away.

That *The Double Dealer* is in a different strain is indicated by the quotation from Horace on its title-page: *"Interdum tamen, & vocem Comœdia tollit."* Thus Congreve announces his more ambitious intention. The seriousness of purpose is seen not merely in the introduction of the villainous characters, Maskwell and Lady Touchwood, but in the manner of presentation of the two lovers Mellefont and Cynthia. As characters they lack individuality, but they stand for a man and a woman in love yet faced with the folly which seems inevitably to attend on their married acquaintances and faced too with the intrigues of the envious. In Act II, just after Lord and Lady Froth have given a fulsome exhibition of connubial affection, Cynthia doubts whether she and Mellefont are well-advised to proceed to marriage:

> MEL. You're thoughtful, *Cynthia?*
>
> CYNT. I'm thinking, tho' Marriage makes Man and Wife one Flesh, it leaves 'em still two Fools; and they become more conspicuous by setting off one another.
>
> MEL. That's only when two Fools meet, and their Follies are oppos'd.
>
> CYNT. Nay, I have known two Wits meet, and by the Opposition of their Wit, render themselves as ridiculous as Fools. 'Tis an odd Game we're going to Play at: What think you of drawing Stakes, and giving over in time?
>
> MEL. No, hang't, that's not endeavouring to win, because it's possible we may lose; since we have shuffled and cut, let's e'en turn up Trump now.
>
> CYNT. Then I find it's like Cards, if either of us have a good Hand it is an Accident of Fortune.
>
> MEL. No, Marriage is rather like a Game of Bowls, Fortune indeed makes the Match, and the two nearest, and sometimes the two farthest are together, but the Game depends intirely upon Judgement.
>
> CYNT. Still it is a Game, and consequently one of us must be a Loser.
>
> MEL. Not at all; only a friendly Trial of Skill, and the Winnings to be laid out in an Entertainment. (II.iii)

As so often in Congreve, the force of the passage depends on its context: it has indeed a powerful ring when the Froths have just been exhibited to us. And the presentation of the lovers' dilemma goes further than this: Cynthia is aware that her powers of perception make life a more serious concern for her than it is for the Froths and the Plyants: she reaches a point in Act III where she can envy the fools, while knowing that her own wit cannot be laid aside:

> 'Tis not so hard to counterfeit Joy in the Depth of Affliction, as to dissemble Mirth in Company of Fools— Why should I call 'em Fools? The World thinks better of

'em; for these have Quality and Education, Wit and fine Conversation, are receiv'd and admir'd by the World—if not, they like and admire themselves—And why is not that true Wisdom, for 'tis Happiness: And for ought I know, we have misapply'd the Name all this while, and mistaken the Thing: Since

If Happiness in Self-content is plac'd,
The Wise are Wretched, and Fools only Bless'd. (III.xii)

There is in this something of the elegiac note that can be heard in *The Way of the World*. If, however, Mellefont and Cynthia are better for the things they say than for the impression they make on us as imagined beings, Maskwell and Lady Touchwood are wholly mechanical pieces of villainy. Congreve was not capable of fully imagining the degree of malignity that he planned for them. He was to do better with Fainall and Mrs. Marwood, partly because their villainy is less and their excuse more powerful: envy and spite and the desire for revenge were of his world, but the fiercer, elemental passion was beyond its scope.

The play's title is an obvious echo of Wycherley, and Congreve certainly means here to expose villainy as well as folly. It has not the bite of Wycherley's best scenes, but Congreve, still aged only twenty-four, suggests that he has more to say than his predecessor. The play is at once an exposure and a programme. It puts in a plea for the rational virtue of Mellefont and Cynthia, it argues for good manners and judgment, it openly proclaims its earnestness without altogether losing a sense of its own small scope. *The Way of the World* was to combine much of this play's serious intent with the gaiety of the intervening *Love for Love*.

There is more vigour, heartier entertainment in *Love for Love* than in any other of Congreve's plays. There are no villains here, no serious threat—despite the many twists and turns of the plot—to the marriage-plans of Valentine and Angelica. The characters, for the first time in Congreve, are vivid: Foresight, the astrologer ready to believe in anything, even his wife's virtue; Sir Sampson Legend, never reluctant to consider trying for a new heir; the sailor Ben, with his remarkable quickness in the uptake; Tattle, the talker who always commits himself farther than he intends; Miss Prue, a juvenile cousin of Mrs. Pinchwife; the ladies Foresight and Frail, whose easy virtue is cheerfully worn—all are individually not outside Wycherley's scope. Wycherley, however, would not have been likely to put them all in a single play. For the secret of this play's popularity is largely in the diversity of its humour. Its contribution to Congreve's development consists in its use of strongly etched figures which are brought into harmony. In *The Way of the World* the characters have less visible outlines, but they retain something of the firmness that is apparent here. It is not only in the subordinate characters that this is found. As Tattle is superior to Brisk or Scandal to Careless, so Valentine and Angelica stand far more clearly before us than Mellefont and Cynthia. They are not so thoughtful as the earlier lovers were: there is almost nothing of the elegiac strain here, and Valentine's assumed madness leads, for the most part, only to grotesque humour. But they are self-assertive, they are not content to be imposed on as Mellefont and Cynthia were. It is Valentine who is responsible for much of the plot, till in the last scenes Angelica takes command and satisfies herself of Valentine's love.

Even in this play, however, we have a touch of the new sentiment. Valentine's gesture in abandoning his inheritance when he believes Angelica will marry his father, and Angelica's cry "Generous *Valentine!*" when she discovers his intention, are equally unconvincing. We should like a hint that Valentine was fairly sure the sacrifice would not in the end be needed, and though we expect Angelica to like and indeed marry Valentine, we find her expression of admiration incompatible with her normal powers of perception. But that may be taking the end of the play too seriously. As in *The Double Dealer,* it is rounded off in a rather cavalier fashion, and certainly Congreve is too fond of elopements in disguise: the coming to terms of the lovers was in any event a settled thing, and the playwright did not concern himself unduly with its achievement. Nevertheless, the terms in which it is done remain appropriate to the comedy of sentiment. We are reminded a little of the noble gesturing at the end of *Love's Last Shift,* where the brothers Worthy and Sir William Wisewoud strive to outdo each other in generosity.

Five years separated the first productions of *Love for Love* and *The Way of the World.* In the interval Congreve had written a tragedy, *The Mourning Bride,* and clearly he came to his last comedy with deliberate steps. The prologue says:

> *He owns, with Toil, he wrought the following Scenes,*

and the dedication describes the play as unsuited to the prevailing taste:

> That it succeeded on the Stage, was almost beyond my
> Expectation; for but little of it was prepar'd for that gen-
> eral Taste which seems now to be predominant in the
> Pallats of our Audience.

That it failed to win much applause at its first performance is usually attributed to its defects in plotting, the thinness of the intrigue in the first four acts and the crowding of incident into the fifth. But not only is bustle wanting: the appreciation of *The Way of the World* needs a sensitivity to emotional overtone that is rare in an audience seeing a new play.[10] If for us this is the play that justifies all Restoration drama, from many of its contemporaries it was simply a less entertaining comedy than Vanbrugh's *The Relapse* (1696) or Farquhar's *The Constant Couple* (1699). Steele, in commendatory verses, echoes Congreve's motto for *The Double Dealer:*

> *By your selected Scenes, and handsome Choice,*
> *Ennobled Comedy exalts her Voice;*

but that was the judgment of a more than usually sympathetic spectator. To the discerning eye, indeed, there is more variety, more planning in *The Way of the World* than in *Love for Love*. The characters are less strongly etched, but their individualities are sure and the differences between them are brought out in the juxtaposition of scenes. It is no accident that the bargaining-scene between Mirabel and Millamant follows immediately after Sir Wilfull has approached Millamant with all the rustic embarrassment of the natural man, or that Mrs. Fainall, the cast mistress still mistress of herself, is placed side-by-side with Mrs. Marwood, the victim of thwarted inclinations. But the colours are subdued. Fainall does not gloat over his villainy as Maskwell did in *The Double Dealer*. Sir Wilfull brings the raw air of Shropshire into the drawing-room, but he does not nearly run away with the play as Ben did in *Love for Love*. Millamant is thoughtful like Cynthia, but not sententious, is in sure command of her speech but not given to pert repartee as on occasion Angelica is. Lady Wishfort is true to her name, but even her languishings and her vituperation have a smoothness and a comic elegance. Witwoud and Petulant are creatures of a summer's fancy, not earth-bound in the way of Tattle. And Mirabel, for all his association with Mrs. Fainall, for all his pretended wooing of Lady Wishfort—which Congreve tactfully leaves outside the action of the play—appears not merely the wit but the thoughtful man.[11] He is no victim of a sudden reformation, like

Cibber's Loveless, but he has a plan for rational living, a plan in which Millamant constitutes a necessary part, a part to be kept in place. And for his own sake, he must see to it that she remains herself, no mere devoted complement to her husband. The bargaining-scenes that appear so frequently in seventeenth-century comedies, from the reign of Charles I right up to this year 1700, seem all anticipations of the meeting of Mirabel and Millamant in Act IV of this play: here Congreve developed the hesitations and the safeguards that he had sketched in the conversation of Mellefont and Cynthia: Restoration comedy had been principally concerned with sex-relations, and here Congreve gave to the dying age a satisfying expression of the attitude it had been fumbling for.

But the final impression the play leaves is perhaps one of suppressed melancholy. At the end of Etherege's *The Man of Mode,* the fortunate Harriet, secure of Dorimant's love, joins a little grossly in the jeering at the cast-off Mrs. Loveit. When Millamant speaks to Mrs. Marwood, there is an echo of this, but Congreve's raillery is altogether less pert: indeed, at the end of this encounter the mocking tone becomes subdued. To Mrs. Marwood's protest that she hates Mirabel, Millamant replies:

> O Madam, why so do I—And yet the Creature loves me, ha, ha, ha. How can one forbear laughing to think of it—I am a Sybil if I am not amaz'd to think what he can see in me. I'll take my Death, I think you are handsomer—and within a Year or two as young.—If you cou'd but stay for me, I shou'd overtake you—But that cannot be—Well, that Thought makes me melancholick—Now I'll be sad. (III.xi)

With Congreve we do not forget the passage of time: its ruins may amuse us, as in Lady Wishfort, but even in her presentation there is a reminder that she is not alone. Sometimes the elegiac note seems to be communicated through the cadence, as when Mirabel speaks in Act II:

> An old Woman's Appetite is deprav'd like that of a Girl—'Tis the Green-Sickness of a second Childhood; and like the faint Offer of a latter Spring, serves but to usher in the Fall; and withers in an affected Bloom. (II.iii)

And in Act I, before we have met Millamant, Fainall and Mirabel are discussing her and this exchange ensues:

FAIN. For a passionate Lover, methinks you are a Man
somewhat too discerning in the Failings of your
Mistress.

MIRA. And for a discerning Man, somewhat too passionate a Lover; for I like her with all her Faults; nay, like
her for her Faults. Her Follies are so natural, or so artful,
that they become her; and those Affectations which in
another Woman wou'd be odious, serve but to make
her more agreeable. I'll tell thee, *Fainall,* she once
us'd me with that Insolence, that in Revenge I took
her to pieces; sifted her, and separated her Failings;
I study'd 'em, and got 'em by Rote. The Catalogue was
so large, that I was not without Hopes, one Day or
other to hate her heartily: To which end I so us'd
my self to think of 'em, that at length, contrary to my
Design and Expectation, they gave me ev'ry Hour less
and less Disturbance; 'till in a few Days it became habitual to me, to remember 'em without being dis-
pleas'd. They are now grown as familiar to me as my
own Frailties; and in all probability in a little time
longer I shall like 'em as well.

FAIN. Marry her, marry her; be half as well acquainted
with her Charms, as you are with her Defects, and my
Life on't, you are your own Man again.

MIRA. Say you so?

FAIN. Ay, ay, I have Experience: I have a Wife, and so
forth. (I.iii.)

Mirabel lovingly considers the twists and turns of his mistress's mind
and delights in his own subjection: there is wisdom in the comic
presentation as well as shrewdness and good phrasing. And the last
words in the scene are given to the man of experience, who has tried
marriage for himself. The acid is there, the shrug that goes with Congreve's wit. Bonamy Dobrée has noted that many of Congreve's set
speeches are just not metrical, that a regular iambic beat is never quite
established.[12] This may be the formal analogue to that undertone of
melancholy which runs through the same speeches, giving to *The Way
of the World* in particular an added dimension within which the
characters move as symbols: there their separateness vanishes and they
become aspects of a single humanity. Congreve, bringing Restoration
comedy into clear focus, brought it also, for a brief moment, into a
larger world.

NOTES

1. From the Preface. The quotation is from *The Dramatick Works of John Dryden, Esq.*, 6 vols. (London, 1762).
2. Cf. Allardyce Nicoll, *A History of English Drama 1660-1900*, I (Cambridge University Press, 1952), 194-195.
3. Quotations from Congreve are from *Comedies by William Congreve*, ed. Bonamy Dobrée (World's Classics, 1929).
4. Quotations from Cibber are from *The Dramatic Works of Colley Cibber, Esq.*, 5 vols. (London, 1777).
5. *A New View of Congreve's Way of the World* (University of Michigan Press, 1958), p. 85.
6. *An Apology for the Life of Mr. Colley Cibber*, 2nd ed. (London, 1740), p. 249.
7. Quoted by F. Dorothy Senior, *The Life and Times of Colley Cibber* (New York, 1928), p. 58, n. 1.
8. *Apology*, pp. 339-40.
9. *The First Modern Comedies: The Significance of Etherege, Wycherley and Congreve* (Harvard University Press, 1959), p. 237.
10. The point was sharply made by Bonamy Dobrée in *Restoration Comedy* (Oxford, 1924), p. 140.
11. Congreve, while keeping our sympathy with Mirabel, recognizes a considerable range of conduct in him. Norman N. Holland, in an otherwise most perceptive study of the play, simplifies notably in labelling Mirabel "a good clever man" (*op. cit.*, p. 160).
12. *Comedies by William Congreve*, ed. Bonamy Dobrée (World's Classics, 1929), p. xxiv.

CLIFFORD LEECH

❀

Restoration Tragedy: A Reconsideration

For those of us who lived through the nineteen-twenties, our attitude
to Restoration drama is linked with our memory of those years. It was
then something of a gesture to express admiration for the comic style
of Wycherley and Congreve, playwrights who still rendered our elders
uneasy. If we look back to the appearance in 1923 of Professor Allardyce Nicoll's standard *History of Restoration Drama*, we find that it
begins with a warning of the dangers of the study: "he who would
now bring the works of Ravenscroft and of Tate to light lies in the
danger of being accused by modern moralists of a perverted judgment
and of an uncultured taste":[1] the dramatic historian of the Restoration, we are reminded, "undoubtedly runs the risk of being accounted
faulty both in critical acumen and in moral probity."[2] We are indeed
fortunate that Professor Nicoll was not deterred, for his book has been
the foundation of Restoration dramatic studies in the last twenty-five
years. But most of us then were not ready to be historians: we went to
the Lyric Theatre, Hammersmith, and saw Dryden and Congreve and
Farquhar: perhaps we did not fully realise our immense good fortune
in seeing Dame Edith Evans in her youth, yet she awed us with her
Millamant, and in her hands even Mrs. Sullen became a creature of
authority and delight: we rebuked our elders for thinking Sheridan
more than second-rate, and we found in the Restoration writers an
independence of mind, a mastery of dramatic prose, a boldness of

From *Durham University Journal*, XI (1950), 106-15. Reprinted by permission of the publishers.

utterance inherited from the Elizabethans combined with an eighteenth-century grace of style. Our enthusiasm at times took us to strange lengths. We seized with delight on Professor Bonamy Dobrée's book on *Restoration Comedy*, which appeared in 1924 and which assured us that the late seventeenth-century playwrights were fundamentally thoughtful men, concerned with the working out of a new, anthropocentric morality: this made it possible for us to laugh at Pinchwife and at sundry other Restoration cuckolds, and to feel that we were engaged in a serious intellectual exercise.

All this is odd to look back upon, for it is no longer necessary to assume an air of defiance when one praises Wycherley. *The Way of the World, Love for Love, The Beaux' Stratagem, The Relapse* can be played and broadcast as part of the normal run of theatrical events. Audiences in London and elsewhere find bawdy no more out of place in an old-fashioned play than in the music-hall. And because defence is not so necessary, enthusiastic praise is rarer. To-day scholars and critics turn more often to the Elizabethans and Jacobeans, and find in Chapman and Webster and Jonson playwrights whose minds were richer and more deeply concerned with the business of living. To-day we enjoy the best Restoration work but are not much inclined to probe into it, to consider whether it should do more than amuse us. It is therefore perhaps time that we made a fresh attempt at appraising this work, seen now in a colder light than when it came as a rediscovery to our theatres nearly thirty years ago. We shall find ourselves impelled at times to be severe, but it is possible that the full stature of Congreve may emerge more surely if we apply both to him and to his contemporaries the supreme question: are these men merely entertainers with a shrewd gift of phrase and a command of dramatic situation, or is their work the embodiment of organised experience? Is a Restoration play a fragment of ribbon-development, a mere echo of the Elizabethan town that has been left behind and a half-hearted warning of the eighteenth century that lies ahead, a wayside patch on the landscape, pretentious and rather slatternly? Or can it be a town, or even a village, with a character of its own, an assured place in the land? Do we, in fact, grow in understanding by reading Dryden or Congreve, as we certainly do by reading Aristophanes or Jonson or Molière?

But before one can turn to the comedies of these men, it is necessary to consider the work in which they were most obviously ambitious, the tragic and quasi-tragic plays of the time. It is true that these have never come back to our theatres as the comedies have done. Critical works will praise *All for Love* and *Venice Preserved* and will describe and account for the heroic plays, but there is no note of challenge in such things: never in this century have we felt especially in tune with the tragic outlook of Dryden and Orrery, Otway and Lee. Nevertheless, one gets a false picture of Restoration drama if due attention is not given to the tragedies and heroic plays. The dramatists often visibly relaxed in their comedies, but when they wrote in verse and in a high style they were conscious of the seriousness of their undertaking. When Nathaniel Lee dedicated his *Theodosius, or The Force of Love* to the Duchess of Richmond, he assured her that "your extraordinary Love for Heroick Poetry is not the least Argument to show the Greatness of your Mind, and fulness of Perfection," and he claimed a high purpose in his writing:

> All I can promise, *Madam*, and be able to perform, is, that your Grace shall never see a Play of mine that shall give Offence to Modesty and Virtue; and what I humbly offer to the World, shall be of use at least, and I hope deserve imitation; which is, or ought to be, I am sure, the Design of all *Tragedies* and *Comedies* both antient and modern.

This was in 1680, and the following year he produced *The Princess of Cleve,* a barbarous adaptation of Madame de Lafayette's courtly novel, interlarded with scenes of the dullest lubricity. This kind of contradiction is characteristic of the time, as we shall see, and need not throw doubt on Lee's profession of good faith to the Duchess of Richmond. *Theodosius* is intended to be a highly moral play: it begins with a solemn scene in which the Emperor of the East and his two young sisters are ceremonially renouncing the world for a life of religion; it has a heroine Athenais who is virtue itself and will not even let her father use the word "whore" in her presence; the play's characters, though pardonably incapable of managing their affairs, are uniformly high-souled; and in the concluding couplet of Act V it is hoped that posterity will say of them:

> No Age with such Examples cou'd compare,
> So great, so good, so virtuous, and so fair!

So we find Dryden in the preface to *All for Love, or The World Well Lost* saying that doubtless the story of Antony and Cleopatra has been frequently dramatised because of "the excellency of the Moral": "the

chief Persons represented, were famous Patterns of unlawful Love;
and their end accordingly was unfortunate." Poetic justice, in fact, was
a law that these playwrights broke only rarely and reluctantly. Occasionally an innocent heroine, like Lee's Athenais or Otway's Monimia,
might have bad luck, or in Dryden's hastily written propaganda-piece
Amboyna the virtuous English might be tortured and killed by their
enemies, but in general there was an effort to suggest that virtue
brought a tangible reward as surely as vice an inescapable punishment:
so the heroic plays, called often "tragedies," might have fortunate end-
ings for the principal characters, and all serious plays aimed at providing a pattern of behaviour, to be admired if not to be emulated.
The hero who renounced love in order to meet the demands of honour, like Dryden's Almanzor, normally contrived to enjoy both; the
hero who yielded to love, like Otway's Jaffeir or Dryden's Montezuma,
paid for it dearly, but came to realise his mistake and was thus able to
show nobility at the play's end.

When these dramatists came to adapt Shakespeare, they often found
him faulty in this respect. Nahum Tate could not allow Cordelia and
Lear to die: the old king was restored, and Cordelia not merely spared
but given a suitable consort in Edgar. Dryden gave Troilus a hero's
death, deserved because he had wrongly doubted Cressida's faith but
ennobling all the same. Shadwell in his version of *Timon* could not
go against the tradition in contriving a happy ending, but he could
invent a faithful mistress for Timon and imply that his treatment of
her made his ending just. We should note that the town approved this
sort of thing: Downes tells us that Shadwell's *Timon* "wonderfully
pleas'd the Court and City; being an Excellent Moral."[3] It is, in fact,
important to remember that the Restoration audience welcomed the
sententious plays of the time. They might be repelled by the too keen
satire of Dryden's *Mr. Limberham, or The Kind Keeper,* and doubtless the critique of *The Country Wife* which Wycherley inserts in *The
Plain Dealer* correctly mirrored the condemnation of that play by
many female judges. They preferred their comedy to leave them undis-
turbed, but they expected a tragic or heroic dramatist to take religion
and morality with the utmost seriousness.

Of course, a dramatist might put in an occasional comic scene for
the sake of variety or for the sake of topical satire, as with Otway's
facetious presentation of Shaftesbury in *Venice Preserved,* or he might
grow for a moment rebellious and cry out against heaven's justice, as
when Antony in *All for Love,* believing Cleopatra dead and learning

that she has been faithful to him, exclaims: "Innocence and Death! This shows not well above." (V.i.) Or he might suddenly endow the grand figures of his story with Restoration manners, so that Eve in Dryden's *The State of Innocence and the Fall of Man,* a never acted play-version of *Paradise Lost,* is for a moment incongruously coy:

> Somewhat forbids me, which I cannot name;
> For ignorant of Guilt, I fear not Shame:
> But some restraining Thought, I know not why,
> Tells me, you long should beg, I long deny.   (II. iii.)

And Dryden's Cleopatra has at times a touch of Millamant or of Pope's Belinda: "she charm'd all Hearts," we are told, as her galley came down the Nile:

> She lay, and leant her Cheek upon her Hand
> And cast a Look so languishingly sweet,
> As if, secure of all Beholders Hearts,
> Neglecting she could take 'em.   (III. i.)

She cries out against marriage and the insipidity of wives when Charmion has given her Antony's message that he will ever respect her:

> Is that a word
> For *Antony* to use to *Cleopatra*?
> Oh that faint word, Respect! how I disdain it!
> Disdain my self, for loving after it!
> He should have kept that word for cold *Octavia*.
> Respect is for a Wife: Am I that thing,
> That dull insipid lump, without desires,
> And without pow'r to give 'em?   (II. i.)

And in her interchanges with Octavia there is a moment when we are reminded of Etherege's Harriet mocking the rejected Mrs. Loveit or of Congreve's Millamant triumphing over the unsuccessful Marwood:

> OCTAV . . .   Shame of our Sex,
>   Dost thou not Blush, to own those black Endearments
>   That make sin pleasing?
> CLEOP.   You may Blush, who want 'em:
>   If bounteous Nature, if indulgent Heav'n
>   Have giv'n me Charms to please the bravest Man;
>   Should I not thank 'em? should I be asham'd,
>   And not be Proud? I am, that he has lov'd me;
>   And, when I love not him, Heav'n change this Face
>   For one like that.   (III. i.)

But these things are incidental to the play's total effect. In general the tragic and heroic plays are written in an entirely distinct mode from the comedies. When a comic plot exists side-by-side with a heroic plot, as in Dryden's *The Spanish Friar* and *Marriage à la Mode*, the two are kept separate in style and in implied attitude: they merely alternate for the sake of variety, and the author pays no attention to the incompatibility of the responses excited. In *Marriage à la Mode* we are given on the one hand a tale of romantic love, persistently thwarted but at length overcoming its obstacles and gaining its reward—a pleasant fairy tale, indeed, dependent on our willingness to believe that a man and a woman can be all-important to one another; on the other hand there is a story, wittily told, which hangs upon the notion that coupling is largely a matter of coincidence. We turn from one to the other as a music-hall audience will welcome the alternation of bawdry and sentiment. There is no fusion but merely the haphazard linking of two separate plays.

The Jacobeans too could use double plots, but in their best work the tragedy was deepened by an undercurrent of dark comedy, so that Othello and Lear are not mere patterns of behaviour but human beings both splendid and absurd, so that a dark laughter reverberates in the distance as our hearts are wrung by Webster's Duchess. Moreover, Jacobean comedy had often a sombre strain in it: Shakespeare's *Troilus and Cressida,* Jonson's *Volpone,* Chapman's *The Widow's Tears* are written by men deeply aware of the human situation but for the moment prepared to see it as mainly ridiculous. This was the strength of the Jacobeans, that in their best tragedies and comedies they looked at human life without blinkers. They did not say: "Today we are writing a tragedy, so we must disregard this or that element in the nature of things." Not that this was deliberate on their part: their critical utterances on the nature of tragedy are most unsatisfactory: they simply wrote plays about human life, in a strain that mood or fashion or an inner compulsion dictated.

And there perhaps we can see one of the difficulties that confronted the Restoration playwrights. They were much more deliberate than the Jacobeans, they wrote long prefaces and vindications and defences, and even in dedications they might theorise concerning what they wrote. They had to be sure of their purposes, they had to try to make an accord between their serious plays and their avowed beliefs. When not being serious, they could be salacious or blasphemous, but they could not write a play which contained a serious challenge to orthodox morality and religion. The tragic effect, however, seems to depend on an anthropocentric view of things, which shows man struggling without avail against the decrees of Fate and arousing in us a sense of pride that a man can do so well when he has been caught in life's trap. The tragic attitude depends indeed on the contradiction that man is a puppet and yet can be admirable. It is not a rational attitude, therefore, and it is inconsistent with orthodox belief. The dramatists of the Restoration wanted to be rational and, within a serious dramatic action, to be consistent. Of all men of his time, Dryden, as we would indeed expect, came nearest to an understanding of the tragic idea. In several of his plays he argues the matter of free will: thus Leonora, Queen of Arragon, in *The Spanish Friar:*

> The Priesthood grossly cheat us with Free-will:
> Will to do what, but what Heaven first decreed?
> Our Actions then are neither good nor ill,
> Since from eternal Causes they proceed:
> Our Passions, Fear and Anger, Love and Hate,
> Mere senseless Engines that are mov'd by Fate;
> Like Ships on stormy Seas without a Guide,
> Tost by the Winds, and driven by the Tide.   (III. ii.)

In *The State of Innocence* there is a long debate on the subject between Adam, Raphael and Gabriel: Adam's persistent questioning is rebuked, and the debate ends with his being told that there could be no reward or punishment if free will did not exist: yet he seems unconvinced, and when the angels depart in a cloud he complains that the bestowal of free will is hardly just:

> Hard State of Life! since Heav'n fore-knows my Will,
> Why am I not ty'd up from doing Ill?
> Why am I trusted with my self at large,
> When he's more able to sustain the Charge?
> Since Angels fell, whose Strength was more than mine,
> 'Twould show more Grace my Frailty to confine.
> Fore-knowing the Success, to leave me free,
> Excuses him, and yet supports not me.   (IV. i.)

We may note here that, as in the famous lines in *Aureng-zebe,* "When I consider Life, 'tis all a Cheat" (IV.i.), Dryden's very clarity of style makes the thought seem commonplace. The Jacobean dramatist can incidentally convey to us an idea of predestination, as when Clermont in *The Revenge of Bussy d'Ambois* sees the ghosts of those he believes yet living and deduces that "all things to be done, as here we live, Are done before all times in th' other life" (V.v.), but Dryden's plainness of statement, his desire to get everything down in straightforward terms, make him the popular lecturer rather than the poet: we do not have to strive after his thought, it comes easily and is too easily recognisable for the platitude it is. But perhaps he expresses himself with more ingenuity and force in the dedication of *The Rival Ladies* to his fellow-playwright, the Earl of Orrery. He praises Orrery's management of his characters and compares his complete control over them with the absolute power over human beings exercised by God:

> Here is no Chance which you have not fore-seen; all your Heroes are more than your Subjects; they are your Creatures. And though they seem to move freely, in all the Sallies of their Passions, yet you make Destinies for them which they cannot shun. They are moved (if I may dare to say so) like the rational Creatures of the Almighty Poet, who walk at Liberty, in their own Opinion, because their Fetters are invisible; when indeed the Prison of their Will is the more sure, for being large: And instead of an absolute Power over their Actions, they have only a wretched Desire of doing that, which they cannot chuse but do.

But though Dryden could thus in a dedication deny free will, and could question it here and there in his plays, he could not deliberately base a tragedy on the assumption that virtue and vice were dictated to men. Nor perhaps can any man, for a world in which men can deserve no praise would only be bitterly ironic. Dryden, experiencing doubts concerning the government of the universe, could still write only plays in which orthodox belief provided the framework and heroes were held up for imitation.

When the theatres were re-opened in 1660, there were many links with the past. We no longer see Restoration drama as a largely French importation: the influence of Corneille is indeed obvious, but it is easy to trace the pre-War English ancestry of Restoration comedy and to see premonitions of the heroic drama in Fletcher and Shirley and in Davenant's Caroline plays. But the War and the Interregnum do mark an important break in the history of English drama. In Ford's *'Tis Pity she's a Whore* and Shirley's *The Cardinal* the Jacobean tragic attitude is precariously maintained: after 1660 it was not possible to **resume** that attitude (except perhaps when the subject of the drama was traditionally established, as in Dryden and Lee's *Oedipus*), and tragedy virtually disappeared from the English stage until the nineteenth century. It is customary to speak of Restoration "tragedies and heroic plays," but the distinction is artificial: rhyme was used for a decade or so, and then blank verse took its place: with the change the heroes became less violently given, but the opposition of love and honour still provided the favourite dilemma, and from Dryden's *The Indian Emperor* of 1665 to his *Love Triumphant, or Nature Will Prevail* of 1693 the governing aim, which he shared with Orrery and Otway and Lee and lesser men, was uniform: the exciting presentation of distressed nobility.

The Jacobean plays were revived after the Restoration, but the only tragic writers that remained long in the repertory were Fletcher and Shakespeare. The men of the Restoration recognised Shakespeare's genius, which they tried to "regularise" in their many adaptations, but it was Fletcher who provided them with a basis for their own style. The tragedies and tragicomedies included in the Beaumont and Fletcher Folios of 1647 and 1679 were plays in which theatrical situations were ingeniously built up for their own sake rather than for any light they might throw on the behaviour of human beings outside the theatre. Thomas Rymer, in his *The Tragedies of the Last Age* of 1678, drew attention to the sheerly theatrical character of *The Maid's Tragedy*: in particular, he noted the scene where the wronged Amintor tells his friend Melantius that Evadne, Melantius' sister, is the King's mistress: each of the friends draws his sword in turn, each in turn finds it impossible to fight the other. Rymer comments that the scene, absurd as a picture of actual behaviour, is made popular in the theatre through the skilful playing of the Restoration actors Hart and Mohun.[4] He might also have seen that it lends itself to the stage, where an audience accustomed to this kind of patterned behaviour sees it very differently from the private reader. In any event, we can find many similar scenes in Restoration tragedy. In Sir Robert Howard's *The Indian Queen*, which Dryden helped to write, the queen Zempoalla and her general Traxalla are respectively in love with their captives Montezuma and Orazia, who love one another: in IV.i the four of them are on the stage, which represents a prison: at first Zempoalla is about to kill Orazia, and Traxalla about to kill Montezuma: neither dares to accomplish the deed lest the other should follow suit: then suddenly there is a change of places, Zempoalla gets between Traxalla and Montezuma, ready to defend Montezuma's life, and Traxalla is then in front of Orazia, whom he is ready to defend: this, of course, is as much an impasse as the preceding situation. The scene does not advance the plot, it is merely an occasion for patterned movement and patterned speech. The characters are meant to arouse enough of our concern merely through the elaborated threat of action, and to give us the same kind of entertainment as to-day we may find in an opera-house. So in Dryden's sequel to this play, *The Indian Emperor, or The Conquest of Mexico by the Spaniards,* Almeria goes to the prison where Cortez lies bound: she is anxious to kill him, but finds herself loving instead. Having been assured by him that his courage comes from innocence, she speaks as follows, with Dryden's stage-directions clearly marking her repeated advances and withdrawals:

> From Innocence? let that then take thy Part.
> Still are thy Looks assur'd—have at thy Heart!
> > [*Holds up the Dagger.*
> I cannot kill thee; sure thou bear'st some Charm,
> > [*Goes back.*
> Or some Divinity holds back my Arm.
> Why do I thus delay to make him bleed?   [*Aside.*
> Can I want Courage for so brave a Deed?
> I've shook it off; my Soul is free from Fear.
> > [*Comes again.*
> And I can now strike any where—but here:
> His Scorn of Death how strangely does it move!
> A Mind so haughty who could chuse but love!
> > [*Goes off.*
> Plead not a Charm, or any God's Command,
> Alas, it is thy Heart that Holds thy Hand:
> In spight of me I love, and see too late
> My Mother's Pride must find my Mother's Fate.
> —Thy Country's Foe, thy Brother's Murderer,
> For shame, *Almeria,* such mad Thoughts forbear:
> It w'onot be, if I once more come on:
> > [*Coming on again.*
> I shall mistake the Breast, and pierce my own.
> > [*Comes with her Dagger down.*   (IV. i.)

With this we can associate the famous and persistent appearances of the Ghost of Almanzor's Mother in *The Conquest of Granada,* and the many passages in *Venice Preserved* where Jaffeir and Belvidera meet only to join each other in lamentation. The rhyme of the earlier plays did, of course, make this patterning more obvious, and it is worth

noting that Dryden in his *Essay of Dramatic Poesy* defends the use of
rhyme by referring to the pleasure that comes from the carrying out
of a pattern, as in "a dance which is well contrived."[5] But in the blank
verse that followed there are often speeches that depend for their
effect on a rhetorical repetition reminiscent of the early Shakespeare
and the University Wits. Thus in Otway's *The Orphan:*

> I'd leave the world for him that hates a Woman.
> Woman the Fountain of all Human Frailty!
> What mighty Ills have not been done by Woman?
> Who was't betray'd the Capitol? A Woman.
> Who lost *Mark Antony* the World? A Woman.
> Who was the cause of a long ten years War,
> And laid at last *Old-Troy* in Ashes? Woman.
> Destructive, damnable, deceitful Woman. (III. i.)

And thus in *All for Love:*

> Who made him cheap at *Rome,* but *Cleopatra?*
> Who made him scorn'd abroad, but *Cleopatra?*
> At *Actium,* who betray'd him? *Cleopatra.*
> Who made his Children Orphans? and poor me
> A wretched Widow? only *Cleopatra.* (III. i.)

When we get this manner of speech in Kyd or Marlowe or in Shakespeare's *Richard III,* it is functional in the play: it brings into focus
Hieronimo's grief or Tamburlaine's ambition or the decrees of Fate
against Richard. But in Dryden and Otway it exists for its own sake, as
indeed do many whole scenes in their plays. Of Otway in particular is
this true. *The Orphan* is a succession of scenes hardly linked by probability or necessity. Why, we ask ourselves as we coldly read the play,
does Acasto grow ill, give solemn, Polonius-like instructions to his sons,
and then recover? Neither illness nor recovery is linked to the main
happenings of the play. Why is the marriage of Castalio and Monimia
kept secret? Even though at one moment Acasto counsels his sons
against marriage, his feelings on the subject do not seem unusually
strong, and we note that he is very ready to agree to his daughter's
marriage. Why does Castalio assure his brother so vehemently at the
beginning of the play that he has no intention of marrying Monimia?
And when Castalio believes that Monimia has simply refused to let
him into her bed-chamber on their wedding-night, it is difficult to see
why his lamentations are quite so crazed. Annoyance or even perturba-
tion we might expect, but for Castalio—before the truth of Polydore's

usurpation is made known to him—the whole world seems at an end. Dryden would never do things like this: in the preface to *All for Love* he takes pride in the play's planning: "every Scene in the Tragedy conducing to the main design, and every Act concluding with a turn of it." The excitement that Dryden produces is certainly operatic, the effect of a frank contrivance, but he did see to it that his patterns interlocked. In *Venice Preserved* there is a more ample plot than in *The Orphan,* so that Otway is not driven to the same expedients for filling out the action. But there too we find an ill-contrived structure. Pierre's virtues are stressed throughout, but they hardly cohere with the intention of wholesale destruction that the rebels proclaim; there seems no point in Jaffeir's leaving Belvidera with the conspirators as a pledge of his fidelity, particularly as it was apparently so easy for him to take her away again; the interviews in Act V where Belvidera successfully begs her father's intervention to save the conspirators' lives, and where Aquilian threatens Antonio into a similar promise, are dramatically irrelevant, for they are not mentioned again and have no effect on the sequence of events; too often, moreover, Otway makes a character describe at length something that has already been presented in action—a fault that even Shakespeare can fall into, as when at the end of *Lear* Edgar tells how he met his father, but here more blameworthy because of the far narrower scope of the play. We should note too the way in which the child of Jaffeir and Belvidera is mentioned both at the beginning and at the end of the play, to underline its parents' woes, and is strangely neglected in all the middle scenes: its parents, we know, were homeless, and Belvidera spent an anxious night as Jaffeir's pledge to the conspirators. The mere mention of this child is as patent and as irritating a device for the extraction of tears as the actual stage-appearances of many a pathetic infant: We may find contradictions in the details of a tragedy by Shakespeare or Webster, but there is more justification there than a mere attempt to work up feeling: Otway was not concerned with a coherent dramatic structure, but aimed at a strenuous emotional exercise. The woes of Jaffeir and Belvidera are not derived from things as they are: they exist to furnish theatrical excitement.

The element of strain in these plays comes out in many of their titles. Only Victorian melodramas and films from the United States can give us labels similar to these: *All for Love, or The World Well Lost; Troilus and Cressida, or Truth Found Too Late; The Orphan, or The Unhappy Marriage; The Fatal Marriage, or The Innocent Adultery;*

The Injured Princess, or The Fatal Wager (a version of *Cymbeline*);
Injured Love, or The Cruel Husband (a version of *The White Devil*);
*Virtue Betrayed; Secret Love; Tyrannick Love; Love Triumphant, or
Nature Will Prevail*. It is a disturbing thought that nearly all of these
were "tragedies" written by leading dramatists of the time.

Yet we cannot deny that such titles were appropriate. Their flamboy-
ance is matched in the scene-descriptions that we find in many plays.
In *The Indian Emperor, Amboyna* and *Venice Preserved* we have
instruments of torture displayed, and in *The Indian Emperor* Montezuma is shown on the rack while he engages in a long disputation with
a Christian priest on the relative merits of their religions.[6] Lee's *Theodosius* begins with this account of the setting and of the ceremonial
that introduces the play:

> *A stately Temple, which represents the Christian Re-
> ligion, as in its first Magnificence: Being but lately estab-
> lish'd at* Rome *and* Constantinople. *The side Scenes shew
> the horrid Tortures with which the* Roman Tyrants *per-
> secuted the Church; and the flat Scene, which is the
> Limit of the Prospect, discovers an Altar richly adorn'd,
> before it* Constantine, *suppos'd kneels, with Command-
> ers about him, gazing at a bloody Cross in the Air, which
> being encompass'd with many Angels, offers it self to
> view, with those Words distinctly written,* (In hoc signo
> vinces!) *Instruments are heard, and many Attendants:
> The Ministers at Divine Service walk busily up and
> down, till* Atticus *the Chief of all the Priests, and Suc-
> cessor of St.* Chrysostom, *in rich Robes, comes forward
> with the Philosopher* Leontine; *the Waiters in Ranks
> bowing all the way before him.*

In the Restoration the word "opera" was used for a play with frequent songs and elaborate scenic devices such as flying machines:
Davenant's version of *Macbeth* and the Davenant-Dryden-Shadwell
version of *The Tempest* fall into the category, as does Shadwell's piece
of brutal horse-play *The Lancashire Witches*. In its use of machines
and other scenic devices, the *Oedipus* of Dryden and Lee is not very
different: ghosts rise from the cellarage and "prodigies" appear in the
sky: in Act II we have this stage-direction:

> *The Cloud draws that veil'd the Heads of the Figures
> in the Sky, and shews 'em Crown'd, with the Names of
> Œdipus and* Jocasta *written above in great Characters of
> Gold.*

And in Act III this:

> *A Flash of Lightning: The Stage is made bright, and*
> *the Ghosts are seen passing betwixt the Trees.*

It is not surprising that the words of the drama struggled to keep up with this. The quieter utterance would hardly make its effect against a sky with prodigies and moving clouds. So we find speeches in this style almost throughout the play:

> Sure 'tis the End of all things! Fate has torn
> The Lock of Time off, and his Head is now
> The ghastly Ball of round Eternity!
> Call you these Peals of Thunder, but the Yawn
> Of bellowing Clouds? By *Jove,* they seem to me
> The World's last Groans; and those vast Sheets of Flame
> Are its last Blaze! The Tapers of the Gods,
> The Sun and Moon, run down like Waxen-Globes;
> The shooting-Stars end all in purple Gellies,
> And *Chaos* is at hand. (II. i.)

That the playwrights were at times impatient with the lavishness of scenic display is suggested in the epilogue, where the entertainment is contemptuously summed up as

> *what your Palates relish most*
> *Charm! Song! and Show! a Murder and a Ghost!*
> *We know not what you can desire or hope,*
> *To please you more, but burning of a* Pope.

The play is not contemptible, and the preface shows that Dryden and Lee had undertaken their ambitious task with due seriousness, but when they reached the epilogue they seem to have recognised uneasily that in the accoutrements of their work they had debased the tragic style. We must always remember that Restoration tragic plays were written for acting in front of painted scenery—sometimes more, sometimes less, elaborate—and that this encouraged the high-flown manner in both writing and acting.

There would appear a paradox between the high moral aim, the concern with distressed nobility, in these plays and the extravagant manner of speech, the lavishness of scene, the elaboration of the affecting moment. We must, however, recognise in the seventeenth century an increasing awareness of personal inadequacy, an increasing desire to live up to extravagant ideas of conduct. We can see it in the baroque style, in the highly self-conscious ceremonial of Charles I's court, in the cult of Platonic Love over which Queen Henrietta Maria presided; we can see it in metaphysical poetry, in the heroic romances of the middle years of the century; we can see it too in Cavalier gallantry and ill-success. When it came to dying, one must not merely make a good end, one must take pleasure in the style of it. We can note from Aphra Behn's comedy *The Roundheads, or The Good Old Cause* that the Cavaliers during the Interregnum loved to call themselves "Heroicks," and to them the exiled Charles II was "the great Heroick."[7] They might dice and drab, or know prison and poverty, but to one part of their minds they were giants who could contemn both their own reduced circumstances and the men of Oliver's faction who held the power. This, I think, to some extent explains the extravagant terms of devotion in which Restoration dedications are written. Poets, of course, were expected to be subservient to patrons, yet in many an instance there is an odd ring of sincerity in the expression of homage. Men were anxious to believe that they lived among the truly great, and the pretence was not altogether unsuccessful. To Dryden, Almanzor and Montezuma were not impossible figures. And with this in mind we can understand such panegyrical writing as appears in Dryden's *Ode to the Memory of Mrs. Anne Killigrew*: when he pays deep homage to members of the royal house and sees Mrs. Killigrew as the leader of the world's poets on the day of judgment, he is offering the same kind of tribute to an idea as when he wrote *The Conquest of Granada*. It is true that neither before nor after the Civil War did men blind themselves all the time: they could behave with everyday commonsense, they could satirise people in high places. But the other impulse was strong and fertile: it could achieve satisfaction in an elaborate tribute to a politician or a king's mistress, or in the creation of characters valiant in their undertakings, stout in their virtue, more than mortal in their powers of endurance. Thus the strained, operatic manner was suited to this presentation of distressed nobility, because the conception of nobility itself was remote from more ordinary hopes and fears and common conditions. Moreover, the heroic manner was valued for its own sake rather than for any end it might achieve: it was therefore appropriate that dramatists should be concerned with the individual scene rather than with the total structure.

But because this attitude of mind had to be kept sharply separate from that of everyday, it was most necessary that the language of tragedy should be persistently high-flown, that words with the vigour of everyday life upon them should be avoided. In the adaptations of

Shakespeare, such words are carefully struck out. Dryden's Cleopatra is no "lass unparallel'd," she cannot compare herself to the milkmaid who does the meanest chores, she cannot become so much woman, and so little queen, as to cry:

> Peace, peace!
> Dost thou not see my baby at my breast,
> That sucks the nurse asleep? (V. ii.)

And because the tragic writing had to strain after the extraordinary effect, the result may be ludicrous not merely in rating but in pathetic passages. Perhaps the supreme example of this is in *Venice Preserved*, when Jaffeir is being led by Belvidera to the Senate, where he is to betray his friends:

> Come, lead me forward now like a tame Lamb
> To Sacrifice, thus in his fatal Garlands,
> Deck'd fine and pleas'd, The Wanton skips and plays,
> *Trots by the enticing flattering Priestess side,*
> *And much transported with his little pride,*
> *Forgets his dear Companions of the plain*
> *Till by Her, bound, Hee's on the Altar layn*
> *Yet then too hardly bleats, such pleasure's in the pain.* (IV. i.)

Jaffeir's description of himself as a skipping and bleating lamb is hardly more surprising than his uncourtly comparison of his wife to an *"enticing flattering Priestess."* Dryden was incapable of giving his heroes such words to speak, but in his stagey management of a pathetic effect he can be almost as grotesque. In *All for Love* Octavia appears with her children, and she tells them to see what their persuasions can do in wresting Antony from Cleopatra:

> You, *Agrippina,* hang upon his Arms;
> And you, *Antonia,* clasp about his Waste:
> If he will shake you off, if he will dash you
> Against the Pavement, you must bear it, Children;
> For you are mine, and I was born to suffer.
> > [*Here the Children go to him,* &c.
> VEN. Was ever sight so moving! Emperor!
> DOLLA. Friend!
> OCTAV. Husband!
> BOTH CHILDR. Father!
> ANT. I am vanquished: take me,
> > *Octavia;* take me, Children; share me all. (III. i.)

This is the penalty of the high-flown style and of the state of mind that demands it.

In this summary account of Restoration tragedy no attempt will be seen to drag any of the plays back to the stage. They served their purpose, ministered to a current taste, and had their day. The rhymed plays did not last long, but Tate's version of *Lear* and Otway's *Venice Preserved* and *The Orphan* were to hold the stage, more or less continuously, until the nineteenth century. Certainly it would be agreeable to see Dryden's *Don Sebastian* or *Aureng-zebe* or *All for Love* in the theatre, done as far as possible in the Restoration style, and perhaps a skilled actress might induce a more favourable attitude towards Belvidera and Otway than cold print can readily contrive. But such performances, if they should take place, would be for the delight and instruction of theatrical antiquarians. We could not expect that they would make the plays any more important to the generality of men.

NOTES

1. *Restoration Drama*, ed. 1928, p. 1.
2. *Ibid.*, p. 2.
3. John Downes, *Roscius Anglicanus*, ed. Summers, N. D., p. 37.
4. *The Tragedies of the Last Age*, ed. 1692, pp. 133-9.
5. *Essays of John Dryden*, ed. Ker, 1926, i. 103.
6. Cf. Montague Summers, *The Restoration Theatre*, 1934, pp. 205f. Plate XVIII in this book reproduces an illustration of a remarkable scene of torture in Settle's *The Empress of Morocco*.
7. Cf. *The Works of Aphra Behn*, ed. Summers, 1915, i. 453.

D. W. JEFFERSON

❀

The Significance of Dryden's Heroic Plays

The rhymed heroic plays are, perhaps, the least understood of all Dryden's works. The general failure to appreciate them is due to the assumption that they are intended, throughout, to be taken seriously— a very natural assumption since Dryden never confessed to any other than a serious and, indeed, orthodox attitude to his subject-matter. In the preface to *The Conquest of Granada*, where he defends his treatment of heroism, he is anxious to show that his work is based on the most respectable ancient and modern precedents. But Dryden could be very disingenuous when it suited his purpose, and this preface, though it probably served as an effective smokescreen against criticism, is by no means a statement of his real views on the subject. The truth is that he had a purpose in these plays which, for want of a better word, may be described as "comic." He chose not to admit it to his public, and his critics ever since have failed to recognise it.

It is instructive to compare Dryden's heroic plays with those of contemporary dramatists; for example, the Earl of Orrery. In Orrery's plays, heroism is always associated with moral idealism. *Mustapha* and *Henry V* are dominated by the theme of self-sacrifice, the triumph of loyalty and friendship over personal desires. There is no violence, no display of heroic force and virtuosity; the action takes place in the moral rather than the physical sphere. This conception of heroism is derived largely from the French romances of Mlle. de Scudéry and

From *Proceedings of the Leeds Philosophical and Literary Society*, V (1940) , 125-39. Reprinted by permission of the publishers.

others. The atmosphere in Crowne's play, *The History of Charles the Eighth of France,* is somewhat different. Here there is vigorous action, but moral idealism is also present. The victorious hero, realising the nobility of his vanquished enemy, behaves with great magnanimity towards him, with the result that they lay down their arms and become friends. In Dryden's plays, this moral emphasis is entirely lacking. What attracted him was the "power" element in heroism. His typical hero, Almanzor, is an irresistible conqueror, a creature of immensely dynamic personality who dominates every situation and reduces his rivals or enemies to pitiful insignificance. The atmosphere is one of violent melodrama.

Why Dryden should have chosen this conception of heroism, is an interesting question, which we must try to answer. We may begin by quoting from the preface to *The Conquest of Granada,* where he tries to justify himself; though, as we have suggested before, his arguments are not to be taken at their face value—

> For, otherwise, what can be more easy for me, than to defend the character of Almanzor, which is one great exception that is made against the play? 'Tis said, that Almanzor is no perfect pattern of Heroick virtue: that he is a contemner of Kings; and that he is made to perform impossibilities.
>
> I must therefore avow, in the first place, from whence I took the Character. The first image I had of him was from the Achilles of Homer; the next from Tasso's Rinaldo (who was a copy of the former), and the third from the Artaban of Monsieur Calprénede: (who has imitated both). The original of these (Achilles) is taken by Homer for his heroe, and is described by him as one, who, in strength and courage surpassed the rest of the Grecian army: but, withall, of so fiery a temper, so impatient of an injury, even from his King and General, that, when his mistress was to be forc'd from him by the command of Agamemnon, he not onely disobey'd it; but returned him an answer full of contumely, and in the most opprobrious terms he could imagine . . . . . Tasso's chief Character, Rinaldo, was a man of the same temper: for, when he had slain Gernando in his heat of passion, he not onely refused to be judg'd by Godfrey, his General, but threat'ned that if he came to seize him, he would right himself by arms upon him . . . .
>
> You see how little these great Authors did esteem the

point of Honour, so much magnify'd by the French, and
so ridiculously ap'd by us. They made their Hero's men
of honour; but so, as not to divest them quite of humane
passions and frailties. They contented themselves to shew
you, what men of great spirits would certainly do, when
they were provok'd, not what they were oblig'd to do by
the strict rules of moral vertue; for my own part, I declare myself for Homer and Tasso; and am more in love
with Achilles and Rinaldo, than with Cyrus and Oroon-
dates. I shall never subject my characters to the French
standard; where love and honour are to be weighed by
drachms and scruples . . . .

Dryden thus screens his hero from criticism by proving that there is
ample precedent for all his excesses. He undoubtedly wanted his readers to believe that Almanzor was intended as another Achilles or another Rinaldo. But no one who has read *The Conquest of Granada*
carefully can possibly accept Almanzor in this way, or believe that Dryden really thought of him in this way himself.

The charge brought against Dryden in his own day, and by later
critics, is that his treatment of heroism carries extravagance to the
point of absurdity. A contemporary critic[1] suggested that "Almanzor
is not more copied from Achilles than from Ancient Pistol." The following paragraph by George Saintsbury, who wrote as an admirer of
Dryden, contains the suggestion that, excellent though the heroic plays
are, they are not free from a certain element of unintentional comedy—

Never, perhaps, was there a better example of what
can and what can not be done by consummate craftsmanship in the teeth of artistic error. That Shakespeare
could have transformed the heroic play, as he transformed everything he touched, is quite possible. Dryden
could not transform it altogether, but he did with it, in
the old phrase, "what a man of mould might," and he
showed, in the doing, of what a mighty mould he was.
With a certain adaptability of temperament, and some
little variety of experience in literature, it is easy, even
with *The Indian Emperor,* easier with *Tyrannic Love,*
and easiest of all with *The Conquest of Granada* to "get
the atmosphere," to submit to the conditions, and to
drive at full speed with the poet in his distinctly wild but
still calculated career. Even when Almeria hectors her
suitors, her sister, her rival, her conquerors, and every-

body; even when Maximin makes a cushion of his assas-
sin, and stabs it now and then to keep it quiet as he
perorates; even when Almanzor makes Drawcansir not so
much a caricature as a faded photograph—it is not impossible to gulp the sense of the ludicrous, and pursue
the triumph of tempestuous petticoat-worship and roist-
ering declamation. And there are passages where no
gulp is necessary. I am not myself fond of the theatre, but
I should like to see one of these plays acted. The very
boards might dissolve in laughter at the first scene or
two; but if this danger could be surmounted, I do not see
why Valeria's modern representative—let us hope she
might have a tithe of Nelly's well-attested charm—should
not speak the famous epilogue (softened, of course) in
a tempest and torrent of cheers.[2]

It is this quality of extravagance bordering on absurdity which
makes Dryden's heroic plays different from the works which he invokes as his models. Saintsbury assumes that it is an unintentional absurdity, but the contention of the present writer is that the plays can
only be understood if we recognise this effect as the result of a conscious artistic purpose. It is, after all, a little unlikely that Dryden,
whose sense of the ludicrous was so keen, should have been capable of
lapsing into gross absurdity himself without realising it. He was one of
the most deliberate of artists.

Dryden's character presents a strange mixture of positive and negative attitudes to life. This is not in itself remarkable, a certain ambivalency being normal in human nature. What is remarkable is that he
could, as it were, exploit this ambivalency in his poetry. He seems to
have taken a pleasure in playing off opposing attitudes against each
other. When his subject is serious, the positive attitude may prevail,
but the negative attitude usually lurks in the background, ready to
show itself at any time unexpectedly.

His position in relation to religion affords an example of this habit.
Dryden was, as he confessed himself, sceptical by nature; and his scepticism was not confined to matters of doctrine. Throughout his work we
continually find passages where the worth-whileness of human existence is called into question, "When I consider life, 'tis all a cheat," is
the best known. Resentment against life, flavoured by a kind of genial
cynicism, is one of the recurring *motifs* in Dryden. It is against this
background of scepticism and pessimism that his religious poems become so interesting. The genuine humility, and desire to believe in
and live according to the Christian faith, which are expressed there,

are all the more moving because his other self is not entirely suppressed. Passages of solemn beauty in *The Hind and the Panther* contrast strangely with touches of wit, where the pagan, earthy side of him
comes out. Prior to the period of the religious poems, when religion,
we may imagine, had not yet become an urgent personal issue for him,
he wrote his dramatic version of Milton's *Paradise Lost*—the opera entitled *The State of Innocence*. Here we have an instance where the intrusion of a negative note into an otherwise respectful presentation of
the subject, has the effect of studied incongruity. Adam is visited by
Gabriel and Raphael, whose task is to instruct him in the mysteries of
the divine purpose. But when the conversation turns on the thorny issue of free-will and divine foreknowledge, it becomes apparent that
Adam is capable of holding his own in debate with the angels; and he
is not prepared to swallow all that they say. Finally, they are compelled
to cut the argument short with a hurried farewell. Adam is left per-
plexed and not a little resentful—

> Hard state of life! Since Heav'n fore-knows my will,
> Why am I not ty'd up from doing ill?
> Why am I trusted with myself at large,
> When hee's more able to sustain the charge?
> Since Angels fell, whose strength was more than mine,
> 'Twould show more grace my frailty to confine.
> Fore-knowing the success, to leave me free,
> Excuses him, and yet supports not me.[3]

Dryden's treatment of heroism shows a similar mixture of attitudes.
He was attracted to this theme because of the ideas of power and
grandeur which it suggested. It filled his mind with large conceptions,
and gave him unlimited opportunities for exercising his gifts of rhetoric. To this extent, then, he *believed* in heroism. But it also stimulated another side of his nature—his satirical and sceptical spirit, and
his sense of the ludicrous. There are a number of passages in the plays
where he deliberately introduces sentiments which have the effect of
pricking the bubble of heroic idealism. Whether the speech is uttered
by a sympathetic character or otherwise does not matter, as it is always
quite apparent that it is Dryden himself who is speaking, and that he
is doing so for his own pleasure. The following lines on love spoken
by Almanzor are a comparatively mild example—

> Love is that madness which all Lovers have;
> But yet 'tis sweet and pleasing so to Rave.
> 'Tis an Enchantment where the reason's bound:

> But Paradice is in th' enchanted ground.
> A Palace void of Envy, Cares and Strife,
> Where gentle hours delude so much of Life.
> To take those Charms away; and set me free
> Is but to send me into misery;
> And Prudence, of whose Cures so much you boast,
> Restores those Pains which that sweet folly lost.[4]

The implication here is that love is very sweet while it lasts, but has no enduring quality. It is an illusion which takes possession of the soul when reason is not in command. The sentiment is not very far removed from that expressed in the speech, "When I consider life 'tis all a cheat"—which Dryden puts into the mouth of his hero, Aurengzebe. (The fact that Aurengzebe is in adversity at the time gives the speech some degree of dramatic appropriateness, but its tone suggests a settled view of life—the view of life which is, in fact, habitual to Dryden.)

There are other passages where a distrust of the spiritual values proper to the heroic code, and a cynical attitude towards human nature in general, are given more blatant expression. Negative comments on Honour occur frequently—

> The points of Honour Poets may produce;
> Trappings of life, for Ornament, not Use:
> Honour, which onely does the name advance,
> Is the meer raving madness of Romance.[5]

> Honor is but an itch of youthful blood,
> Of doing acts extravagantly good;
> We call that Vertue, which is only heat
> That reigns in Youth, till age findes out the cheat.[6]

These definitions are offered by persons of unheroic disposition. Let us turn to a character who might be expected to speak well of Honour—

> CYDARIA: What is this Honour which does Love controul
> CORTEZ: A raging Fit of Vertue in the Soul;
>   A painful burden, which great minds must bear
>   Obtain'd with danger, and posses'd with fear—[7]

A much more positive attitude, but even here there is the suggestion that honour may, after all, be only quixotic folly.

General comments on life are very plentiful in the heroic plays.

However superficially appropriate to the person speaking and to his or her situation, they usually give the impression of having been put there for non-dramatic reasons. Dryden deliberately uses every occasion that presents itself for saying those things which he enjoys saying, and his comments have added piquancy because they seem all wrong in such a setting.

It is in his characterisation that the intrusion of satirical or comic attitudes is most interesting.

The idea of the aggressive, invincible hero appealed to Dryden, but he realised that, with its essential unreality and extravagance, it could easily lead to absurdity. He was not merely aware of these possibilities, but, in the person of Almanzor, he exploited them. This does not mean that he resorted to burlesque. Burlesque merely belittles; its object is entirely negative. Dryden developed both the grandiose and the comic aspects of his theme at the same time, the one being continually modified by the other. His methods are worthy of analysis. They are akin to those with which we are familiar in the later, satirical poetry.

Dryden makes Almanzor an immensely convincing figure. The power and solid weight of his verse suffice to convey an impression of irresistible force of character—

> No man has more contempt than I, of breath;
> But, whence hast thou the right to give me death?
> Obey'd as Soveraign by thy Subjects be;
> But know that I alone am King of me.
> I am as free as Nature first made man,
> 'Ere the base Laws of Servitude began,
> When wild in woods the noble Savage ran.[8]

But there is more here than simple heroic rhetoric. There is statement and argument, and these elements make the effect more complex. Dryden finds in his subject not merely poetical stimulus, but also intellectual amusement. He endows his hero with first-rate powers of debating, with which he makes him expound his own unique nature. It is here that Almanzor becomes "comic." The claims he makes for himself are so monstrous—and yet so convincing, because the whole weight of his overwhelming personality is behind them—that we accept him as a creature apart from the human species; a prodigy, at the same time magnificent and grotesque.

Dryden displays great skill in giving a show of plausibility to a completely outrageous argument—

> BOABDELIN: Since, then, no pow'r above your own you know,
> Mankind shou'd use you like a common foe.
> You shou'd be hunted like a Beast of Prey;
> By your own law, I take your life away.
> ALMANZOR: My laws are made but only for my sake;
> No King against himself a Law can make.
> If thou pretend'st to be a Prince like me,
> Blame not an Act which should thy Pattern be.
> I saw th' oppresst, and thought it did belong
> To a King's office to redress the wrong:
> I brought that Succour, which thou ought'st to bring
> And so, in Nature, am thy Subjects' King.[9]

His gift of arguing in verse has always been recognised, but the extent to which he exercised it in the heroic plays has not been sufficiently realised. We shall have occasion to quote several more examples later in this essay.

The imagery of Almanzor's speeches deserves attention. Van Doren, the author of what is perhaps the standard critical estimate of Dryden to-day, remarks that he was somewhat deficient in imagery; but this statement is only true—and then not wholly so—of the satirical and controversial poems, where imagery is not called for to any great extent, and which, moreover, were the product of the poet's later years, when his style, though admirable in its vigour and lucidity, was perhaps less colourful than that of his earlier period. Far from being deficient in imagery, Dryden was very rich in it, and it is of a remarkably original quality. In Almanzor's speeches it is used as a direct instrument in characterisation.

The passage quoted below is one which has been referred to by more than one critic as an example of Dryden at his worst. In the opinion of the present writer, this view is the result of the usual failure to understand Dryden's purpose in these plays. The speech occurs in the scene where Almanzor first meets Almahide, and suddenly falls in love with her. His manner of falling in love is entirely in keeping with his tempestuous nature—

> I'me pleas'd and pain'd since first her eyes I saw,
> As I were stung with some *Tarantula*:
> Armes, and the dusty field, I less admire;
> And soften strangely in some new desire;
> Honour burns in me, not so fiercely bright,
> But pale as fires when master'd by the light.
> Ev'n while I speak and look, I change yet more;

> And now am nothing that I was before.
> I'm numm'd, and fix'd, and scarce my eye-balls move;
> I fear it is the Lethargy of Love!
> 'Tis he; I feel him now in every part:
> Like a new Lord, he vaunts about my Heart,
> Surveys in state each corner of my Brest,
> While poor fierce I, that was, am dispossesst.
> I'm bound; but I will rowze my rage again:
> And though no hope of Liberty remaine,
> I'll fright my Keeper when I shake my chaine.[10]

Dryden parodies and exaggerates the conventional psychology of love, the imagery being deliberately made crude to suggest an emotional upheaval of more than normal violence. The passage, if closely examined, exhibits a considerable variety of effects. Lines like—

> But pale as fires when master'd by the light

> While poor fierce I, that was, am dispossesst

have the authentic ring of serious poetry, while in—

> I'll fright my Keeper when I shake my chaine

we have an unexpected image which borders on the comic.

Almanzor's speech of withering invective against Abdalla, at the end of the same scene, derives much of its force and point from the imagery—

ABDALLA:	Your boldness to your services I give:
	Now take it as your full reward to live.
ALMANZOR:	To live!
	If from thy hands alone my death can be,
	I am immortal; and a god to thee.
	If I would kill thee now, thy fate's so low,
	That I must stoop 'ere I can give the blow.
	But mine is fix'd so far above thy Crown,
	That all thy men,
	Pil'd on thy back can never pull it down.
	But at my ease thy destiny I send,
	By ceasing from this hour to be thy friend.
	Like Heav'n I need but onely to stand still;
	And, not concurring in thy life, I kill.
	Thou canst no title to my duty bring:
	I'm not thy Subject, and my Soul's thy King.
	Farewell, when I am gone,

> There's not a starr of thine dare stay with thee:
> I'le whistle thy tame fortune after me:
> And whirl fate with me wheresoe're I fly,
> As winds drive storms before 'em in the sky.[11]

The effect is one of gigantic contrast. While Abdalla is dwarfed and annihilated, Almanzor takes on prodigious stature; he becomes the vehicle of a terrific dynamic power, before which creatures like Abdalla are scattered like chaff before the wind. There is at least one image which is frankly comic, and at least one example of unmistakably "metaphysical" wit. But in its carefully-devised extravagance, the whole passage might justly be said to be in the best metaphysical manner.

It is easy to see how different Dryden's treatment of Almanzor is from, say, Marlowe's treatment of Tamburlaine. For Dryden heroic virtuosity is an idea to be played with; an opportunity for poetry, but also an opportunity for wit. The "power" element in the hero may fill his mind with grandiose conceptions, and so inspire magnificent rhetoric; but it also tempts his essentially plastic mind to indulge in effects of exaggeration or distortion.

It is doubtful whether this dual treatment makes for dramatic success. The intention is probably too subtle to be appreciated by the average playgoer, and it might be difficult to convey in the acting. We have no evidence that it was fully grasped by any of Dryden's contemporaries.

In the character of Almanzor, we see a mixture of the splendid and the grotesque. In some of the minor characters, it is the latter quality which predominates. There were certain types of character which offered themselves as admirable subjects for such treatment—Boabdelin, the wretched king of Granada, whose weakness and vacillation appear doubly contemptible in comparison with Almanzor's superhuman strength; his counterpart, the Emperor in *Aurengzebe,* who is as wilful and autocratic as he is impotent; the villainous characters, Abdalla in *The Conquest of Granada,* Morat in *Aurengzebe,* and Maximin in *Tyrannic Love.* Dryden makes excellent capital out of the ridiculous figure of the Emperor who, in spite of his decrepit condition, does not consider himself too old for love. The scene in which he quarrels violently with his Empress has been described by Mr. T. S. Eliot as "admirable purple comedy"—

> EMPEROR: 'Tis true, of Marriage-bands I'm weary grown;
> Love scorns all ties, but those that are his own.

> Chains, that are drag'd, must needs uneasie prove:
> For there's a God-like liberty in Love.

Nourmahal's reply is exquisitely insulting—

> What's Love to you?
> The bloom of Beauty, other years demands;
> Nor will be gather'd by such wither'd hands;
> You importune it with a false desire;
> Which sparkles out, and makes no solid fire.
> This impudence of Age, whence can it spring?
> All you expect, and yet you nothing bring:
> Eager to ask, when you are past a grant;
> Nice in providing what you cannot want.[12]

In another context, she says of him—

> He only moved and talked, but did not live.

When the Emperor catches one of his courtiers making advances, as he supposes, to the lady he covets, his resentment is expressed with magnificent absurdity—

> Did he my Slave, presume to look so high?
> That crawling Insect, who from Mud began,
> Warm'd by my Beams, and kindl'd into Man?
> Durst he, who does but for my pleasure live,
> Intrench on Love, my great Prerogative?[13]

Dryden is admirable in expressions of gross conceit and self-complacency. Here, his power of creating an effect of spurious plausibility by ingenious argument is frequently brought into play. The scene in which Nourmahal first sees Indamora, the object of her husband's attentions, contains a brilliant example. Nourmahal is struck by her remarkable beauty, and tries to explain to herself how so formidable a rival to her own charms could possibly exist—

> A fairer Creature, did my eyes ne'r see!
> Sure she was form'd by Heav'n, in spite to me!
> Some Angel copi'd, while I slept, each grace,
> And molded ev'ry feature from my face.
> Such Majesty does from her forehead rise,
> Her cheeks such blushes cast, such rays her eyes,
> Nor I, nor Envy, can a blemish find;
> The Palace is, without, too well desgn'd:
> Conduct me in, for I will view thy mind.

> Speak, if thou hast a Soul, that I may see,
> If Heav'n can make throughout, another Me.

Indamora, who has been asleep, wakes, and Nourmahal is reassured
by the fear and humility in her manner, that as far as "soul" is concerned, she has nothing to lose by the comparison—

> The Palm is, by the Foes confession, mine.
> But I disdain what basely you resign.
> Heav'n did, by me, the outward model build:
> Its inward work, the Soul, with rubbish fill'd.
> Yet, Oh! th' imperfect Piece moves more delight;
> 'Tis gilded o'r with Youth, to catch the sight.
> The Gods have poorly robbed my Virgin bloom,
> And what I am, by what I was, o'rcome.
> Traitress, restore my Beauty and my Charms,
> Nor steal my Conquest with my proper Arms.[14]

In the following speech by Morat, Aurengzebe's villainous brother
who resents his position as a younger son, the imagery is of a peculiar
flavour—

> for when great Souls are giv'n,
> They bear the marks of Sov'reignty from Heav'n.
> My Elder Brothers my fore-runners came;
> Rough-drafts of Nature, ill-design'd and lame.
> Blown off, like Blossoms, never made to bear;
> Till I came, finish'd; her last-labour'd care.[15]

The heroic plays and, indeed, the whole of Dryden's work, abound
in a kind of imagery, the effect of which is to represent the human
species, and processes relating to the creation or generation of the
species, as absurd or monstrous. Such imagery corresponds to an habitual mental attitude in Dryden—his delight in thinking ignobly of the
soul. It is deliberately used with comic intent.

Here is Aurengzebe's description of his brother—

> When thou wert form'd, Heav'n did a man begin;
> But the brute Soul, by chance, was shuffl'd in.[16]

Nourmahal on Indamora (quoted in full above)—

> Heav'n did, by me, the outward model build.
> Its inward work, the Soul, with rubbish fill'd.

The Emperor's description of his subjects—

> The Vulgar, a scarce animated Clod,[16]

and

> The little Emmets with the humane Soul.[16]

His definition of children—

> Children the blind effect of Love and Chance.[16]

Dryden enjoys overturning human standards in favour of the sensual self-sufficiency of the brute creation—

> Reason's nice taste does our delights destroy:
> Brutes are more bless'd who grossly feed on joy.[17]

> Or make thy Orders with my reason sute
> Or let me live by Sense a glorious Brute—[16]

We have already noticed his use of novel and striking imagery as an instrument of characterisation. Its effect is usually to distort the character and give it a grotesque quality. In the following lines spoken by Maximin, who expresses resentment because love has come inopportunely into his life, the images have been deliberately chosen to make his emotional condition absurd—

> This Love which never could my youth engage,
> Peeps out his coward head to dare my age.
> Where hast thou been thus long, thou sleeping form,
> That wak'st like drowsie Sea-men in a storm?
> A sullen hour thou chusest for thy birth:
> My Love shoots up in tempests as the earth
> Is stirr'd and loosen'd in a blustring wind,
> Whose blasts to waiting flowers her womb unbind[18]

There is a touch of oddity in the dying speech of Abdalla—

ABDELMELECH: Now ask your Life.
ABDALLA: 'Tis gone: that busy thing,
      The Soul, is packing up, and just on wing.
      Like parting Swallows, when they seek the Spring.[19]

The piquancy of the image is often enhanced by Dryden's splendid powers of statement, his ability to create an impression of weight and importance. For example—a description of a "heavy father"—

> It is a murdering will!
> That whirls along with an impetuous sway;
> And like chain-shot, sweeps all things in its way.[20]

Almanzor on Boabdelin—

> The word that I have giv'n shall stand like Fate;
> Not like the King's, that weathercock of State.
> He stands so high, with so unfixt a mind,
> Two Factions turn him with each blast of wind.[21]

Sometimes an image which is fine in itself becomes absurd in its context—

> Let my Crown go; he never will return;
> I, like a Phoenix, in my Nest will burn.[22]

The speaker is Boabdelin.

More examples may be given of Dryden's witty use of casuistical argument. Some of the best scenes in the heroic plays consist of debates, in which the protagonists—often quarrelling lovers—play a game of skilful wrangling. The scenes between Lyndaraxa and her helplessly amorous victim, Abdelmelech, usually take this form. There is often a mischievous, and sometimes a frankly comic, purpose in Dryden's handling of these debates. The following conversation between Montezuma and the Spaniards, on the subject of the proposed Christianisation of Mexico, is typical—

> PIZARRO: The Soveraign Priest,—
> Who represents on Earth the pow'r of Heaven,
> Has this your Empire to our Monarch given.
>
> MONTEZUMA: Ill does he represent the Powers above,
> Who nourishes debate, not Preaches love;
> Besides, what greater folly can be shown?
>
> He gives another what is not his own.
>
> VASQUEZ: His pow'r must needs unquestion'd be below,
> For he in Heaven as Empire can bestow.
>
> MONTEZUMA: Empires in Heaven he with more ease may give,
> And you perhaps would with less thanks receive;
> But Heaven has need of no such Vice-roy here,
> It self bestows the Crowns that Monarchs wear.
>
> PIZARRO: You wrong his power as you mistake our end,
> Who came thus far Religion to extend.
>
> MONTEZUMA: He, who Religion truely understands,
> Knows its extent must be in Men, not Lands.

ODMAR: But who are those that truth must propagate
Within the confines of my Father's state?

VASQUEZ: Religious Men, who hither must be sent
As awful Guides of Heavenly Government;
To teach you Penance, Fasts, and Abstinence,
To punish Bodies for the Soul's offence.

MONTEZUMA: Cheaply you sin, and punish crimes with ease,
Not as th' offended, but th' offenders please.
First injure Heaven, and when its wrath is due,
Your selves prescribe it how to punish you.

ODMAR: What numbers of these Holy Men must come?

PIZARRO: You shall not want, each Village shall have some
Who, though the Royal Dignity they own,
Are equal to it, and depend on none.

GUYOMAR: Depend on none! You treat them sure in state,
For 'tis their plenty does their pride create.

MONTEZUMA: Those ghostly Kings would parcel out my pow'r,
And all the fatness of my Land devour;
That Monarch sits not safely on his Throne,
Who bears, within, a power that shocks his own.
They teach obedience to Imperial sway,
But think it sin if they themselves obey.[23]

The passage in which Almanzor asserts his claim to Almahide, Boabdelin's betrothed, contains a remarkable mixture of logic-chopping,
metaphysical wit, and rhetoric—

ALMAHIDE: Alas it is in vain;
Fate for each other did not us ordain.
The chances of this day too clearly show
That Heav'n took care that it should not be so.

ALMANZOR: Would Heav'n had quite forgot me this one day,
But fate's yet hot—
I'le make it take a bent another way.
(*He walks swiftly and discomposedly, studying.*)
I bring a claim which does his right remove:
You're his by promise, but you're mine by Love.
'Tis all but Ceremony which is past:
The knot's to tie which is to make you fast.
Fate gave not to *Boabdelin* that pow'r;
He woo'd you but as my Ambassadour.

ALMAHIDE: Our Souls are ty'd by holy Vows above.

ALMANZOR: He sign'd but his: but I will seal my love.
I love you better, with more Zeale than he.

ALMAHIDE: This day—
I gave my faith to him, he his to me.

ALMANZOR: Good Heav'n thy book of fate before me lay,
But to tear out the journal of this day.
Or, if the order of the world below
Will not the gap of one whole day allow,
Give me that Minute when she made her vow.
"That Minute, ev'n the happy, from their bliss
      might give;
"And those, who live in griefe, a shorter time
      would live.
So small a link, if broke, th' eternal chain
Would, like divided waters, joyn again.
It wonnot be; the fugitive is gone,
Prest by the crowd of following Minutes on;
That precious Moment's out of Nature fled,
And on the heap of common rubbish layd,
Of things that once have been, and are decay'd.[24]

There are some admirable examples of audacious and crushing repartee—

DON ARCOS: Since thus you have resolv'd, henceforth prepare
For all the last extremities of war:
My King his hope from heavens assistance draws:

ALMANZOR: The *Moors* have Heav'n, and me, t'assist their cause.[25]

EMPEROR: You may be pleas'd your Politiques to spare:
I'm old enough, and can my self take care.

INDAMORA: Advice from me was, I confess, too bold:
Y'are old enough it may be, sir, too old.[26]

Debate and verbal skirmishing are not confined to a few scenes; they
dominate the larger part of the heroic plays. The reader of Dryden
learns to look to them as a more important source of pleasure than the
more dramatic elements in the action.

We are now in a position to sum up our conclusions regarding these
plays. It is quite clear from the examples given—and numerous as they
are, they are merely a selection—that Dryden deliberately used heroic

melodrama as a playground for his powers of wit and rhetoric. In choosing this subject-matter he was not going against his nature, as Van Doren suggests. On the contrary, the theme was peculiarly suited to his temperament, and his treatment of it was calculated to the last degree. When he began to write heroic plays, he did not become immediately aware of the possibilities of his material. He was probably attracted to it, in the first instance, merely because it gave him a chance to "let himself go." *The Indian Queen* (in which he collaborated with Sir Robert Howard) contains scarcely any of the elements to which we have referred, though there is a slight tendency towards the comic in Zempoalla. Undercurrents begin to appear in *The Indian Emperor*. Montezuma's tirade against the gods, for example, has some of the flavour of Maximin's much more extravagant outbursts—

> Take, gods, that Soul ye did in spight create,
> And made it great to be unfortunate:
> Ill Fate for me unjustly you provide,
> Great Souls are Sparks of your own Heavenly Pride:
> That lust of power we from your god-heads have,
> You're bound to please those Appetites you gave.[27]

The development is carried further in *Tyrannic Love,* where Maximin is entirely grotesque, and it reaches its height in *The Conquest of Granada* and *Aurengzebe*. In the latter play, most of the important characters—the Emperor, Nourmahal, Morat—are comic. Aurengzebe, the hero, is a serious figure, an upholder of virtue and loyalty, but his character is modified significantly by frequent expressions of disillusion and resentment against life, all in Dryden's favourite vein.

It is because the heroic plays are completely unreal that it was possible for Dryden to play with his material in this way. The characters, the emotions, the sentiments, are entirely artificial—but in the positive sense of that word. Dryden, as Van Doren points out, had no real insight into human feelings or the springs of human action; he could never have become a dramatist in the Shakespearian manner. But what Van Doren fails to realise is that Dryden was aware of his own limitations, and deliberately chose subject-matter which lent itself to artificial treatment. The theme is so far removed from reality, his version of heroism so cut off from serious values and ideals, that it was possible for him to exploit his material in whatever way suited his fancy.

Dryden composed these plays between 1664 and 1675, and they represent his main poetical output during this period. They have an important place in his development as a poet, because it is in them, especially in *The Conquest of Granada* and *Aurengzebe,* that his great powers are first exercised to the full. The Dryden of the early poems—even *Annus Mirabilis*—was still immature. His individuality had not yet emerged. In the heroic plays he seems to have found a medium in which his personality could develop itself freely. Nearly all the qualities which later made him such a superb satirist were developed at this stage, including the satirical spirit itself. His methods of comic portraiture, for example, were carried over from the plays into the poems, as the imagery in the following lines from *Mac-Flecknoe* clearly demonstrates—

> Some Beams of Wit on other Souls may fall,
> Strike through and make a lucid intervall;
> But Sh—'s genuine night admits no ray,
> His rising Fogs prevail upon The Day:
> Besides, his goodly Fabrick fills the eye
> And seems design'd for thoughtless Majesty:
> Thoughtless as Monarch Oakes that shade the plain,
> And, spread in solemn state, supinely reign.

His powers of debating in verse were exercised in the heroic plays many years before the composition of *The Hind and the Panther.* Critics of Dryden have erred seriously in their failure to trace the continuity between these two phases of his work.

But the Dryden of the heroic plays is different in many ways from the later Dryden: much richer in imagery, much more given to poetical and intellectual exuberance. This is due partly to the difference of subject-matter—the plays gave more scope for free indulgence in fantasy than the satires, which are concerned with topical actualities—and partly to the fact that the plays are earlier work. The metaphysical quality of this earlier style is especially notable. That Dryden was influenced by the metaphysical poets has always been realised, but the examples cited have usually been from those poems in which he was still largely imitative. The examples in the plays, which are much richer and more individual, have been neglected. Dryden differs from the other metaphysical poets in several rspects. His images and ideas are not obscure or complicated. On the contrary, the whole effect of his style is to make everything palpable and obvious. While the reader of a poem by Donne is immediately struck by the unusualness of the intellectual content, Dryden's poetry, being essentially rhetorical, makes its first impact on the ear rather than on the mind. Of the two qualities, magniloquence and wit, the former appears to predominate. It is, perhaps, on this account that his metaphysical qualities have been missed.

NOTES

1. Martin Clifford, whom Dr. Johnson quotes in his life of Dryden.
2. Introd. to selection of Dryden's plays in the Mermaid Series.
3. *The State of Innocence*, IV.
4. *The Conquest of Granada*, Part II, III, 3.
5. *Aurengzebe*, II.
6. *The Indian Queen*, III.
7. *The Indian Emperor*, II, 2.
8. *The Conquest of Granada*, Part I, I.
9. *The Conquest of Granada*, Part I, I.
10. *The Conquest of Granada*, Part I, III.
11. *The Conquest of Granada*, Part I, III.
12. *Aurengzebe*, II.
13. *Aurengzebe*, II.
14. *Aurengzebe*, V.
15. *Aurengzebe*, V.
16. *Aurengzebe*, III.
17. *Aurengzebe*, V.
18. *Tyrannic Love*, III.
19. *The Conquest of Granada*, Part II, IV.
20. *The Conquest of Granada*, Part I, V.
21. *The Conquest of Granada*, Part I, III.
22. *The Conquest of Granada*, Part II, I.
23. *The Indian Emperor*, I, 2.
24. *The Conquest of Granada*, Part I, III.
25. *The Conquest of Granada*, Part I, I.
26. *Aurengzebe*, II.
27. *The Indian Emperor*, II.

ARTHUR C. KIRSCH

❊

The Significance of Dryden's *Aureng-Zebe*

The second decade of the Restoration witnessed two significant changes in the development of serious drama: the advent of sentimental heroes and domestic situations, and the abandonment of rhyme. The changes are particularly interesting because they seem to be related. They can be seen in all the serious plays of the decade, but their relationship is perhaps most clear in Dryden's *Aureng-Zebe* (1676), the play which stands midway between *The Conquest of Granada* (1672) and *All for Love* (1678), the former a rhymed play whose hero exemplifies an aristocratic code of glory and self-aggrandizement, the latter an unrhymed play whose hero is guided by standards of sentiment and self-indulgence.

I   Sentiment and the Fall of Glory

Aureng-Zebe gathers up many themes and characters long familiar in Dryden's rhymed plays. The Emperor is a variation upon the old Montezuma in *The Indian Emperour,* debasing himself and imperiling his kingdom by a love he cannot control. Nourmahal is a duplicate of the lustful and villainous Zempoalla in *The Indian Queen,* and Arimant, who sues in vain for the heroine's love, is a carbon copy of the equally unsuccessful Acacis of *The Indian Queen.* Indamora is a slightly weaker version of Almahide, the heroine of *The Conquest of*

From *ELH: A Journal of English Literary History,* XXIX (1962), 160-74. Reprinted by permission of The Johns Hopkins Press.

Granada; Melisinda, a considerably more pathetic copy of Valeria, the self-denying mistress of *Tyrannic Love.* Aureng-Zebe and Morat repeat the contrast of virtue and vice embodied by Guyomar Odmar in *The Indian Emperour.*

But if the characters are old the way in which they are treated is new. Dr. Johnson commented that "The personages [in *Aureng-Zebe*] are imperial; but the dialogue is often domestick, and therefore susceptible of sentiments accommodated to familiar incidents."[1] The clearest verification of his observation is to be found in the character of Melisinda. Melisinda is descended from the unrequited lovers of Dryden's earlier plays, but she also anticipates Octavia in *All for Love.* She is a wife and she cannot thrive, as her predecessors had, by meriting the love which her rival possesses. When Morat first reveals his infidelity, Melisinda *"retires, weeping, to the side of the Theatre."* (sig. [G3])[2] Afterwards she tells Morat plaintively of her love for him. Morat replies:

> You say you love me; let that love be shown.
> 'Tis in your power to make my happiness.
> *Mel.* Speak quickly: to command me is to bless.
> *Mor.* To *Indamora* you my Suit must move:
> You'll sure speak kindly of the man you love.

But Melisinda is not such stuff as the old heroines were made of, though Morat himself, of course, is hardly the hero to inspire her. She answers:

> Oh! rather let me perish by your hand,
> Than break my heart, by this unkind command . . .
> Try, if you please, my Rival's heart to win:
> I'll bear the pain, but not promote the sin.

Morat then casts her off, and she weeps again. At this point the Emperor intrudes upon them and notices her tears. Rather than have him think that her marriage has been violated and that her "Lord" is "unkind," she says:

> Believe not Rumor, but your self; and see
> The kindness 'twixt my plighted Lord and me.
>   [*Kissing* Morat.
> This is our State; thus happily we live;
> These are the quarrels which we take and give.
> I had no other way to force a Kiss.   (*Aside* to Mor.)
> Forgive my last Farewel to you, and Bliss.
>   [*Exit.* (sigs. [H4]-I)

The sentimentality of this farewell is particularly important because the scene is not isolated, as such scenes usually were in Dryden's other plays. The domestic sentimentality with which Melisinda is portrayed pervades the entire play.

The most significant evidence of this domesticity is the contrast between Morat and his brother, Aureng-Zebe. With the partial exception of Guyomar in *The Indian Emperour*, Aureng-Zebe is like no other hero in Dryden's previous plays. Before Aureng-Zebe Dryden's heroes had been distinguished by their capacity for passion, frequently expressed in rant, by their primitivistic if not primitive natures (both Montezuma and Almanzor are characterized as children of nature), and by their constant desire to prove their worth in love as well as in war. None of them were temperate men: if they denied themselves the physical satisfaction of love they did so, as Almanzor made clear, "because I dare." (*Conquest of Granada*, Part 2, sig. N2) They lived not by virtue, in any conventional sense, but by their pride. They conformed only to their own most extravagant conceptions of individual power, to what Corneille and other French writers termed *la gloire*, and like the Cornélian heroes, they sought not approval but admiration.[3]

To such motives and aspirations Aureng-Zebe is essentially immune. He is described, in contrast to all his brothers, as a man

> . . . by no strong passion sway'd,
> Except his Love, more temp'rate is, and weigh'd: . . .
> He sums their Virtues in himself alone,
> And adds the greatest, of a Loyal Son.   (sig. B2v)

The moment he appears on stage he kneels to his father and kisses his hand, exclaiming:

> Once more 'tis given me to behold your face:
> The best of Kings and Fathers to embrace.
> Pardon my tears; 'tis joy which bids 'em flow,
> A joy which never was sincere till now.   (sig. C)

Since his love for Indamora is his one "strong passion," he is at first enraged to learn that his father has become his rival, and he threatens to rebel against him to protect Indamora from imprisonment. But she chastens him:

> Lose not the Honour you have early wonn;
> But stand the blameless pattern of a Son. . . .

> My suff'rings for you make your heart my due:
> Be worthy me, as I am worthy you.

Aureng-Zebe rises to the challenge:

> My Virtue was surpris'd into a Crime.
> Strong Virtue, like strong Nature, struggles still:
> Exerts itself, and then throws off the ill.
> I to a Son's and Lover's praise aspire:
> And must fulfil the parts which both require.   (sig. C3v)

For the remainder of the play he does so; he refuses to cede to his father his right to Indamora's love, and at the same time he refuses to sully the "glory"—the word is his—of his name by rebelling against him.

Despite his protestations about the strength of his virtue, Aureng-Zebe is what Indamora calls him, "the blameless pattern of a Son." The enormous capacity for passion of all Dryden's previous heroes—a capacity which Aureng-Zebe is allowed to demonstrate only with the emotion of jealousy—is gone; Aureng-Zebe is a temperate man. Gone too are the roughness which characterized the earlier heroes and the rant which was the emblem of their heroic pride. Aureng-Zebe's failure to embody these qualities would not alone signify Dryden's departure from his earlier conception of heroic drama: Guyomar, for example, had been drawn on similar lines in *The Indian Emperour*. But Guyomar shared the stage with Cortez; Aureng-Zebe is the only hero of the play which bears his name. All the marks of heroic virtue which he lacks are appropriated by Morat, and in Morat the quest for personal glory which had distinguished such characters as Almanzor and Montezuma is stigmatized as unmistakable evidence of villainy. Dryden thus splits the hero, and in the process he irrevocably undermines the heroic *ethos* which had animated his earlier plays.

The change is discernible the moment Morat makes his first appearance. He is a soldier, proud in his power of arms, triumphant in his speech:

> To me, the cries of fighting Fields are Charms:
> Keen be my Sab[r]e, and of proof my Arms.
> I ask no other blessing of my Stars:
> No prize but Fame, nor Mistris but the Wars.   (sig. F2)

He also aspires to greatness:

> Me-thinks all pleasure is in greatness found.
> Kings, like Heav'ns Eye, should spread their beams around.
> Pleas'd to be seen while Glory's race they run.   (sig. F2v)

But his designs upon the state are unscrupulous; and the maxims by which he proposes to rule are the hallmarks of political villany. Like his heroic forbears, he is a child of nature, but of a nature which Dryden now makes clear is nasty, solitary and brutish, the reverse of the natural paradise which nourished the virtues of Montezuma and Almanzor. Aureng-Zebe remarks to Morat:

> When thou wert form'd, Heav'n did a Man begin;
> But the brute Soul, by chance, was shuffl'd in.
> In Woods and Wilds thy Monar[c]hy maintain:
> Where valiant Beasts, by force and rapine, reign.
> In Life's next Scene, if Transmigration be,
> Some Bear or Lion is reserv'd for thee.   (sig. F4v) [4]

But this is not the worst of the indignities which Morat's grandeur must suffer. In what is certainly one of the most extraordinary scenes in all of Dryden's heroic drama, Indamora successfully persuades Morat to abandon forever the corrupt code by which he lives. Morat argues that usurpation by force eventually justifies itself:

> But who by force a Scepter does obtain,
> Shows he can govern that which he could gain.

Indamora replies that such a doctrine is an invitation to an anarchy of power, and Morat begins his retreat:

> I without guilt, would mount the Royal Seat;
> But yet 'tis necessary to be great.
> IND. All Greatness is in Virtue understood:
>   'Tis onely necessary to be good.
>   Tell me, what is't at which great Spirits aim,
>   What most your self desire?
> MOR. —Renown, and Fame,
>   And Pow'r, as uncontrol'd as is my will.
> IND. How you confound desires of good and ill!
>   For true renown is still with Virtue joyn'd;
>   But lust of Pow'r lets loose th'unbridl'd mind.
>   Yours is a Soul irregularly great,
>   Which wanting temper, yet abounds with heat:
>   So strong, yet so unequal pulses beat.
>   A Sun which does, through vapours dimnly shine:
>   What pity 'tis you are not all Divine! . . .
>   Dare to be great, without a guilty Crown;
>   View it, and lay the bright temptation down:
>   'Tis base to seize on all, because you may;

> That's Empire, that which I can give away:
> There's joy when to wild Will you Laws prescribe,
> When you bid Fortune carry back her Bribe:
> A joy, which none but greatest minds can taste;
> A Fame, which will to endless Ages last.
> MOR. Renown, and Fame, in vain, I courted long;
> And still pursu'd 'em, though directed wrong. . . .
> Unjust Dominion I no more pursue;
> I quit all other claims, but those to you.   (sigs. K2v-[K3])

Morat does not give up his claims to Indamora, even at his death, but he signifies his reclamation by renouncing his "pleasure to destroy" and by showing generous feelings towards both his brother and Indamora herself. (sigs. [K3]-K3v)

There are, of course, many scenes in heroic drama in which the villain converts to virtue on his deathbed. But Morat's capitulation involves far more than himself. With his fall from grandeur, and with Aureng-Zebe's corresponding rise to the virtues of love and piety, Dryden, in effect, recognized the exhaustion of the form of drama which only four years before he had acclaimed as the equal of the tragedies of the last age. *Aureng-Zebe* does not mark a total break with the earlier plays. The peripatetic stage pattern remains, as it was to remain in the drama for years to come; and though the super-hero is clearly repudiated, some of his principles survive. Both Aureng-Zebe and Indamora seek to make themselves worthy of each other, and love and honor are still the principal catch-words. The play closes, in fact, with the Emperor giving Aureng-Zebe Indamora's hand as his "just [reward] of Love and Honour." (sig. M3v) But if the topics are the same —the *"mistaken Topicks of Tragedy,"* Dryden was later to call them— the purposes for which they are used have begun to change. Pity and the capacity for tears have begun to supersede the union of private and public pride as the credentials of heroism, and the focal scenes are those which occasion a display of these sentiments rather than those which demonstrate grandeur and evoke admiration.[5] The virtues which Indamora and Aureng-Zebe insist upon are those of the private life, and there is no corresponding emphasis upon public responsibility. Aureng-Zebe is less the best of subjects than he is the best of sons, one of the first heralds of the paragons of filial devotion that abound in eighteenth-century plays.[6] In Morat's case even the antinomy of love and honor itself begins to be sapped at its roots, for he gives up an honor which, though corrupted, still bears the marks of the old heroic grandeur; and he gives it up *for* love. This is the first time in all of Dryden's drama that love and honor constitute a real antithesis, and the victory of love in this context spells the end of the heroic play. Two years later, Antony also gives up honor, and he does so all for love.

II   Rhyme and Decorum

The exploitation of sentiment in *Aureng-Zebe* is reflected in the structure of its verse. Saintsbury pointed out that "There is in *Aurengzebe* a great tendency toward enjambment; and as soon as this tendency gets the upper hand, a recurrence to blank verse is, in English dramatic writing, tolerably certain."[7] Dryden himself is aware that this is happening, for he complains in the prologue to the play that he

> Grows weary of his long-lov'd Mistris, Rhyme.
> Passion's too fierce to be in Fetters bound,
> And Nature flies him like Enchanted Ground.   (sig. [a2])

In the dedication he remarks that *"If I must be condemn'd to Rhyme, I should find some ease in my change of punishment. I desire to be no longer the* Sisyphus *of the Stage; to rowl up a Stone with endless labour (which to follow the proverb, gathers no Mosse) and which is perpetually falling down again."* (sig. [A4]) At a distance of three centuries we may overlook the importance of these statements, since our own prejudices about the failure of rhymed verse in English drama may lead us to believe that Dryden was simply acknowledging an obvious fact. But in order to understand the significance of what he is saying we must appreciate how central rhyme had been both in his theory and practice of heroic drama.

Dryden's first discussion of rhyme appears as early as 1664 in his dedication of *The Rival Ladies* to the Earl of Orrery. He points out that rhyme is *"not natural"* only *"when the Poet either makes a Vicious choice of Words, or places them for Rhyme (sic) sake so unnaturally, as no Man would in ordinary Speaking . . ."* He states further that

> the Excellence and Dignity of it, were never fully known
> till Mr. Waller *taught it; He first made Writing easily an
> Art: First shew'd us to conclude the Sense, most commonly, in Distichs; which in the Verse of those before
> him, runs on for so many Lines together, that the Reader*

is out of Breath to overtake it. This sweetness of Mr.
Wallers Lyrick Poesie was afterwards follow'd in the
Epick by Sir John Denham, in his Coopers-Hill: a Poem
which your Lordship knows for the Majesty of the Style,
is, and ever will be the exact Standard of good Writing.
But if we owe the Invention of it to Mr. Waller, *we are*
acknowledging for the Noblest use of it to Sir William
D'avenant; who at once brought it upon the Stage, and
made it perfect, in the Siege of Rhodes.

(sig. [A4]; Ker, I, 7)[8]

Having established the literary excellence of this form of verse, and
its attendant dignity and majesty, Dryden considers the subjects which
are appropriate to it. He acknowledges the common objection that
"Rhyme is only an Embroidery of Sence, to make that which is ordi-
nary in it self pass for excellent with less Examination," but he concludes that such a defect is caused by an abuse of rhyme: *". . . as the*
Best Medicines may lose their Virtue, by being ill applied, so is it with
Verse, if a fit Subject be not chosen for it. Neither must the Argument
alone, but the Characters, and Persons be great and noble; Otherwise,
(as Scaliger *says of* Claudian) *the Poet will be, Ignobiliore* materiâ de-
pressus. *The Scenes, which, in my Opinion, most commend it, are those*
of Argumentation and Discourse, on the result of which the doing or
not doing some considerable action should depend." (sig. A4v; Ker, I,
8-9) T. S. Eliot has suggested that Dryden defended the rhymed couplet
"because it was the form of verse which came most natural to him,"[9]
and the suggestion is persuasive. The argument of the dedication to
The Rival Ladies reads suspiciously as if Dryden were trying to parlay
his instinct for rhyme into a full-fledged theory of drama; all the sali-
ent features of his later theory are present, even the epic analogy,
which is implied in the reference to Denham's *Cooper's Hill.* But in
any case, the essay stresses the literary perfection of verse which had
been practiced by Denham and Waller and ennobled on the stage by
Sir William D'avenant, and its argument is controlled throughout by
the principle of decorum of style. At its inception, therefore, Dryden's
theory of the heroic play constituted a commitment to rhyme and an
exploration of the subjects suitable to it.

The following year, in the preface to *Four New Plays,* Sir Robert
Howard objected to rhymed plays, arguing that since a play, unlike a
poem, "is presented as the present Effect of Accidents not thought of,"
rhymed verse and rhymed repartee were unnatural, appearing rather

as the premeditation of the author than as the natural result of the dialogue and conversation of characters. He added that "the dispute is not which way a Man may write best in, but which is most proper for the Subject he writes upon . . ."[10] In *Of Dramatick Poesie* (1668) Crites reiterates Howard's position, offering a series of arguments terminating in the assertion that since people do not speak in rhyme and since drama must imitate the conversation of people, rhyme has no place in serious drama. Crites recommends that blank verse, which is "nearest Nature," should be preferred. Neander's response is an appeal to decorum: "I answer you . . . by distinguishing betwixt what is nearest to the nature of Comedy, which is the imitation of common persons and ordinary speaking, and what is nearest to the nature of a serious Play: this last is indeed the representation of Nature, but 'tis Nature wrought up to an higher pitch. The Plot, the Characters, the Wit, the Passions, the Descriptions, are all exalted above the level of common converse, as high as the imagination of the Poet can carry them, with proportion to verisimility. Tragedy we know is wont to image to us the minds and fortunes of noble persons, and to portray these exactly, Heroick Rhime is nearest Nature, as being the noblest kind of modern verse." (sigs. I-I2v, Kv; Ker, I, 90-93, 100-01) As in the dedication of *The Rival Ladies* the burden of Dryden's argument lies in his insistence that the style be suited to the purpose of the genre. Thus, a serious play is "nearest Nature" when, in certain respects, it is farthest from it; decorum, not illusion, is the measure of artistic perfection. As Dryden explains, "A Play . . . to be like Nature, is to be set above it; as Statues which are plac'd on high are made greater then the life, that they may descend to the sight in their just proportion;" (sig. K2; Ker, I, 102) and the artifice of rhyme, "the noblest kind of modern verse," is the means by which this aesthetic distance can best be achieved.

In "A Defence of an Essay of Dramatique Poesie" Dryden amplifies this position. Howard had repeated his objections to rhyme in the preface to *The Duke of Lerma,* and Dryden replied with a searching exposition of his belief that, above all, "a play is supposed to be the work of the poet." (Ker, I, 114) In support of this conviction he argued that " 'Tis true, that to imitate well is a poet's work; but to affect the soul, and excite the passions, and, above all, to move admiration (which is the delight of serious plays), a bare imitation will not serve. The converse, therefore, which a poet is to imitate, must be heightened with all the arts and ornaments of poesy; and must be such as, strictly considered, could never be supposed spoken by any without premeditation." (Ker. I, 113-14) This passage provides further evidence that in Dryden's mind the heroic play was inseparable from "all the arts and ornaments of poesy," and that rhymed verse was intimately associated with the stipulated end of heroic drama, the creation of epic admiration.

In the preface to *The Conquest of Granada* Dryden once again justifies rhyme—this time confident that it was *"already in possession of the Stage."* He remarks that *"it is very clear to all, who understand Poetry, that serious Playes ought not to imitate Conversation too nearly;"* and he adds that *". . . it was onely custome which cozen'd us so long: we thought, because* Shakespear *and* Fletcher *went no farther, that there the Pillars of Poetry were to be erected. That, because they excellently describ'd Passion without Rhyme, therefore Rhyme was not capable of describing it.* (sigs. a2-a2v; Ker, I, 148-49) Rhymed heroic verse, *"the last perfection of Art,"* was clearly Dryden's bid for dramatic fame. He wrote in the preface to *Annus Mirabilis* (1667) that he preferred Virgil to Ovid because Virgil, speaking usually in his own person, *"thereby gains more liberty then the other, to express his thoughts with all the graces of elocution, to write more figuratively, and to confess, as well the labour as the force of his imagination."* (sig. A8; Ker, I, 15-16) The self-conscious employment of artifice had a long history in the drama and criticism of Jonson, Fletcher and their followers, including D'avenant. Dryden was an heir to this tradition, and the rhymed heroic play was his attempt to preserve it by perfecting upon the English stage a language of tragedy that would *"confess as well the labour as the force of his imagination."*

But the practice of such a language, as Dryden had repeatedly argued, was contingent upon a conception of tragedy which could justify it. Consequently, his admission in the prologue to *Aureng-Zebe* that he is weary of rhyme and that "Passion's too fierce to be in Fetters bound" is not primarily a confession of impatience with the heroic couplet itself—Dryden continued to use rhyme in other genres—but rather a critical recognition that the purpose of serious drama was changing and that therefore the artifice of rhyme could no longer exercise its proper function in the theatre.[11] The same principle of decorum by which Dryden had justified rhyme for the representation of grandeur and glory compelled him to acknowledge its inappropriateness for the portrayal of sentiment and piety.

In both its form and substance, therefore, *Aureng-Zebe* represents a turning point in Dryden's dramatic career; and the domesticity, senti-

mental characterizations and appeals to pity and tears which are evident in *Aureng-Zebe* become increasingly dominant in the plays which
immediately follow it: particularly in *All for Love* (1678) and *Troilus
and Cressida* (1679).[12] *All for Love* is professedly designed "to work
up the pity [of the original story] to a greater heighth . . ." (sig. b)
Octavia is introduced as a stock if uninviting symbol of the family and
the scene in which she appears *"leading Antony's two little Daughters"*
(sig. [F3]) is a paradigm of sentimental drama. Cleopatra, who complains that "Nature meant" her to be "A Wife, a silly harmless
houshold Dove, / Fond without art; and kind without deceit," (sig.
[G4]) is a drastically domesticated version of Shakespeare's heroine;
and Antony, who Dryden notes is not "altogether wicked, because he
could not then be pitied," (sig. b) is as different from Shakepeare's hero
as he is from the heroical hero of Dryden's earlier plays. Indecisive,
and the constant prey of conflicting sentiments, Antony is thrown by
the successive pleas of Ventidius, Octavia, Dolabella and Cleopatra
into alternating postures of grief and hope; and his capacity to assume
such postures with extravagance and tears becomes the final measure
of his heroism. Dryden describes him accurately in the prologue:

> *His Heroe, whom you Wits his Bully call,*
> *Bates of his mettle; and scarce rants at all:*
> *He's somewhat lewd; but a well-meaning [m]ind;*
> *Weeps much; fights little; but is wond'rous kind.*   (sig.χ)

To an extent, the description applies to every major character in the
play, all of whom, with the exception of Alexas, an unregenerate villain, demonstrate their worth by fighting little and weeping much.[13]

   Troilus and Cressida shows a similar orientation towards sentimental effects. Cressida, like Cleopatra, is made transparently faithful; and Troilus, like Antony, is portrayed in a series of tableaux of
grief and hope; Hector, the play's most exemplary character, numbers
as a principal heroic virtue his devotion as a husband and a brother.
All three characters, but especially the men, are distinguished by their
ability to feel compassion for one another. Hector is valiant, but Andromache's highest praise of him is that his "Soul is proof to all things
but to kindness." (sig. I2) Troilus, younger and more demonstrative
than Hector, shows his mettle by tears and distraction. During their
farewell scene he and Cressida *"both weep over each other,"* (sig. G)
and after Cressida kills herself to prove her fidelity to him, he demonstrates his own love by the extremity of his grief:

> . . . she dy'd for me;
> And like a woman, I lament for her:
> Distraction pulls me several ways at once,
> Here pity calls me to weep out my eyes;
> Despair then turns me back upon my self,
> And bids me seek no more, but finish here:
>   [*Sword to his breast.*   (sig. K2v)

The play's most celebrated scene, added by Dryden at the suggestion of Betterton, shows Troilus and Hector debating whether to surrender Cressida to the Greeks. The dispute has the same turns and counter-turns as the rhymed debates in Dryden's earlier plays, but the crux of the argument is now plainly the point of pity rather than the point of honor. After Troilus agrees to give Cressida up, Hector tells him, "I pity thee, indeed I pity thee," and Troilus answers:

> Do; for I need it: let me lean my head
> Upon thy bosome; all my peace dwells there;
> Thou art some God, or much much more then man!

In a final turn, Hector offers to fight to keep Cressida in Troy, but Troilus refuses: "That you have pitied me is my reward," and Hector concedes: "The triumph of this kindeness be thy own." (sig. F4v) [14]

The reward of pity and the triumph of kindness in *All for Love* and *Troilus and Cressida* are the natural results of the process which begins in *Aureng-Zebe*. There are specific resemblances between *Aureng-Zebe* and the later plays: the give and take of compassion between Indamora and Melisinda looks forward to the debates between Antony and Ventidius and between Hector and Troilus; Indamora's praise of Aureng-Zebe's capacity for pity anticipates Andromache's praise of Hector's responsiveness to kindness; Melisinda's abandonment is a model for Octavia's. But more important than the particular analogues is the major shift of emphasis in *Aureng-Zebe* which makes the later developments possible. Morat's conversion and the repudiation of his aspirations to personal glory, Aureng-Zebe's temperance and family loyalty, Melisinda's unrelieved distress, and the general disposition of all the exemplary characters to demonstrate their virtue through tears and compassion mark Dryden's distinct departure from his earlier ideals of heroic drama and pave the way for the stress upon domestic piety and compassion that characterizes both his own subsequent plays and the plays of the dramatists who succeeded him.

Dryden, of course, was not alone in creating this orientation, nor did

he exploit it as extensively as his younger contemporaries, Lee and Otway, but *Aureng-Zebe* is a testimony to his sensitivity to its dramatur-
gical consequences. In the history of the late seventeenth-century English theatre *Aureng-Zebe* stands out as an important anticipation of the
sentimental drama that flourished in the following century.

NOTES

1. *Lives of the English Poets*, ed. G. B. Hill (Oxford, 1905) , I, 360-61.
2. References to Dryden's plays are to the texts of the first editions.
3. For a full discussion of these points see my article, "Dryden, Corneille
   and the Heroic Play," *Modern Philology*, LIX (1962).
4. Aureng-Zebe uses similar language in condemning Nourmahal when he
   realizes that she is trying to seduce him:

   > Hence, hence, and to some barbarous Climate fly,
   > Which onely Brutes in humane form does yield,
   > And Man grows wild in Nature's common Field.   (sigs. H2-H2v)

   Cf. Montezuma's account of his wild upbringing (*The Indian Queen,* in
   Sir Robert Howard, *Four New Plays* [1665], sig. Z2v) and Almanzor's
   boast of kinship with the "noble Savage." (*The Conquest of Granada*,
   Part I, sig. [A4]) .
5. This change of focus is evident not only in the scenes and speeches that
   have been cited, but throughout *Aureng-Zebe*. Compassion is a constant
   touchstone of virtue in the play. During their first scene together Indamora tells Melisinda that because she is "Distress'd" herself, she "therefore can compassion take, and give," and Melisinda, in return, promises
   to "pay the charity" which Indamora has "lent [her] grief." (sigs. F, Fv)
   In a later scene, when their fates seem to have been reversed again,
   Melisinda remarks:

   > Madam, the strange reverse of Fate you see:
   > I piti'd you, now you may pity me.   (sig. [G4])

   Indamora praises Arimant for his "generous Pity" (sig. C4v) and tells
   Morat when she pleads for Aureng-Zebe's life:

   > Had Heav'n the Crown for *Aureng-Zebe* design'd,
   > Pity, for you, had pierc'd his generous mind.
   > Pity does with a Noble Nature suit:
   > A Brother's life had suffer'd no dispute.   (sig. [G3])

   Aureng-Zebe confirms Indamora's judgment by taking pity upon Nourmahal, who he thinks is his enemy, (sig. E) and upon the Emperor, who
   he knows has been his rival. (sig. I4v)
       All the virtuous characters, moreover, demonstrate their compassion by
   crying. Aureng-Zebe sheds tears when he first sees his father, (sig. C)
   and weeps as a means of earning Indamora's forgiveness after a quarrel.
   (sig. [I4]) Indamora kneels to Nourmahal in tears, (sig Lv) and weeps
   at Morat's death, as she explains to the jealous Aureng-Zebe in tribute
   to her own redemptive powers:

   > Those tears you saw, that tenderness I show'd,

> Were just effects of grief and gratitude.
> He di'd my Convert.   (sig. M)

Melisinda is described as "bath'd in tears" before the audience ever sees her, (sig. E4v) and the moment she does appear, Indamora greets her as a personification of grief:

> When graceful sorrow in her pomp appears,
> Sure she is dress'd in *Melisinda*'s tears.   (sig. F)

On one occasion Melisinda even delivers a lecture on the beneficence of tears:

> *Ind.* I'm stupifi'd with sorrow, past relief
> Of tears: parch'd up, and wither'd with my grief.
> *Mel.* Dry mourning will decays more deadly bring,
> As a North Wind burns a too forward Spring.
> Give sorrow vent, and let the sluces go.   (sig.[K4])

6. The emphasis upon family relationships throughout *Aurenge-Zebe* is notable. For the first time in Dryden's plays, family piety becomes an essential means of differentiating virtue and vice. The virtuous characters in the play are uniformly conscious of their domestic obligations. Aureng-Zebe, as we have seen, is the best of sons; Indamora promises to be the best of daughters-in-law; and Melisinda, as Dryden remarks of her in the dedication, is "*a Woman passionately loving of her husband, patient of injuries and contempt, and constant in her kindness, to the last. . . .*" (sig. *a*) On the other hand, the Emperor is loyal neither to his son nor to his wife; Morat is both unconstant and brutal to his wife; and Nourmahal, who boasts that "Love sure's a name that's more Divine than Wife," (Sig. G) entertains desires that are incestuous as well as unfaithful.

7. *Dryden* (London, 1881), p. 57.

8. With the exception of "A Defence of an Essay of Dramatique Poesie," quotations from Dryden's criticism are from the texts of the first editions, but I have also cited page references from *Essays of John Dryden*, ed. W. P. Ker, 2 vols. (Oxford, 1926). Quotations from "A Defence" are from Ker's text.

9. *John Dryden* (New York, 1932), p. 37.

10. *Critical Essays of the Seventeenth Century*, ed. J. E. Spingarn (Oxford, 1908), II, 101, 102.

11. Judging by the stage effects in *Aureng-Zebe* itself, and by the form of heroism the play supports, audiences began to demand a sense of illusion rather than of artifice, domesticated heroes whom they could sympathize with rather than admire. Under such circumstances, as Dryden seems increasingly to have realized, Sir Robert Howard's arguments were valid. Dryden fully disavowed the style of the rhymed heroic play in the preface to *Troilus and Cressida* (1679) and the dedication of *The Spanish Fryar* (1681); see Ker, I, 222-24, 245-47. For a discussion of the aesthetic consequences of this change of taste see Earl R. Wasserman, "The Pleasures of Tragedy," *ELH*, XIV (1947), 283-307.

12. The material of *Oedipus* (1679), which Dryden wrote in collaboration with Lee, was less amenable to sentimental treatment, although Dryden

made the most of his opportunities. Oedipus and Jocasta are reduced to figures of sensational distress, and a new sub-plot is introduced dealing with the pathetic circumstances of the lovers, Euridice and Adrastus.

13. The tears of the men in *All for Love* are especially conspicuous. Antony weeps three times onstage (sigs. C, [F4], I3v-[I4]) and once his "falling tear" is reported. (sig. D) Dolabella cries when Antony exiles him, (sigs. I3v-[I4]) and even Ventidius cries twice, once in grief for Antony (sig. C) and once in joy over Antony's family reunion:

> My joy stops at my tongue;
> But it has found two chanels here for one,
> And bubbles out above.   (sig. G)

14. In analyzing the aim of tragedy in the preface to *Troilus and Cressida*, Dryden says that ". . . *when we see that the most virtuous, as well as the greatest, are not exempt from . . . misfortunes, that consideration moves pity in us: and insensibly works us to be helpfull to, and tender over the distress'd, which is the noblest and most God-like of moral virtues*," (sig. a2v; Ker, I, 210) a statement which relates Dryden's growing concern with pity to contemporary benevolist theories. See R. S. Crane, "Suggestions toward a Genealogy of the 'Man of Feeling,'" *ELH*, I (1934), pp. 205-30.

ALINE MACKENZIE TAYLOR

❀

Venice Preserv'd

Although *Venice Preserv'd* is the play on which Otway's fame rests most securely, it has not received unqualified praise from his admirers. The highest eulogy of it is tempered with censure, if only a vague suggestion that despite its sweep and passion, there is something in it which is fundamentally not quite right. As to what this something is, there is not much agreement. Hazlitt, for example, thinks that the play is marred by "a voluptuous effeminacy of sentiment and mawkish distress, which strikes directly at the root of that mental fortitude and heroic cast of thought which alone makes tragedy endurable."[1] Mr. Bonamy Dobrée objects to Otway's "pity-mongering on behalf of love [which] undermines the emotional structure," and his "exploring not man's courage so much as his capacity for feeling, even for self-torture." The play "is unrelieved by any element of strong sanity," its dignity "resides almost wholly in Pierre, about whom there is really something fine. . . ." He adds: "The theme of unfortunate love bulks far too large in it, and though Belvidera supplies a necessary element, one cannot refrain from wishing her away."[2]

The root of the difficulty seems to be the political bias of what is otherwise a tragedy of private life. Behind Mr. Dobrée's criticism of *Venice Preserv'd* lies an irritation with a plot in which political events are decided by domestic issues. This same irritation is reflected in the

From *Next to Shakespeare: Otway's Venice Preserv'd and The Orphan* (Durham: Duke University Press, 1950), pp. 39-72. Reprinted by permission of Duke University Press.

opinion of Sir A. W. Ward. If Mr. Dobrée, like Hazlitt, wants conspiracy without sentiment, Ward wants romance without politics. "The
most striking and characteristic beauty of *Venice Preserved* [he says]
. . . consists . . . in the exquisitely natural tenderness of the love-
scenes between Jaffier and Belvidera, and in the consummate art of
the great scene in which she saves her father and the Senate." The
great flaw of the play lies in "the infusion of political virulence into
his 'historical' tragedy [which] could not but detract from its artistic
effect, and indeed is so grossly contrived as to give offence to any un-
prejudiced mind."[3] This is a serious charge against the play and includes in its scope more than the comic relief, against which many critics have raised deprecating voices. It implies that Otway has relied too
heavily upon the extraneous interest which contemporary political
events lent to his play, and that he did not succeed in welding this
occasional interest into an artistic unity. Ward's criticism brings out
clearly the discordant elements which it would seem no purely aesthetic point of view can reduce to harmony. A purely political point
of view is equally unsatisfactory. Sir Edmund Gosse complains that
"the only point in which any weakness can be traced [in the plot of
Venice Preserv'd] is the motive actuating Jaffier to join the conspirators. The revenge of a merely private wrong upon a whole commonwealth is scarcely sane enough for the dignity of tragedy."[4] In
1711 Joseph Addison had voiced nearly the same criticism.[5]

The nineteenth-century criticism of *Venice Preserv'd* leaves a baffled
reader unsatisfied. It fails to account for the former popularity of the
play, and it fails likewise to account for the conflicting impressions
which a modern reader derives from the text: the vigorous political
bias of the fable and the overlush sentiment of the domestic plot; the
farcical Nicky-Nacky scenes and the somber tone of the tragedy. Unless these conflicting impressions can be reduced to harmony, it is impossible to evaluate the dramatic effectiveness of *Venice Preserv'd*.

For the modern reader, the first great difficulty lies in finding a
point of view from which the principal characters may be seen in just
perspective against the background of the Spanish conspiracy in the
Venetian Republic. Two friends, Jaffier and Pierre, engage in the
plot to subvert Venice. Jaffier, under the influence of Belvidera, betrays both his friend and the conspirators to the senate—on condition
that their lives be spared. Pierre and the conspirators are condemned
to death. On the scaffold, Jaffier in atonement stabs first Pierre and

then himself. Belvidera goes mad. The conspiracy is crushed; the senate is saved. But are one's sympathies to lie with the bloodthirsty conspirators whom Jaffier and Pierre join, or with the perfidious senate that Belvidera saves? If with the conspiracy, how are Jaffier and Belvidera to be regarded? If with the senate, how Pierre? The turmoil of passions and conflict of interests do not seem to permit the reader's interpreting the whole play from any single point of view that the modern mind can easily assume. To regard the action through the eyes of one character in it, or to read into it one's own political views, leaves too much in the play unaccounted for.

Since *Venice Preserv'd* won royal favor at its *première*[6] and was stigmatized as a Tory play thereafter, it seems clear that the point of view from which the action may be seen to best advantage is that of its first audience. That point of view is by no means easy to determine. *Venice Preserv'd* was first performed in February, 1682, just as the panic and hysteria of the Popish Plot were beginning to subside and the political issues were becoming clear. It must have been composed during the crisis, while the nation was divided into factions, and political feeling was veering suddenly, as the fortunes of his Majesty rose and those of the Earl of Shaftesbury declined. At the time very few good heads in England could perceive the principles which were at stake, so much was obscured by the smoke of controversy. *Venice Preserv'd,* with its conflict of senate and conspirators, is bound up with the English political crisis of 1678-1682, and the interpretation of the play is determined by the fortunes of the King's party, whose manifesto it became.[7]

Otway was abroad with the army in the autumn of 1678,[8] when "Dr." Titus Oates's disclosure of the Horrid Popish Plot was substantiated by the murder of Sir Edmundbury Godfrey, the seizure of Edward Coleman's treasonable correspondence with the Père la Chaise, and the exposure of the Earl of Danby, which revealed an intrigue between Charles II himself and Louis that "agreed well with Coleman's letters." Otway returned to England early in 1679, to find the nation at the height of an anti-Catholic panic. A few very astute men, Charles II for one, may have surmised the truth. For the majority of Englishmen, the country was threatened by invasion from France, Spain, Ireland, and Wales; the King was to be murdered with particular ceremony; the city of London was to be fired; the protestants were to be put to the sword; and the Roman Catholic Church was to be reestablished. The Papists, Jesuits, and the Roman Catholic Duke of

York were at the bottom of the mischief; and under the influence of the terror, England became violently protestant and "Whig." Old Cavalier and old Parliamentarian alike were united by the terror of Rome, and the King stood practically alone, surrounded only by a small band of unpopular counselors. Otway, returning home to take up his old profession of making plays, could scarcely have found the condition of the nation encouraging. The theater was falling upon evil days. As Dryden put it, the Plot, like Pharaoh's lean kine, had swallowed up all the lesser plots of the stage. But if Otway was casting about for the subject of a new play, there was one ready to hand. In February, 1679, the popular panic had elicited a second edition of the English translation of Saint-Réal's *History of the Spanish Conspiracy against the State of Venice* (first edition, 1675).[9] The plot of the Spanish Marquis of Bedamar acquired topical interest from the plot divulged by Oates and described in countless pamphlets of the time. In the spring of 1679, however, Otway had other work on hand. He was busy preparing *Caius Marius* for the stage (D.G., August, 1679), in writing *The Poet's Complaint of His Muse* (published in February, 1680), and *The Souldiers Fortune* (D.G., March, 1806), and in finishing *The Orphan* (D.G., ca. March, 1680). By March, 1680, at least, he was free, and so it may be assumed that during the next two years he was engaged principally in composing *Venice Preserv'd* and seeing it through its first performance.

In March, 1680, the nation was dominantly Whig in sentiment. The followers of the Earl of Shaftesbury, it is true, had had one setback the preceding year. The trials and arrests and executions for treason, which followed Oates's disclosures, had culminated in the summer of 1679 when Sir George Wakeman, physician to the Queen, was acquitted by the Lord Chief Justice Scroggs, at some risk of personal danger from infuriated Whigs. Matters were quieting down for the Catholics, and emboldened by Wakeman's acquittal, they tried to turn the tables on their enemies. In October, 1679, they professed to discover a Presbyterian Plot against the state. They could scarcely have chosen a more inopportune time for their discovery. The Earl of Shaftesbury had been encountering some difficulties, as a result of the stand he took on Scottish affairs. In August, 1679, the Duke of Monmouth, who had been sent to Scotland to quell the Covenanters, returned victorious to England at the head of his army at the very moment that Charles lay seriously ill at Windsor. The peaceable part of the nation, thoroughly frightened by the royal illness and by the presence of the army, raised the cry that " 'Forty-one' is come again," and recoiled before the threat of civil war. The cleavage between monarchy men and parliament men, growing since March, 1679, when Shaftesbury and Halifax had quarreled, deepened, and Shaftesbury's adherents seemed to be losing some of their hold on the nation. This was the moment at which the Catholics came forward with their sham counterplot, the exposure of which fanned popular feeling against them once more and enabled Shaftesbury's party to recover its ground. Whig power was manifested in the elaborate Pope-burning of November 17, 1679. Whig strategy, outlined and rehearsed in the Green-Ribbon Club, crystallized in the Exclusion Bill and its alternatives, the schemes for the King's divorce and the royal acknowledgment of the Duke of Monmouth as heir to the crown. The second Whig Parliament, which finally met in October, 1680, had all the characteristics of a revolutionary assembly. After October, however, the tide began to turn slowly, though to all appearances Whig sentiment still dominated the country. When the Second Exclusion Bill was brought before the Houses in November, 1680, it found its real opponent in the Marquis of Halifax, who alone defeated it after fifteen debating speeches in which he answered his uncle, Shaftesbury, clause by clause, as the King lolled by the fireplace and listened. It was becoming clear that the real plot in the state emanated, not from the Romanist minority, but from the Whigs of whom Shaftesbury was the chief and Dr. Titus Oates the tool. Henceforward a party began to form around Charles and the Duke of York. In January, 1681, the King was able to prorogue the fractious Parliament.

While the battle raged in Parliament, one event occurred in the theater which is of some significance for Otway and *Venice Preserv'd*. Nathaniel Lee, who had come over to Dorset Garden about 1678 and produced there in succession three innocuous plays, took heart from the Whiggish temper of the times, and produced, in December, 1680, a play on the republican conspiracy in ancient Rome—*Lucius Junius Brutus*. Unfortunately for Lee, the Second Exclusion Bill had just been defeated in November; the time was scarcely auspicious for the dramatic representation of republican idealism. *Lucius Junius Brutus* was forbidden the stage on December 11, 1680, because of its "very Scandalous Expressions & Reflections upon ye Government"[10]—that is, upon Kings and their followers. In the interim of more than a year between the *premières* of *Lucius Junius Brutus* and of *Venice Preserv'd*, Otway had ample time to benefit by his fellow dramatist's fiasco.[11] During the course of 1681, moreover, political issues became much clearer. The Parliament at Oxford (March 21-28) left no doubt that the King's party had triumphed over the Earl of Shaftesbury's. After the debacle of March 28, the power of the Whigs was broken; in July their leader was arrested, and in November brought to trial—only to be acquitted by a packed jury. In November, 1681, the Tory poet laureate stated concisely, for all Englishmen to read, the political principles that were involved in the conflict of the past three years.

In treating the Spanish conspiracy against Venice, Otway set himself a most delicate task, that of trying to capitalize on popular sentiment at a time when it was veering wildly. The Spanish plot in Venice afforded an obvious parallel for the Popish Plot in England, but unfortunately the Popish Plot, which professed to be one thing, turned out to be something quite different, a sham plot masking a real one. If Otway conceived the plan of *Venice Preserv'd* on his return from the Continent in 1679, the idea of the conspiracy might well have engrossed his attention. By 1682, however, the Popish Plot was three years old; it was recognized as essentially a Whig plot against the royal prerogative, and the terrors it raised had given place to partisan feeling which concentrated upon the Earl of Shaftesbury and Charles II. If the modern reader of *Venice Preserv'd* finds it difficult to discover the point of view of the play, it may be well to remember that contemporary Englishmen, "pelted at with impudent, horrid libels," found it difficult to follow the course of events from 1679 to 1682, that many playwrights of the day tried to capitalize on public sentiment and to woo official favor, and that most of them succeeded only in having their plays forbidden the stage.[12] When so many others failed, *Venice Preserv'd* is all the more remarkable for its brilliant *première* and its continued popularity. In the secret of its success lies the clue to its interpretation.

> It has been observed by others, that this poet has founded his tragedy of Venice Preserved on so wrong a plot, that the greatest characters in it are those of rebels and traitors. Had the hero of his play discovered the same good qualities in the defence of his country, that he showed for its ruin and subversion, the audience could not enough pity and admire him: but as he is now represented, we can only say of him what the Roman historian says of Catiline, that his fall would have been glorious had he so fallen in the service of his country.[13]

Addison, perhaps, let his Whiggish prejudices color his criticism, and yet the objections he raised in 1711 go to the heart of the problem that

confronted Otway in composing *Venice Preserv'd*. How, in an age
when monarchy was absolute, and when a political crisis was dividing
England into factions, was it possible for a playwright to make both his
heroes conspirators against the state, evoke the sympathy of the audience for them, and yet not lay himself open to charges of sedition or
of republican idealism?

It is in the motivation of his conspirator-heroes that Otway came
squarely to grips with his problem. He kept the middle way between
two pitfalls, either of which might have ruined his play in 1682. His
two heroes engage in conspiracy, but on the one hand they avoid all
suspicion that they do so for political principle—which smacks of the
Good Old Cause, Innovation, and Whiggery—and, on the other, that
they do so for no principle at all—which would make them no better
than political malcontents, soldiers of fortune eager for the loot which
an upheaval in the state promises them. These conspirator-heroes have
principles, but their principles are personal and stem entirely from the
heroic code of honor. Political principles are thus transmuted into
personal motives, and ideals of personal conduct are completely detached from matters of state.[14]

In establishing the motives of Jaffier on purely personal grounds,
Otway faced a task not too difficult of accomplishment. Jaffier is a conspirator from personal emotion pure and simple. In the opening scene
he is shown in a violent altercation with Priuli, who nurses a three-year
feud with him. Jaffier, like Othello, had received as an intimate
into the house of the Venetian senator, and, having saved Belvidera's
life during the festivities of the Wedding of the Adriatic, had married
her without the consent of her unreasonable old father. For three years
thereafter he had taxed his "little fortune" to the utmost in order to
maintain a style which becomes a daughter of the great Priuli. When
the scene opens, he faces complete ruin and is apparently asking his
father-in-law to pay off his creditors. Priuli replies tartly:

> Home and be humble, study to retrench;
> Discharge the lazy Vermin of thy Hall,
> Those Pageants of thy Folly,
> Reduce the glittering Trappings of thy Wife
> To humble Weeds, fit for thy little state;
> Then to some suburb Cottage both retire;
> Drudge to feed loathsome life: Get Brats, and Starve—
> Home, home, I say—
>
>   (I, 104-111)

and he goes off abruptly. Jaffier, left alone, finds it extremely difficult
to keep his composure:

> Yes, if my heart would let me—
> This proud, this swelling heart: Home I would go,
> But that my Dores are hatefull to my eyes,
> Fill'd and damn'd up with gaping Creditors,
> Watchful as Fowlers when their Game will spring;
> I have now not 50 Ducats in the World,
> Yet still I am in love, and pleas'd with Ruin.
>   (I, 111-117)

In this mood Pierre finds him. His remark on Jaffier's melancholy
elicits a reply which sets him discoursing on the paradox that honesty
is a cheat. In the course of an argument, so adroit that Jaffier cannot
suspect he is being persuaded, Pierre recalls the theft of his own mistress and the injustice meted out to him by the senate on that occasion,
interspersing his account with telling references to the public abuses
with which his private wrongs are bound up. Chafing under personal
injury and unmerited disgrace, he is a conspirator out of resentment
rather than principle; and it is very important for the plot that he is
so. His pique influences Jaffier as no rational argument ever could, for
it strikes a sympathetic note and prepares him to lend a willing ear to
exhortations to vengeance, especially when Pierre's account of his own
grievances is followed immediately by a story that touches Jaffier more
nearly:

> I past this very moment by thy dores,
> And found them guarded by a Troop of Villains;
> The sons of public Rapine were destroying:
> They told me, by the sentence of the Law
> They had Commission to seize all thy fortune,
> Nay more, *Priuli*'s cruel hand hath sign'd it. . . .
>   (I, 232-237)

Jaffier is resigned to his fate, but Pierre continues:

> Curse thy dull Stars, and the worse Fate of *Venice*,
> Where Brothers, Friends, and Fathers, all are False;
> Where there's no trust, no truth; where Innocence
> Stoop's under vile Oppression; and Vice lords it:
> Hadst thou but seen, as I did, how at last
> Thy beauteous *Belvidera*, like a Wretch
> That's doom'd to Banishment, came weeping forth . . .
>   (I, 252-258)

Jaffier breaks down in tears. Pierre urges him to express himself in a different fashion: "Out with't, Swear a little—" (l. 296). Jaffier, wound up to the point of swearing, concludes with *"Priuli—is—a Senator!"*

PIERRE. A Dog!
JAFF. Agreed.
PIERRE. Shoot him.
JAFF. With all my heart.
No more: Where shall we meet at Night?
PIERRE. I'l tell thee;
On the Ryalto. . . .

(II, 299-302)

When the appointment is made, it is merely a matter of Pierre's so laying open the plot that Jaffier will not shy off suddenly, and he becomes a conspirator through his resentment of Priuli and his friendship for Pierre.

The importance of the part played by Pierre in persuading Jaffier to join the conspiracy can scarcely be exaggerated, for Jaffier's resentment would not have driven him to rebellion without the influence of the single-minded Pierre. "Now thanks Heav'n," he exclaims, when the news of the disaster is brought to him. "For what?" asks Pierre. "That I am not worth a Ducat" (l. 251). . . . "There's a secret Pride in bravely dying."

PIERRE. Rats die in Holes and Corners, Dogs run mad;
Man knows a braver Remedy for Sorrow:
Revenge! the Attribute of Gods, they stampt it
With their great Image on our Natures; dye!
Consider well the Cause that calls upon thee:
And if thou art base enough, die then: Remember
Thy *Belvidera* suffers: *Belvidera!*
Dye—Damn first—

(I, 285-292)

The cheerful matter-of-factness of Pierre's bravado is so irresistible that Jaffier is swept away by it and joins the conspiracy. No political principle at all is involved in his step.

Despite his talk about liberty and public wrongs, Pierre likewise is no political idealist. He has no truck with ideals at all; he is motivated simply by personal loyalties. The first words Jaffier addresses to him:

I'm thinking *Pierre,* how that damn'd starving Quality
Call'd Honesty, got footing in the World

(I, 123-124)

give Pierre an opening to discourse paradoxically on the natural wickedness of human nature and to point out that notions of virtue were
set up by a few clever wicked men as a means of keeping the many
foolish virtuous ones in convenient subjection:

> Why, pow'rful Villainy first set it up,
> For its own ease and safety: Honest men
> Are the soft easy Cushions on which Knaves
> Repose and fatten: Were all mankind Villains,
> They'd starve each other; Lawyers wou'd want practice,
> Cut-Throats Rewards: Each man would kill his Brother
> Himself, none would be paid or hang'd for Murder:
> Honesty was a Cheat invented first
> To bind the Hands of bold deserving Rogues,
> That Fools and Cowards might sit safe in Power,
> And lord it uncontroul'd above their Betters.
> JAFF. Then Honesty is but a Notion.
> PIERRE. Nothing else,
> Like wit, much talkt of, not to be defin'd:
> He that pretends to most too, has least share in't;
> 'Tis a ragged Virtue: Honesty! no more on't.

Jaffier, not a little startled by his friend's doctrine, asks, "Sure thou art
Honest?" "So indeed men think me," Pierre replies, and goes on to
explain that he is a rogue and a villain none the less,

> A fine gay bold fac'd Villain, as thou seest me;
> 'Tis true, I pay my debts when they'r contracted;
> I steal from no man; would not cut a Throat
> To gain admission to a great man's purse,
> Or a Whores bed; I'de not betray my Friend,
> To get his Place or Fortune: I scorn to flatter
> A Blown-up Fool above me, or Crush the wretch beneath me,
> Yet, *Jaffeir,* for all this I am a Villain.

> (I, 143-150)

Jaffier cannot comprehend the term "villain," and this occasions further explanation by Pierre:

> Yes a most notorious Villain:
> To see the suffering's of my fellow Creatures,
> And own my self a Man: To see our Senators
> Cheat the deluded people with a shew
> Of Liberty, which yet they ne'r must taste of;
> They say, by them our hands are free from Fetters,

> Yet whom they please they lay in basest bonds;
> Bring whom they please to Infamy and Sorrow;
> Drive us like Wracks down the rough Tide of Power,
> Whilst no hold's left to save us from Destruction;
> All that bear this are Villains; and I one,
> Not to rouse up at the great Call of Nature,
> And check the Growth of these Domestick spoilers,
> That make us slaves and tell us 'tis our Charter.
> (I,151-164)

In reply, Jaffier bursts out, rather irrelevantly:

> Oh *Aquilina!* Friend, to lose such Beauty,
> The Dearest Purchase of thy noble Labours;
> She was thy Right by Conquest, as by Love.
> (I, 165-167)

When *Venice Preserv'd* is taken in its entirety, Pierre can be regarded only as the cavalier, the gentleman-soldier motivated by the
code of honor. He joins the conspiracy to avenge a personal injury,
not an injustice meted out to him by the senate which has blighted his
career as a soldier, but something far more heroic. A senator has stolen
Pierre's mistress, Aquilina. The gentleman's code has been violated, for
when Pierre chastised him for his depredations a private quarrel became an issue of state:

> The matter was complain'd of in the Senate,
> I summon'd to appear, and censur'd basely,
> For violating something they call *priviledge*—
> This was the Recompence of my service:
> Would I'd been rather beaten by a Coward!
> (I, 194-198)

Pierre's obedience to the gentleman's code is declared by the senate to
be a violation of senatorial privilege; the privileges of gentlemen are
under fire from the political group in power—and what gentleman in
1682 would not rally to the defense?[15] Especially when Pierre continues:

> A Souldier's Mistress *Jaffier's* his Religion,
> When that's prophan'd, all other Tyes are broken,
> That even dissolves all former bonds of service,
> And from that hour I think myself as free
> To be the Foe as e're the Friend of *Venice*—
> Nay, Dear Revenge, when e're thou call'st I am ready.
> (I, 199-204)

Pierre in taking his revenge may be censured from the point of view of a modern liberal, but scarcely from that of seventeenth-century gentlemen for whom the play was written. Although the strict loyalist would have it that no loyal subject may avenge even the greatest injury upon the sacred person of the King, who according to both the Constitution and the theory of Divine Right can do no wrong, Pierre is not guilty of *lèse-majesté* in this personal sense—Antonio is only a senator.[16] Pierre and Jaffier plot against the state under the provocation of personal injury, but the state to them means Antonio and Priuli, and the satisfaction that they seek is only that which is sanctioned by the gentleman's code. That the motives which Otway assigns for their joining the conspirators are from the modern point of view highly personal and selfish would offer no difficulty for the cynical and disillusioned contemporaries of La Rochefoucauld.

Yet in establishing the motives of Pierre on purely personal grounds, Otway was not so successful as he was with Jaffier, for there still lingers more than a suggestion of political idealism about the stalwart, bold, plain-spoken soldier, the staunch but exacting friend. At the close of the play the reader may remain in some doubt whether Otway escaped entirely from the mold provided for Pierre by Brutus on the one hand, and by Cassius and the Captain Jacques Pierre of Saint-Réal on the other. Pierre's heroic motives are challenged at two points in the plot, and the final impression of his character does much to obliterate the impression created by the account of Aquilina and Antonio in the first act. Pierre's argument persuading Jaffier to join the conspiracy first impugns his heroic motive for revenge and suggests a note of political idealism in his character:

> Nay, It's a Cause thou wilt be fond of *Jaffeir*.
> For it is founded on the noblest Basis,
> Our Liberties, our natural Inheritance;
> There's no Religion, no Hypocrisie in't;
> Wee'l do the Business, and ne'r fast and pray for't:
> Openly act a deed, the World shall gaze
> With wonder at, and envy when it is done.
> JAFF.   For Liberty!
> PIERRE.   For Liberty my Friend:
> Thou shalt be freed from base *Priuli's* Tyranny,
> And thy sequestred Fortunes heal'd again:
> I shall be freed from opprobrious Wrongs,
> That press me now, and bend my Spirit downward:
> All *Venice* free, and every growing Merit

Succeed to its just Right: Fools shall be pull'd
From Wisdoms Seat; those baleful unclean Birds,
Those Lazy-Owls, who (perch'd near Fortunes Top)
Sit only watchful with their heavy Wings
To cuff down new fledg'd Virtues, that would rise
To nobler heights, and make the Grove harmonious.

(II, 153-171)

This argument is so curious a blend of the selfish and the idealistic
that it gives ample grounds for a reader who wishes to see in Pierre
either the "patriot" or the malcontent. The more it is scrutinized, the
more impossible it becomes not to ask the question, Why does Pierre
take such pains to secure Jaffier for his enterprise if neither political
ideal nor material gain is at stake, but merely revenge for a personal
injury? Otway tries to make it clear that Pierre brings Jaffier into the
conspiracy out of friendship. When he confronts Jaffier after the betrayal in the fourth act, he recalls the time

when first my foolish heart took pity
On thy misfortunes, sought thee in thy miseries,
Reliev'd thy wants, and rais'd thee from the State
Of wretchedness in which thy fate had plung'd thee
To rank thee in my list of noble friends,
All I receiv'd in surety for thy truth,
Were unregarded oaths; and this, this dagger,
Given with a worthless pledge, thou since hast stoln.

(IV, 355-362)

In the second act, when Pierre introduces Jaffier to the conspirators, it
is with the words,

I've brought my All into the publick Stock;
I had but one Friend, and him I'l share amongst you!

(II, 309-310)

In the third act Pierre's friendship is put to the test when he refuses to
listen to the well-grounded suspicions of Renault and champions his
already faithless friend against the entire body of conspirators as they
menace him with drawn swords. It may be supposed that the plain-
minded soldier Pierre thinks only of the heroic code of loyalty to
friends and revenge for personal injury, that he therefore regards it as
an office of friendship to bring Jaffier, injured like himself, over to the
conspirators.

But there is yet another point in the play at which Otway has had to

exert all his cunning to prevent Pierre from becoming a political idealist. As Pierre stands before the senate, betrayed to his death by the
man he has befriended, his staunchness may suggest that he has something more at heart than a personal grievance and personal loyalties
—in short, that he has a political ideal. Pierre's firmness and gallantry
under trial, combined with the perfidy of the senators—not to say of
Jaffier—win the greatest sympathy for him at the moment and do much
to discredit Jaffier. Otway has righted the balance by the subsequent
action of the play—Pierre's striking Jaffier across the face, an affront
that was unforgiveable according to the code of honor, and Jaffier's
atoning for his treachery by stabbing Pierre on the scaffold. Otway further dissipates the too great sympathy for Pierre by the pitiful fate of
Belvidera. But for the moment at least Pierre does rise to the heights
of the disinterested rebel before the perfidious senate. A note of political idealism is inherent in his character, and it is largely the emphasis
that Otway has put on Aquilina and Antonio in the first act that pre-
vents this note from becoming a dominant trait. Since the interpretation of Pierre as the Restoration Cavalier is bound up so closely with
Aquilina and Antonio, the analysis of his character cannot be complete
without a consideration of the Nicky-Nacky scenes, their political significance, and their relation to the main action of *Venice Preserv'd*.

The Nicky-Nacky scenes furnish one of the curiosities to be found
in the history of taste. Their popularity in their own day is attested by
the fact that they suggested the title for a poem by Mrs. Behn, "The
Cabal at Nickey Nackeys,"[17] and that they provoked a poem entitled
"Satyr" from a Whig who admired Shadwell.[18] By 1718, however,
Nicky Nacky had been banned the stage: "the miserable Farce *under
Plot*" of *Venice Preserv'd*, as Gildon remarked at that time, "has been
left out for many Years."[19] By 1784 Davies deplored "the necessity of
expunging what was written to please a court faction, but has become
in process of time, odious and disgusting."[20] The Nicky-Nacky scenes
appealed to audiences of Otway's own time but were damned by all
subsequent ones until the revival of the play in Paris in 1895, when
they were pronounced highly comic.

Whether or not the Nicky-Nacky scenes are comic is so much a matter of taste that those critics who have attempted to justify them on
grounds of their comic qualities must not be disputed. But it is a
curious reflection that this obscene and ribald subplot, which evoked
only disgust in the critics of the eighteenth century, should later have

raised an aesthetic problem. In 1779 Dr. Johnson judged *Venice Pre-serv'd* "a tragedy which still continues to be one of the favourites of the public, notwithstanding the want of morality in the original de-sign, and the despicable scenes of vile comedy with which he has diversified his tragic action."[21] In the nineteenth century, however, Taine could praise the Shakespearean quality of "la grande bouffonerie amère, le sentiment cru de la bassesse humaine,"[22] and Goethe, in a conversation with Henry Crabb Robinson, could say that "the comic scenes are particularly good. . . . It is they alone which account for, and go near to justify the conspiracy: for we see in them how utterly unfit for government the senate had become."[23]

Now, a skeptical reader may question whether Otway intended to justify rebellion by these scenes, as Goethe suggests, and thereby lay himself open to the charge of sedition and the certainty of having his play forbidden the stage by the Lord Chamberlain, as Lee did by his too great republican zeal in *Lucius Junius Brutus*. In 1682 a conspiracy against the state was not to be regarded with sympathetic eyes, though gentlemen might be involved in it, even the blood royal. Yet the Nicky-Nacky scenes do have a political significance. They contain a most venomous onslaught on the Earl of Shaftesbury and the closest and most deliberate political parallel in the play. Antonio—the name itself is but a contemptuous familiarity for Anthony Ashley Cooper[24] —is a "fine speaker in the Senate";[25] he is sixty-one years old (III, 40); and the scandals of his private life are well known to the Duke, and to Priuli, who treats him with marked contempt.[26] He loves to call his fellow senators by their titles (V, 122). He makes a fine speech about the existence of a plot in the state, which parodies ridiculously a reso-lution passed by the first Whig Parliament at the height of the Popish Terror. And there are more recondite allusions, such as the order to search the apartments of Aquilina "with decency" (IV, 203), which Davies declared was an allusion to "the search made in the Earl of Shaftesbury's apartments for treasonable papers. . . . The report given out was that a female friend of his lordship was discovered under his bed, or in a closet."[27] And lest the similarity between Antonio and Shaftesbury should be missed in performance, there is the Prologue, with its marked allusion to the King of Poland, to put the identity of the two beyond question.[28] It is very likely that, to Otway's first audi-ence, any artistic function these scenes may have had was of secondary importance to the satiric purpose—the savage pillorying of the first Earl of Shaftesbury. Yet the fact that they stand in the play as Otway left it

requires that they be considered as part of an artistic whole. It remains
to be seen whether Otway succeeded in making this ephemeral political
interest serve the artistic effect of his whole play.

The Nicky-Nacky scenes present a delicate problem in the analysis
of dramatic technique in its relation to the rapidly veering political
sentiment of the years from 1679 to 1682. In the original Prologue
Otway disclaimed any resemblance between the conspiracy of his play
and the recent plot in the state:

> In these distracted times, when each man dreads
> The bloudy stratagems of busie heads;
> When we have fear'd three years we know not what,
> Till Witnesses begin to die o'th'rot,
> What made our Poet meddle with a Plot?
> Was't that he fansy'd, for the very sake
> And name of Plot, his trifling Play might take?
> For there's not in't one Inch-board Evidence,
> But 'tis, he says, to reason plain and sense,
> And that he thinks a plausible defence.
> Were Truth by Sense and Reason to be tri'd,
> Sure all our Swearers might be laid aside:
> No, of such Tools our Author has no need,
> To make his Plot, or make his Play succeed. . . .

The disclaimer was judicious, for in 1682 the political implications of
the Marquis of Bedamar's conspiracy against the Republic of Venice
were very different from the implications of that conspiracy in 1679,
when the Popish Plot was generally accepted as being what Titus Oates
said it was. In 1682 political events had outstripped the significance of
the Spanish conspiracy, and political feeling was for the most part concentrated on the person of Lord Shaftesbury. Otway saved the topical-
ity of his play by bringing this feeling to a focus in the character of
Antonio, whose buffoonery with his mistress Aquilina forms the action
of the Nicky-Nacky scenes. "The black Bills," "the Spanish Pilgrims
cast a-shore in Wales," the "murther'd Magistrate," to which he refers
in the Prologue, were old matters, and of such tools he truly had no
need. In the Prologue he takes care to point out the elements in the
play to which he wishes his audience to attach a topical significance:
the "Army rais'd, though under ground"; the "Traitour . . . that's
very old,"

> Turbulent, subtle, mischievous and bold,
> Bloudy, revengefull, and to crown his part,
> Loves fumbling with a Wench with all his heart;

and finally, the "Senatour that keeps a Whore,"

> In *Venice* none a higher office bore; . . .
> Oh *Poland, Poland!* had it been thy lot,
> T'have heard in time of this Venetian Plot,
> Thou surely chosen hadst one King from thence,
> And honour'd them as thou hast *England* since.

The unmistakable allusion to Shaftesbury's recent "election" to the crown of Poland makes it clear that the senator Antonio and Shaftesbury are one. And few Tories who had read Dryden's *Absalom and Achitophel* three months earlier[29] would miss seeing in the traitor who is "turbulent, subtle, mischievous and bold," the sinister traits of Achitophel. From the Prologue it appears that, in February, 1682, Otway wished *Venice Preserv'd* to be regarded in the light, not of the conflict of conspiracy and senate, but of two characters, Antonio the senator and Renault the conspirator, both of whom represent the Earl of Shaftesbury.

The political significance of the Nicky-Nacky scenes, taken in themselves, is clear, and their function in the play with regard to the political sentiment of the day is understandable. But when these scenes are considered in relation to the political significance of the rest of the play, difficulties of interpretation arise on all sides. Unfortunately, it is this Prologue as much as anything else in the play that confuses the clear-cut political significance of the Nicky-Nacky scenes, the conspiracy, and the senate. Shaftesbury is represented not only by Antonio but by Renault as well, and this identification seems in effect to identify the conspiracy with the senate. But if there is no significance in the opposition of the senate and conspirators, there is no significance in Jaffier's betraying the conspirators, in Belvidera's saving the senate, in Pierre's loyalty to his comrades, and the whole play becomes politically little more than an elaborate hoax, the plot a house of cards that falls with the slightest breath of inquiry.

For a Tory audience of 1682, the identification of Shaftesbury with Antonio the Venetian senator and with Renault the French chief of plotters should have raised no difficulties. Antonio and Renault are different aspects of the same person, and there is a subtle political significance in this identification. Antonio ridicules Shaftesbury's open maneuvers in the Whig Parliament, which he controlled before March, 1681; Renault heightens the sinister and subterranean activities of the Whig chief in the notorious Green-Ribbon Club, where all the Whig strategy was worked out and rehearsed before it came to light in the swift maneuvers of the Whigs in Parliament. Furthermore, Shaftesbury as leader of the Whigs was heir to the political theory of the Commonwealth. In this theory, the senate of the Venetian Republic had long served as a model for improving the English government.[30] Shaftesbury himself was suspected of trying to remodel Parliament after the fashion of the Venetian senate and to reduce the functions of the King to those of the Doge—as Dryden put it, to "melt him to that golden calf, a state."[31] Venice was inextricably bound up with the ideas of parliamentary government and liberty, as opposed to monarchy and the royal prerogative.[32] But there is an even subtler significance. The identification of Shaftesbury with both the Venetian senator and the French plotter finds its *raison d'être* in the Tory argument which identified the political principles of Covenanter, Cromwellian, or Whig, with the political principles of the Liguers in the French wars of religion.[33] The corollary to this argument was propounded after the Parliament at Oxford by those Tory pamphleteers who were pleased to see in the horrid Popish Plot nothing but a mask for a Whig plot against the royal prerogative. The two groups, Whig Plotter and Popish Plotter, Cromwellian and Liguer, might be distinct as groups, but there was nothing to distinguish them in ideology; they held the same principles and called them by different names. Consequently, against Shaftesbury's Whig Parliament and his Green-Ribbon Club, as against Antonio and his Venetian senate and Renault and his plot, conspiracy lost all taint of treason, and treachery most of its odium.

Antonio and Renault are obverse and reverse of the same coin; between them there is nothing to choose. Neither character wins any sympathy for the party he represents, but on the contrary each contributes to its odiousness. If this identification of Antonio and Renault with Shaftesbury confuses the political allegory for the modern reader, it nonetheless contributes to that shifting of our ill wishes between senate and conspirators, which Henry Hallam noted as a defect in the play when we read it, "though it does not, as is shown by experience, interfere with the spectators' interest."[34] It has indeed a subtle artistic purpose, for it distracts attention from the fable, with the dangerous political implications of the conspiracy against the state, and concentrates it on the plot, the swaying back and forth of the emotions of love, friendship, and filial affection which leads to the "full repose" of the catastrophe.[35] If Renault and Antonio both represent Shaftesbury, one takes sides with neither conspirators nor senate and condemns neither Pierre and Jaffier for joining the conspiracy nor Belvidera for saving the senate. All sympathy becomes divorced from the political opponents and rests with the three principals, in their misfortunes representative of the respectable, peaceable part of the nation, who are caught in the circumstances produced by a gigantic fraud and forced into courses of action that they would never have taken if left to their own devices.

This shifting of our ill wishes between senate and conspiracy is essential to the emotional structure of the plot. It is intensified by Antonio, but it does not depend on him. The cruelty of Priuli and the treachery of Renault, the blood-thirstiness of the conspirators and the perfidy of the senate are adequate motivation for ill wishes toward each body. Hence, when the animosities aroused by Lord Shaftesbury had subsided, Antonio and the Nicky-Nacky scenes could be removed from the play, and the main action would sustain only the slightest injury. Pierre, however, acquired an unwonted political significance and emerged as the republican idealist of the stage.[36]

Mr. Dobrée has remarked that even if Otway "included the farcical [Nicky-Nacky] scenes at the King's request, he did not feel that they were amiss as part of his structure."[37] In view of the political temper of 1682, they are a necessary part of the structure. They bear witness to the consummate craftsmanship of Otway who thus capitalized on an ephemeral political feeling, gave it the significance of a political argument, and wrought the extraneous element so cunningly into the texture of his play that it served the artistic effect of the whole.

The plot of *Venice Preserv'd* is so contrived that the audience's ill wishes for both the senate and the conspiracy sway back and forth with the alternate triumph of love or friendship or filial affection. Attention is consequently distracted from the political conflict and focused on the conflict of emotions in which the three principal characters are destroyed. As the plot develops, it becomes clear that each of these characters is dominated, as it were, by a *passion maîtresse*. Pierre acknowledges a friendship for Jaffier that induces him to bring his friend into the conspiracy and a soldier's honor that keeps him loyal to his conspirator comrades. Belvidera, who at the opening of the play is the almost passive object of Jaffier's love, as well as the real object of the injuries intended Jaffier by Priuli and by Renault, is thereafter impelled to act by filial devotion. Jaffier, smarting under the injury first of Priuli and then of Renault, is torn between love for Belvidera and friendship for Pierre. Although Belvidera becomes so powerful under

Otway's hands that she decides the fate not only of Venice but of the other characters as well, Jaffier, in whom the conflicting emotions of love and friendship find their battleground, is the central character of the play.[38] The swaying back and forth of his emotions is accompanied by the alternating supremacy of Pierre and Belvidera in deciding his actions. It is made concrete in a tangible object, the dagger, which, as it passes from Jaffier to Renault, then to Pierre, and back to Jaffier, becomes by virtue of its associations an indispensable adjunct to the plot, the heroic element in Jaffier's emotions, and the symbol of his word of honor.

In the first act love and friendship are in a harmonious equilibrium. Belvidera and Pierre have equal but unconflicting claims to Jaffier's attention, and it is not until Pierre has roused Jaffier to a sense of his injuries and to the proper manner of resenting them, that the balance seems likely to be overset. Pierre secures Jaffier's acquiescence to the notion that Priuli should be shot, and makes the appointment to meet on the Rialto at midnight; but Pierre, as it appears later, is by no means confident of his success (II, 77-78). Belvidera's entry, after Pierre's departure, confirms Jaffier's sense of injury and his conviction that Pierre was right. He must attempt, cost what it may, to spare her the fate Priuli has prepared.

The second act opens with an irrelevant scene between Pierre and Aquilina, in the course of which he repudiates her and announces that she is to keep Antonio from prying about the house, that he has friends coming, and that she is to "give order that whoever in my name /Comes here, receive Admittance." Although her house shelters the conspirators, it is clear that she is not of their councils. The scene shifts to the Rialto. Jaffier, alone, is haunted by a sense of the desperateness of his midnight meeting, and Pierre on arriving senses his state immediately. He opens his business by asking after Belvidera and gives Jaffier a purse with the debonair comment that "Marriage is Chargeable." Jaffier accepts it as though it were a bribe. Pierre asks pertinently whether Priuli has relented, and when Jaffier winds up the imprecations which this question evokes with "oh for a curse to kill with," Pierre remarks simply, "Daggers, Daggers are much better." Jaffier gives a startled "Ha!" and Pierre repeats, "Daggers."

JAFF.   But where are they?
PIERRE.   Oh, a Thousand
    May be disposed in honest hands in *Venice.*
JAFF.   Thou talk'st in Clouds.

> PIERRE.   But yet a Heart half wrong'd
> As thine has bin, would find the meaning, *Jaffeir* [*sic*].
>   (II, 124-127)

Jaffier either cannot, or will not, find the meaning, and his reply fore-shadows the catastrophe of the play:

> A thousand Daggers,   all in honest hands;
> And have not I a Friend will stick one here?
> PIERRE.   Yes, if I thought thou wert not to be cherisht
> To a nobler purpose, I'd be that Friend.
>   (II, 128-131)

Jaffier is now more than half committed, it seems to Pierre, who goes straight to the business in hand. If Jaffier will pledge himself to secrecy, he shall know where those friends are who can wield the thousand daggers. And as the scene closes, the two go out together, Pierre secure of his proselyte.

The mention of the dagger marks the first step in the ascendancy of Pierre over Jaffier, but the equipoise between Jaffier's love for Belvidera and his friendship for Pierre is not overset until Pierre introduces him to the conspirators as a friend who knows the details of the matter in hand. The conspirators receive the news in consternation: "How! all betray'd." Pierre reassures them by saying that he wears "a Dagger here," and that if the conspirators find Jaffier worthless after they have "seen and searcht," he will recover the secret by stabbing his friend. At that, Jaffier enters *"with a Dagger."* The conspirators greet him with coolness, not to say with mistrust and hostility (l. 332)—all save Bedamar. Jaffier assures them of the deeds he will perform, while Renault takes his measure and remarks, "You talk this well, Sir" (l. 331). "Nay," replies Jaffier, "—by Heav'n I'l do this," and boasts for nine lines, until Bedamar out of admiration embraces him. Renault remarks coolly, "I never lov'd these huggers" (l. 342). To win Renault's approv l, Jaffier sacrifices love to friendship in a manner which astonishes others besides Bedamar (l. 353). He hands Belvidera over to the Ambassa 'or and his lieutenant as a hostage for his good behavior, and with 'er his dagger. Completely confounded by this inexplicable behavior, Belvidera is led away by Bedamar and Renault, breaks from them begging for an explanation, and is recaptured and dragged off the stage. The second act comes to a close in this sensational scene, which signifies the triumph of friendship over love in their contest for Jaffier's loyalty.

The resentment which under the influence of Pierre drove Jaffier to the conspirators yields shortly to a second resentment which under the influence of Belvidera drives him from them, and the third act represents this swing back of the pendulum. It opens with a noisy scene between Antonio and Aquilina, and when peace is restored to the house by the ejection of Antonio, Belvidera enters to lament Jaffier's strange treatment of her and to inform the audience of Renault's attempt to violate his trust. Jaffier finds her, and, in the long scene which follows, he listens to her reproaches, and at last under her persuasions reveals the conspiracy, urging her to await its outcome patiently. The effect on Belvidera is swift and decided. Her father as a senator is to be murdered in the universal massacre, and she exercises all her power to save his life. She has one trump card, and she plays it to the best advantage —but not at once. She first points out—with good reason—that the men Jaffier is associating with are "such a crew" as "take a Ruffian's Wages, to cut the Throats of Wretches as they sleep" (l. 164). Jaffier, impervious to reason, insists that he has "engag'd/With Men of Souls: fit to reform the ills/Of all Mankind" (l. 167 ff.). Belvidera retorts with a question about Renault and finally reveals his perfidy. Jaffier's whole outlook suffers a sudden change, and, in the shock of revelation, he promises to take her out of the clutches of such iniquity. Just as Pierre won his friend to the side of the conspirators once he appointed to meet him, so Belvidera has won her point once Jaffier promises to come for her "at Twelve," thereby inadvertently revoking his pledge of fidelity to the conspirators. The dagger, symbol of that pledge, remains in the hands of Renault, however, and serves to motivate subsequent action.[39]

While Jaffier is still under the influence of Belvidera's last words, Pierre finds him, hears about Renault, and is rightly shocked. The announcement that Bedamar has commissioned Renault to take charge of the proceedings at the second meeting only intensifies Jaffier's sense of outrage. When Renault appears, Jaffier menaces him with words of faintly veiled enmity. The conspirators enter, and Jaffier suddenly realizes what he was not before aware of, that he is

> beset with cursed Fiends,
> That wait to Damn me: What a Devil's man,
> When he forgets his nature. . . .
>   (II, 302-304)

As Renault takes charge of the meeting and gives orders for slaughter and bloodshed for its own sake, Jaffier, hearing for the first time the details of the plot, is so horrified and revolted that his confusion is observed (l. 355). A few minutes later he steals from the assembly. His departure arouses the suspicions of the conspirators, and when Renault's harangue is finished, they surround Pierre menacingly. As Renault, who has divined Jaffier's purpose, says significantly, "I wear a dagger" —the same that Jaffier had given him with Belvidera—and adds, "I could wish it buried in his heart," Pierre, staunch friend that he is, snatches Jaffier's dagger from Renault, hides it in his own tunic, drives Renault from the scene, and cows the other conspirators into making their peace. The full irony of Pierre's loyalty is brought out in the following scene, for Jaffier, led by Belvidera, is on his way to the senate, where he is to give a full account of the conspiracy.

Up to this point, the opening of the fourth act, love and friendship, represented in the persons of Belvidera and Pierre, have alternated in their supremacy. Now love triumphs momentarily as Jaffier hands over an account of the conspiracy, with a list of the conspirators and thus confirms the intelligence that Priuli has already had from some "unknown hand" (IV, 110-128).[40] Jaffier makes one condition: that he himself is to receive full pardon and the lives of the conspirators are to be spared. But no sooner has he revealed the plot than he begins to repent it. As he is led away, it is clear that the two emotions which have held alternate sway over him are coming to a sharp conflict. The crisis comes when Jaffier is led back on the stage to confront Pierre. The two are brought face to face, and Pierre mistakenly thinks that Jaffier is sharing their general fate. When he learns that Jaffier has betrayed them, he casts the traitor off and demands honorable death of the senators. As the conspirators file out, Jaffier rushes to Pierre, and pleads. Pierre in reply strikes him across the face and flings down the dagger he took from Renault when he defended his friend's good faith. Pierre's action, his scorn for Jaffier and his contempt for his own life should he owe it to a traitor, succeeds in unnerving Jaffier and marks the final stage in the conflict between love and friendship.

As Jaffier takes up the dagger, his sense of violated faith to Pierre comes into mortal conflict with the influence of Belvidera. When Belvidera appears, he describes to her his interview with Pierre; he dwells on the humiliation of it, and his self-abasement is almost pathological. Belvidera urges him to forgive his friend, especially since Pierre has been sentenced to die on the wheel. Jaffier's nerves are screwed to the cracking point, and he wreaks his feelings on Belvidera. She was the pledge of his good faith, and she persuaded him to revoke that pledge, to betray his friend to death. Honor requires that she shall atone for it. And the dagger which was the symbol of his worthless pledge must do the work. In the course of a long and overlush scene, he makes three vain attempts to stab her. The scene closes on his commanding her to use her influence with her father to save Pierre's life. Belvidera succeeds in her mission, but Priuli's intervention comes too late to save Pierre. Jaffier seeks her out, but it is only to part. As he enters, with the dagger in his hand, she senses his purpose and pleads with him to stay—or at least to leave his dagger with her—but he replies, "Resolve to see me go or see me fall." The bell tolls for the execution, and he rushes out to find Pierre on the scaffold. The two friends are reconciled, and Pierre requests one last favor of Jaffier, who engages immediately to sacrifice Belvidera. But that is not Pierre's intention; it is that Jaffier should atone for his treachery by saving him from a felon's death. Jaffier stabs Pierre to the heart with the dagger which was the token of his broken faith. Then he stabs himself, and the scene closes with the triumph of friendship.[41] Belvidera, the innocent cause of the disaster, goes mad with the horror of it, and Priuli is left a prey to grief and remorse.

It was with good reason that Charles Gildon in the early eighteenth century singled out *Venice Preserv'd* as a great example of neoclassic dramatic theory.[42] Any summary of the action brings to mind Dryden's words, that "every alteration or crossing of a design, every new-sprung passion, and turn of it, is a part of the action, and much the noblest, except we conceive nothing to be action till the players come to blows."[43] The plot of *Venice Preserv'd* has for its theme the heroic conflict of love and friendship, but every possible variation is played upon that theme until the harmony is brought to the "full repose" in the deaths of Jaffier, Pierre, and Belvidera. There is no great variety among the emotions that are evoked but a subtle change of tension in a few dominant ones. The unity of effect is concentrated in the conflict of heroic sentiment, so that not even the ribald Nicky-Nacky scenes can dissipate it.

Dryden gave it as his opinion that "the painting of the hero's mind" was more "properly the [dramatic] poet's work than the strength of his body,"[44] and that the hero of a tragedy was the one on whom the pity and terror were principally, if not wholly, founded.[45] Otway's heroes were interpreted many times during the next two centuries, and some of these interpretations show curiously whither Dryden's theory was leading. For Otway's own audience, Pierre and Jaffier could appear

only as two gentlemen, pushed to the extreme and engaging in conspiracy as the only possible alternative to dying like rats in holes. Beyond that, Pierre figures very well as the cavalier soldier of fortune,
and Jaffier as the heroic lover, "whose Swellings and Blustring upon
the Stage," as Addison sarcastically put it, "very much recommends
them to the fair Part of their Audience."[46]

Jaffier, however, is not so much the heroic lover that he became out-
moded when the fashion changed. He figures quite well as the man of
feeling, the *schoene seele,* too delicate to cope with the gross realities
of life. "Tell me why, good Heav'n," he exclaims in the first act,

> Thou mad'st me what I am, with all the Spirit,
> Aspiring thoughts and Elegant desires
> That fill the happiest Man? Ah! rather why
> Didst thou not form me sordid as my Fate,
> Base minded, dull, and fit to carry Burdens?
> Why have I sence to know the Curse that's on me?
> Is this just dealing, Nature?
>   (I, 308-314) [47]

Jaffier, the man of feeling, found favor with those audiences whose
taste was formed in the school of Richardson. It is an interpretation
which accompanies the spread of Lord Shaftesbury's ideas of virtue and
which finds its best expression in the lines of Lord Lyttelton:

> In wretched Jaffier, we with pity view
> A mind to honour false, to virtue true.
> In the wild storm of struggling passions tost,
> Yet saving innocence, though fame was lost;
> Greatly forgetting what he ow'd his friend—
> His country, which had wrong'd him, to defend.[48]

Although this interpretation may be wrested from the text, it finds
no favor with the modern reader—indeed, it only serves to damn Jaffier further in modern eyes. This hero, Jaffier, who joins a conspiracy
from purely personal motives, and who betrays it for the same, is he
not something worse than a rebel and a traitor? Is he not a weakling,
a selfish and vindictive sentimentalist devoid of all moral fiber? What
is the mildest judgment that can be passed on a hero whose boastful
efforts to dispel the mistrust of a band of strangers and desperadoes he
would fain make one of, conclude with words of pathetically baffled
egotism:

> Oh did you but know me,
> I need not talk thus!
>
> (II, 339-340)

who of his own free choice hands his wife over as a pledge for his good faith to men he has never seen before; who announces to her that he is going to kill her father and adds complacently,

> How rich and beauteous will the face
> Of Ruin look, when these wide streets run blood;
> I and the glorious Partner's of my Fortune
> Shouting, and striding o'er the prostrate Dead;
> Still to new waste; whilst thou, far off in safety
> Smiling, shalt see the wonders of our daring;
> And when night comes, with Praise and Love receive me
>
> (III, ii, 143-149)

who on turning informer, can find space in his remorse to ruminate upon himself—

> I've done a deed will make my Story hereafter
> Quoted in competition with all ill ones:
> The History of my wickedness shall run
> Down through the low traditions of the vulgar,
> And Boys be taught to tell the tale of *Jaffeir* [*sic*]
>
> (IV, 207-211)

who meets his friend's contempt for his treachery with the protest,

> I have not wrong'd thee, by these tears I have not.
> But still am honest, true, and hope too, valiant;
> My mind still full of thee: therefore still noble
>
> (IV, 304-306)

and who finally, turning on his wife in a torrent of vindictive fury, tells her she is responsible for his bad faith and *"offers to stab her again"* (IV, 515)?

The sentimental interpretation of Jaffier suppresses all his bolder and more heroic traits. It may serve as an ironic commentary on Dryden's notion of what a hero should be. But the modern attitude not only repudiates everything sentimental, it ignores all the heroic conventions as well. In *Venice Preserv'd* political issues are treated as merely an extension of Jaffier's domestic concerns. Jaffier is molded to the will of Belvidera; he joins the conspiracy as an alternative to imposing his ruined fortunes on her; he betrays the conspiracy under her persuasions. And by a strange perversity, Belvidera becomes the pawn in Jaffier's game of politics. From the modern point of view, Jaffier's relation to Belvidera is utterly impossible. A wife cannot be chattel security for a man's good faith, and ever since 1770, protests have been raised against Belvidera's being given as a hostage to Renault.[49] On the other hand, to those who find the conspiracy glorious in itself, Belvidera's influence over Jaffier is pernicious—a rebel like Lord Byron called her "that maudlin bitch of chaste lewdness and blubbering curiosity . . . whom I utterly despise, abhor, and detest."[50] To a writer like Mrs. Parsons, the tragedy of *Venice Preserv'd* is "the shame and downfall brought upon an originally noble nature, by excessive uxoriousness—a unique theme . . . in acting drama."[51] Very few modern readers would agree with Lord Lyttelton's estimate of Belvidera and Jaffier;[52] fewer still would see Belvidera and Jaffier from the point of view of an age when a monarch held councils of state in his mistresses' drawing-rooms, when a secret treaty could be negotiated by a clever woman, when a royal mistress could be indicted as a political nuisance.

It is difficult for the modern reader, brought up on the democratic ideal of the individual's responsibility for his share in the government, to maintain the mood of political irresponsibility and detachment which is necessary if the conspiracy of *Venice Preserv'd* is to be regarded in the light of Jaffier's personal sentiments. Indeed, it has been the fate of *Venice Preserv'd* as a stage play that the senate and the conspiracy have taken their political coloring from contemporary events. As a result, the heroes, instead of imposing a personal interpretation on the political issues in the play, have had a political interpretation imposed upon them and have been regarded as villainous or glorious, according to the political sympathies of the critic and audience. Either judgment must necessarily obscure much in a tragedy whose real significance is to be found only when a balance of sympathy is maintained among the three principal characters—a balance which is maintained only when ill wishes shift freely back and forth between senate and conspirators.

"I will not defend everything in his *Venice Preserved*," Dryden wrote in 1695, "but I must bear this testimony to his memory, that the passions are truly touched in it, though perhaps there is somewhat to be desired, both in the grounds of them, and in the height and elegance of expression; but nature is there, which is the greatest beauty."[53] Otway's verse has at different times been praised for its naturalness, censured for its vulgarity, or condemned for its bombast; and in the present day, Mr. Bonamy Dobrée has said that "one thing, and one thing only could have saved [*Venice Preserv'd*]—a higher poetic potential."[54]

For the reader who comes to Otway in the study, the verse is undistinguished enough. In 1757, however, a critic declared that Otway's "striking passages were in every mouth," and in 1779 Dr. Johnson repeated the statement.[55] From 1701 to 1790 innumerable passages culled from his plays made their appearance in collections of "Natural and Sublime Thoughts." But a modern reader, who leafs through these collections looking for poetry phrased with the matchless melody and simplicity of the Elizabethans, finds only platitudes. There are Chamont's speech on the hag, which Addison praised, Castalio's speech on absence, and Pierre's speech on Liberty; but removed from their context in the plays, they appear sadly wanting in style and in imagination. Clearly it was the actor's influence, his delivery behind the footlights, and not the critics' study of the printed page, which won so large a place for Otway in the Elegant Extracts of the century.[56]

Otway intended his verse to be spoken by certain actors in Betterton's Company;[57] it was adapted to a particular style of acting; its full effect can be recaptured only by conjuring up the conditions under which it was originally delivered. A musician once said that it was impossible to set Shelley's poetry to music, the verse itself having such melody that musical notation could only detract from it. And it is significant that the words of many of the Elizabethan madrigals, supremely lovely when sung with the arabesques of counterpoint and "division sweet," seem poor things when read aloud from the cold print, the voice of the singers departed. Different styles of acting and of stage delivery from those of Betterton's Company at Dorset Garden must inevitably have modified the effect produced by Otway's verse and indirectly influenced critical opinions of it. It may be impossible in reading the plays to recapture the effect his verse produced when it was spoken by great actors and actresses, trained in all the refinements of elocution; but it is possible to regard his verse primarily as a vehicle for the actor, something intended to reach the ear directly through the medium of the actor's voice.

Gildon once remarked that Mrs. Barry could never pronounce the words "Ah! poor Castalio!" without tears;[58] but her tears, one may well believe, arose from the situation and not from the words themselves. Otway's phrases, apart from the situations in which they take their rise, have little to recommend them. His verse is "dramatic." There is nothing purely poetic, such as modern readers of Shakespeare and Webster have been taught to seek in poetic plays. Even the "rants" had their place in a style of acting which placed more emphasis on elocution than on pantomime. But if Otway's verse takes its significance from the situations of his plays, here again the mere reader faces a difficulty. As Dryden pointed out, Otway may succeed in touching the passions, but there is "somewhat to be desired" not only in the expression of those passions but also in "the grounds of them."

In Otway's situations there is an unresolved conflict between heroic convention and domesticity. Two decades after Dryden wrote his criticism, Addison pointed out that

> Otway has followed nature in the language of his tragedy, and therefore shines in the passionate parts, more than any other of our English poets. As there is something familiar and domestic in the fable of his tragedy, more than in those of any other poet, he has little pomp, but great force, in his expressions.[59]

In the present day Mr. Bonamy Dobrée says, "he stands out from his contemporaries—he is probably the most read of them nowadays—because he is less artificial than they are."[60] Less artificial than his contemporaries Otway certainly is, yet it must be said of both *The Orphan* and *Venice Preserv'd* that their naturalness is rooted in artificiality. Both plays are built upon central situations which are pre-eminently artificial: the gay rake Polydore with his superstitious regard for marriage and his substitution for Castalio, Jaffier's giving Belvidera to the conspirators as hostage for his loyalty. In Otway's plays the heroic is disintegrating under the weight of the pathetic but the heroic convention is nonetheless a powerful influence; between it and the pathetic, though there may be a truce, there cannot be a peace. The very naturalness of speech and sentiment stands over against the sensationalism of the plot of *Venice Preserv'd*: the fatal dagger which dominates the crucial actions, the tolling bell for Pierre's execution, which invariably struck terror to the hearts of eighteenth-century audiences,[61] and the public execution with Jaffier's last office of friendship on the scaffold. This inherent artificiality of plot is a complete antithesis to its domesticity—the ruined fortunes of Jaffier, the malleability of his temper which makes him so susceptible to the influence of Pierre and of Belvidera. This antithesis is at the bottom of the great diversity of opinion

about Otway's plots and verse. The eighteenth century saw the domesticity and naturalness. "There is nothing more moving than the Loves
of Belvidera and Jaffier," Charles Gildon said;[62] Davies felt that "the
conjugal affection of Belvidera, in circumstances of the most trying
nature, is the boast of the English stage";[63] and Mrs. Inchbald re-
echoed their sentiments:

> The connubial state of Jaffier and Belvidera causes that
> sympathy in their grief from beholders, which neither
> the harmonious numbers of the poet, nor the exquisite
> acting of the performers, could awaken, merely on the
> part of two lovers.[64]

Among complacent, middle-class Victorians, however—the most domesticated of people—few would agree that a bankruptcy might be
revenged by a conspiracy, or that a wife was proper security for a man's
good faith. The very fact that Jaffier regards his political life as no
more than a projection of his private and domestic affairs—a perfectly
understandable arrangement for the king of a heroic play, or for
Charles II—raises difficulties for more earthbound spirits. Where older
critics saw naturalness and domestic virtues, modern critics see only
bombast, artificiality, and excessive sentiment. The taste of their times,
which permits them to see certain qualities in Otway's work, has
blinded them completely to others.

The "natural artificiality" of Otway's plots is reflected in his style.
Although his verse is as colloquial as it may be without becoming
prose, there are long passages which undoubtedly provided ranting
actors with an opportunity to step forward and declaim. There are also
triplets and couplets, which enabled them, at the close of the scene, to
rime themselves harmoniously off the stage. Both the rants and the
rimes are glaringly out of harmony with "natural verse" and with
natural acting. For the full effect of Otway's verse, as well as of his
situations, the balance between the natural and the artificial must be
kept true. That balance could be maintained only when the actor's
style was declamatory rather than pantomimic, formal rather than
realistic, when it gave full weight to the heroic as well as to the natural
in sentiment. Hence it is that Otway's plays were least popular with
the Ryans, the Keans, the Macreadys, most successful with the Better-
tons, the Wilkses, the Kembles, and with Garrick, who, naturalistic as
he sometimes was, yet inherited the grace and dignity of that vanish-
ing *beau monde* of which Otway's plays were one expression, when

gentlemen were "grace incarnate, far from the boor now hustling us in another sphere; beautifully mannered, every gesture dulcet." The naturalness of Otway has its roots in the highly artificial conventions which formed no small part of the life of the Restoration world. If his verse fails to produce any great effect in the study, one may well believe that it was intended to produce an effect nowhere but in the playhouse, and if changes in taste have had much to do with estimates of his verse, so also different styles of acting—themselves a manifestation of the taste of their day—have contributed their share to those estimates.

NOTES

1. *Lectures on the Literature of the Age of Elizabeth* (*Works,* ed. Waller and Glover, V, 354-355) .
2. *Restoration Tragedy,* pp. 141-148.
3. *History of English Dramatic Literature,* III, 418, 416.
4. *Seventeenth Century Studies,* p. 294.
5. *Spectator,* No. 39, April 14, 1711 (quoted on p. xxx below) . By the middle of the eighteenth century Addison's charge had become one of the clichés of criticism (cf. Johnson, *Idler,* No. 60, June 9, 1759; *Lives of the Poets,* ed. Hill, I, 245-246; *Biographia Dramatica,* 1782; Preface to *Venice Preserv'd,* in *Cumberland's British Theatre,* London, *ca.* 1825-1855; and Ghosh, ed., *Works of Otway,* I, 60) .
6. For details of the *première,* see Taylor, *Next to Shakespeare,* p. 145.
7. The following summary of political events is based on John Pollock, *The Popish Plot* (London, 1903) ; G. M. Trevelyan, *England under the Stuarts* (London, 1920) ; C. H. Firth, "The Stewart Restoration," and John Pollock, "The Policy of Charles II and James II," in *The Cambridge Modern History;* W. D. Christie, *A Life of Anthony Ashley Cooper, First Earl of Shaftesbury* (London, 1871) , 2 vols.
8. See Ghosh, ed., *Works of Otway,* I, 23; Ham, *Otway and Lee,* pp. 91-94; Charles Dalton, ed., *English Army Lists and Commission Registers* (London, 1892) , I, 208-222.
9. César Vischard, Abbé de Saint-Réal, *La Conjuration des Espagnols contre la République de Venise en l'année MCDXVIII* (Paris, 1674; licensed Dec. 21, 1674) . Translated as *A Conspiracy of the Spaniards against the State of Venice* (*Term Catalogues,* Easter, May 10, 1675; second edition, Hilary, Feb. 18, 1679) .
    Saint-Réal accompanied the Duchess of Mazarin when she came to reside in London in 1675, a fact which may have contributed to the popularity of his book in England.
10. Allardyce Nicoll, *Restoration Drama,* p. 10; cf. Ham, *Otway and Lee,* p. 129.
11. For Otway's indebtedness to Lee, see Ham, *Otway and Lee,* pp. 195 ff.

12. For a list of plays banned from the stage for political reasons, see Nicoll, *Restoration Drama*, p. 10.
13. *Spectator*, No. 39, April 14, 1711.
14. This motive recurs frequently in the plays of Beaumont and Fletcher. It is used with great effect in Bulwer's *Richelieu* (cf. Westland Marston's description of Macready in the title role, *Our Recent Actors*, Boston, 1888, p. 48).
15. Cf. Colley Cibber's story of James II's interference in the quarrel between a courtier and William Smith, the impersonator of Pierre (*An Apology for His Life*, Everyman Edition [London, 1938] p. 46).
16. On Pierre's motives for conspiracy, cf. A. J. Toynbee's analysis of Catiline and Marius, *A Study of History* (Oxford, 1939), V, 70-72.
17. *Poems upon Several Occasions* (1684), in *Works of Aphra Behn*, ed. Montague Summers (London, 1925), VI, 211. This poem had appeared as a song in her play, *The Roundheads* (Act IV, scene iii), staged about December, 1681.
18. *Poems on Affairs of State, From 1640 to this present Year, 1704* (1704), III, 123.
19. *Art of Poetry*, I, 237.
20. *Dramatic Miscellanies*, III, 223.
21. *Lives of the Poets*, ed. Hill, I, 245.
22. *Histoire de la littérature anglaise* (Paris, 1863), II, 654.
23. Robinson, *Diary*, ed. Thomas Sadler (Boston, 1870), I, 121.
24. Played by Anthony Leigh, King Charles's "own actor" (Cibber, *Apology*, p. 80). Lord Shaftesbury is frequently referred to as either "Tony" or Anthony (cf. Mrs. Behn, *The Roundheads*, ed. Summers, I, 354, and *Somers's Tracts*, ed. Sir Walter Scott, London, 1809-1815, VIII, 313, *et passim*).
25. See the *Dramatis Personæ* of *Venice Preserv'd*.
26. Cf. IV, 196-197 and V, 122; and Christie, *Life of Shaftesbury*, II, 428-437.
27. *Dramatic Miscellanies*, III, 217; cf. *The Medal*, 1. 37.
28. Prologue, 11. 29-37; cf. "A Modest Vindication of the Earl of Shaftesbury: in a Letter to a Friend, concerning his being Elected King of Poland" (1681), *Somers's Tracts*, VIII, 313-314; "The Last Will and Testament of Anthony K. of Poland" (1682), in *Poems on Affairs of State* (1703), II, 119-122.
29. Published Nov. 17, 1681.
30. Zera S. Fink, "Venice and English Political Thought in the Seventeenth Century," *Modern Philology*, XXXVIII (1940-1941), 155 ff.; and *The Classical Republicans* (Evanston, Ill., 1945), pp. 143-148. Cf. J. R. Moore, "Contemporary Satire in *Venice Preserved*," *Publications of the Modern Language Association*, XLIII (1928), 161-181.
31. *Absalom and Achitophel*, 1. 65.
32. "Il n'y eut jamais de Monarchie si absolue dans le Monde, que l'empire avec lequel le Sénat de Venise gouverne cette République. On y fait une différence infinie jusques dans les moindres choses entre les Nobles, et ceux qui ne le sont pas" (Saint-Réal, *La Conjuration de Espagnols, Oeuvres*, Amsterdam, 1740, III, 166).

33. Dryden had hit upon the parallel as early as 1660 when he was reading Davila's *Historia della Guerre Civili di Francia*, on which *The Duke of Guise* is based (see *Astræa Redux*, 1660, ll. 97-102, and *Vindication*, ed. Scott and Saintsbury, VII, 145-149; see also Louis I. Bredvold, *The Intellectual Milieu of John Dryden* (Ann Arbor, 1934).

34. *Introduction to the Literature of Europe* (London, 1855), IV, 285.

35. Dryden, *Essay of Dramatic Poesy*, ed. Ker, I, 41.

36. See Taylor, *Next to Shakespeare*, pp. 151, 154 ff., 161-164, 198-208.

37. *Restoration Tragedy*, p. 43. In 1752 Samuel Derrick started a tradition that the Nicky-Nacky scenes were written at the "particular command" of Charles II to "satirize the Earl of Shaftesbury" (*Dramatic Censor*, p. 2). For evidence which may lead one to believe that the Nicky-Nacky scenes represent an inspiration later than that of the main action, see Aline Mackenzie, "*Venice Preserv'd* Reconsidered," *Tulane Studies in English* (New Orleans, Tulane University, 1949), I, 81-118.

38. For the effect of this emotional structure of the scenes when Garrick and Barry supported Mrs. Cibber, see Francis Gentleman, *The Dramatic Censor* (1770), I, 334-335, and Arthur Murphy, *Life of David Garrick* (London, 1801), I, 137-144. See also Taylor, *Next to Shakespeare*, pp. 167-180.

39. These details are brought out by the stage directions in the texts published by Wm. Oxberry (*The New English Drama*, London, 1818, Vol. IV), and by Thomas Hailes Lacy (*Lacy's Acting Edition of Plays*, London, n.d., Vol. XXXII).

40. See Alfred Johnson, *Lafosse, Otway, Saint-Réal* (Paris, 1901), p. 108; Ghosh, ed., *Works of Otway*, I, 59-60; *Dramatic Censor* (1770), I, 325-326.

41. Cf. the actor Warde's concealment of the dagger (praised by the *Dublin Theatrical Observer*, Jan. 26, 1821, quoted on p. 229, below). What "token" Jaffier entrusts to the Officer on the scaffold (V, 474-477), is not clear. It may be the dagger which Belvidera asks Jaffier to leave with her in the preceding scene (V, 324-334). This seems likely in view (1) of the business indicated in IV, 377, 480, 496, 502, 515, 523, and (2) of the stage directions in V, 481-502, where the ghost of Jaffier rises, then sinks, the Officer enters, and "*the Ghosts of Jaff. and Peirr. rise together, both bloody.*" If the dagger is the "token," then it motivates the Officer's entry (V, 494) and Belvidera's second vision, and it brings out clearly the full significance of the dagger as the symbol of Jaffier's word of honor. This surmise, however, is substantiated neither by directions in any acting text I have seen, nor by descriptions of performances.

42. He preferred *The Orphan*, but invariably mentioned *Venice Preserv'd* at the same time (*Art of Poetry*, I, 237, 248; see Taylor, *Next to Shakespeare*, pp. 256-258).

43. *Essay of Dramatic Poesy*, ed. Ker, I, 64.

44. *Ibid.*

45. Preface to *Troilus and Cressida* (1679), ed. Ker, I, 216.

46. *Spectator*, No. 39, April 14, 1711.

47. Cf. *Absalom and Achitophel*, ll. 448-457.

48. "To a Young Lady, with the Tragedy of 'Venice Preserved'" (*The English Poets*, ed. Alexander Chalmers, London, 1810, XIV, 186). On Jaffier's "betrayal," cf. Dryden, *Of Heroic Plays* (ed. Ker, I, 155-157).

49. *Dramatic Censor* (1770), I, 320, 323; cf. Fanny Kemble, *Record of a Girlhood* (London, 1878), II, 85-86.

50. Byron to Murray, April 2, 1817 (*Letters and Journals*, ed. R. E. Prothero, IV, 91).

51. Mrs. Clement Parsons, *The Incomparable Siddons* (London, 1909), p. 82. Cf. *Edinburgh Dramatic Review*, April 13, 1824, and the London *Times*, June 14, 1904.

52. "To a Young Lady, with the Tragedy of *Venice Preserved*," English Poets, XIV, 186; cf. Davies, *Dramatic Miscellanies*, III, 213-229.

53. Preface to *De arte graphica* (1695), ed. Ker, II, 145.

54. *Restoration Tragedy*, p. 147.

55. *Morning Chronicle*, March 8-10, 1757; *Lives of the Poets*, ed. Hill, I, 246.

56. *The Elegant Extracts*, Compiled by Vicissimus Knox (London, 1790), which appeared after Otway's popularity had passed its peak, contains only three passages from the plays; but compare *The Beauties of the English Stage*, 1737 (see Taylor, *Next to Shakespeare*, p. 4 n. 6 and p. 245 n. 1). Cf. the critique of the Phoenix Revival of *Venice Preserv'd* (London *Times*, Dec. 5, 1920): "Many new generations ought to get a chance of seeing and hearing it.

"We say hearing it, because the play is remarkable, even more than for its action, for the nobility of its verse and the richness of its vocabulary. It shows what a fine instrument the English language, at any rate, once was. You miss Shakespeare's peculiar lyric touch, but its blank verse has a fine full swell, is never in the least like prose cut into lengths."

For comments by nineteenth-century playgoing critics, see Taylor, *Next to Shakespeare*, pp. 227, 228 n., 242 f.

57. Gildon, *Art of Poetry*, I, 258. Cf. "Essay on the Art, Rise and Progress of the Stage," *Works of Shakespeare*, ed. Rowe (1714), IX, xliii.

58. *Art of Poetry*, I, 290.

59. *Spectator*, No. 39, April 14, 1711.

60. *Restoration Tragedy*, p. 132.

61. On the effect of the bell, see *Spectator*, No. 44, April 20, 1711; Arthur Murphy, *Life of Garrick*, I, 143, 168; Hazlitt, "On a Sun-Dial" (*Works*, ed. Waller and Glover, XII, 57).

62. *Art of Poetry*, I, 202.

63. *Dramatic Miscellanies*, III, 221.

64. Preface to *Venice Preserved, British Drama*, ed. Mrs. Inchbald, Vol. XII.

JOHN LOFTIS

❀

The Political Strain in Augustan Drama

Apart from governmental restrictions, there was nothing to prevent
Augustan dramatists from turning satirical attention to political subjects, no inhibitory sense of propriety, such as kept religious subjects
out of comedy if not out of tragedy. There was a relative freedom of
expression, on the stage as in the press; there were well-defined and
powerful opposing factions, numerically small and compact enough to
be susceptible to adroit propaganda; and there was admiration for
verbal ingenuity, even a willingness to examine it and applaud or
damn it as deserved with a certain tolerance for difference of opinion.
The age is remarkable for the political eminence enjoyed by literary
men, just as it is remarkable for the literary eminence enjoyed by
politicians, which is not the same thing. A political age, it produced a
political drama—but a political drama that is clever rather than profound.

Wit there is in abundance, and adroit allusion to famous personalities; but not convincing treatment of the most important political
relationships. The political themes are on the one hand narrowly
partisan and on the other generalized to the point of being platitudi-
nous. At the one extreme there is the personal allusiveness of *The
Beggar's Opera;* at the other the oratorical dramatization of political
theory in *Tamerlane.* The dramatists failed to express lively conflicts
embodying rival political philosophies.

From *The Politics of Drama in Augustan England* (Oxford: Oxford University Press, 1963), pp. 154-61. Reprinted by permission of the Clarendon
Press, Oxford.

That they did not was in part owing to the nature of politics at the time. From a condition of opposition on fundamental issues, politics became progressively a matter of rivalries turning on personalities and the interests of factions.[1] As early as the reign of Queen Anne, there were signs of weakening in the ideological differences between Tories and Whigs—as appears, among other ways, in the instance of the Tories' cheering *Cato,* and this at the height of their resurgence in the Queen's last years. The long ascendancy of Walpole encouraged an indifference to political ideas. In England, as in Lilliput, political principle became obscured by faction, and the English theatres produced the drama we would expect of Lilliput.

Political events caused changes in emphasis in both tragedy and comedy; but these changes came without much reference to distinctions between Whig and Tory. There is an emphasis in Restoration tragedy on the evils arising from disregard of the royal prerogative; an emphasis in tragedy produced after the Revolution on the evils arising from despotism. Dryden depicted the horrors of mob rule; Addison of tyrannical rule. *Cato* is the most famous instance in which a Roman points a political moral to the English, but there are many others, including a series of dramatizations of the heroic resistance made by Lucius Junius Brutus to the despotism of Tarquin. Tragedies celebrating the limitation of royal power, of constitutional monarchy as conceived by Locke, are abundant after the Revolution; tragedies celebrating the bounties that arise from the exercise of the royal prerogative or depicting the horrors that arise from the infringement of it are non-existent. Dramatists, to be sure, had a lively conception of the balance of powers as the foundation of English liberties; but they were far more sensitive to infringements on the powers of Lords and Commons than to infringements on those of the Sovereign. A dramatization of the history of the royal martyr Charles I appeared, but characteristically his impolitic and arbitrary acts are reprehended at the same time that his fate is deplored. It was William III, symbol of liberation from tyranny, who was the favoured hero of the dramatists. The absence of tragedies celebrating passive obedience and divine right provides a gauge of the intellectual bankruptcy of the older form of Toryism in the eighteenth century.

The social assumptions of Restoration comedy, which were related to political animosities, persisted long after the Revolution. Hatred of the dissenters as latter-day Puritans and of the business community which had supported Cromwell and which in its bustling prosperity

was a threat to aristocratic privilege, this hatred determined the direction of satire in comedy for some two decades after 1688, animating
personal rivalries depicted in the plays of, among others, Congreve,
Vanbrugh, and Farquhar. It is worth noting that these three dramatists
were Whigs, the two former indeed members of the Whig Kit-Cat
Club. The social attitudes that dominated comedy until about 1710
(inherited from Royalist attitudes of the Restoration) were then not
held merely by Tory reactionaries. Thereafter, with the parliamentary
and journalistic debates that preceded and followed the Treaty of
Utrecht in 1713, Whig doctrine began to influence characterization,
satire, and even in some comedies pronouncements by normative characters. This is intermittent in the second and third decades of the
eighteenth century, reversions to the older attitudes frequently occur-
ring; but by the fourth decade the new attitudes, which in origin certainly were Whig, are so widespread in comedy that it would seem
gratuitous to associate them with the programme of any political
group. Just as before 1710 the attitudes that were Royalist in origin
are so widespread in comedy as not to admit of association with the
Tory party, so after 1730 the new attitudes may not properly be called
Whig, even though they were Whiggish in origin.[2]

It has been argued that sentimentalism, so prominent in early eighteenth-century drama, is an expression of Whiggism.[3] It would seem to
me that we have overstated the differences between Whigs and Tories
on this as on other aesthetic subjects. There are, of course, some affinities between the conception of human nature responsible for sentimentalism and the theological liberalism we associate with Whiggism.[4]
Sentimentalism (which in its eighteenth-century sense I assume to be
the interpretation of character, motive, and incident with reference
to moral philosophy emphasizing innate benevolence[5]) is in its essential nature, with its glossing over of Original Sin and human depravity,
incompatible with High Church orthodoxy and thus, logically at least,
with Toryism. Swift, who represents so articulately the High Church
mentality, expresses in his writings the very antithesis of the "sentimental" assumption that men are fundamentally benevolent.[6] The
single person most influential in bringing to focus moral philosophy
with this emphasis was the third Earl of Shaftesbury, liberal in theological opinion to the point of deism, the grandson of the man usually
described as the founder of the Whig party.

All this notwithstanding, sentimentalism was an aspect of ethical
thought and Whiggism of political thought; and the two were quite

distinct from one another. The reasons for conceiving of sentimentalism in drama as an expression of Whiggism will be seen to be ambiguous if we examine, not the logical implications of ideas, but the political activities and the plays of individual dramatists. I have mentioned Congreve, Vanbrugh, and Farquhar as Whig dramatists who preserved into the eighteenth century, or to the eve of it, the social attitudes of the Restoration. They were, at the same time, dramatists who resisted, and in the case of Vanbrugh satirized, the encroachments of sentimentalism. Vanbrugh's *The Relapse,* the sequel to Cibber's *Love's Last Shift,* is the most destructive of the contemporary critiques of dramatic sentimentalism; and it is destructive because of the honesty and audacity with which it examines the assumptions underlying Cibber's denouement. Since all the important dramatists who revealed political bias in Anne's and George I's reigns were Whigs, it is impossible to contrast attitudes toward sentimentalism expressed by adherents of the two parties. The Whig dramatists active during these reigns —Vanbrugh, Farquhar, Rowe, Steele, Mrs. Centlivre, Thomas Baker, William Burnaby, Charles Johnson, Addison, and Cibber (Whig at least after 1714) —included sentimental episodes in their plays so irregularly, if at all, that we can scarcely think of those episodes as a corollary of their political affiliation. And the rout of the Tories was so complete after the accession of George I that they soon lost whatever cohesiveness as a political unit they had had. By the mid-1720's the significant political distinction was the one between the Walpole Whigs and the opposition.[7] Thus to associate sentimentalism with the Whig party of George I's and George II's reigns, without reference to the antagonism among Whigs between Court and Country parties, is to oversimplify; it is in fact to emphasize a political terminology which does not coincide with the political conditions of that time. Since most of those who were writing in the later years of George I and the earlier years of George II were Whigs, even if in opposition, it is easy to show that the expressions of sentimentalism (by Thomson, Dodsley, and Fielding, among many others) were by Whigs; but this seems to be little more than saying (what is undoubtedly true) that sentimentalism became pervasive in English literature at a time when the Whigs enjoyed an overwhelming ascendancy in English politics.

Like sentimentalism, neoclassicism would seem on first impression to be an aesthetic subject having political implications. There was a frequent metaphorical association of neoclassicism with France, which represented to the English both formalism in critical theory and absolutism in government. As early as Dryden's *Essay of Dramatic Poesy* some such association is implied,[8] and as late as Joseph Warton's *The Enthusiast* it is made epigrammatically.[9] French tyranny, even in art, and English freedom; these are contrasted, though not always in language carrying the same evaluations, through a century of English criticism. Often the contrast is described as being between French order and English anarchy (at least in art) ; but whatever the sympathies of the writer, the terms of the opposition remain fairly constant. The accomplishment of French seventeenth-century drama was such that English men of letters had to give respectful attention to it, whatever the conclusions they reached on the critical theory it embodied.

The metaphorical comparisons would suggest that the Tories, who were more sympathetic to absolutism in government and to the French than were the Whigs, would have been the more firm neoclassicists. Yet I see no evidence that this is true. The party affiliations did not noticeably affect dramatic criticism in its theoretical aspects. From the rough and tumble of party rivalries in the theatres, no clear, logical opposition of principles in dramatic theory emerges: the Tories did not as a group support classical regularity in drama, nor did the Whigs with any consistency oppose French tyranny in its dramatic application. Dennis, a strong Whig who wrote tragedies glorifying the Whig theory of government, was among the nation's firmest admirers of classical regularity in drama—of the "tyranny" of French rules. He criticized the Whig Addison for his maladroit adherence to some of the rules and departure from others in *Cato;* and he roundly denounced the Whig Steele for his violation of the doctrine of kinds in *The Conscious Lovers.* Of the critical essays that Addison contributed to *The Spectator,* one famous group, on *Paradise Lost,* is neoclassical in assumptions and another famous group, on "the pleasures of the imagination," is not at all, but rather provides a theoretical basis in aesthetics for much subsequent imaginative and critical writing in opposition to neoclassicism. Steele was inconsistent in his attitude toward the neoclassical rules, now observing them, now ignoring or even denouncing them. In short, Dennis, Addison, and Steele, all three of them Whig dramatists, disagreed as thoroughly on the critical principles as they did on most other subjects except politics. And their disagreement illustrates a general absence of correlation between political and literary assumptions. To impose a pattern of association between political conviction and literary theory, with reference to support for or opposition to the doctrines of French formalism, is to inflate the importance of a metaphor beyond reasonable proportions and to ignore exceptions more important than the cases comprehended.

There are important correlations between the political and critical attitudes of the Augustan age, but they are fundamental ones which exist without much reference to the division between Whig and Tory. The body of common agreement, and of common change in both political and critical opinions with the passage of time, seems much more impressive than any critical disagreements we may associate with partisan political affiliations. Attitudes toward the neoclassical doctrine of decorum in characterization provide an instance of a parallel between critical and political assumptions so fundamental as to have little relevance to party differences. Dryden's and Rymer's conceptions of propriety in characterization rest on assumptions that are critical and political alike: that drama should imitate the ideal order of society, conceived to be an hierarchical and rather rigid structure. The later relaxation in the conceptions of propriety evident in the eighteenth-century experiments in domestic tragedy came from a weakening in the conviction that drama should imitate an ideal order and from the social dislocations accompanying the growth of the mercantile community. The sympathetic hearing that Lillo's *The London Merchant* received would have been impossible in Dryden's time. Lillo, it is true, was a Whig, Dryden had been a Tory; but the Whigs of Charles's reign no more held Lillo's critical and political convictions than the Tories of the 1730's held those of Dryden. The evidence in critical theory seems to me to emphasize ideological affinities between Whigs and Tories rather than differences.

The most obvious impact of politics on the drama is in the practical area of propaganda. Effective propaganda must be emphatic, and Augustan drama written in the service of party or faction is emphatic indeed. The political motive led to intensification, whether of tragic seriousness or of comic satire; it led to the avoidance of ambiguity and even of subtlety. Augustan tragedy is at best declamatory, and when the tragedians were at pains to make their plays point a political moral, they made their characters mouth lectures of a preternatural seriousness. We note and are repelled by an assurance of statement in Augustan tragedy, a positiveness that leaves little room for the uncertainties that are so prominent in human experience and hence in the greatest tragedies. To be sure, the propagandistic purpose was not the only reason, perhaps not even the most important reason, for the declamatory tone and the simplification of tragic issues. The Enlightenment was notoriously an age of intellectual self-confidence; and the Lockeian political system that controlled tragedy after 1688 was a tidy system, encouraging an intellectual tidiness in the plays. But it seems clear enough that a propagandistic purpose led frequently to exaggerated earnestness, over-emphatic statement, and over-simplified argument. And this would seem to be a major reason why the plays are remarkable chiefly as a chronicle of their age.

NOTES

1. Cf. L. B. Namier's discussion of the absence of political issues in the mid-eighteenth century: *The Structure of Politics at the Accession of George III*, 2nd ed. (London, 1957), pp. 133-4; *England in the Age of the American Revolution* (London, 1930), pp. 206-7.
2. John Loftis, *Comedy and Society from Congreve to Fielding* (Stanford, 1959), *passim*.
3. Cf. C. A. Moore, "Whig Panegyric Verse, 1700-1760: A Phase of Sentimentalism," *PMLA*, xli (1926), 362-401.
4. On the religious and intellectual background of sentimentalism, see Ronald S. Crane, "Suggestions toward a Genealogy of 'The Man of Feeling,'" *ELH, A Journal of English Literary History*, i (1934), 205-30; Ernest L. Tuveson, "The Importance of Shaftesbury," *ibid.*, xx (1953), 267-99; and Martin C. Battestin, *The Moral Basis of Fielding's Art* (Middletown, Conn., 1959), Ch. V.
5. For my conception of sentimentalism, see *Comedy and Society from Congreve to Fielding*, pp. 127-8.
6. See Ernest L. Tuveson, "Swift: The Dean as Satirist," *University of Toronto Quarterly*, xxii (1953), 368-75; and Roland Mushat Frye, "Swift's Yahoo and the Christian Symbols for Sin," *Journal of the History of Ideas*, xv (1954), 201-17.
7. C. B. Realey, *The Early Opposition to Sir Robert Walpole* (Lawrence, Kansas, 1931), Ch. V; Keith Feiling, *The Second Tory Party* (London, 1938), Ch. II.
8. Cf. *Essays of John Dryden*, ed. W. P. Ker (Oxford, 1900), i. 67-79.
9. Ll. 25 ff. For further discussion of associations between political and critical theory, see Samuel Kliger, *The Goths in England* (Cambridge, Mass., 1952), pp. 3-6.

JOHN HARRINGTON SMITH

❀

Shadwell, the Ladies,
and the Change in Comedy[1]

The change which took place in the spirit and method of English comedy in the late seventeenth (or early eighteenth) century has always engaged the interest of students of the drama. But the authorities who have endeavored to define this change, chart it chronologically, and determine why it came about have not been able to agree on any of these points. The uncertainty about such matters may be seen, for instance, in the shift of ground which has taken place as to the question of when the change may be said to have begun. I do not by any means intend the following account to be definitive; but, roughly speaking, the view at first, when the ball was started rolling by A. W. Ward, was that Steele (more particularly in *The lying lover* [1703]) introduced it;[2] later, the date was pushed back to Vanbrugh's *Aesop* (1697);[3] then to Cibber's *Love's last shift* (1696);[4] then to two plays (one an Elizabethan adaptation) earlier than Cibber;[5] then to more plays before 1696;[6] still more recently the first signs of the change have been pushed still further back by Professor Croissant, who, in a number of plays of various types between 1660 and 1696, finds evidence that "romanticism and sentimentalism maintained themselves in the theater throughout the Restoration."[7] When findings are as diverse as this, perhaps still another essay at the subject may seem justified.

To begin with, it is necessary to determine precisely what quality in

From *Modern Philology*, XLVI (1948), 22-33. Reprinted by permission of The University of Chicago Press. Copyright, 1948, by The University of Chicago Press.

the changed comedy makes it fundamentally different from the kind of comedy that had dominated the scene in the reign of Charles II. Uncertainty as to this point will inevitably produce just such uncertainty as to the date at which the new spirit began in plays as appears in the cycle, from Ward to Croissant, sketched above. Furthermore, until this date is settled upon, one does not know at about what date to look for causes, which (since causes must precede effects) would have to be such as could be shown to have been operative at a date at least slightly earlier than the plays in which the new spirit is found. The three parts of the problem (characteristics, date, causes) are thus closely dependent on one another; and it is only from a just view of the first that valid conclusions can be reached as to the second and third.

It is not an easy matter, however, to fix upon that quality (or those qualities) which should be searched for and, when found, hailed as certain evidence of the anti-Restoration spirit in comedy. The difficulty arises from the fact that—at least when full-blown—the "sentimental" manner is not an entity but a complex of elements. All these are to be found in the new comedy as a whole, but not necessarily in every play of the class: the combination of elements is not inevitable—one or more may be lacking, though the play may be clearly anti-Restoration, for all that. It does not do, then, to insist upon an element not of universal distribution in the class—"pity," for instance; it was thus that Ward withheld the accolade until Steele's second play and, in consequence, seemed to rule out many an earlier comedy which, though it happened to lack this element, was, all the same, clearly not in the manner of Wycherley or Etherege. On the other hand, one should not define too liberally—as, it seems to me, happens when the term "sentimental" is stretched to include motifs in dramas which, since they make initially no pretense whatever of representing things as they are, would be more properly called "romantic": to find—for instance—a favorable view of human nature or distresses with which the audience is asked to sympathize in a romantic drama should surprise no one, the muse of romance being, in any period, like nothing but herself and perfectly consistent in such matters. "Sentimental" comedy has, certainly, generic resemblances to romance and, no doubt, in some sort is indebted to it; but it seems to me that the term has no point unless applied exclusively to comedies of contemporary life. Unless this distinction is observed, we may find ourselves using "sentimental" as a label for plays like *As you like it* or *The two gentlemen of Verona*

—or even *Everyman,* a play to which the term has actually been applied by one writer on the subject.[8]

In fact, "sentimental" has been used in such a variety of ways that it had better be banished from this discussion and the problem stated in other terms. What we need is a reliable differentia, inclusive enough but not so inclusive and indiscriminate as to blur all distinctions, for recognizing the type of comedy of contemporary life which came to triumph after 1700, as opposed to that which flourished in the sixteen-seventies. "Pity" is not sufficiently universal in distribution to serve this purpose—though this technique differs enough, in all conscience, from that of Wycherley. I am not inclined, either, to set up my rest upon "benevolence." It is a more specialized concept than "pity," which it frequently includes; also, it is more widely distributed in comedy.[9] But still—at least prior to 1750—it is only one of the modes in which the reaction against the comic method of Etherege and Wycherley expressed itself.

It seems to me, on the other hand, that the essence of that reaction was the replacement of the comic method of the Restoration, which featured realism and satire and in which the writer's interest in whether reform was accomplished thereby was merely incidental, with a method which put reform first and meant to accomplish it by representing not things as they were but standards as they ought to be, personified in characters who should be examples for imitation by the audience. Let us call this the "exemplary" method. It is most clearly seen in the change in fashion as regards heroes and heroines in the plays—in the replacement of the gay, intriguing spark by the "man of sense"; the lively, elusive, and (at least professedly) antimatrimonial heroine favored in the earlier comedy by a type that was serious, sententious, sincere. However, the method is likewise apparent in the reclaimed rake and coquette, for these become "examples" as soon as they are brought to a sense of their folly and of their best subsequent course.

If this be a really reliable touchstone for the "change in comedy" (and I think I can testify that it is, from extensive and strenuous reading in the plays to 1750), then I suggest 1688-89 as the date by which the new comic method had established itself as a rival, on at least equal terms, with the old; and I offer as causes, not those commonly cited by the authorities, but two which I think will have something of an air of novelty about them. It is Shadwell and "the ladies" (by which term I mean the respectable female patrons of the theater in the period) who should, it seems to me, be viewed as the chief enemies of the old mode and the motivators of its replacement by something more edifying, if—unhappily—distinctly less entertaining.

Opposition to the strictly nonexemplary mood which dominated comedy in the early Restoration was first voiced by Shadwell; and at the time he was in a minority of one. The great comic theme of the first decade of Charles's reign was the love-game, in which a gay hero and heroine, both of whom, in accordance with the inflexible code of the time, make a point of seeming not to be serious about anything, carry on a witty courtship action which always ends—sometimes to their surprise, for they have been scoffing at matrimony, but never to the surprise of the dramatist or the audience—in an agreement to marry. The flowering of this motif in the Restoration period was inevitable, considering the tradition which had been established in earlier plays and considering also the "platonic mode," which had been introduced at court in the time of Charles I and was still to be seen in heroic plays, and against which both sexes presumably felt themselves to be in revolt—but of these matters I cannot speak more fully in this place. It was Dryden who first tested the temper of his age with a love-action characterized by jesting and intrigue rather than by sighs and protestations, in *The wild gallant* (January, 1663).[10] James Howard's *The English mounsieur,* before July of the same year, developed and advanced the motif; the duel between Wellbred and Lady Wealthy established the essentials of the love-game as it was to be played in many a comedy of the period.[11] Etherege made improvements on the formula in *The comical revenge* (January, 1664), epitomizing the gallants of his time in Sir Frederick Frollick. March, 1667, saw the love-game exemplified in Cavendish's *The humorous lovers* and brilliantly furthered in Dryden's *Secret love,* in which Celadon and Florimel far surpass, in wit, sophistication, and seeming scorn of the conventions, any couple which had yet been seen on the contemporary stage. James Howard's "mad couple," Philidor and Mirida, in *All mistaken,* acted in September of the same year, were a mere caricature of Celadon and Florimel, designed to cater to the lowest tastes of the audience. But Etherege fully re-established the credit of the gay love-duel in *She woud if she coud* (February, 1668) ; in May, Sedley added to its prestige in *The Mulberry-Garden,* which contains some exquisite courtship in the gay manner; and in June appeared *An evening's love,* in which Dryden gave the stage Wildblood and Jacinta—in the vein of his own Celadon and Florimel, but a bit wilder.

This was the state of affairs when Shadwell made his appearance upon the scene with his first play, *The sullen lovers* (May, 1668). In Lovell and Caroline he made certain concessions to the now established convention—their love passages are gay enough—but he did not permit them to jeer wittily at the eternal verities. And in his preface he attacked the reigning couple in comedy, describing the gay hero as "a Swearing, Drinking, Whoring, Ruffian" and the gay heroine as "an impudent ill-bred tomrig"; "and these are the fine people of the play."[12] He returned to the attack in the preface and prologue to *The royal shepherdess* (1669), in both of which Collier's *Short view* is foreshadowed:

> I find, it pleases most to see Vice incouraged, by bringing the Characters of debauch'd People upon the Stage, and making them pass for fine Gentlemen, who openly profess Swearing, Drinking, Whoring, breaking Windows, beating Constables, etc.

> It is a Vertuous Play, you will confess,
> Where Vicious men meet their deserv'd success.
> Not like our Modern ones, where still we find,
> Poets are onely to the Ruffians kind;
> And give them still the Ladies in the Play,
> But 'faith their Ladies are as bad as they.

Having thus come face to face with the proposition that it is the business of comedy not to reflect the contemporary scene but rather to encourage virtue and discourage vice, Shadwell proceeded to put the principle into practice in his second major comedy, *The humorists* (December, 1670). He has an eye to poetic justice throughout; and in Raymond and Theodosia he is obviously aiming at a couple who should express his judgment upon and, if possible, counteract the influence of the gay couple. There is no love-game: the hero is an honest lover, no intriguer; the heroine is sincere and serious. This experiment in the exemplary vein was not well received in the theater; but it may have done something to encourage the production, a few months later, of Revet's *The town-shifts,* a charming comedy, with love but no love-game.[13]

Shadwell returned to his crusade in *The miser* (January, 1672), with a hero and heroine on the same pattern as the former pair, but more formidably exemplary. The heroine's high standards of modesty, sincerity, and virtue are insisted upon; the hero is not only a sincere lover but one who, though formerly irregular in his conduct and a fashionable railer against matrimony, has come to see the folly of these ways and is now virtuous on principle. In contrast are two sparks of the fashionable stamp; and Shadwell emphasizes the hero's superiority.

At this point, however, he deserted the exemplary method for the opposite one—that of realism and satire. This shift was in response to a change now in progress in the moral climate of comedy. In the first decade of the Restoration, comedy had been comparatively chaste.[14] Heroes in love-games had frequently been encumbered with kept mistresses, but little stress had been placed on these. The play which, it would seem, opened the eyes of the dramatists to the possibilities of cynical sex intrigue was Betterton's *The amorous widow* (ca. 1670), in its minor plot an adaptation of Molière's *George Dandin ou le mari confondu*, with its trio of inadequate bourgeois husband, intriguing wife, and predatory gallant. Molière implies that Dandin has been cuckolded before the final curtain, though he is not explicit on this point; Betterton likewise leaves the question unsettled. But the ultimate fate of the ridiculous husband in this action was unmistakable; and the rank and file of English writers, unhampered by any notion of decorum, soon began to outdo Molière in their treatments of the theme.[15]

Shadwell was as ready as anyone to exploit the new fashion in tone and subject matter. The example of Wycherley, who made his first appearance on the stage in 1671 with *Love in a wood*, more hard-hitting than any comedy that had thus far appeared and with one extraordinarily frank sex-comedy scene,[16] doubtless helped to show him that stronger measures than he had employed thus far could be taken with vice and folly. Into *The miser* he introduced an ugly scene of the cuckolding sort (though the trio are here an elderly cully, a whore, and a bully). And in *Epsom Wells* (December, 1672), he discarded the exemplary method entirely for a love-game action modeled upon that in Etherege's *She woud* (a play which, his preface to *The humorists* shows, he greatly admired) and a cynical subplot dealing with the cuckolding of a pair of cits.

Wycherley now, in 1675, produced *The country wife*, which conferred such authority upon the cuckolding theme as to give it, for the decade which followed, a decided advantage over the love-game or any other motif. There was to follow, in the next year, the superb love-duel between Dorimant and Harriet in Etherege's *The man of mode*. But no comparable pair were to be seen thereafter until Congreve; and it was not as a lover that Dorimant impressed Etherege's contem-

poraries but as the betrayer of Mrs. Loveit and seducer of Bellinda.
The joint effect of these two plays, reinforced by *The plain-dealer*,
which followed before the end of 1676, was too great to be resisted by
the less talented writers of the time; they immediately began to turn
out copies of Horner and Dorimant, with an assortment of unfaithful
wives, stupid husbands, and foolish virgins as materials for the gallant.
Shadwell succumbed with the rest—having, we may suppose, quite as
much instinctive sympathy with this method as with the other. At least
The virtuoso (1676), is not only his most Wycherleyan comedy but his
strongest. His next, *A true widow,* two years later, finds him beginning
to emerge from this influence; but, on the whole, in this, his middle
phase, Shadwell does not oppose the comedy dominant in his time but
is a component of it.

Here, then, let us leave him for the present and turn to the ladies;
for respectable females, it seems, did attend the theater from the beginning of the period and not merely when a tragicomedy or heroic
play was to be performed. My guesses as to their tastes in theatrical
entertainment and the measures which they took to enforce them are
based almost entirely on passages in plays, prologues, prefaces, and the
like. Still, from such sources alone it seems clear that the ladies had
more to do with the shaping of comedy in the period than has hitherto
been supposed.

For the first decade and a half I have no evidence that they found
fault with the offerings of the comic writers; and, indeed, with the love-
game they would have had little reason to quarrel. It should not have
shocked them to hear true love spoken of as lightly as doubtless they
spoke of it themselves. Besides, the issue in this type of comic action
is always marriage, which from the female point of view could scarcely
have been unsatisfactory. The oncoming of the era of rampant free
gallantry, however, would certainly have struck the ladies as a change
for the worse, for now the gallant comes completely to overshadow the
heroine. If he marries at play's end, it is with an air of lordly conde-
scension (as in Mrs. Behn's *Rover* and *City-heiress,* Dryden's *The kind
keeper,* Leanerd's *The rambling justice*); and as likely as not he may
be a cuckold-maker and nothing more (as in *The country wife,*
Rawlins' *Tom Essence,* D'Urfey's *A fond husband,* Otway's *Friendship
in fashion*). It could scarcely please the ladies to see such a hero go
scot-free at play's end—an unwholesome example, this, for gallants in
real life! And they could not have failed to resent the stress of these
plays on the failings of their sex—female hypocrisy and vice (when the

wife in the play leagued with the gallant against the husband) or weakness (when the gallant overcame the woman's resistance).

Whether or not the ladies analyzed their feelings in these terms, their reaction to the full-blown cuckolding play was both unfavorable and immediate. It was, in fact, *The country wife* that elicited their first protest. The evidence for this is furnished by Wycherley himself in his next play, *The plain-dealer,* in which the hypocrite Olivia is made to speak with horror of a member of her sex who had been "seen at The Country Wife after the first day"—as for herself, she would not think of patronizing Wycherley's filthy piece. From this it seems clear that respectable female society had put the play under a ban (though the view which the author would like to establish is that truly virtuous female playgoers would not protest so much). *The plain-dealer* was no less frank, and it also "lost its reputation with the ladies of stricter lives in the playhouse."[17] Again the author was irked at the ladies' presuming to sit in judgment upon his work, and when he printed he tried to pay them off by ironically dedicating not to them but to the celebrated procuress, Mother Bennett—no prude or hypocrite she! But since he wrote and printed no more plays, his quarrel with the ladies went no further.

The next writer to draw their fire was Mrs. Aphra Behn, the preface to whose *Sir Patient Fancy* (1678) indicates that this play was likewise boycotted by the ladies; she refers to its "loss of fame" with them and tries to be sarcastic at their expense.[18] In her defense she comes ultimately to the proposition that she had to write for a living and so might have been excused for having given the audience what it had shown it wanted. She had indeed not miscalculated greatly. The fact was that, although the ladies did not like the cuckolding theme, the gallants did; it is to their taste that comedy in these years is written, and the ladies may consider themselves lucky if they get a curt nod in the prologue. "Ladies, there's no bawdy in't," writes Otway in the prologue to *Friendship in fashion* (1680). But he seems to mean only that he has eschewed the *double entendre,* a form of wit which (as evidenced by various prologues of the time, including some to which I shall come presently) the ladies found especially offensive; as to plot, the play is as thoroughly Wycherleyan as any gallant in the pit could wish. The dominance of masculine taste at this time is suggested by the prologue to D'Urfey's *The virtuous wife* (1679), which shows the author's anxiety lest the gallants should damn the play for disappointing them of their accustomed fare:

> A Virtuous Wife! Why what a damn'd mistake
> The poet's in, to think this play can take?

In the next decade the ladies begin to gain in influence. Highly interesting and suggestive of their activities is the prologue to Ravenscroft's *Dame Dobson* (1683). It reveals that, when his greatest success, *The London cuckolds,* was produced in 1681, the ladies actually banded into a faction to voice their protests in the theater—"made visits with design to cry it down." Ravenscroft at least claims that he has framed the present play to meet their specifications. The prologue also makes clear the allocation of the contending factions, male and female, into sections of the theater—"pit" for gallants and "boxes" for ladies. It runs, in part:

> Gallants, I vow I am quite out of heart,
> There's not one smutty Jest in all my part.
> Here's not one scene of tickling Rallery;
> There we quite lose the Pit and Gallery.
> His London cuckolds did afford you sport.
> That pleas'd the Town, and did divert the Court.
> But 'cause some squeamish Females of renown
> Made visits with design to cry it down,
> He swore in's Rage he would their humour fit
> And write the next without one word of Wit.
> No line in this will tempt your minds to Evil.
> It's true, 'tis dull, but then 'tis very civil.
> No double sense shall now your thoughts beguile,
> Make Lady Blush, nor Ogling Gallants Smile.

Pit and boxes are also seen as opposed factions in the prologue to D'Urfey's *The banditti* (1686). The author has kept the play clean, he assures the ladies, and he asks them to stand his friend against the gallants, who may be expected to dislike it:

> Upon my Credit no Lewd word is there
> If you dare trust the Credit of a Player:
> He begs you will your Conquering Forces use
> Against the Dragons of the Lower House,
> To pleasure whom he not one scene contrives,
> No, if a smutty Scene would save their Lives.

In the years immediately following, it becomes (if one can judge from dramatists' prefaces) a matter of routine for the ladies to protest plays written in the old cynical way. Mrs. Behn's *The luckey chance,* the preface shows, had to struggle for success under the handicap of a report that the play was bawdy, which, widely circulated, kept the ladies from attending. She was thereby goaded into going to great lengths in her defense, which falls under several headings. The play, she tries to show, could not well have been indecent, for she had had it read by several "Ladys of very great quality," who had found it unobjectionable; and, further,

> it being a Comedy of Intrigue Dr. Davenant out of Respect to the Commands he had from Court, to take great Care that no Indecency should be in Plays, sent for it and nicely look't it over, putting out anything he but imagin'd the Critiks would play with. After that, Sir Roger L'Estrange read it and licens'd it, and found no such Faults as 'tis charg'd with: Then Mr. Killigrew, who more severe than any, from the strict Order he had, perus'd it with great Circumspection.[19]

In the second place, she argues (with something of a shift of ground) that the play was no worse than those of male authors for the theater, in many of whose plays (and she cites chapter and verse) cuckoldings had passed unchallenged. She is being subjected to persecution because of her sex: "All I ask, is the Priviledge for my Masculine Part the Poet in me . . . to tread in those successful Paths my Predecessors have so long thriv'd in." But these paths were not to be successful much longer.

Sedley's *Bellamira* (1687) attained to at least a moderate success but was strenuously objected to on the score of indecency. Sedley expresses surprise at this. The main features of his plot (it is from Terence's *Eunuch*) were, he says, in a passage which shows that a female boycott had been applied,

> so essential that they cou'd not be omitted, nor well fitted to our Stage without some expressions or Metaphors, which by persons of a ticklish imagination, or overquick sense that way, seem'd too lascivious for modest Ears; I confess after the Plays I have seen lately Crowded by that fair Sex: the exception did not a little surprise me.

And he invites the reader, "Go in and judge for thy self, see what the Modesty of this year takes offense at." Such passages indicate that the writer is now on the defensive, the boxes gaining in influence. Through failure to observe this fact, D'Urfey's *A fool's preferment,* acted the next year, expired before reaching a third day. In the dedication the author attributes this failure to reports spread by "some certain, very nice, Persons, especially one" who told their Majesties the play "was so obscene, that it was not fit to be Acted; when, I can prove, there has not, these seven years, been any Comedy so free from it." But the play scarcely supports this statement or lends credence to an attempt of D'Urfey to attribute the malice of his female enemies to an attack which he makes on basset. It has a very ugly intrigue feature.

Besides thus setting themselves up as unwilling to patronize comedy which was obscene or cynical, the ladies, it seems to me, may well have played a positive role in encouraging the infiltration of comedy of contemporary life by themes hitherto indigenous to romantic and other forms of "sympathetic" drama. This development is too large a matter to be more than barely suggested here. But even in the heydey of the cuckolding play there begin to appear in comedies with the scene London such figures as the virtuous girl who resists a would-be seducer and thus brings him to propose marriage[20] and the wife who stands the shock of courtship by a spark and so wins the audience's admiration and his also.[21] Constancy in love begins to be regarded with more respect by comic writers; and the sincere suitor, instead of being laughed at, as young Bellair had been by Dorimant and Medley in *The man of mode,* may now dominate his play—as Farewel in *Sir Courtly Nice* (1685). This drift in comedy in the later sixteen-seventies and early eighties is doubtless to be attributed in part to the inability of the lesser writers to realize and appreciate the spirit of comedy as written by Etherege and Wycherley and so maintain the integrity of the genre. But no doubt this softening was, at least in part, in response to the wishes of the ladies, who would have been certain to like *Sir Courtly Nice* as much as they disliked Mrs. Behn's *The luckey chance.* And certainly the gallants had not requested any trend toward the sympathetic in comedy. By now we know what kind of thing *they* liked.

With the line between pit and boxes sharply drawn and the issue in doubt as to whether comedy would continue to stress a cynical treatment of human nature or would succumb to the sympathetic mood, we are now ready to examine the years 1688-89. The plays here are of extraordinary interest. James Carlile's *The fortune-hunters,* for instance, testifies to his awareness of the now equally authoritative demands of the male and female factions in the audience by furnishing a rowdy love-game for the pit, and, no less emphasized, a romantic

couple, obviously for the ladies. But these years are chiefly of importance as marking the return of Shadwell to the stage after a long absence. In 1681 his *The Lancashire witches* had testified to his emer-
gence from Wycherley's influence: there is no brutal sexuality in the
play, and his two heroes are honest lovers. However, their superiority
to the rake type is not stressed, and, on the whole, this is one of Shadwell's weakest performances. When he returns in the year of the
Glorious Revolution, the play is one of his strongest—*The squire of
Alsatia*. It marks his return to the exemplary mood, but the formula is
different. In *The humorists* and *The miser* he had created heroes who
were "examples" from the very start of the play; in *The squire*, Bel-
fond Jr. becomes one at play's end by virtue of his reclamation from
rakish courses. And this, it should be noted, is largely through female
influence; for, though the sensible counsels of his adoptive father play
their part in his reformation, it is brought about mainly by the requirements of the serious heroine Isabella, who would not take him
otherwise. In essence this formula was new. Something approaching it
had been seen earlier in the period, in the reformation of the gay hero
Ramble in Crowne's *The country wit* (1676). But in *The squire* it is
for the first time deliberately applied to the schooling of the rake of
the day, whether on the stage or in the audience; and Shadwell deserves to be credited with a kind of patent on the motif, which was to
be used subsequently in dozens of plays. His *Bury Fair* (1689) is no
less interesting. Here Lord Bellamy is the perfect example of what a
gentleman should be; and his superiority to Wildish, who stands for
what had been the conception of the man of sense a decade or two
before, is insisted on throughout.

Nor was it Shadwell alone who pushed the exemplary method at this
time. In *Love for money* (December, 1689),[22] D'Urfey expresses all the
virtues that he could call to mind in Young Merriton and Mirtilla, the
pair of true lovers, and the more for the edification of his audience
includes a contrasting pair, the libertine Jack Amorous and the mer-
cenary Betty Jiltall, who in the end learn that their lack of principle
does not pay. In this place should perhaps be mentioned, also,
Crowne's *The English friar* (1689 or 1690),[23] in which Crowne arranges
for a coquette the same sort of discipline and reclamation that Shadwell had applied to a rake in *The squire*; and this is similarly a "first"
in the use of a motif that was to appear frequently later.

Exemplary comedy had thus been solidly founded by the beginning
of the last decade of the century; and, since the ladies had for long

been anxious to see risqué wit, facetious lovemaking, and perhaps even coquetry replaced on the stage by decency, sincerity, and honest love, a tacit alliance between their party and the reforming dramatists was the result. And in the nineties, despite the endeavors of Southerne, Congreve, Vanbrugh, and others to keep the old kind of comedy alive and despite, also, the gallants in the audience, who would have been sure to encourage them in this, the influence of the exemplary dramatists and the ladies progressively triumphs. By and large, the love-game languishes, while constancy and sincerity take its place; cuckold-making comes to be frowned upon; "examples," by which the authors intend to show rakes and coquettes the path to reform, are met with abundantly. Meanwhile, the ladies, it may be noted, were not idle but kept·the pressure on dramatists who tried to stick to the old way: by the middle of the decade the weight of their displeasure had been felt by Congreve himself,[24] Crowne,[25] Granville,[26] and D'Urfey.[27]

But I do not intend here to pursue comedy into the nineties, which, with a few glorious exceptions, was a time to make the judicious grieve. The issue was really settled before the decade began. And if this is true, then the influences which have usually been credited with having brought about the change in comedy are too late in date to have done more than confirm it and determine this or that phase in which it was later to express itself. Influence of reforming pamphleteers? Collier, of course, came too late to be thought of as having initiated a change, and Professor Krutch shows that the "moral and ascetic objection to the theater" was "but tentative and sporadic between 1660 and 1698."[28] Influence of the court? William and Mary were certainly an improvement on their predecessors, but surely no monarch before Anne could be said to have made any move to clean up the theater. Influence of the "middle class"? Professor Krutch shows that the societies for the reformation of manners began to think of the theater as early as 1694,[29] but attempts on their part to exert pressure by prosecuting dramatists and actors date from 1698 and after.[30] As for audience pressure by citizens, the epilogue to Love's last shift (1696) shows that at least by this date they did indeed attend the theater, where they sat in the middle gallery. But the cits who patronized the theater would not be those who inveighed against it or wished to reform it. Even after 1700, comedy gives little evidence of having been written to please what members of this class might be in the audience; Steele's Sealand, in The conscious lovers, is quite exceptional; in the main the cit is about as severely treated in comedy after 1700 as before. For at least the first half of the eighteenth century the dominant faction in the audience was, as it had been in Charles II's time, the *beau monde*.[31]

As to "benevolence," the state of the case is much the same, but this appears only when the term is used with the requisite precision. It has been defined by Professor Crane[32] as a " 'general kindness' to all men because they are men"—this being thought of as not merely rational but emotional and given to expressing itself in pity and compassion; natural—not foreign or alien—to the human species; and hence capable of giving pleasure and self-satisfaction in its exercise. He shows that these essentials of the doctrine as it is found in the eighteenth century had been asserted in sermons by Latitudinarian churchmen long before the end of the seventeenth, so that it would have been in ample time to have exerted a mollifying influence upon comedy as early as 1688-89, or even earlier.

As a matter of fact, however, I do not find evidence of it in plays until a decade after this date. Distinctions have to be made. The teary scene in Steele's *The lying lover,* in which the erring Young Bookwit weeps with his father and is converted, is on a basis of benevolence, as the epilogue to the play shows. But not all conversions, even in comedy of contemporary life, should automatically be assumed to be on this basis. Scapegrace sons may surely be reformed without it in the drama, as in life; and, since in life some tears are appropriate on these occasions, a few may naturally be expected on the stage. Thus Shadwell, in allowing tears in a conversion of a son by a father in *The scowrers* (1691), would seem only to be copying nature, without asking himself whether his audience were possessed of an innate sympathy for their species which might be stimulated to their benefit. The difference between the scenes in the two plays is that Steele's is exemplary and benevolist, Shadwell's only exemplary.

The most mischievous type of confusion, however, is that in which benevolence is read into those standbys of the romantic or "sympathetic" mood in literature which merely happen to resemble it—for instance, the motif in which a strayed lover or husband is brought back into the right path. I do not—for example—find benevolence in *Love's last shift,* Loveless' reunion with Amanda seeming to me to show it no more than does the reunion of Posthumus and Imogen in *Cymbeline.* The only difference is that Cibber treats the motif in a comedy of contemporary life. But, to come at once to the point, I find the first trace of recognizable benevolence in the comedy of the period in a play which is of the same year as Collier's *Short view*—Farquhar's *Love and a bottle* (1698).[33]

It would seem, then, that most of the credit (or blame!) for the change in comedy should be divided between Shadwell, who, in order to correct the dubious morality of the plays of his contemporaries, invented the exemplary method, and the ladies, who were revolted by the Wycherleyan phase of comedy and fought it by protest and boycott until—as is always likely to happen in any age—they got their way.

NOTES

1. This paper is based on one entitled " 'The ladies' and the change in the temper of comedy, from Wycherley to Steele," read before the English Drama discussion group of the Modern Language Association at the last annual meeting of the association at Detroit. I have amplified it somewhat, but anything like satisfactory presentation of the whole course of comedy in the period, the setting in which Shadwell and the ladies carried on their operations, is beyond the scope of an article. I can only apologize for such assertions in the following as I have been compelled by limitations of space to leave without adequate support; I hope, however, that most, if not all, of these will be made good in my book "The gay couple in Restoration comedy," to be published in the coming fall by the Harvard University Press.
2. *English dramatic literature* (London, 1899) , III, 495.
3. O. Waterhouse, "The development of English sentimental comedy in the eighteenth century," *Anglia*, XXX (1907) , 155-58.
4. De Witt C. Croissant, "Studies in the work of Colley Cibber," *University of Kansas Bull., Humanistic Studies*, I (1912-15) , 29, 44 ff.
5. Ernest Bernbaum, *The drama of sensibility* (Cambridge, 1915), chap. iv, pp. 50-52, 63-64, 70-71.
6. Allardyce Nicoll, *A history of Restoration drama* (Cambridge, 1923) , pp. 251 ff.
7. De Witt C. Croissant, "Early sentimental comedy," in *The Parrott presentation volume* (Princeton, 1935) , p. 71.
8. Frederick T. Wood, "The beginnings and significance of sentimental comedy," *Anglia*, LV (1931) , 368-92: "The first traces of sentimental comedy are to be found as far back as the Morality Plays. . . . In *Everyman*, it is true, the hero finally has to answer the summons of Death, but he achieves a moral triumph in realizing that the only measure of achievement in life is Good Deeds, which is, after all, the tenor of the greater part of the sentimental plays of the eighteenth century. No matter which of the definitions of sentimental comedy we accept, these plays will answer to them all. By their very conception, as upheld in their name, they presented a moral problem; confidence in the goodness of human nature is their most marked characteristic, and the central figure

. . . is designed to appeal to the sympathy of the spectators" (pp. 373, 375).

9. I shall briefly discuss "benevolence" at a later point in the paper.

10. Unless otherwise noted, dates throughout are dates of first performance according to Nicoll.

11. But this credit to Howard holds good only if the first printed edition (1674) faithfully represents the play as produced at the earlier date. In the eleven-year interim he may have revised the play and borrowed from Etherege in the process. My guess would be, however, that the edition is fairly trustworthy and that the borrowing was the other way.

12. The passage is usually taken as an attack on Dryden's *Secret love,* but *All mistaken* is the only preceding play that could have justified it.

13. The interest of this play was recognized long ago, in C. M. Scheurer, "An early sentimental comedy," *Anglia,* XXXVII (1913), 125-28. In a number of ways it forecasts subsequent developments in eighteenth-century comedy in really surprising fashion. But Revet arrives at these effects merely through being good-natured and sympathetic; he means neither to rebuke the gay couple nor to present examples for imitation by his audience. In other words, he is not "exemplary," whereas with Shadwell the case is otherwise.

14. I can think of but one cuckolding in new plays (1660-69), and this single instance is in Wilson's *The cheats* (1663), a Jonsonian comedy of humors and intrigue which has no love-game and, in fact, nothing of the post-Restoration air about it at all. Killigrew's *The parson's wedding,* acted in 1664, is very bawdy, but it was written before the Civil Wars. There is also a cynical intrigue in Dryden's *Sir Martin Mar-all,* but it is in the minor plot.

15. Adultery figures, for instance, in Arrowsmith's *The reformation* (1673), and Anon., *The Mall* (1674).

16. Act IV, scene 2: Sir Simon Addleplot, as "Jonas," and Lady Flippant.

17. Wycherley, in the dedication of the play.

18. "I Printed this Play with all the impatient haste one ought to do, who would be vindicated from the most unjust and silly aspersion, Woman could invent to cast on Woman. . . . That it was Baudy, the least and most Excusable fault in the Men writers, to whose Plays they all crowd . . . but how so Cruell an unkindness came into their imaginations I can by no means guess; unless by those whose Lovers by long absence, or those whom Age or Ugliness have rendered a little distant from those things they would fain imagin here—But if such as these durst profane their Chast ears with hearing it over again, or taking it into their serious Consideration in their Cabinets; they would find nothing that the most innocent Virgins can have cause to blush at."

19. Dr. Charles D'Avenant and Charles Killigrew were two of the co-proprietors of the United Theatre Royal at this time; Killigrew was also Master of the Revels. L'Estrange was licenser of the press.

The lady is protesting a good deal in this passage. Any "charge" by James II to D'Avenant and Killigrew, it is safe to say, need not be taken too seriously; and the licenser would have been on the lookout for sedition but scarcely for cuckoldings. The play is one of Mrs. Behn's naughtiest.

20. See, for example, the Bellamour-Isabella plot in Shadwell's *A true widow* (1678) and compare with Ludovico-Otrante in Rhodes's *Flora's vagaries* (1663) , or Salerno-Leandra in Stapylton's *The slighted maid* (1663).

21. See the Welford-Christina plot in D'Urfey's *Squire Oldsapp* (1678) and compare with Iberio-Pyramena in *The Slighted maid* or Almanzor-Almahide in Dryden's *The conquest of Granada, Part II* (1670) .

22. So dated by Nicoll. Harbage, *Annals of English drama, 975-1700* (1934) and Montague Summers, *A bibliography of Restoration drama* (London, n.d.) , date the play 1690.

23. Harbage and Summers give it the earlier, Nicoll the later, date.

24. *The double-dealer* (1693) . Congreve's preface reveals that the ladies had taken offense at Lady Froth and Lady Plyant. Strangely enough, they do not seem to have minded Mrs. Fondlewife in *The old bachelor*, but this might have been because she was a cit, not a person of quality.

25. *The married beau* (1694). Crowne's answer in his preface is a rather surly one: "In the play a lady's virtue is vanquish'd by temptation, and she is led out to be debauch'd, and not long after, returns and confesses her sin: This offends some ladies, but 'tis hard to know which offends them, the sin or the confession, the latter example perhaps they like worst. If the sin be the offence, the ladies have led my muse astray, by going so often to see the same assaults and conquests more grossly represented in other plays."

26. *The she-gallants* (1695) . This play they evidently damned, for Downes (*Roscius Anglicanus*, ed. Summers [London, n.d.], p. 45) says that it was well acted, but "offending the Ears of some Ladies who set up for Chastity, it made its exit."

27. *Don Quixote, Part Third* (1695) . In his preface D'Urfey attributes its failure to a variety of causes, one of which was offense unintentionally given to the boxes. When he "heard the Ladies were prejudic'd about some Actions and Sayings in Mary the Buxome's and Sancho's Parts" he was "extremely concern'd." He is sorry to have disobliged "that essential part of the Audience."

28. *Comedy and conscience after the Restoration* (New York, 1924) , p. 92.

29. *Ibid.,* p. 163.

30. *Ibid.,* p. 169.

31. Nicoll (*A history of early eighteenth century drama* [Cambridge, Eng., 1929]) by no means overstates the case when he warns: "It must not be presumed . . .that even in the last portion of this period [1700-1750] the atmosphere of the theatre was middle class rather than aristocratic" (p. 8) .

32. R. S. Crane, "Suggestions toward a genealogy of the 'Man of feeling,' " *ELH*, I (1934), 205-30.

33. In my forthcoming book I discuss the role of benevolence and furnish a list of such instances of its occurrence as I have found in comedies to 1750. The list is, on the whole, not a long one, benevolence being not very widely distributed in the comedy of the period.

ERNEST TUVESON

❀

The Importance of Shaftesbury

I

It has generally been acknowledged that the third Earl of Shaftesbury exercised an immense influence on the eighteenth century.[1] His collected works, the *Characteristics*, went through eleven editions between 1711 and 1790; and the list of authors who demonstrated the influence of Shaftesbury would include a majority of those published in the eighteenth century. Yet there is a puzzle about Shaftesbury's effect on his own and later times. It was long assumed that this influence consisted in his originality, the newness of his theory of the "moral sense" in particular, as well as his "preromantic" and supposedly original glorification of external nature. The notable growth in altruism in eighteenth century literature, says Professor C. A. Moore, "is to be traced largely, I think, to the *Characteristics* . . . of Lord Shaftesbury," and he adds, "It has long since been established that his system of philosophy constitutes a turning point in the history of pure speculation, especially in ethics."[2] In more recent years, however, this view has been challenged. Professor R. S. Crane has shown that the essentials of the "moral sense" theory were being preached by "Latitudinarian" divines even before Shaftesbury was born. He writes:

> If we wish to understand the origins and the widespread
> diffusion in the eighteenth century of the ideas which
> issued in the cult of sensibility, we must look, I believe,
> to a period considerably earlier than that in which

From *ELH: A Journal of English Literary History*, XX (1953), 267-99. Reprinted by permission of The Johns Hopkins Press.

> Shaftesbury wrote and take into account the propaganda
> of a group of persons whose opportunities for moulding
> the thoughts of ordinary Englishmen were much greater
> than those of even the most aristocratic of deists.[3]

It can be shown as well that the exaltation and adoration of external nature was anticipated by and reflected a complex of ideas that the new science in combination with religion had already prepared.[4]

Must we, then, give up Shaftesbury as "original"? And if we do, how are we to account for the astonishing influence which he exerted? The answers to these questions, I believe, lie along other lines than have usually been suggested. In the world of thought, the whole is greater than the sum of the parts; and if the age that followed Shaftesbury was to a considerable extent *Characteristical,* it was not because his ideas separately were new or startling, but because he constructed of many elements a complete and artistically consistent whole, in a setting which had not previously existed.

As to the "moral sense" theory. There was as Professor Crane indicates, a cloud of divines who to some extent advanced the propositions that virtue is centered in a natural impulse towards humanitarian feeling for and sympathy with one's fellows, and that the exercise of this virtue is accompanied by an inward feeling of satisfaction and joy, while the spectacle of distress produces sympathetic pain. Yet, however striking these statements may be in themselves, we must remember that they were embedded in a context which did much to reduce their revolutionary effect.

Let us consider as examples two influential members of what is loosely called the "Cambridge Platonist" group. John Norris's *The Theory and Regulation of Love* (1694) postulates a "moral Gravity" of the soul, impressed on it by God Himself. This gravity

> will be its *Connaturality* to all Good, or Good in general,
> that is to God as its primary adequate Object, and to par-
> ticular Goods, only so far as they have something of the
> common Nature of Good, something of God in them.[5]

The image borrowed from the new philosophy, which makes goodness seem as inevitable in men as the operation of natural law in the cosmos, is striking and apparently radical enough; yet the theory is not what it seems to be. For Norris still sees good as merely participation in a transcendental God. The "moral gravity," it appears, is the result of a spiritual ascent. "From the Original Pravity and Degeneracy of our Nature, among *all* these particular Goods, that which we most eagerly propend to, is *sensual* Good."[6] The "Animal" impressions are formed first, "Sensuality comes to be *Adult* and *Mature*, when our discourses are but *young* and *imperfect*." When we arrive at an age for reflection we have, therefore, to "unravel the Prejudices of our Youth, and *unlive* our former Life . . . ," and we are assured that it is not an easy job. This curious theory, with its mixture of new science, psychology, and old theology, represents in sum a partly scientific, partly Neoplatonic version of the doctrine of original sin. At no time did Norris, despite his seemingly radical phrase "moral gravity," really absorb morality into nature, or identify the end of existence with conduct in this world. Against this view Norris's friend Henry More advanced another account of moral action, also seemingly radical in its imagery.

> For, as the eye, . . . if it be vitiated in it self, cannot rightly discern the Condition of the visible Object it fixes its Sight upon; so the Mind of Man, let him set himself never so diligently to contemplate any *Moral* or *Intelligible* Object, if she be made dim by Moral Corruptions and Impurities, will not be able or free to close with what is best in the Circumstances that lye before her, being held captive by the Vices the Party has not yet purified himself from . . . our being redeemed into an Ability or freedom of chusing what is best, is not from *mere attention* to the Object, but from Purification, *Illumination,* and *real Regeneration* into the *Divine Image.*[7]

Here are two liberal clergymen who speak indeed of "goodness" as "natural," as natural as gravity in the physical world, or as seeing in the animal; yet the images certainly are not to be taken by themselves. Platonized Christianity, though modified by Cartesianism and early Newtonianism, nevertheless did not lose sight of *"Purification, Illumination,* and *real Regeneration"* as essential before the "divine Image" can be complete.

Other preachers, of a later generation, do in fact carry the naturalizing tendency further; but we see, if we read the works of these divines, that the basic Christian pattern is always to be discerned in the background. Isaac Barrow, one of the most extreme of them all, can exclaim:

> In fine, the wisest observers of man's nature have pro-
> nounced him to be a creature gentle and sociable, inclin-
> able to and fit for conversation, apt to keep good order,
> to observe rules of justice, to embrace any sort of vertue, if
> well managed; if instructed by good discipline, if guided
> by good example, if living under the influence of wise
> laws and virtuous governours. Fierceness, rudeness, craft,
> malice, all perverse and intractable, all mischievous and
> vitious dispositions do grow among men (like weeds in
> any, even the best soil) and overspread the earth from
> neglect of good education; from ill conduct, ill custome,
> ill example; ('tis the comparison of Saint *Chrysostome,*
> and of Plutarch.)[8]

The combination of a Father and a pagan philosopher as authorities
should remind us that such ideas go back very far and derive from the
amalgamation of classical philosophy with Christianity which early
began to take place. That man has some—perhaps a fairly large—
capacity for goodness was part of orthodox Christian theology. But we
must always view such statements against the whole background. Barrow, for instance, frequently points out that the soul must undergo a
spiritual awakening before its goodness can be released:

> If also being, through divine grace awakened out of that
> drowsie state (which naturally in great measure hath
> seised upon all men) he discovereth his moral or spiritual
> wants, and imperfections; he is then apt to breathe and
> endeavour a nearer similitude to God. . . .[9]

The sacrifice of the Cross is essential to that "rousing." We must seek
divine illumination "to enflame us with ardent love unto thee, and
to direct our steps in obedience to thy Laws through the gloomy shades
of this world, into that region of eternal light and bliss, where thou
reignest in perfect Glory and Majesty, . . ."[10] In the famous sermon
"The Nature, Properties and Acts of Charity," which has been considered a very close approach to the theory of natural benevolence, we
find him telling his hearers that we cannot disregard any man as "contemptible," for the reason that "Every man is of a divine extraction,
and allied to heaven by nature and by grace, as the Son of God, and
Brother of God Incarnate."[11] Such a theory of altruism, a version of
the great tradition of Christian charity and brotherhood, is still some
distance from a consistently naturalistic one. On other occasions he
shows his remoteness from the "social" doctrine of Shaftesbury and

the eighteenth century when he praises the virtues of solitude quite in the old tradition, implying that in it is to be found the climax of religion; man is "social" by nature because of his potentialities as a son of God, but he manifests the true glory of his nature in his solitary immediate relation to God.

It would be a fatal mistake to assume that the Christian and other worldly elements in the thinking of these preachers were mere vestigial remains, so to speak, hanging on to a new, secular, optimistic opinion about human nature. However great their "latitude"—and of course to such conservatives as Swift it seemed dangerously wide—they were never really out of touch with the great traditional belief that men are destined to recover, by supernatural aid, from a disastrous cosmic fall into a transcendental state. Thus it would be easy, on the basis of isolated passages alone, to place Samuel Parker among the most completely naturalistic benevolists. In attempting to defend the existence of a divinely ordained law of nature against the attacks of skepticism, he cites such facts as strength of parental feeling, and that "as for the Generality of Men their hearts are so tender and their natural affections so humane, that they cannot but pity and commiserate the afflicted with a kind of fatal and mechanical sympathy."[12] Before we conclude that such a remark anticipates the man of feeling, however, we should recall that elsewhere he very emphatically asserts that the instincts are insufficient guides.

> God may possibly have put some secret Notices into the Minds of Men for the greater security of Justice and Honesty in the world; but then, beside that there is no way to prove the Certainty or demonstrate the Obligation of any such inward Record, this plainly resolves the Authority of the Law of Nature into uncertain and unaccountable Principles, or such as may be pretended and, when they are, ought to be admitted without any Proof or Evidence of Reason. . . .[13]

Many other examples might be cited.[14] But in sum they would, I think, show that, while the Latitudinarian preaching certainly had much to do with bringing about a new emphasis on altruism, it did not present a really new concept of human nature.

The Anglican apologists were on the *qui vive* against opinions of many kinds which they regarded as erroneous. They strongly emphasized free will and the possibility of the general access to grace, in opposition to the extreme of "total depravity." They were aware of the fact that for some time there had been a tendency to depreciate "right reason" as a reliable governor of personal conduct. Montaigne could remark that reason, like wax, takes any form imposed on it. Such skeptical idealists as Rochester were led into an attitude resembling romantic irony, seeing in reason a faculty which serves only to make men worse than the animals whose impulses they share; as Mackenzie, much later, puts the view:

> Men must have passions; paint them, if you can;
> Where less the brute enjoys, and more the man.
> To combat passion when our reasons rise,
> Reasons are better passions in disguise. . . .
> The world's dull reason, sober, cool, and pure,
> The world's dull reason is a knave demure.[15]

To combat this attitude, destructive alike of belief in the divine possibilities of the soul and of the concept of the "dignity of man," it was necessary to show that the universe as a whole is "rational" and that human behavior, even though man stands in need of assistance from beyond himself, is not truly anarchic.

The school of Hobbes, of course, powerfully reinforced the tradition of doubt, and it was said that every aspiring bachelor of divinity broke a spear against the steel cap of the sage of Malmesbury. He represented what was thought of as the "naturalistic" school, and the culmination of the skepticism about reason. But he was more easily condemned than answered. The powerful realism or apparent realism, of his demonstration that crass self-interest, however dressed up, is the true motive of all actions, could not be answered except by descending into the deep subrational drives of human nature. To answer Hobbes involved showing that this subrational part of our nature has more than one drive, that it can be good and "social" instead of warring and chaotic.

In answering these and other attacks, the Anglican divines were polemicists, it must be remembered, and the polemicist is notoriously prone to exaggerate in making whatever point he immediately has in hand. Defending religion did for many reasons involve defending the relative natural goodness of human beings; but while this fact certainly is important, it should not obscure our recognition that the polemical treatises and sermons are not representative of the whole views of both preachers and congregations. A most important result of the complex of thought in this time was a largely unconscious drift among these preachers towards a kind of Pelagianism: the proposition that the potentialities of human nature remain, and that corruption has entered from a long accumulation of pejorative changes in customs, educations, etc. Yet theological Pelagianism, although a heresy, remains within religion, and implies need for grace and redemption; and one can say no more than that it hovered in the air, and was hardly more than a vague omen of what was to come.[16] It is undoubtedly true, however, that a vague Christian Pelagianism could easily prepare the way for the powerful secular development of Pelagianism which is dominant in our own time. Contributing to the drift was the great mass of new information about other cultures that had been reaching Western Europe since the time of Henry the Navigator, which was making people realize more and more the real importance of environment and training on personality; this was the age of Locke, and the old faith in innate ideas went out with astounding rapidity.

Before a new sensibility could arise, however, a kind of catalytic agent was necessary to precipitate these undefined and unintegrated elements. That agent was supplied, in considerable part, by Shaftesbury. He did it by combining the spiritual idealism of the divines with the "naturalistic" view of the psychologists, and by applying consistently the full implications of the new world-view in science to the problems of ethics. It is usually said that he defends the "natural goodness" of man. In a general way this is true, but only if we remember that "goodness" has for him a new kind of meaning. It would be more accurate to say that Shaftesbury represents the human being as naturally adapted, with a kind of psychological ethical fitness, to live in his surroundings. The new philosophy depicted a universe of a myriad of parts, harmoniously operating according to immutable laws; it is not a universe in need of transformation or salvation, but one perfect and complete. The sum of these operations represent the *raison d'être* of the whole: the *process* is the final cause, not eternal principles rising above the flux.

It is logical to assume, therefore, that the human being, as an operating part of the great Whole, must be so constructed that in all his action he will, if he behaves "naturally," do those things which will promote his happiness and the happiness of the universe. With Shaftesbury we take the difficult step that this conclusion involves: with Shaftesbury we begin to see conduct in terms of what we should now call "normal" instead of in terms of obedience to divine or natural law; and with Shaftesbury we begin to think of departures from desirable behavior as the "abnormal" and "maladjustment" rather than "sin." The villains become environment and training, rather than the hereditary "degenerate nature of man," as Swift puts it.

Yet Shaftesbury was intensely aware of the fact that, to the human view at least, society in his time was far from being the ideal harmonious system it should be. Mandeville did Shaftesbury a great injustice by caricaturing him as a retiring patrician, favored by a gentle education, viewing through rose-colored glasses a world which he did not understand. The truth is that the noble philosopher remarkably anticipated Rousseau's passionate indictment of the social order, as we see in such passages as this:

> Tho however we may, in passing by, observe, that whilst we see in all other Creatures around us so great a proportionableness, constancy and regularity in all their passions and affections; so great a harmony, and such an adherence to Nature; no failure in the care of the Offspring, or of the Society (if living in Society). . . . Man in the mean time, vicious and unconsonant man, lives out of all rule and proportion, contradicts his Principles, breaks the Order and Oeconomy of all his Passions, and lives at odds with his whole Species, and with Nature: so that it is next to a Prodigy to see a Man in the World who lives NATURALLY, and as A MAN.[17]

The last clause, of course, has the stinger, for in it Shaftesbury uncompromisingly asserts that it is coming back to nature, not rising above her, that will solve the ethical problem.

Why, then, is there an air of hope about the whole work of Shaftesbury, an air of "enthusiasm" which was to infect future generations? Here the real purpose of the moralist has been misunderstood. It seems that he was not writing a mere complacent defense of the universe, or seeking to rehabilitate the aesthetic side of life as against "mechanism." His real goal was much larger. Shaftesbury, the heir to the great Whig tradition of his grandfather, thought of himself as carrying on, in the field of morals, the work of the reformer. In *The Moralists* (1709) he speaks of the

> Grace or Beauty in that original Native Liberty, which sets us free from so many inborn Tyrannys, gives us the Privilege of Ourselves, and makes us our own, and Independent. . . . A sort of Property, which, methinks, is as material to us to the full, as that which secures us our Lands, or Revenues.[18]

Now that security of estate and freedom of thought have been established after the Glorious Revolution, and the way is clear to remove fanaticism from religion, a great prospect for the betterment of life is opening up; the way is open to free men from the perversions engendered by religious dogmas and zeal, from false, derogatory ideas of human nature, and from artificial customs which separate man from nature, God from nature, and all three from the unity in which they should exist. Above all, if men are to be "natural" and therefore happy, they must stop connecting morality with meretricious ideas of the future life, which remove the emphasis from nature and its harmony. But argument and attack were not Shaftesbury's method; rather, he envisioned something like therapy, the treatment of an urbane and insinuating style, the application of raillery rather than the traditional satire, the artistic presentation of external nature and encouragement of the communion of the mind with landscape untouched by man.

In an age intoxicated by the wonders of mechanism, it was necessary to show how this adaptation of the moral nature to environment could work. If man is to be represented as merely "natural" how can the presence of the impulse to good within the mind be explained without resorting to some such hypothesis as that reason is the "candle of the Lord"? And if good behavior is "natural," how can it be reconciled with so abstruse a faculty as advanced logical thought?

I have suggested that Shaftesbury combined a tradition of spiritual idealism with naturalistic psychology. The first he inherited from the Cambridge Platonists, at least in large part. We have seen how Henry More reduced the moral action to a kind of process, thus showing the influence of the new philosophy. In the *Enchiridion Ethicum,* he describes virtue as "rather a Power than a Habit."[19] This "power" is manifested in a "boniform Faculty," which More calls, borrowing but changing in connotation an Aristotelian phrase, the "very Eye of the Soul." This boniform faculty is the manifestation in action of "right reason," but—most importantly—it does not consist of innate propositions, or reasoning therefrom. Indeed, these things are at best crutches for the numerous race in whom the boniform faculty is regrettably weak. The highest kind of moral judgment consists in a kind of superintuition, but one which is emphatically not a purely natural endowment. It has affinities with the "mens" or "intellectus angelicus" of Ficino's Christian Neoplatonism, and More once defines it as a divine power "by which we are lifted up and cleave unto God," which produces a "ravishing" and supra-worldly pleasure in those lofty spirits who have it. Those who belong to this group can perceive a "symmetry of the passions" as immediately as the average man perceives a parallelism of lines. It appears that More describes a kind of "moral sense"; his emphasis on a "power" rather than a reasoning faculty is part of his movement away from the "clear and distinct ideas" of Descartes, that philosopher who came to seem to him an *ignis fatuus,* and this movement More shared with his age. The idea, nevertheless, remains firmly embedded in a concept of the universe both other worldly and aspirational. The process of moral intuition is the result of an extensive purification of the soul from its corruption by matter.

Shaftesbury's innovation was the naturalization of this moral faculty. The moral intuition, in the successful developed personality, is the original, not final state of man. In other words, the ancient picture is turned upside down: the task of the human being is to retain a natural and original moral sense, instead of to attain it by a long course of redemption. Exactly how could such a natural moral sense be shown to exist? Fortunately, there was available a means of implementing the idea in terms of the master of the new psychology himself.

The older idea that Locke was a complete empiricist has been challenged in recent years.[20] In saying that the soul at birth is like a blank sheet of paper, he meant only that ideas are not somehow mysteriously present in us before we have any contact with the outside world. He did not, however, mean to imply that our ideas are formed by a purely passive action, through the automatic effect of sense impressions. In fact the mind plays the decisive part in cognition. It is autonomous, the ever alert observer, combining, separating, creating order out of the chaos of sensations which constantly are borne in upon it. First it is an *observer:* all mental action, to Locke, is ultimately a matter of "perceiving." He reduces the whole of thought to three kinds of "perception":

> 1. The perception of ideas in our minds. 2. The perception of the signification of signs. 3. The perception of the connexion or repugnance, agreement or disagreement, that there is between any of our ideas.[21]

Certainly the independent power of the mind in the second and third kinds of thinking cannot be denied, and it is possible that it has some creative function even with regard to the first; and when sensations associate themselves arbitrarily, without the mind's ordering control, we have "association of ideas," the manifestation of irrationality and even insanity. By identifying "perception" and "understanding," therefore, Locke placed the pivot of intellectual action in the imagination, and not without reason did Berkeley object to Locke's attempt to show that abstractions can be made, independent of any one image. The image, indeed, is the very center of the mental process. A constant procession of images pass before the mind, even when it is not experiencing directly, and even in sleep.[22]

If Locke had presented a convincing epistemology, he had, it was feared, set forth a wholly inadequate system of ethics—or, some thought, none in fact at all. Practical morality, according to him, depends on the fear of eternal punishment threatened by the Supreme Being for those who disobey His revealed will.[23] Shaftesbury, the disciple of the Cambridge Platonists, objected to the proposition that good and evil are not absolutes but rather mere arbitrary commandments of God, which to be known, must be revealed. Certainly it seemed, further, if good and evil are absolutes, they must have their representative faculty in man's mind; he surely is not left helpless to drift without a moral rudder. Much of Shaftesbury's aversion to his teacher Locke arises from his horror of Locke's calloused attitude towards the moral problem. Yet the calm confidence which earlier philosophers, such as Lord Herbert of Cherbury, had displayed in innate ideas, was no more. How, without invoking a supernatural and mystical power, could the absolute standard of right and wrong be brought into relation to human life?

The solution lay at hand in the adaptation of Locke's own system to moral idealism of the kind Henry More had displayed. If the mind perceives the connection, repugnance, etc., of ideas derived from sensation, why should not this process apply to morality as well? Why should not the mind perceive the harmony or repugnance of images of action and passions, just as it perceives the difference between a triangle and a circle? And so Shaftesbury, in the *Inquiry concerning Virtue,* combines the two:

> In a Creature capable of forming general Notions of things, not only the sensible things that offer themselves to the sense, are the objects of the Affections; but the very *actions* themselves, and the affections of Pity, Charity, Kindness, Justice, and so their contraries, being brought into the Mind by reflection, become Objects; . . . .[24]

The imagination, as in Locke, makes possible the action; the similarity to Locke's "perception" is evident.

> And thus the several Motions, Inclinations, Passions,
> Dispositions, and consequent Carriage and Behavior of
> Creatures in the various Parts of Life, being in several
> scenes represented to the Mind, which readily discerns
> the good and the ill towards the species or Public; it
> proves afterwards a new work for the affection, either
> virtuously and soundly to incline to, and affect what is
> just and right; and disaffect what is contrary; or, vitiously
> and corruptly to affect what is ill, and disregard or hate
> what is worthy and good.

The actual "moral sense" is not in itself an emotion. It is an action of
the mind in viewing the "several scenes" of behavior, etc.; the affections follow, and should be properly related as effect to cause. Shaftesbury implies that the actual recognition of good and evil is in itself
sound. The process goes wrong when the affections get out of kilter
with the perceptions, and the wrong passion, or the right passion to
excess becomes attached to an intuition. But a powerful natural impulse should produce the normal kind of reaction: the reflex action
must be distorted by long habit before it goes wrong. The affection in
turn is a drive to action. Here of course something like instrumental
reason has its place. The affection may produce the right intention but,
because of poor judgment, inappropriate action may be taken. It is
important, nevertheless, to recognize that "reason" here is a means of
implementation rather than the judicial governor of basic decisions.

Shaftesbury's conception of the affections also clearly shows the influence of Locke. The latter reduced emotion to pleasure and pain, which
he identified with good and evil for the individual.[25] Things, whether
experienced in the present or only as images in reflection, produce
thoughts of pain and pleasure, and "our ideas of love and hatred are
but the dispositions of the mind, in respect of pleasure and pain in
general, however caused in us." The various emotions—love, joy, sorrow, etc.,—are states of mind, "easiness" or "uneasiness." These conscious states of pleasure or pain enable us, among other things, to be
sure that we exist separately from the objects which we perceive. Locke
even hints at a kind of moral sense: shame, he says, "is an uneasiness
of the mind upon the thought of having done something which is indecent, or will lessen the valued esteem which others have for us," and
a father delighting in the well-being of his children need only call up
that idea into reflection to have pleasure.

Locke, however, had separated knowledge from moral decisions.

Morality, he did admit, may be theoretically as certain as knowledge—but only when moral propositions are abstractions.

> And hence it follows that moral knowledge is as capable of real certainty as mathematics. For certainty being but the perception of the agreement or disagreement of our ideas, and demonstration nothing but the perception of such agreement, by the intervention of other ideas or mediums; our moral ideas, as well as mathematical, being archetypes themselves, and so adequate and complete ideas; all the agreement or disagreement which we shall find in them will produce real knowledge, as well as in mathematical figures.[26]

But of course Locke is speaking only of "archetypes," abstracted from concrete events. The kind of adaptation of archetype to experience which Kant was to make lay far in the future, but Shaftesbury as well as other philosophers groped for something of the kind. They thought they had found what they wanted in the seeming fact that men have a capacity for observing the "harmony" among images of passions and actions as certain as their capacity for knowing the existence and differences between things of the outside world. Such a belief fitted in perfectly with the rising conviction that the universe is a great system in which each smallest part operates in perfect mathematical harmony with all the other parts. It is not surprising that Shaftesbury thought there could be an "arithmetic" of the moral sense.

The later versions of the *Inquiry* and other works, however, contain a very important modification of the "moral sense." At first Shaftesbury seemed to identify it with Locke's third, "complex" form of understanding. Later he suggested that moral ideas are more like Locke's first class of perception, so immediate and direct are the impressions they make on the mind.

> Is there then, said he, a natural Beauty of *Figures,* and is there not as natural a one of ACTIONS? No sooner the Eye opens upon *Figures,* the Ear to *Sounds,* than straight the *Beautiful* results, and *Grace* and *Harmony* are known and acknowledged. No sooner are ACTIONS view'd no sooner the *human Affections* and *Passions* discern'd (and they are most of 'em as soon discern'd as felt) than straight *an inward* EYE distinguishes and sees the *Fair* and *Shapely,* the *amiable* and *Admirable,* apart from the Deform'd *the Foul, the Odious,* or *the Despicable.* . . .[27]

The addition of the analogy with aesthetic experience makes it even clearer that the "moral sense" is a naturalized "spiritual eye" of the kind More and others had described. The point is even more emphatic in the later editions of the *Inquiry*, which have three added paragraphs, beginning as follows:

> The Case is the same in the *mental* or *moral* subjects, as in the ordinary *Bodys*, or common Subjects of *Sense*. The Shapes, Motions, Colours, and Proportions of these latter being presented to our Eye; there naturally results a Beauty or Deformity, according to the different Measure, Arrangement, and Disposition of their several Parts. . . .[28]

In the next of these added paragraphs, Shaftesbury tells us that the mind is continually observing other minds; in the third, that as the forms and images of things continually move before our senses, "even when we sleep" (a statement obviously suggested by Locke) so the forms and images of the "moral and intellectual kind" continually move before the mind, even when the objects themselves are absent.

The extremely "aesthetic" form of the moral sense theory, then, was an afterthought in Shaftesbury, but it is the form in which his theory is best known. He was not the first to suggest such an analogy.[29] There may be several reasons for the desire to reduce the moral sense to a reflex so immediate. For one thing, the age increasingly was impressed by the essential importance of the direct sense impression. The fashion for study of epistemology itself betrays this preoccupation, as well as the central place given images in thinking. Again, in this time the standards of taste, at least on the level of forms, seemed absolutely decisive; More, to take one example, often appeals to aesthetic comparisons to make more nebulous matters seem clear-cut. Finally, the desire to take the moral intuition out of the field of "ratiocination" altogether, to remove it from any possible contamination by innate ideas, would tend to make the analogy with immediate sensation tempting.

Many questions remained unanswered. There was, most difficult of all, still the problem of relativism. Granted that there is some kind of innate potentiality for sensing good and bad, are its contents really absolute and immutable, even where development of the personality has been "natural"? These issues, as we shall see, were to prove more than troublesome. But Shaftesbury had made his contribution by combining in a system the deepest desires and beliefs of his age. He had effectually severed morality from righteousness; the supernatural had been absorbed into the natural. He had furthered the process by which, as Panofsky has said, the dualism between Christian and classical "ceased to be real, . . . because the very principle of reality was shifted to the subjective human consciousness."[30]

II

Consequences of the first importance follow from the new *kind* of thinking about man and society and the universe which I have sketched, and in no field more than in literature. In this section I shall try to outline very generally a few of the results of the position Shaftesbury represents (though not necessarily Shaftesbury's direct influence), as we see them in some eighteenth century writing. The full consequences of great changes in thought do not become evident until some time after they have taken place, and the examples cited not unnaturally come several decades after Shaftesbury's death.

Attention has been so completely concentrated on Shaftesbury's "natural goodness" theory that few realize how much of his work is devoted to the study of the "ill" in human nature (the very term is significant in that he does not use "evil" or "sin"). A reading of the *Inquiry*, however, reveals a catalogue of something like case studies in abnormal psychology, presented with an acuteness of insight and a sympathetic power which deserve recognition. Perhaps it was in this field that Shaftesbury was most "original." His two main contributions may be, first, the conception of undesirable behavior as "maladjustment" —to use a modern term; and second, the call for study of states of mind in themselves, impartially and so to speak from within.

The cause of "unsocial" behavior, as we have seen, is described as the disharmony of the moral perception with the drives to action. Shaftesbury's immediate purpose was to show, by imaginative presentation of states of mind, that these dislocations of the personality produce an "uneasiness" such as Locke describes. Thus Shaftesbury departed from the tradition of morality handbooks, with their listings of virtues and vices considered with relation to a given natural or divine law. He did preserve the names of the virtues and vices, but they are only specialized forms of two great basic impulses. In a broader sense Shaftesbury attempted to study the personality to find what causes produce such results—logically enough if the villain is not the will but the external factors which have warped the growth of the mind. Thus he stands in the tradition of objective study of nature—which from Bacon's time on included as a desideratum the natural history of man. The reform of an ill society would require first of all clearing away the false notions about man which have caused infinite mischief. The principal source of "ill" states of mind is the undue strengthening of man's natural and in its place wholly desirable impulse of self-interest. Shaftesbury, describing the basic impulses as self-love and the social sense, combined the two great views of ethics in the Restoration period: the Hobbesian and the Latitudinarian. His style is adapted to the gradations of this self-interest: as he proceeds through the forms which its excess may take, ranging from the slight to the pathological, there is an increasing emotional tension; and at the last, with the "unnatural" emotions, we experience unrelieved horror, which arises from participation with the experiencing mind itself. No one can read these descriptions and feel that the author is the complacent aristocrat of fable.

The progress is from something like "neuroses" to the "psychopathic." Locke pointed out, as he discussed association of ideas, that we all have vagaries in our thinking; the difference between our everyday eccentricities and madness is one of degree. Much the same kind of distinction applies to Shaftesbury's division of the "ill" emotions into those which merely represent over-action of self-interest and those in which the drives to action have become twisted into something tragically self-defeating.

> Now if these SELFISH PASSIONS, besides what other ill they
> are the occasion of, are withal the certain means of losing
> us our *natural Affections;* then 'tis evident, That they
> must be the certain means of losing us the chief Enjoyment of Life, and raising in us those horrid and unnatural Passions, and that Savageness of Temper, which
> makes the GREATEST OF MISERIES, and the most wretched
> State of Life.[31]

Shaftesbury's isolation of sadism as a psychopathological condition and his serious interest in it, which anticipates later developments in literature, is an example of this method:

> To see the Sufferance of an Enemy with Cruel Delight
> may proceed from the height of Anger, Revenge, Fear,
> and other extended Self-Passions: But to delight in the
> Torture and pain of other Creatures indifferently, Natives or Foreigners, of our own or of another Species,

> Kindred or no Kindred, known or unknown; to feed,
> as it were, on Death, and be entertain'd with dying
> agonys. . . .[32]

He asks whether the unnatural passions may not carry with them a sort of pleasure, barbarous as it is—nevertheless a real kind of satisfaction, from tyranny, sadism, and the like. He grants that this is the fact, but going in subtlety far beyond the crude analysis of Hobbes, finds it is the very perversion of the mind that produces the pleasure:

> For as the cruellest bodily Pains do by Intervals of As-
> suagement, produce (as has been shewn) the highest
> bodily Pleasure; so the fiercest and most raging Torments
> of the Mind, do, by certain Moments of Relief, afford the
> greatest of mental Enjoyments, to those who know little
> of the truer kind.[33]

Such a theory is susceptible of other interpretations, however, and this fact perhaps as much as anything illustrates the real weakness in an ethics grounded on the subjective consciousness. The pleasures of perversity were to provide material for the "Satanist" school of writers. The parallel of physical and mental pleasure and pain, and the obvious implication that the most intense pleasure can derive from the extreme pathological, could have startling results. How can we distinguish "true" from "false" pleasure if the test is the quantity of sensation: how can one be "falser" than the other? Shaftesbury's own "arithmetic" of the moral sense would betray him here. Not without reason did Archibald Campbell ridicule the pretensions of those "refined spirits" who affect to follow only a "disinterested moral sense," for, as Campbell says, the self-approval which follows a generous action provides a pleasure and is the real motive of action, however loftily disguised.[34]

Shaftesbury's rhetoric in his character sketches often anticipates later developments in literature. His subsequent shortening and smoothing of the following passage from the 1699 edition of the *Inquiry,* for example, obscure its kinship of mood and language and imagery with descriptions of heroic villains we find in later romantic fiction:

> How thorow and deep must that Melancholy be, where
> there is nothing softning or pleasing from the side of
> Friendship to allay or divert it when once risen: no flat-
> tering view or imagination of kindness, or affection from

any part; but where every thing around is gastly and horrid, every thing in appearance hostile, and, as it were, *bent* against a privat and single being, who is divided from, and at war with the rest of Nature, in a disagreement and irreconciliation with every thing, and with the Order and Government of the Universe? 'Tis thus at last that a Mind becomes a Wilderness where all is laid waste, everything fair and goodly remov'd, and nothing extant but what is dismal and horrid. Now if any thing that but looks desert, or that feels like banishment or expulsion from human Commerce, be so heavy to bear; what must it be to be thus estranged from Mankind, and to be after this manner in a Desert, and in the horridest of Solitudes, even when in the midst of Society; and to live with Mankind as with a foren Species and as with those Creatures that are most remote from Man, and such as he has the most cause to fear?[35]

But there is a deep contradiction in the very use of "unnatural" to describe pathological states of mind. How, in a universe perfectly planned and operating, can there be anything not ultimately harmonious? Shaftesbury was one of the philosophers who encouraged that intoxication with the Whole which was to lead to Voltaire's bitter protest in the letter on the Lisbon earthquake. There must be a *"Resignation, . . . a Sacrifice and mutual yielding of Natures one to another,"* and all "Inferiour Natures" must be subjected to the "Superiour Nature of the World." "The Central Powers, which hold the lasting Orbs in their just Poize and Movement, must not be controul'd to save a fleeting Form, and rescue from the Precipice a puny Animal. . . ."[36] Some such scheme, it appears, operates in the human as well as all other systems, and the intersection of the majestic, impersonal forces can produce there, too, what seem to finite eyes disasters. He does suggest, with a sly trace of raillery, that even those who see nature as imperfect may have their use. " 'Twas not its [nature's] Intention to leave us without some Pattern of Imperfection; such as we perceive in Minds like these, perplex'd with froward thought."[37]

The theory has, however, a very important potentiality. The study of the "ill" in all its varieties is a means of determining, by contrast, what is "natural." Literary theory soon reflected the concept. But the theory, like others of Shaftesbury's, could be carried to lengths of which the moralist never dreamed. It is one thing to rise to the level of the great over-all Plan and ask with Pope

THE IMPORTANCE OF SHAFTESBURY

> If plagues or earthquakes break not Heav'n's design,
> Why then a Borgia, or a Catiline?

It is quite another to look at the matter from the viewpoint of the Borgia or the Catiline, as we do in this passage from the Marquis de Sade:

> C'étaient des monstres, m'objectent les sots. Oui, selon nos moeurs et nôtre façon de penser; mais relativement aux grandes vue de la nature sur nous, ils n'étaient que les instruments de ses desseins; c'était pour accomplir ses lois qu'elle les avait doués de ses caractères féroces et sanguinaires.[38]

Is not the "monster," in being a monster, living according to his nature, and is he not therefore among the new enlightened who seek the "natural"?

The necessity for sympathetic, imaginative representation of the mind and experience is a vital part of Shaftesbury's philosophy. Of the early philosophical writings which Horace mentions in the *Ars Poetica*, he says:

> 'Twas not enough that these Pieces treated fundamentally of *Morals*, and in consequence pointed out *real Characters* and *Manners*: They exhibited 'em *alive*, and set the Countenances and Complexions of Men plainly in view. And by this means they not only taught us to know *Others;* but, what was principal and of highest virtue in 'em, they taught us to know Our-selves.[39]

The best poet, Shaftesbury tells an author to whom he addresses "Advice,"

> describes no Qualitys or Virtues; censures no Manners: makes no Encomium, nor gives Characters himself; but brings his actors still in view. 'Tis they who shew themselves. For the poet is a second Maker: a just PROMETHEUS, under Jove.[40]

He is a maker, because, like the Deity, he is a "moral Artist," and it is a fundamental principle in Shaftesbury that the world is to be considered as a work of art. The creation of the poet presents through the imagination a series of scenes, appealing through artful arrangement to the moral sense; the business of the poet is to present the scenes so effectively that the sense will operate of itself, and he should not tell in so many words and abstractions what the "moral" is. Distinguishing the "unnatural" from the "natural" therefore is a matter of arousing response and not giving formal instruction. Aesthetic form is inseparable from truth as images are from thought. One of Shaftesbury's principal differences from his old tutor Locke is the fact that the one was by nature aesthetic in response, the other not; but it was, as we have seen, Locke's own epistemology, with its basis of "perception," that did a vital service in promoting the cult of the imagination. Shaftesbury here as elsewhere began to draw out the consequences of this epistemology.

These forms of art supplement and extend our primary source of knowledge about man—ourselves. Even that "rectification" of society which so much concerned Shaftesbury is found to depend in considerable part on introspection.

> But the knowledg of our Passions in their very Seeds, the measuring well the Growth and Progress of Enthusiasm, and the judging rightly of its natural Force . . . may teach us to oppose more successfully those Delusions which . . . come arm'd with the specious Pretext of moral certainty. . . .[41]

Thus Shaftesbury cast his *Advice to an Author* as a "soliloquy," a form to which he gives the highest praise. He expands the Socratic tradition of "Know thyself." Not meditations or essays written with one eye on the audience, he says—but true soliloquy, self-examination to the very depths of the soul, is what is needed. One thinks involuntarily of Rousseau's *Confessions*. He praises *Hamlet* in a significant but neglected piece of criticism as "one continu'd *Moral*: a Series of deep Reflections, drawn from *one* Mouth, upon the Subject of *one* single Accident and Calamity naturally fitted to move Horrour and Compassion."[42] Here, it may be, is the beginning of the change in the tradition of *Hamlet* criticism, wherein the play moves from a tragedy of action to that of an inward and subjective revelation, the *"one"* absorbing everything.

In this tradition is the critic William Richardson, who came much later in the century and was influenced by such followers of Shaftesbury as Lord Kames and Reid (although he refers to Shaftesbury directly, too). In the Introduction to the *Lectures on Shakespeare's Dramatic Characters,* he dilates upon the points made briefly in Shaftesbury. Our "internal feelings" are the beginning of our understanding of human nature. But they are far from sufficient to give us the insight we need.

> We judge of mankind by referring their actions to the
> passions and principles that influence our own behav-
> iour. We have no other guide, since the nature of the
> passions and faculties of the mind are [*sic*] not discerni-
> ble by the senses.[43]

Shaftesbury had lightly assumed that we continually observe other
minds, recreating their experience as our inner sense observes the
"scenes" representing their characteristics and qualities. But this simple idea, like so many derived from Locke, had all manner of com-
plexities lurking in it. Shaftesbury himself suggested that we need the
second maker under Jove to extend our knowledge. Richardson explains that there are many barriers between our minds and those of
others. We ourselves are seldom "indifferent" while we observe others;
we are biassed, and we can seldom see all that is going on from external actions and signs; our memories are fallible; and the emotions
which are weak in us are srong in others, and *vice versa,* so that we unconsciously distort our picture of others' characters.

> If we measure the minds of others precisely by our own,
> . . . our theories must necessarily be inadequate. But,
> by considering the copy and portrait of minds different
> from our own, and by reflecting on these latent and
> unexerted principles, augmented and promoted by im-
> agination, we may discover many new tints, and uncom-
> mon features. Now, that class of poetical writers that
> excel by imitating the passions, might contribute in this
> respect to rectify and enlarge the sentiments of the phi-
> losopher; and if so, they would have the additional merit
> of conducting us to the temple of truth, by an easier and
> more agreeable path, than mere metaphysics.[44]

Thus carrying observers, so to speak, into the very minds of other personalities—as wide a range of personalities as possible—becomes a primary function of art. This vicarious introspection sets, moreover, a
new task for literature, one which powerfully encourages a "psychological" approach.

It was inevitable that Shakespeare should become the ideal poet of
this new ideal kind. His principal characters come to be seen as types
of the relations between the social passions, self-interest, and society;
his method is praised as the pattern of that sympathetic imagination
which was essential to the poet. A new school of criticism came into
being: "An exercise no less adapted to improve the heart, than to in-

form the understanding," Richardson boasts of his essays. The kind of
effect the poet is to produce is indicated in a famous passage from another pioneer critic of this group:

> The reader will perceive that I distinguish between
> *mental impressions* and the *understanding*. . . . There
> are none of us unconscious of certain feelings or sensa-
> tions of mind, which do not seem to have passed through
> the understanding; the effects, I suppose, of some secret
> influences from without, acting upon a certain mental
> sense, and producing feelings and passions in just cor-
> respondence to the force and variety of those influences
> on the one hand, and to the quickness of our sensibility
> on the other.[45]

The conception that poetry may produce "certain feelings or sensations of mind, which do not seem to have passed through the understanding" owes much, I think it is clear, to the kind of thinking Shaftesbury did so much to inaugurate.

The new critical method may be seen at work in relation to a peculiar problem which arose from the new secularized Pelagianism. If the
fall is really the fall of society, what becomes of those rare spirits who
seemingly cannot do anything other than live according to nature—
what becomes of them in a world where the great majority live "out of
all rule and proportion"? That there is an aesthetic value in this situation Shaftesbury himself hinted.

> The very Disturbances which belong to natural Affection,
> though they may be wholly contrary to Pleasure, yield
> still a Contentment and Satisfaction greater than the
> Pleasures of indulg'd Sense. . . . We continue pleas'd
> even with this melancholy Aspect or Sense of Virtue. Her
> Beauty supports it-self under a Cloud, and in the midst
> of surrounding Calamitys.[46]

The problem is twofold. There is the conflict of the natural man
with an unnatural world, and there is the difficulty of ascertaining a
desirable balance between sensibility and self-interest. Shaftesbury unmistakably implies that in some cases unbalance of the moral sense and
the emotions is due to temperament; there may be need for patterns of
imperfection, and he suggests, again, that the moral sense may be too
tender. May there be need, also, for patterns of perfection?

Hamlet soon became the image of this dilemma. Mackenzie, who probably led the way in the "sentimental" interpretation of this hero, explains that

> Naturally of the most virtuous and most amiable disposition, the circumstances in which he was placed unhinged those principles of action which, in another situation, would have delighted mankind, and made himself happy. Finding such a character in real life, of a person endowed with feelings so delicate as to border on weakness, with sensibility too exquisite to allow of determined action, he has placed it where it could be best exhibited, in scenes of wonder, of terror, and of indignation, where its varying emotions might be most strongly marked amidst the workings of imagination, and the war of the passions.[47]

Hamlet is, indeed, as Mackenzie says, a new kind of tragedy if we accept this interpretation. The plot and the other characters are reduced to mere contrasting "scenes" against which the sensibility of the hero is exhibited.

In *Mirror* No. 39 Mackenzie goes so far as to suggest that the fall of society is responsible for many of the most affecting tragedies. Unfortunately, "honest ambition" for recognition is accompanied by "delicacy of taste and sentiment" out of place in the present world. In earlier times, when mankind was uncorrupted by excessive luxury and refinement, there could be confidence that recognition would be given where it was due; but now a man of true worth, seeing himself set aside in favor of the worthless and contemptible, gives way to despair, and is "in danger of changing . . . into a morose and surly misanthrope." Mackenzie implies that reason is a power of the mind, one of many potentialities which can be "brought into action as chance or circumstances direct." In the imperfect state of society in which we find ourselves, it is the part of prudence to adjust ourselves with cheerfulness and good humor (the Shaftesburian tone is obvious in the emphasis on these qualities) and "firmly rise above injustice, and refuse to retreat into the passive virtues."

Perhaps it is the absence of the revolutionary or even reforming spirit that is the keynote to Mackenzie's puzzling combination of idealistic sensibility and hard-headed prudence. He condemns at once the unnatural society and the fine spirit who is too "natural" for it. The story of Emilia (*Mirror* No. 101), a girl whose "delicacy and fineness of feeling" lead her to an irreconcilable conflict with Mrs. Grundy, pro-

duces no more than an effect of hysterical emotion; the difficulty arises
from the ambivalence of the author's attitude, which is at once passionately sympathetic with the sensitive heroine and condemnatory of
her perfect sensibility. We miss the single effect of melancholy beauty
which unfallen goodness in a fallen society could produce. The Man
of Feeling himself represents the dilemma. He has had, significantly,
a sheltered life, his remarkable moral sense has unfolded without ob-
stacle, and from his conflict with a selfish and cruel society Mackenzie
tries to extract the essence of tragedy. The situation is presented during the stagecoach conversation of chapter 33. The stranger enthusi-
astically maintains that the "poetical inclination" has at least one advantage—"the causes of human depravity vanish before the romantic
enthusiasm [the poet] professes, and many who are not able to reach
the Parnassian heights, may yet approach so near as to be bettered by
the air of the climate." To which the now disillusioned Harley replies:
"I have always thought so; but this is an argument of the prudent
against it; they urge the danger of unfitness for the world." The suggestion that the poet, although hopelessly ineffectual in the world as it is,
may yet have his function as a "pattern of perfection" both etherealizes
the nature of poetry and emphasizes its evocative rather than its com-
municative aspect.

Richardson's essay on the character of Hamlet shows the relation of
his view to the Shaftesbury school:

> On reviewing the analysis now given, a sense of virtue, if
> I may use the language of an eminent philosopher, with-
> out professing myself of his sect, seems to be the ruling
> principle in the character of Hamlet. In other men, it
> may appear with the ensigns of high authority: in Ham-
> let, it possesses absolute power.[48]

So delicate is this sense of virtue that it governs his every action, his
every personal relation:

> It even sharpens his penetration; and, if unexpectedly he
> discerns turpitude or impropriety in any character, it in-
> clines him to think more deeply of their transgression,
> than if his sentiments were less refined. . . . As it excites
> uncommon pain and abhorrence on the appearance of
> perfidious and inhuman actions, it provokes and stimu-
> lates his resentment; yet, attentive to justice, and con-
> cerned in the interests of human nature, it governs the
> impetuosity of that unruly passion.

Hamlet's sufferings caused by this acute sensibility occupy an essay devoted to the paradox of the pathological "amiable." The whole play takes on a new character, and to go from Johnson's criticism, with its concern about plot, characterization and outcome, to that of Richardson is to go from one age to another. In Richardson's analysis is the germ of the melancholy of Werther, and there is the anticipation of his death: one can hardly escape the suspicion that Richardson and Mackenzie secretly feel that suicide would have been a really appropriate ending to the play. Strange dilemma! That the most "natural," the most harmonious and sensitive to moral beauty, should so fail, so come to cross purposes with the order of the world! "We love, we almost revere the character of Hamlet; and grieve for his sufferings. But we must at the same time confess, that his weaknesses, are the cause of his disappointments and early death."

That a strong sensibility produces "weakness" in action became a commonplace. In Thomas Whately's *Remarks on Some of the Characters of Shakespeare* it even transforms Macbeth. This critic, significantly, tells us that the emphasis on "fable" in criticism is erroneous, and that "character" is the real center of a play.[49] In line with this principle, he studies *Macbeth* and *Richard III*. The former hero he finds to be a "man of sensibility" led astray by what Shaftesbury would have called the "zeal" introduced by the weird sisters' suggestions. He shows indecision and fear everywhere, as is to be expected from a man of "gentle and amiable qualities." Richard, on the other hand, shows firmness and courage, for he "is totally destitute of every softer feeling."[50] Irresolute, showing the "symptoms of a feeble mind," Macbeth is yet, in an absolute sense, by far the more admirable, for he has a strong sense of virtue, whereas Richard has none. It is not merely the conflict within himself that weakens Macbeth, moreover; it would be easy to turn him the other way and see a Hamlet in him. The conclusion is that the noblest of men are by a strange paradox the weakest of men, and that a strong moral sense means an inevitably tragic life.

More celebrated theories of Hamlet carry on these themes. The sense of the fatal conflict of highly developed sensibility with real facts underlies Goethe's account of the hero, in *Wilhelm Meister*. "The feeling for the good and graceful," we learn, "had unfolded in him together with his consciousness of his high birth." The natural development is strongly emphasized; he was "polished by nature, courteous from the heart." But such a soul, so perfect in itself, comes into inevitable conflict with the necessity for action, for he "is endowed more properly with sentiment than with a character." Hamlet is, when we consider the setting of the discussion in the novel, plainly the image of that conflict which Mackenzie's stranger in the stagecoach suggests.

Coleridge's view is more purely psychological, and more straightforwardly analyzes Hamlet in terms going back to Shaftesbury's modification of the Locke epistemology. There must, in the healthy mind, be a balance between "the impressions of outward objects and the inward operations of the intellect: if there be an overbalance in the contemplative faculty, man becomes the creature of meditation, and loses the power of action."[51] The *Notes on the Tragedies of Shakespeare* makes the process more explicit. "In Hamlet this balance does not exist—his thoughts, images and fancy being far more vivid than his perceptions, and his very perceptions instantly passing thro' the medium of his contemplations, and acquiring as they pass a form and color not naturally their own."[52] It is logical that the stream of images passing before the inner sense could be too vivid and be transformed too much in the process of imaginative working.

The function of Shakespeare thus appeared in a new light. Coleridge sees Shakespeare as providing those "patterns of imperfection" which the new philosophy of man called for: "conceiving characters out of his own intellectual and moral faculties, by conceiving any one intellectual or moral faculty in morbid excess and then placing himself, thus mutilated and diseased, under given circumstances." Among the important results of this new criticism were lifting characters out of plays and making them, as it were, living beings—represented by the tendency to write separate studies of Shakespeare's *dramatis personae;* and the increasing decline of emphasis on dramatic action as such, implicit in Shaftesbury's remark about *Hamlet's* being a long soliloquy and culminating in the romantic aversion to seeing Shakespeare's plays performed. The distant descendant of the theory of the function of the poet is, perhaps, to be seen in T. S. Eliot's theory of the "objective correlative," in his remark that

> If you examine any of Shakespeare's more successful tragedies, you will find this exact equivalence; you will find that the state of mind of Lady Macbeth walking in her sleep has been communicated to you by a skilful accumulation of imagined sensory impressions; the words of Macbeth on hearing of his wife's death strike us as if,

given the sequence of events, these words were automatically released by the last event in the series.

Communication of a state of mind by "imagined sensory impressions"
is indeed in keeping with Shaftesbury's vision of the poet as a "second maker under Jove"; vicarious experience is the purpose of poetry.

If Hamlet was the supreme symbol of the tragedy of the natural in
a degenerate world, there was another figure who as a kind of foil was
to loom especially large in romantic literature. William Richardson
adumbrates the type in describing Jaques as the frustrated benevolist,
but one whose mental history has been different from that of Hamlet.
Even the prince, in whom the conflict of his sense of virtue with society is the ruling principle, eventually is led into violence; but his
hesitations are "amiable." In Jaques, on the other hand, the result
of frustration of a keen sense of benevolence has been less amiable.
Richardson starts from the doctrine of the "ruling passion." What if
the dominating impulse in a person is the "social and beneficent Affections," and what if those affections are so strong as to be irresistible
—and then, as they come into conflict with an uncongenial, selfish
world, are twisted into evil ways? The result of this thwarting of the
"natural" will be misanthropy. The social affections lead men to society, and society being what it is, to dissipations and regrets. Jaques
accordingly turned into a "dissipated and sensual libertine," and, like
la Rochefoucauld's old roué (but for different reasons) into a gloomy
moralist as well. This "white" melancholy (as distinguished from the
"black" melancholy of the true villain) is, then, really a good impulse
perverted by its contact with a world to which it should be suited, but,
because of the evil of society, is not.[53]

The Byronic hero, I might suggest, often shows this kind of thwarting of the exceptional moral sense.

> With more capacity for love than earth
> Bestows on most of mortal mould and birth,
> His early dreams of good outstripp'd the truth,
> And troubled manhood follow'd baffled youth;
> With thought of years in phantom chase misspent,
> And wasted powers for better purpose lent; . . .
> Too high for common selfishness, he could
> At times resign his own for others' good,
> But not in pity, not because he ought,
> But in some strange perversity of thought,

That sway'd him onward with a secret pride,
To do what few or none would do beside. . . .[54]

The few examples sketched above give some idea of the changes which the complex of thought which Shaftesbury pioneered could produce. All of them assume the continued existence of the system of society as it exists. Obviously, however, another road was open. Could it be that a "root and branch" reformation of the social order is necessary to release the supposed normal state of mankind? It would be outside the limits of this paper to show that there is little in Rousseau that is not in Shaftesbury also, but that the French moralist carries things much farther than does the English one. Both were optimists in a deeper sense; it is not that all *is* well, but that all *can be* well in society. They both declare the eternal possibility of living "NATURALLY, and as a MAN." The enchanting prospect they offer is that nature is always before and within men, divinely harmonious, beautiful and serene, and that every generation, if it will only awaken from the nightmare dreams of the past, can find happiness and freedom in this life and on this earth.

NOTES

1. Two recent books deal with Shaftesbury and his influence: A. O. Aldridge, *Shaftesbury and the Deist Manifesto* (Transactions of the American Philosophical Society, 1951); and R. L. Brett, *The Third Earl of Shaftesbury* (London, 1951). Since these studies, as well as the still essential book of Fowler, *Shaftesbury and Hutcheson*, give detailed accounts of this author's life and writings, I am not repeating this material. I am trying only to suggest a new interpretation of Shaftesbury's relationship to his own time, especially to the Cambridge Platonists and to Locke, and to suggest some new lines which study of his influence may take. In suggesting these lines I am not trying to define direct and exact "sources," but rather significant changes which the *kind* of thinking Shaftesbury pioneered helped to produce. It is to be remembered, however, that we can assume nearly every educated man of the eighteenth century had some acquaintance with the *Characteristics* of Lord Shaftesbury, just as nearly every educated person today has some acquaintance with the writings of, say, John Dewey.
2. "Shaftesbury and the Ethical Poets in England, 1700-1760," *PMLA*, 31 (1916), 264 ff.; and see also W. E. Alderman, "Shaftesbury and the Doctrine of Moral Sense in the Eighteenth Century," *PMLA*, 46 (1931), 1087 ff.
3. "Suggestions toward a Genealogy of the 'Man of Feeling,'" *ELH*, 1 (1934), 207.

4. See F. E. L. Priestley, "Newton and the Romantic Concept of Nature," *UTQ*, 17 (1948), 323 ff.; Miss Marjorie Nicolson's books, especially *The Breaking of the Circle* (Evanston, 1950) ; and an article of the writer, "Space, Deity, and the 'Natural Sublime,'" in *MLQ*, March 1951.

5. Pages 9-10.

6. P. 55.

7. *Ibid.*, pp. 156-8.

8. *Works of Isaac Barrow*, ed. Tillotson (London, 1696) , II: 107-8.

9. *Ibid.*, 105.

10. *Ibid.*, I: 11-12.

11. *Ibid.*, I: 356.

12. *A Demonstration of the Divine Authority of the Law of Nature, and of the Christian Religion* (London, 1681) , 55.

13. *Ibid.*, 5.

14. Archbishop Tenison, for example, contrasts the "generous Spirit of Charity," a soul that animates society and makes it possible, with the self-love which is becoming all too prevalent; but this state of affairs is to be expected since St. Paul predicted that "the nigher [men] are to the Last Judgment, the more Criminal they grow." *A Sermon against Self-Love* (London, 1689) , 12. It is Christian charity, not benevolence, of which he speaks, and it cannot be equated with the social feeling of Shaftesbury or Rousseau. The idea that the growth of self-interest argues the approach of the Judgment, furthermore, is a very old one among theologians. Again, we find one of the most "liberal" of the Latitudinarians, Archbishop Tillotson, describing how God in His mercy has provided, by the "abundance and *Grace* of the Gospel, so powerful a *Remedy* for this hereditary Disease of our corrupt and degenerate Nature." *Six Sermons*, 2d ed. (London, 1694) , 51. It is "common humanity," to be sure, that makes us concerned for the welfare of our families, etc., but this fact does not argue innate goodness of men.

15. *The Pursuits of Happiness* (London, 1771) .

16. It is interesting to note that Tillotson carefully guards himself against the imputation of this heresy by emphasizing that the "disease of the depravity of human nature" is transmitted by traduction, from parent to child, and not by imitation. His student Thomas Burnet was one of the first to go the whole way in saying that the fall was a gradual affair, really consisting in the corruption of society.

17. *Inquiry concerning Virtue*, p. 99. This first, "imperfect" edition, now extremely rare, published though it was without Shaftesbury's knowledge, often gives us more immediately and more impressively the very spirit of its author than does the later, "polished" *Inquiry concerning Virtue, or Merit* as published in the *Characteristics*.

18. *Characteristics* (London, 1737), II. 252.

19. *An Account of Virtue: Or, Dr. Henry Moore's Abridgment of Morals, Put into English,* tr. Edward Southwell (London, 1690), 11.

20. This assumption may be the most serious fault in Mr. Brett's recent book on Shaftesbury—which otherwise has many acute insights. To oppose Shaftesbury as the champion of the belief that perception involves

a "creative process" over against Locke as the philosopher of "passive association" seems to me misleading. The close connection of Shaftesbury's theory with Locke's epistemology has not, so far as I know, been pointed out. Locke in fact is the fountain head of the two great schools of thought about the mental life; on one side, he leads to the romantic psychology and ethics inaugurated by Shaftesbury—on the other, to the Hartley associationist school, depending on which element in his thought is stressed at the expense of the other.

21. *An Essay concerning Human Understanding,* ed. A. C. Fraser (Oxford, 1914) , II: xxi: 5.

22. The implications for literature of this yoking of the image to thought are of course incalculable. Shaftesbury and Addison immediately show the results. Philocles, in Shaftesbury's *The Moralists,* says that he must have a "kind of material Object," an "Image" in mind before he can love a person or an abstraction; he has been in love, for example, with the "People of old Rome" under the form of a beautiful youth "call'd *the* GENIUS *of the People." Characteristics,* II: 242 ff. This should be the lower rung of the Platonic ladder of beauty, which should ascend to the immaterial pure Idea, but the ladder is never completed. Later, when Shaftesbury presents his very important idea of the organic unity of the universe, he cites as an authority Locke's *Essay,* IV: vi: 11, where it is shown that we cannot understand the essence of any object unless we perceive its intricate physical integration into the workings of the universal machine; we perceive a collection of related images. See *The Moralists,* in *ed. cit.,* II: 285 ff. And in one of the most significant passages of all Shaftesbury's works, in the late *Miscellaneous Reflections,* he sets forth his version of the "scale or catalogue of beauty" (the equivalence of the terms is interesting for a Platonist) in the form of greater and greater combinations of images into patterns, in both the animate and inanimate worlds. *Ed. Cit.,* III: 182-3, footnote. The spirit, the enthusiasm, the language, are Neoplatonic, but the substance has much of Locke in it.

23. On the objections to Locke's ethics, see my article "The Origins of the 'Moral Sense,' " in *HLQ,* XI (1948) , 241-59.

24. P. 27.

25. *Essay,* II: xx.

26. *Essay,* IV: iv: 7.

27. *The Moralists,* in *Characteristics,* II: 414 f.

28. *Characteristics,* II: 28 ff.

29. Thomas Burnet, in three pamphlets directed against Locke (first in 1697, the second and third in 1699) , appears to have originated the comparison. He wrote in 1697: "This I am sure of, that the Distinction, suppose of Gratitude and Ingratitude, Fidelity, and Infidelity, . . . and such others, is as sudden without any Ratiocination, and as sensible and piercing, as the difference I feel from the Scent of a Rose, and of Assafoetida. . . ." For an account of these pamphlets and of Locke's reaction thereto—a reaction which may be assumed in large part to Shaftesbury also—see my article, cited above.

30. *Studies in Iconology* (New York, 1939), 229. It may be well to say a little about the question of Shaftesbury's attitude towards religion, a problem which has rather unnecessarily vexed his critics and biographers from his own century onwards. Of his dislike for and fear of any strong religious belief involving any form of "mystery" or supernatural faith there can be no doubt. It is true that in the preface to Whichcote's Sermons, and in some letters he speaks of the Anglican state church in respectful and even affectionate terms; but careful reading of these passages will show, I think, that it is the absence of "zeal" and the generally good therapeutic effect which belief in providence may have that he means. Of his certainty that the universe is God's creation, in which He is imminent, there is no doubt, either. But no one who takes revealed religion seriously can look on Shaftesbury as a confrere. The really governing fact is that, as I have tried to point out, his basic assumptions about the nature of man rule out original sin and the belief in a supernatural destiny as the true goal of life. And as Swift says, "So I affirm original sin, and that men are now liable to be damned for Adam's sin, to be the foundation of the whole Christian religion." It must be added that Shaftesbury was not argumentative. To attack religion dogmatically would be a manifestation of that very "zeal" which he felt had produced so much damage. Better is the convincing presentation, in imaginative form, of the truth about men, accompanied by a raillery against superstition. Shaftesbury's artistic achievement in the latter form has never been studied satisfactorily.

31. *Characteristics*, II: 163.

32. *Ibid.*, II: 164.

33. *Ibid.*, II: 169.

34. *An Enquiry into the Original of Moral Virtue* (Edinburgh, 1733), 324 ff.

35. Pp. 193-4. The psychological state, the warfare of the mind with itself, is the essence of the horror in this passage, rather than pride, a sense of disobedience to God, or remorse, as in Milton's Satan, or Marlowe's Faustus.

36. *Characteristics*, II: 214-15.

37. *Ibid.*, II: 283.

38. Quoted by Mario Praz, *The Romantic Agony*, tr. Angus Davidson (London, 1951), 98. Diderot, as is well known, expressed similar ideas.

39. *Ibid.*, I: 194. And so Shaftesbury casts his own work in artistic forms, such as dialogues and "soliloquies," a fact which accounts at once for its suggestiveness and its vagueness. One must always remember that Shaftesbury was, by choice, no systematizer, and that, not isolated statements, but as in creative works, the effect of the whole is what counts.

40. *Ibid.*, I: 2007. The applicability of this statement to Shaftesbury's own work, even the *Inquiry*, is worth noting. He is not a judicial moralist.

41. *Ibid.*, I: 43. Professor R. D. Havens has pointed out that as early as 1725 Henry Baker wrote a "natural History of myself, truly pointing out the Turn and Disposition of my Soul at the Time it gave them [the poems he was publishing] birth." The shift to introspection, as Professor Havens indicates, is noteworthy. It comes fourteen years after the publica-

tion of the *Characteristics,* when the reading of Shaftesbury was ubiquitous. "Unusual Opinions in 1725 and 1726," *PQ,* 30 (1951) , 447. In line with this change in presentation of character, attention may be called to Professor Edward Hooker's article "Humour in the Age of Pope," *HLQ,* 11 (1948) , 361 ff. The attitude changes from one of condemnation according to an objective standard, to sympathetic depiction of diversity. This change is entirely in accord with Shaftesbury's principle.

42. *Ibid.,* I: 275-6.
43. (Sixth edition, London, 1812) . For an account of this book and its evolution, see R. W. Babcock, "William Richardson's Criticism of Shakespeare," *JEGP,* 29 (1929) , 117 ff.
44. *Ibid.,* pp. 19-20. On the history of the sympathetic imagination, see W. J. Bate, "The Sympathetic Imagination in Eighteenth Century English Criticism," *ELH,* 12 (1945) , 144 ff.
45. Maurice Morgann, *An Essay on the Dramatic Character of Sir John Falstaff* (London, 1825), 6-7.
46. *Op. cit.,* II: 106.
47. *Mirror,* No. 99.
48. *Op. cit.,* 117.
49. (London, 1785) , Introduction.
50. *Ibid.,* 15.
51. Bristol Lecture III, in *Coleridge's Shakespearean Criticism,* ed. Raysor (London, 1930) , II: 272.
52. *Ibid.,* I: 37.
53. Richardson, *op. cit.,* 168 ff.
54. *Lara,* I: xvii. The last four lines recall Richardson's analysis of that supreme example of misanthropy, Timon at Athens, whose morbid condition is supposed to result from a combination of a ruling passion—desire for eminence—with a strong sense of benevolence. The new casuistry could indeed adopt many forms!

PAUL E. PARNELL

❀

The Sentimental Mask

Fifty years after the modern study of sentimentalism was inaugurated by Ernest Bernbaum, the problem remains whether the term has ever been satisfactorily defined or described. Two recent developments reveal some of the difficulties: Arthur Sherbo in *The English Sentimental Drama* takes five basic criteria considered by most authorities as typical, and shows that they may all apply to plays demonstrably not sentimental.[1] John Harrington Smith, in the preface to *The Gay Couple in Restoration Comedy* (1948), announces that he has completely avoided the term "sentimental" as too vague to be of much value.[2] Yet Ronald Crane, writing fourteen years before, assumed the essential traits of sentimentalism to be fairly clear,[3] and Norman Holland has implied that two criteria borrowed from Bernbaum and Krutch still supply an adequate definition.[4] There is not even agreement whether sentimentality is a positive or negative quality. Krutch and Sherbo feel that it is false and dishonest, therefore bad.[5] Crane concedes that it is somewhat limited intellectually, but emphasizes its humanitarianism and emotional warmth, especially the "self-approving joy" that makes virtue satisfying.[6] Bernbaum vacillates between sympathy and contempt.[7]

If sentimentalism is hard to define, the word nevertheless means something vivid and unmistakable to its users. Who can read Cumberland's *The West Indian* (1771), or Lillo's *The London Merchant*

From *PMLA*, LXXVIII (1963), 529-35. Reprinted by permission of the Modern Language Association of America.

(1731) and forget that mawkish sweetness, that unctuous virtue, those interminable repentances? Surely there is something unique here that can be distinguished from other literary experiences. And yet the definitions offered by critics have lacked an essential clarity. Sentimentality has something to do with the enjoyment of tears, with the insistence on material rewards for virtue, with an everyday kindliness that may possibly be "spontaneous" (Crane) or "calculated" (Sherbo), with a middle-class emphasis that often features, inconsistently, a titled cast.[8] Criticism so far has simply not defined the basic relationship between sentimentalism and virtue or morality; nor has it explained why the term, if occupied with man's noblest ideals, carries a generally unfavorable connotation. A further investigation is clearly required.

A few passages from Richard Steele and Samuel Richardson suggest a new approach. First, from the Epilogue to Steele's play *The Lying Lover* (1703):

> . . . Laughter's a distorted passion, born
> Of sudden self-esteem and sudden scorn;
> Which, when 'tis o'er, the men in pleasure wise,
> Both him that moved it and themselves despise;
> While generous pity of a painted woe
> Makes us ourselves both more approve and know.[9]

Ordinary comedy, in Steele's view, raises the self-esteem of the spectator by provoking scorn of other people's faults. But then there is a delayed reaction: after he has thought about the comedy a little, he sees that the criticism applies to him too, and so he feels less important and less worthy. Since Steele is interested in feeling as virtuous as possible, he resents such a presentation and despises the person who perpetrated it. On the other hand, pity for dramatically presented woe has no uncomfortable aftermath. It gives the spectator the feeling that he is of sterling character, that the more he knows himself the more he will find to admire. The personal emphasis is illuminating, since the sentimentalist usually alleges himself to be altruistically concerned with others. Steele asserts in *The Christian Hero,* "How unwilling are we to Eradicate the . . . Satisfaction of Self-Admiration . . . the most senseless and stupid of all our Infirmities."[10] But it is clear that altruism of the sentimental sort is a means of further promoting self-admiration. Steele says elsewhere in the same tract, "Christianity has that in it, which makes Men pity, not scorn the Wicked, and by a beautiful kind of Ignorance of themselves, think those Wretches their Equals."[11]

Here the assumption of one's own virtue is absolute; the Christian belief that all men are sinners in the eye of God becomes a generous
self-delusion, for the purpose of lifting up the morally inferior, who
might otherwise be too disgusting. One sees that Bernbaum's principle
of "perfectibility of human nature" needs qualification. It is not human nature in general that is perfectible: it is one's own nature, and
that is very nearly perfect now. Steele never considers the possibility
that he himself might be one of the wicked. One easily infers that if
"those Wretches" thought themselves in any way the equals of their
condescending betters, the sentimental-Christian mask would quickly
fall off. One such scene shows up in Steele's own correspondence. He
is writing to Mrs. Charlotte Clayton: "I Sincerely assure you, that I do
not Seek this Station upon any other View but to do good to others,
and if I do not gett it, you will See my Opposers repent that they
would not let me be Humble, For I shall then think myself obliged
to show them what place among mankind I am really in."12

Here we see beneath the altruism his snobbishness, both moral and
social, his conviction that there are limits beyond which Christian
virtue cannot be carried, his opportunism, his effectual confession that
the humility was just a pose he assumed out of decency, but a pose
that ought not to be maintained for a moment if his interests are
threatened. But it is important to see that Steele does not think of
himself as a hypocrite; on the contrary, he shows a certain moral fervor
all through the passage. He is a sincere and dedicated altruist, his
"opposers" are enemies of the light. It is just that Steele, like most
sentimentalists, is playing a double game: he wants to think of himself as continuously virtuous, and he wants to get the job too. And
these inconsistent desires require a continuous reinterpretation of
every circumstance so as to emphasize the virtue and ignore the un-
scrupulousness. This reinterpretation is a conscious process, and as
logical as the sentimentalist can make it; but, by a necessary inconsistency, the sentimentalist can never admit to himself that his argument is a rationalization, or else it would fail of its designed effect:
a clearing of his conscience and a conviction of his own sinlessness and
altruism. Thus sentimental thinking is balanced delicately between
hypocrisy and sincerity, simplicity and duplicity, self-consciousness
and spontaneity. Unquestionably, the sentimentalist sees himself as
sincerely, simply, and spontaneously virtuous, but only achieves this
belief at the cost of a constant demonstration to himself that his mask
of virtue and his face are one.

What is the nature of this mask? It can take many forms, but all are

clearly related to the assumption of moral perfection. The Epilogue
to *The Lying Lover* gives one hint:

> What is that touch within which nature gave[?]
> . . . .
> 'Tis that pure joy which guardian angels know,
> . . . .
> When they the good protect, the ill oppose.

Thus the sentimentalist may feel that when he intervenes on the side
of virtue against debauchery and evil, he is directly inspired by
Heaven, and is a kind of guardian angel. Richardson, describing his
heroine in the preface to *Clarissa*, is even more explicit: "As far as is
consistent with human frailty, and as far as she could be perfect, considering the people she had to deal with, and those with whom she
was inseparably connected, she *is* perfect. To have been impeccable,
must have . . . carried our idea of her from woman to angel" [italics
Richardson's].[13] Plainly, though, she falls short of an angel by very
little; he is careful to put most of the blame on the "people she had
to deal with," and no more blame can be put on her than the bare
minimum consistent with "human frailty." In fact, as a virtuous "Ex-
emplar to her sex," she is somehow raised above the human race. And
at the same time she is envied and hated for it, just as Pamela is for
her celebrated "virtue." Sentimental heroines may be abused, scorned,
or even violated; but whatever happens, they die or live triumphant,
and work to reclaim the errant. It must be evident that the sentimentalist in many respects aspires to the attributes of Christ—sinlessness, while ostensibly taking the blame on himself for the sins of others, humility that suffers in silence, altruism, lack of ambition—and at
the same time the power to save such as repent, and the will to damn
the others. Of course the assumption of the Christlike mask gives him
considerable leeway, since he can be either humble or almighty, as the
Steele quotation indicates. The choice of means depends largely on
the possibly opportunistic end in view.

The validity of such assumptions cannot finally be demonstrated
within the space of an article. But examination of a few key scenes
from plays usually regarded as sentimental (ranging in date from
1696 to 1731) provides a test for these criteria. Even so limited a study
may possibly discover evidence applicable on a wider scale.

First, Steele's *Conscious Lovers* (1722) offers a splendid example of
almost pure reinterpretation of motives. In this play Bevil Junior, in

obedience to his father's wishes, has become engaged to Lucinda, who is loved by his friend Myrtle. Bevil Junior really loves the beautiful and penniless Indiana whom he secretly maintains, after rescuing her from a compromising situation. Evil-minded persons might infer that he is keeping her, but Bevil is so noble that such imputations are of course unfair. On the morning of the wedding-day Bevil, still engaged to Lucinda, and already dressed in his wedding-clothes, decides he wants to visit Indiana. One might suppose that such an impulse would be hard to justify. He is in danger of being followed and detected, and his being dressed so elegantly ought to arouse her suspicion. But he wants to see her, and so he lectures himself as follows:

> We must often . . . go on in our good offices, even under the displeasure of those to whom we do them, in compassion to their weaknesses and mistakes.—But all this while poor Indiana is tortured with the doubt of me. She has no support or comfort but in my fidelity, yet sees me daily pressed to marriage with another . . . [If she does, it is not his fault. He has told her nothing, and she has no other direct means of finding out.] The religious vow to my father restrains me from ever marrying without his approbation, yet that confines me not from seeing a virtuous woman . . . the pure delight of my eyes and the guiltless joy of my heart. (p. 301)

This is a true *locus classicus* of sentimental thinking. He cites only those aspects of his action that will be favorable to himself: his generosity, his fidelity to obligation, his love of virtue in others, his tender regard for her ambiguous status. On the other hand, he refuses to recognize the imprudence and irresponsibility of his action. He may be correct in stressing his superiority of position, which is primarily practical—she cannot help herself, and he *can* help her (and furthermore he has not taken any steps to make her independent of him)—but he uses this independence to build up an assumption of his own moral superiority. His moral dominance becomes so overwhelming that he finds an obligation to persevere, whether his actions are appreciated or even welcome. He must go on managing his friends with the same loving pity a parent feels for a child; or to put it more honestly, he feels a right to manipulate his friends as he pleases, provided that he can state his objectives to himself in sufficiently noble terms. But he is not a hypocrite, nor does his rationalizing proceed from an un-

easy conscience. He is a sentimentalist, for whom a spontaneous reinterpretation of motives has become a conviction, a way of life.

A few scenes later his complacency is rudely shattered when his
friend Myrtle, convinced Bevil intends to marry Lucinda after all,
challenges him to a duel. At first fighting seems the only solution. But
this tactic is so crude, and so destructive to Bevil's whole opportunistic
fabric, that he can accept it only under the strain of an extreme emotion. At the first slight respite, the emotion that is supposed to dominate
in sentimental plays is brought to heel by his "reason." He decides to
show Myrtle Lucinda's letter, which he had felt obliged hitherto to
keep secret, "except I could . . . serve him, and her, by disobeying
her . . . more than I should by complying with her directions" (p.
330). Opportunism could be no franker. He manages to defend his
action, however, by an apology to Myrtle for "perhaps too much regard to a false point of honour" (p. 333). A disillusioned commentator
might observe that Bevil has got himself out of a nasty predicament
by committing an impropriety, when a little frankness earlier would
have forestalled the whole crisis. He might appropriately take some
of the blame on himself, instead of abusing "honor"; but guilt is precisely what his whole intellectual orientation is designed to avoid. He
therefore justifies himself by virtuous considerations: if Myrtle had
found the letter about a man he had killed, it would have been worse
than death to him. Myrtle, fortunately, is taken aback by this unexpected revelation, and shame at his own hastiness keeps him from resenting the violation of a confidence. Bevil now easily recovers control
of the situation: "[*Aside.*] When . . . he has seen himself thoroughly,
he will deserve to be assisted towards obtaining Lucinda" (p. 334).
Bevil's basically false estimation of his own qualities does not keep
him from applying a very shrewd mind throughout to the attainment
of his goals. Even in the scene just quoted, Bevil's mind is already
moving ahead to the match between Myrtle and Lucinda, because
they love and deserve each other, and also because Bevil will not be
free to marry Indiana until his fiancée Lucinda is taken off his hands.

Another example of reinterpretation may be seen in Amanda's acceptance of the "bed trick" in *Love's Last Shift* (1696) as a means of
reclaiming her husband. After a good deal of cavilling at the risks of
the scheme, she finally consents after she has glorified the moral purpose of the plan thus: "Oh! to reclaim the Man I'm bound by Heaven
to Love . . . were such a sweet Revenge . . . so vast a Triumph of
rewarded Constancy, as might persuade the looser part of Womankind

ev'n to forsake themselves, and fall in Love with Virtue."[14] One would hardly suspect that she was herself to imitate the "looser part of womankind" for an evening. Later, during the decidedly questionable "seduction" scene, she again shows her ability to find virtue where she wants to find it. When Loveless vows to pursue her, though to the hazard of his life, Amanda murmurs, "Oh, were this Courage shewn but in a better Cause" (I, 49). And in the ensuing scenes her skill in maneuvering her husband to the desired repentance is clearly to be admired, and is probably to be taken as proof of her superior virtue. That is, virtue here involves skill in managing people toward her own ends. Even her fainting may be taken as a stratagem allowable in the circumstances, since she recovers quickly with the cryptic (or businesslike) comment, "It is done," as soon as her husband starts to yield. As for her emotionalism, she does not begin to weep until *after* her husband has repented.

In the two examples already cited, the sentimentalist has been seen managing other people for the furthering of his own interests and theirs. In both cases the sentimentalist clearly regards the person to be managed as his inferior, both in understanding and in virtue. Hence it is not surprising that sentimentalists often invoke the relationship between parent and child, with its similar indications of love and discipline. And as love in this relationship may be spontaneously felt, or may be a means of concealing a naked advantage, so the sentimentalist may play a game of spiritual coercion while seeming to exude nothing but love. A conspicuous example is Lady Easy in Cibber's *The Careless Husband* (1704). She finds her husband, with his wig off, and the maid asleep on two chairs in his bedroom—as close an approximation to actual adultery as could be presented on the eighteenth-century stage. What should she do? The temptation is strong to "yield to her emotions," that is, simply faint, or give him a tongue-lashing. But she controls herself until she thinks of a stratagem; then she takes off her lace "steinkirk" collar, and lays it on his bare head. This is an extremely shrewd move, that lets him know he has been discovered, but does not let him know the extent of her knowledge. He cannot get off by blustering through it, because she has not made any formal accusation. In fact, he is not in her confidence at all, and if he lets the matter ride, he may find himself faced with a suit for separate maintenance. The only thing he can do is what he does—come to her and confess.

Her behavior, however, demands more careful scrutiny. First, she rationalizes his behavior in the most favorable manner possible. "Duty

. . . forbids me to insult" (I, 390), although she has conceded a few lines before that her indulgence for him might make her insults ineffective. That is, it may not be really duty at all, but timidity—in the circumstances, a fault and not a virtue. She then casts the blame on herself: nature has not formed her with the "Thousand little Requisites'" that arouse love. Then she observes that he is bareheaded, and exposed to the "unwholesome Air." He may catch cold, or "Heav'n offended" may send him some "languishing Distemper" (I,390), and in this case she is not disposed to accept Heaven's decrees. Hence the steinkirk. Now if she wants in fact to protect his head from a draft, a lace collar is not nearly so effective as his own wig, which must be lying nearby. But she does not replace his wig because such action would not yield her any advantage, and it is this advantage that she seeks, rather than any protection of his health. Lady Easy has almost completely misrepresented to herself her own motives. She has ignored her intense desire to hold her husband, a need seriously inhibited by an inability, arising from her timidity, to face him down in a direct altercation. Presumably she senses the advantages of her action with the steinkirk, but she cannot represent the action to herself as a conscious contrivance. Instead she has to recast her motives completely in terms of virtue, love, and wifely submissiveness, when in reality her emotion is directed toward possession, an intention that is the exact reverse of altruism. The purpose of this rationalizing appears to be a heightening of self-esteem. And it is this ambition to think of herself as more virtuous than she really is that antagonizes the modern reader. Her position is unfortunate and arouses sympathy; her action is an adroit means of exploiting a painful situation, and so the reader applauds her discreet stratagem; but her justification of the action is insufferable.

And the misrepresentation continues into the reconciliation scene. When Sir Charles decides to make a clean breast of it and asks her to discharge the guilty maid, Lady Easy bursts into tears: "Distract me not with this Excess of Goodness." Obviously his actions show only a bare minimum of goodness; but this is his cue to say, "Praise me not, lest I reflect how little I have deserv'd it," a true statement that concedes her superior generosity of spirit. Sir Charles then gets his contrition off his chest and concludes with "Receive me then intire at last," to which she exclaims joyfully, and a little unguardedly, "O the dear Reward of long-desiring Love!" Whether or not he may be considered "intire," she has attained her goal, which is less spiritual than material. And when Sir Charles again insists that the maid be discharged, Lady Easy again objects, but this time for reasons of pure policy. A peremptory discharge might cause scandal and make the maid hate Lady Easy forever after. These shrewd reasons are not disguised with virtue, possibly because a virtuous rationalization would be lost on a delinquent maid, possibly because the avoidance of scandal is inherently virtuous. Sir Charles at least sees virtue in it: "Still my Superior every way" (I, 394-395). Or is he implying that in both practical resourcefulness and in virtue she is equally excellent? As in the other two plays discussed, there seems to be a parallel between virtue and superiority of tactics.

Like Amanda in *Love's Last Shift,* Lady Easy has channeled all her emotions so that they are wholly devoted to demonstrating the warmth and intensity of her own virtue: Lady Easy as guardian angel. This emotion could not of course be expressed by laughter, and yet it is so strong that it must break out some way, and tears are the logical solution. Tears may also imply a self-esteem so strong as to be self-admiration; but whatever the specific situation, it may be theorized that tears show an intense preoccupation with oneself.

In each of the three situations so far considered, there has been a scene where the less sentimental character has repented of his misdeeds and asked forgiveness of the more sentimental character. And in each of these cases, the character who has established a virtuous dominance has assured the other that his sins have been forgiven, and that he may now make a fresh start. One thing is reasonably clear in these and other repentance scenes, so frequent in sentimental drama: the erring person does not primarily or emphatically ask forgiveness of God; he really humiliates himself before the leading sentimental character. This behavior is in keeping with the sentimentalist's assuming the part of Christ, or at least Christ's vicegerent; he feels himself able to dispense forgiveness and is happy when someone confirms his judgment of himself. Usually in such scenes the repentant one admits he has been not only evil, but also stupid, ill-advised, and immature, whereas he now sees that the sentimentalist is at once more sensible, more practical, and more virtuous. The sins of the one repenting are exaggerated, and the virtues of the one forgiving are praised beyond measure. The sentimentalist, confronted with this flattering image of his own virtue, responds with a display of Christian humility and turns the compliment aside almost as if he found it too pleasant to believe. He may even exact a vow of secrecy from the other, so that his virtue will not be publicized. But fame, however delicious, is not really necessary. If the sentimentalist can feel that his moral dominion has been irrefutably established in this instance, he has a strong proof that he is as good and as powerfully influential as he wants to believe he is. The sentimentalist has in large part substituted the ideal of ecstatic self-approval for the former ideal of glorious reputation.[15]

But the pleasures of bestowing forgiveness, with its richly satisfying heightening of self-esteem, cannot be indulged without someone to forgive. Hence the value of the sinner to the sentimentalist. Sometimes it seems as though the sin is not the worst evil, but the refusing to ask the sentimentalist's pardon for it afterward. And so long as the act of abasement is practiced with sufficient assiduity, the usually stuffy and prudish sentimentalist can forgive an amazing amount of wrongdoing. Here it is appropriate to glance at possibly the most conspicuous example of abasement in sentimental literature: the prison scenes of *The London Merchant* (1731), by George Lillo. Just before his execution George Barnwell humiliates himself before the employer he has robbed, the friend who has shielded him, and the girl who has loved and sacrificed for him in vain. By this time Barnwell has committed fornication, breach of trust, robbery, and murder—and moreover murder of a relative and benefactor. Nevertheless, all may be forgiven him because he admits himself wrong with such vehemence and goes to such extremes in self-humiliation. He weeps bitter, self-accusing tears. He throws himself on the ground, exclaiming: "Are those honest arms . . . fit to embrace . . . a murderer? These iron fetters only shall clasp, and flinty pavement bear me . . . even these too good for such a bloody monster."[16]

When the still faithful Maria appears, he says the one thing that will abase himself and flatter her self-esteem: "Think how much beneath your self you condescend, to regard me now" (p. 103). He finally brands himself a wicked wretch who can justify his existence only by serving as a horrid example to others tempted like him. Such a person may yet be admired in the sentimental scheme of things because he repents, and because he makes all his three friends seem so virtuous and forgiving. His seductress Millwood, on the other hand, will not play the game. She followed her inclinations as everyone else does, she happened to be caught, and she will not say she is sorry. Such a person cannot help us "ourselves both more approve and know." In fact, she raises some very serious questions about the virtue of the virtuous. Hence, even though her charges are partly true, she cannot be saved.

She will not humiliate herself before God and, what is more important, before the virtuous. She will not accept gratefully the pity of the
complacent.[17]

In less serious cases, the person who repents need not kneel or
grovel, in action or word. Myrtle in Steele's *Conscious Lovers* only
stammers out an apology, and all effusive language is kept to a minimum. But he has admitted himself to be wrong, Bevil Junior to be
right, and has conceded further that "right" implies virtue. That is all
Bevil requires. Thus the virtuous person in sentimental plays enjoys
the satisfaction of humiliating his opponents, and of taking them
captive by converting them to his own ideas.

But while all this is happening onstage, what should the spectator
be thinking? Of course he is on the side of virtue and presumably believes himself virtuous. Therefore he begins to identify with the hero
or heroine, and the dramatist encourages him by always showing the
hero or heroine in a favorable light, no matter how unsavory the implications of his actions might appear to an unbiased judge. Consequently, the spectator sees the development of the main character as
an apotheosis of virtue and finds in this exaltation a glorification of
himself; since by this time spectator is fully identified with hero. A
sense of positive illumination follows this revelation of virtue in the
alter ego onstage. Now the spectator can really "approve and know"
himself, and in this steadfast conviction of his own moral loftiness, can
put into practice that other line of Steele's: "Christianity makes Men
pity, not scorn the Wicked."

One thing more remains to be said about the sentimentalist. Ostensibly there is no more loyal supporter of religion. After all, if he patterns his life on Christ, what more can we ask? But if this emulation
of Christ is only a self-deception for primarily egoistic reasons, then his
attitude is presumptuous rather than admirable. And in that case, sentimentalism might be said to make a distinct step away from traditional
Christianity. The substitution of oneself for Christ is to a certain degree the substitution of a god one finds irresistibly attractive (oneself)
for a god one is no longer willing to worship (Christ). If we must be
"insensibly betrayed into morality, by bribing the fancy with beautiful
and agreeable images" of virtue,[18] as Steele said, we have probably
abandoned the morality and embraced the merely agreeable. There is
no doubt that we want the bribe; it is not so certain that we want the
morality or the religion. Actually there is no room in sentimentalism
for the awareness of sin and the real sense of humility that Christianity

is ordinarily thought to demand. Neither has sentimentalism room for theology, dogma, or ethical speculation. All that has been swept away and replaced with the sentimentalist's own virtue.

And it must not be thought that the sentimentalist is all-forgiving and overflowing with human kindness. That is merely how he thinks of himself. On the contrary, he can be malicious toward those who oppose his ideas or labor to defeat his ends. A common type in sentimental comedy is the hateful character whom everyone wants destroyed. At the end of the play, he is cornered (in *The West Indian,* the Fulmers and Lady Rusport; in *The Conscious Lovers,* Cimberton; in *The London Merchant,* Millwood). Should he be forgiven? His faults seem too gross, but sentimentalists grudgingly give him that chance. To everyone's relief, he refuses; and then the punishment everyone has hoped for may be administered with a clear conscience.

In conclusion, sentimentality seems, from the evidence collected, to have an actual but ambiguous connection with morality. Sentimentality is a state of mind based on the assumption that one's own character is perfect, or as near perfection as necessary, or if certain grave faults seem to emerge, they must not be regarded as inherent. The sentimentalist believes it is the part of Christian morality to see himself as a moral paragon whose behavior is in many respects Christlike; and he consents to indulge in mutual admiration with every person who will reciprocate. The sentimentalist will venture to "forgive" and "save" every erring mortal who will abase himself, theoretically before God, but mainly before him, the sentimentalist; and he will venture to damn every erring mortal who will not so abase himself. The first trait of sentimentality, then, is self-esteem raised to the presumptuous level of self-adoration, self-worship; and since love is a basic Christian attribute, the sentimentalist drenches all his relationships with professions of charity and altruism. Since no one is in fact perfect, and faults and limitations occur, even in sentimental behavior, they have to be explained away by a constant process of reinterpretation. The sentimentalist spends half his time justifying his morally ambiguous actions and the other half exclaiming over the beauties of Christian virtue, including his own. But, although the process of rationalization is more or less conscious, the sentimentalist is so determined to convince himself, and so successful, that he cannot be called a hypocrite. He may share with the hypocrite a determination to keep his opportunism intact; but, unlike the person of conscious duplicity, he feels obliged to wear at all times his sentimental mask.

NOTES

1. East Lansing, Mich., 1957, pp. 22-30.
2. Cambridge, Mass., 1948, p. vii.
3. R. S. Crane, "Suggestions toward a Genealogy of the 'Man of Feeling,'" *ELH*, I (1934), 206.
4. Holland, *The First Modern Comedies* (Cambridge, Mass., 1959), p. 113. For Krutch and Bernbaum, see notes 5 and 7 below.
5. Joseph Wood Krutch, *Comedy and Conscience after the Restoration* (New York, 1949), p. 252; Sherbo, p. 166.
6. Crane, I, 205-230.
7. Ernest Bernbaum, *The Drama of Sensibility* (Boston, 1915). At times he speaks of a new development in the sentimental genre as an "advance" (p. 103) and observes that Steele in *The Tender Husband* "failed to use a good opportunity to enlarge the scope of the genre" (p. 101). He means that Steele could have made the subplot sentimental too, and declined. Later the movement is condemned almost without restriction: "True comedy was dead. The comic spirit . . . sought a mean refuge in farce or lived a slavish existence as the subordinate element in sentimental comedy" (p. 267). But the concluding dialogue between "Master Softheart and Sir Hardhead" that immediately follows avoids a definite conclusion (pp. 268-279).
8. Sherbo, p. 6.
9. *Richard Steele*, ed. G. A. Aitken (London, 1894), p. 187.
10. *Tracts and Pamphlets by Richard Steele*, ed. Rae Blanchard (Baltimore, Md., 1944), p. 28.
11. *Tracts*, p. 47.
12. *The Correspondence of Richard Steele*, ed. Rae Blanchard (London, 1941), p. 108.
13. Samuel Richardson, *Clarissa* (Oxford, 1930), I, xiii-xiv (Shakespeare Head edition).
14. *Plays Written by Mr. [Colley] Cibber* (London, 1721), I, 30. All volume and page references to Cibbers plays are to this edition.
15. For further illustration, see the passage quoted by Crane, I, 206, and *Tatler*, Nos. 92, 97, and 138.
16. George Lillo, *The London Merchant and Fatal Curiosity*, ed. A. W. Ward (Boston, 1906), p. 98.
17. Millwood claims that she is fated to ill-fortune (pp. 109-110). But Lillo here seems to be reviving the medieval warning against the dangers of despair. Barnwell's comments in the same scene show that she might be saved if she would only repent; but the awful consequences of sin without repentance (i.e., humiliation before the sentimentalist) have to be shown.
18. *Tatler*, No. 98.

BERTRAND H. BRONSON

❀

The Beggar's Opera

According to thrice-told report (a "most sweet robe of durance"), we owe it to Jonathan Swift's belief that a "Newgate pastoral" would make an "odd, pretty sort of thing" that *The Beggar's Opera* came into being. A more appropriate parentage could hardly be invented: the work is just what ought to have resulted from the impregnation of John Gay's somewhat feminine mind by the robust ironic intelligence of the Dean. That the union was brilliantly successful we do not need to be reminded. The play "was received with greater applause than was ever known. . . . The ladies carried about with them the favourite songs of it in fans, and houses were furnished with it in screens." For two hundred years and more it has given unceasing delight.

Reasons for this extraordinary success are not immediately apparent in the fable itself. A rascally thieftaker and receiver of stolen goods discovers that his daughter is married to a highwayman. Deliberation convinces him that he stands to win more by the reward for the highwayman's death than by what the latter may bring him if allowed to go free. Knowing that his son-in-law is promiscuously fond of women, he bribes two jades to put the man off his guard while constables rush in and arrest him. The highwayman is lodged in Newgate, but promptly gains his liberty through the Keeper's daughter, another sweetheart. Soon after escape, he is again betrayed by his fatal weak-

From *Studies in the Comic* (Berkeley: University of California Press, 1941), pp. 197-231. Reprinted by permission of the publishers.

ness, again confined, and condemned at once to be hanged. His last hours are disturbed by the wrangling of his two chief loves, the thief-taker's and the gaoler's daughters, both of whom get admittance to his cell. Their importunity reconciles him to the idea of dying, and his resolution is confirmed by the appearance of four more "wives," each with a child. At this point, in order that the piece may not end un-happily, a reprieve is cried, and the play closes with a general dance.

On the face of it, there is nothing in this farcical plot—or no-plot—to bespeak consideration. How could such a scarecrow have been filled with vitality enough to last two centuries and to show every promise—if the world endure so long—of lasting for another, besides producing a nu-merous progeny, from *The Village Opera* of Charles Johnson to the Savoy Operas of Gilbert and Sullivan? Out of what textiles have the garments been woven that so miraculously cover this tawdry frame, and what is the magic that has kept them fresh?

It is not a facile formula that will account for such a wonder. From how many and what various fields Gay collected his elements, the careful investigations of several scholars in recent years have taught us.[1] French *Comédie en vaudevilles*, realistic Elizabethan comedy, the Italian tradition of Harlequin and Columbine, recent operatic fash-ions with both Italian features and elements of the English masque, contemporary news sheets and popular song—all these and more sup-plied Gay with the simples which his own genius enabled him to compound with such extraordinary felicity.

After so much patient research on *The Beggar's Opera,* it may well seem that the squirrel's granary is full and the harvest done. We must not be ambitious now to add anything considerable in the way of in-formation to what scholarship has already amassed. Coming after those who have "led away the corn," we ought to be satisfied if, gleaning here and there, we may "find an ear of any goodly word that they have left." One or two aspects of the subject do await fuller illustration. But, in addition, reading the play in the light of all that is known about it, we may still feel that its continued popularity poses questions that invite further scrutiny of its pages. Exploring once again the familiar configurations of character and scene, and meditating upon the way in which they exfoliate or, like concentric rings in water, are forced outward by some inner generative impulse into wider and wider areas, can we not press closer than heretofore toward the secret of their vitality? May we not, in considering afresh the appeals that evoked response when the play was young, as well as those which are still potent, sharpen our perception of its peculiar qualities, and, in so doing, enrich our understanding of the ways of the comic spirit? The effort is surely worth the cost.

I

Before passing to broader considerations of enduring value, our attention may reasonably be engaged by certain matters which were of importance to the play's first audiences but which now are generally overlooked or ignored. Without any pretense to an exhaustive summary of the findings of scholarship, we may at once note a few of the reasons why *The Beggar's Opera* should have captured the favor of its immediate public. We know that its political implications made part of its appeal. An audience that could interpret Addison's *Cato* as a tract for the times was not slow to catch the allusion to Walpole in a catalogue of thieves which included *"Robin of Bagshot, alias Gorgon, alias Bluff Bob, alias Carbuncle, alias Bob Booty."* The First Minister's methods of political bribery, his success in amassing a private fortune, were easily read into an account of the tricks of gangsters. A recent quarrel with Townshend was perceived in the Peachum-Lockit dispute. Walpole's personal habits were understood in the remark, "He spends his life among women"; and Macheath's passion for the whole sex would have been interpreted in the same way even if Gay had not pointed it in that direction by transparent insinuation.

Then, too, the habitual Philistinism of the British attitude toward certain forms of art found cheap support in the gibes against the absurdities of opera. Gay asks to be forgiven for not making his own opera throughout unnatural, like those in vogue. He has omitted Recitative, he declares, but he has introduced all the favorite operatic similes: "the *Swallow,* the *Moth,* the *Bee,* the *Ship,* the *Flower";* and in his avoidance of catastrophe he has followed good operatic tradition: "for you must allow, that in this kind of Drama, 'tis no matter how absurdly things are brought about," and an Opera "must end happily."

A matter not so frequently adverted to is the debt of *The Beggar's Opera* to Durfey's *Pills to Purge Melancholy* for some of its immediate popularity. Durfey's collection, in its third, six-volume, edition, had but recently appeared. It had gathered a vast quantity of songs from current and late Restoration plays, from single sheets and printed broadside ballads, incidentally including at least two-thirds of the

sixty-nine tunes which Gay used in *The Beggar's Opera*. The *Pills*
were familiar to most of the male part, at least, of Gay's audience. A
large majority of the tunes he chose were associated with amorous
words, and not infrequently Gay kept phrases, refrain lines or half
lines, or followed the earlier verbal patterns, for his new lyrics. There
is no doubt that he thus won the amused attention of all whose tastes
had made them familiar with the originals. In the printed text of the
play, the titles alone of many of the airs would suggest the content of
the songs: "O Jenny, O Jenny, where hast thou been"; "Thomas, I
cannot"; "When once I lay with another man's wife," and so on. He
makes use of Congreve's familiar and wittily naughty song, "A Soldier
and a Sailor," and keeps a line of the refrain of the catchy but obscene
"Tom Tinker's my true-love": "This way, and that way, and which
way I will." Similar play is made with the phrase "what I dare not
name" in Mrs. Peachum's "If Love the virgin's heart invade," and, in
other songs, with "Pretty Poll," "Over the hills and far away," and
"How d'you do again." One of the best-loved songs in the play, Macheath's "If the heart of a man is deprest with Cares," is closely modeled
on its original, a song in *The Modern Prophets,* the first stanza of
which is as follows:

> Would you have a young Virgin of fifteen Years,
> You must tickle her Fancy with sweets and dears,
> Ever toying, and playing, and sweetly, sweetly,
> Sing a Love Sonnet, and charm her Ears:
>> Wittily, prettily talk her down,
>> Chase her, and praise her, if fair or brown,
>>> Sooth her, and smooth her,
>>> And teaze her, and please her,
> And touch but her Smicket, and all's your own.

A good deal subtler is the transformation of Durfey's song in *The
Country Wake,* called "The Mouse Trap." Durfey bewails the ham-
pering effect of marriage on a man's liberty. In contrast to the carefree
frolics of bachelor days, he describes the married state in terms like
the following:

> We're just like a Mouse in a Trap,
>> Or Vermin caught in a Gin:
> We Sweat and Fret, and try to Escape,
>> And Curse the sad Hour we came in.
>
> This was the worst Plague could ensue,
>> I'm Mew'd in a smoky House;

> I us'd to Tope a Bottle or two,
>   But now 'tis small Beer with my Spouse.

Remembrance of these words gives additional piquancy to Mrs. Peach-um's praise of marriage. Only *after* a woman is married, she declares, does she win her freedom. Maidens are like unminted gold, with no currency: but

> A Wife's like a Guinea in Gold,
>   Stampt with the Name of her Spouse;
>   Now here, now there; is bought, or is sold;
>   And is current in every House.

There is a similar reversal, but in the opposite direction, in Polly's song, "Virgins are like the fair Flower." The words in *Dioclesian,* set to Purcell's exquisite melody, conclude as follows:

> Iń fair Aurelia's Arms, leáve me expiring,
>   To be Imbalm'd with the sweets of her Breath;
>   To the last moment I'll still be desiring;
>   Never had Hero so glorious a Death.

Keeping this image in mind, listen to Polly's comment on the cropping of the fair flower.

> But, when once pluck'd, 'tis no longer alluring,
>   To *Covent-Garden* 'tis sent (as yet sweet,)
>   There fades, and shrinks, and grows past all enduring,
>   Rots, stinks, and dies, and is trod under feet.

For the tune of "Our Polly is a sad Slut," no less than six sets of words, for the most part high-spirited and indecent, are to be found in Dur-fey's *Pills.* In all of them the idea of women "flinging themselves away" is not far to seek, so that the knowing ear would find a large allowance. Gay has not followed any of the six closely; the talk of Polly's fashion-able apparel comes nearest to a song of a fashion called the Button'd Smock, in which occur the ensuing lines:

> For some will have the out-side fine,
>   To make the braver show;
>   But she will have her *Holland* Smock
>   That's Button'd down below.

For a number of his other lyrics Gay has taken hints from the sub-ject matter of the original songs. Macheath's disillusioned comment on the power of money, "If you at an Office solicit your Due," is based on two songs of worldly advice to the same tune in Durfey: "Advice to the Ladies" ("Ladies of *London*, both Wealthy and Fair") and "Advice to the Beaus" ("All Jolly Rakehells that Sup at the *Rose*"). "Come, Sweet Lass" begins with an identical line. With the substitution of "Polly" for "Shepherd," Polly's "When my Hero in Court appears" ends with the original four-line refrain:

> And alás poór Shépherd,
> Alack and a welladay;
> Before I was in Love,
> Oh every month was *May*.

Macheath's "But Valour the stronger grows, The stronger Liquor we're drinking" is set to the ancient drinking song of "Old Simon the King":

> For drinking will make a man Quaff,
> Quaffing will make a man Sing;
> Singing will make a man Laugh,
> And laughing long life doth bring.

That universal favorite, "Fill ev'ry Glass," derives from a curious drinking song in Durfey celebrating Marlborough, Eugene, and d'Auverquerque, the words in French but accompanied with an English version. The song begins, "Que chacun remplisse son verre"; or, according to the Durfey translation, "Fill ev'ry glass"; its last stanza is particularly in the mood of Gay:

> Si nous a [i]mions autant la Gloire
> Que boire nous serions des Heros;
> Car parmi les verres [et] le [s] Pots,
> Nous sommes seurs [*sic*] de la victoire.

Lucy's confession to her father, "When young at the Bar," is a rare example of debasement by Gay of his original. Little remains of the charm of Purcell's song in *The Fairy Queen*, except subject and inviolably lovely melody, to which the words had been these:

> If Love's a sweet Passion, why does it Torment?
> If a bitter, oh tell me! whence comes my content;
> Since I suffer with Pleasure, why should I complain,
> Or grieve at my Fate, when I know 'tis in vain?
> Yet so pleasing the Pain is, so soft is the Dart,
> That at once it both wounds me, and tickles my Heart.

This song, incidentally, had gained a well-deserved popularity by the turn of the century. It appears on broadsides as well as in Durfey, and its title stands above many another ballad to designate the tune to which the new words should be sung.

Having brought his hero as it were to the foot of the gallows, Gay cast about for some piece of music that would rise to the needs of this important occasion. He found just what he wanted in Lewis Ramondon's "Hymn upon the Execution of two Criminals," a dirge in three-two time with appropriately lugubrious words, which may be seen in Durfey's final volume of the *Pills*. Its introductory stanzas will sufficiently display its character:

> All you that must take a leap in the Dark,
> Pity the Fate of *Lawson* and *Clark;*
> Cheated by Hope, by Mercy amus'd,
> Betray'd by the sinful ways we us'd:
> Cropp'd in our Prime of Strength and Youth,
> Who can but weep at so sad a Truth;
>   *Cropp'd in our Prime,* &c.
>
> Once we thought 'twould never be Night,
> But now alass 'twill never be light;
> Heavenly mercy shine on our Souls,
> Death draws near, hark, *Sepúlchres* Bell Toles:
> Nature is stronger in Youth than in Age,
> Grant us thy Spirit Lord Grief to asswage.
>   [*Grant us thy Spirit,* &c.]

These melancholy measures Gay divided for a grand trio between his three principals, Macheath, Polly, and Lucy, not neglecting the admirable hint of St. Sepulchre's bell for operatic effect: "But hark!" sings Macheath, "I hear the Toll of the Bell." Whereupon they all echo in chorus, "Tol de rol lol"!

II

In the course of the opera Gay has introduced among the arias sundry duettos in the proper contemporary operatic manner, to vary the entertainment and underline the burlesque. Polly and her mother share one, Polly and Macheath three, and Polly and Lucy another three. There is likewise due use of a chorus at several points, and, for an echo of operatic ballet, three dances are introduced, including Macheath's cotillion of ladies and the grotesque dance of prisoners in chains. Thus most of the musical elements of real opera are used by Gay, in his fashion. To introduce recitative he would have had to

employ the services of a composer. What he does, instead, is to suggest a parody of recitative in Macheath's meditations in the condemned hold. The Ladies, as the Beggar announces in the Introduction, always reckon a Prison Scene "charmingly pathetick"; and in
this affecting passage is would not do to allow his hero to express
himself in ordinary fashion. Here Gay constructs a medley, linking
phrases out of nine familiar melodies (including one from Purcell's
Bonduca, Farinel's *Ground*, Carey's *Sally*, the popular "Why are mine
Eyes still flowing," and *Chevy Chase* and other ballad tunes) and
rising to *Greensleeves* by way of closing aria. The fun of this sequence
was considerably lessened in the late Hammersmith production (otherwise admirable) by the omission of more than half the excerpts. The
omissions unfortunately resulted also in obscuring Gay's equating of
his hero's courage with the amount of liquor he contained at the moment. Macheath tugs at the bottle after nearly every phrase. Raising
his spirits with a brimmer, he boldly chants (to Purcell's air of "Brit-
ons, strike home"),

> Since I must swing,—I scorn, I scorn to wince or whine;

but his next words are,

> But now again my Spirits sink,

and he promptly endeavors to "raise them high with wine." After another phrase or two, he turns to brandy for further assistance. Thus he
ascends by degrees to his ironic aria (omitted at Hammersmith):

> Since Laws were made for ev'ry Degree,
>   To curb Vice in others, as well as me,
>   I wonder we han't better Company,
>   Upon *Tyburn* Tree!

But the effect soon wears off: "O Leave me to Thought!" he entreats
Polly and Lucy in the trio which follows:

> I fear! I doubt!
> I tremble! I droop—See, my Courage is out,
>   [*Turns up the empty Bottle.*

POLLY.   No token of Love?

MACHEATH   See, my Courage is out.
>   [*Turns up the empty Pot.*

The whole scene is treated as the most extravagant burlesque, and
it is time to pursue the hint which Gay has dropped earlier about

pathetic prison scenes, and inquire whether anything in particular lies behind the burlesque here.

Considering the amount of minute investigation accorded *The Beggar's Opera*, one wonders that no student appears to have examined the contemporary operas of Händel, Buononcini, and Ariosti, to learn whether general parody anywhere becomes specific. For if the search has been made, the results of it, whether positive or negative, have nowhere been announced in print. Schultz, indeed, has noted Sir John Hawkins' observation, that "possibly Macheath's appearance in Newgate fetters might be supposed to ridicule the prison scene in *Coriolanus*, performed a few years before."[2] But Hawkins flouted the notion generally of burlesque in Gay's play, and Schultz did not—or could not—verify his suggestion here. F. W. Bateson, in a recent edition of *The Beggar's Opera*,[3] converted "possibly" into "probably" and amplified the note: "a hit probably at the prison scene in Attilio Ariosti's opera, *Caius Marius Coriolanus*, produced in 1723." A glance at Burney's History supplies the fuller reference and the date. *Marcius* has been miscopied *Marius;* but the fact is irrelevant, for the opera was doubtless known simply as Coriolano. Suggestion of any specific parody in this direction thus rests where Hawkins left it in 1776.

Schultz has caught one other allusion in the Beggar's preliminary statement: "I have observ'd such a nice Impartiality to our two Ladies, that it is impossible for either of them to take Offence." "This," Schultz observes, "seems to have no bearing on Polly and Lucy"; and he continues with the correct explanation, though vaguely expressed: "it is clearly a reference to the quarrel between two rival singers, Cuzzoni and Faustina, in 1727, over the leading part in an Italian opera." Now this quarrel was the most notorious event in the annals of the operatic stage during the two years preceding the appearance of Gay's work. Faustina Bordoni was imported in the spring of 1726 at the fabulous salary of £2500. Cuzzoni, already established, was receiving £2000. Cuzzoni, in spite of what Burney calls her "native warble" and "a perfect shake," was dumpy and singularly unattractive in personality. Faustina seems to have been an appealing creature, and pleasing to the eye, as well as the possessor of an equally miraculous voice. Fashionable London at once took sides. Lampoons were published on both parts in the papers, and the friends of the two singers met in the theater to hiss their enemies off the stage in turn, until the universal clamor broke up the performance. Matters came to a hysterical climax when, in a performance of Buononcini's *Astyanax*, in the spring of

1727, the rivals actually resorted to mutual scratching and hair pulling
on the stage. Nobody could possibly have remained ignorant of this
notorious dispute. Gay's allusion to it goes much beyond an introductory reference. The rivalry of Polly and Lucy, in this view, takes on
added comic significance:

> LUCY. If you are determin'd, Madam, to raise a Dis-
> turbance in the Prison, I shall be oblig'd to send for
> the Turnkey to show you the Door. I am sorry,
> Madam, you force me to be so ill-bred.
> POLLY. Give me leave to tell you, Madam: These forward
> Airs don't become you in the least, Madam . . .
>   [Then a song:]
> LUCY.   Why how now, Madam Flirt?
>   If you thus must chatter;
>   And are for flinging Dirt,
>   Let's try who best can spatter;
>   Madam *Flirt!*
>
> POLLY.   Why how now, saucy Jade;
>   Sure the Wench is tipsy;
>   How can you see me made   [*To him.*
>   The Scoff of such a Gipsy?
>   Saucy Jade!   [*To her.*

In this song, the monosyllable *Dirt* occupies a running passage nearly
three bars long, in true bravura style, and in strong contrast to the
usual note-for-syllable habit of the settings. The quarrel subsequently
works toward a fateful climax. "I could murder that impudent happy
Strumpet," cries Lucy; and she proceeds to make the attempt. In a
speech which is the exact counterpart in English of contemporary
Italian operatic recitative, she declares: "Jealousy, Rage, Love and
Fear are at once tearing me to pieces. How am I weather-beaten, and
shatter'd with distresses!" This launches her naturally upon her next
aria, built on the figure of the Ship ("I'm like a Skiff on the Ocean
tost"), and rising to its climax:

> Revenge, Revenge, Revenge,
> Shall appease my restless Sprite.

In the right operatic tradition, she has prepared a poison draught
against Polly's arrival; and, dropping to speech again, she says:

> I have the Rats-bane ready.—I run no Risque; for I can
> lay her Death upon the Ginn [this of Cuzzoni!].—But say,

I were to be hang'd—I never could be hang'd for any
thing that would give me greater Comfort, than the
poysoning that Slut.

Polly enters, and there is pretense of a reconciliation, Lucy recommending—pleasantly enough, in the light of her intentions—a "quieting Draught." "I wish," she says pointedly, "I wish all our Quarrels
might have so comfortable a Reconciliation"—a patent allusion to
matter outside the play.

But Faustina and Cuzzoni will take us yet further. When Faustina
arrived early in 1726, the very first task which Händel set himself was
to write an opera in which both stars could sing, and in which neither
could claim that the other's role was better than her own. The job
seems to have taken him nearly a month! and a handsome piece of
work it was, in which the arias were shaped as by the hand of an ex-
pert *couturier* to display the special excellences of each voice. The
recitatives were evenly divided, and the duets so artfully contrived
that now Faustina and now Cuzzoni had the foremost part. Each lady
had as well a duet with the leading man. The opera was *Alessandro*.
It opened on May 5, and proved so popular that, instead of the usual
twice, it was performed thrice a week for the rest of the season. The
plot is very largely taken up with the rivalry of Rossane and Lisaura
for the love of Alessandro, who, outwardly at least, vacillates deplor-
ably between them, inclining to the nearer, and not fixing upon Rossane until the last possible moment. "How happy could [he] be with
either, Were t'other dear charmer away!" Throughout the three[4] acts
of the opera, the ladies consequently live upon the rack, singing all
the while of their pains and doubts and jealousy. "How sweet love
would be," sings Lisaura, "were it not for jealousy with its icy poison."
There is no close parody in *The Beggar's Opera* of any particular
scene in *Alessandro,* but a kind of condensed parody occurs here and
there of broader vistas. Thus, in *Alessandro,* there is a scene in which
the hero comes back from martial exploits to his two loves. Alessandro greets Rossane with a loving embrace, and is well received, whilst
Lisaura watches with inward rage. Then he turns to Lisaura with the
words: "Delightful Lisaura, no less gladly do I return to thee." There-
upon, Rossane starts away in jealous wrath. Alessandro follows her,
and Lisaura exclaims that she cannot longer endure this unworthy
treatment: "More unstable is this inconstant one than the wave, more
easily set in motion than a leaf." So in balder fashion do Polly and
Lucy bid for Macheath's notice:

POLLY.	Hither, dear Husband, turn your Eyes.
LUCY.	Bestow one glance to cheer me.
POLLY.	Think with that Look, thy *Polly* dyes.
LUCY.	O shun me not—but hear me.
POLLY.	'Tis *Polly* sues.
LUCY.	—'Tis *Lucy* speaks.
POLLY.	Is thus true Love requited?
LUCY.	My Heart is bursting.
POLLY.	—Mine too breaks.
LUCY.	Must I
POLLY.	—Must I be slighted?

Again, in the third act of Händel's opera, the women meet by themselves to take stock of the situation. "Let us leave jealousy, deceit, and trickery, fair Lisaura," says Rossane; "let us both equally love the conqueror of the world, and let Alessandro's heart fall to her who shall have the better hap in true loving constancy." "In vain you try to put me down with your fine boasting," replies Lisaura; "as for me, I would imitate the fair flower which turns toward the sun's brightness, and finds solace in admiring his beauty. Yet I differ in that I long for what consumes me, whilst the flower only follows that which gives it life." Similarly, Gay's ladies meet to discuss their mutual unhappiness. "Ah, *Polly! Polly!*" cries Lucy; " 'tis I am the unhappy Wife; and he loves you as if you were only his Mistress." "Sure, Madam," Polly answers, "you cannot think me so happy as to be the Object of your Jealousy.—A Man is always afraid of a Woman who loves him too well—so that I must expect to be neglected and avoided." "Then," says Lucy, "our Cases, my dear *Polly*, are exactly alike. Both of us indeed have been too fond." Rossane, however, has premonitions of felicity, and in a brilliant aria she describes her feelings in images comparable to those in which Lucy earlier expresses Polly's good fortune. While like the rudderless skiff, cries Lucy, "I lye rolling and tossing all Night, That *Polly* lyes sporting on Seas of Delight!" "Si nella calma azurro," sings Rossane, "brilla il mar, se splende il sole, e i rai fan tremolar tranquilla l'onda."

All this makes something of an Alexander out of Macheath, and indeed the two heroes have significant traits in common. Both have attained their greatest successes in the same manner—by force of arms— and both tower above their associates in magnanimity. The parallel is hinted by Swift in a letter to Gay. "I wish," Swift writes, "Macheath, when he was going to be hanged, had imitated Alexander the Great

when he was dying. I would have had his fellow-rogues desire his commands about a successor, and he to answer, Let it be the most worthy,
etc." (March 28, 1728). But Alexander's death was not in the opera.
What was in the opera was Alessandro's passion for the sex, and his
reluctance to say no to a pretty face. He comes upon the sleeping
Rossane and thinks to obtain a kiss. But Lisaura is on the watch and
promptly comes forward. When Alessandro perceives her, "Come," he
says, "beautiful Lisaura, and console the distresses of a sorrowful
heart." Rossane awakes at that moment, but feigns continued slumber.
Mockingly, Lisaura repeats the words she has just heard him use to
her rival: "Let me kiss you, lovely rubies": and departs with disdain.
Alessandro turns back to Rossane for solace of his pains. She in turn
picks up the words he has just addressed to Lisaura, pointing them
against him with scorn: "Proud eyes beloved, let me no longer languish,"—and mockingly abandons him. "What honor," he exclaims
ironically, "is given to the world's conqueror! Alexander made a mock
by two stubborn women!" So, at a great remove, sings Macheath:

> One wife is too much for most husbands to hear,
> But two at a time there's no mortal can bear.
> This way, and that way, and which way I will,
> What would comfort the one, t'other wife would take ill.

Until someone can make a careful examination of the whole file of
Italian operas that were produced in London before 1728, it will not
be possible to draw up an exact account of Gay's use of them. The
operas of Ariosti and Buononcini have not been accessible to the
present writer, but a cursory inspection of Händel's operas alone is
enough to reveal a good many interesting parallels. Thus, in several
of them the poisoned cup appears. *Flavio* (1723) has a scene of quarreling fathers. *Ottone* (1723) has a pirate, a daring, resourceful, wild
fellow, who might almost have given hints for Macheath. *Ottone* was
very popular, its phrases, according to Burney, passing current among
musical people almost as the *bons mots* of a wit circulate in society.
In *Giulio Cesare* (1724) there is a scene in a seraglio in which the
tyrant Ptolemy gets into a genial frame, forgets his mistrust, and lays
aside his sword, whereupon, at a sign from Cornelia, Sextus rushes in
and attempts to stab him. In outline, this is close to the capture of
Macheath.

Hawkins may have had a special reason for suggesting *Coriolano* as
the original of the prison scene in *The Beggar's Opera*. But he could

have pointed equally to several of Händel's operas for prison scenes
that the ladies might have considered "charmingly pathetick." *Silla*
(1714) has an affecting one; *Tamerlano* (1724), a fine and popular
opera, of which the favorite songs were separately published by Walsh,
has another, involving a cup of poison. Radamisto, in the opera of
that name (1720), is condemned to death by the tyrant Tiridate. Zeno-
bia, Radamisto's love, is given the choice of marrying Tiridate or of
carrying death to her lover. She enters the prison with the poisoned
bowl and, as she approaches Radamisto, tries to drink it herself. Unable to move because of his shackles, he can do nothing to prevent her.
But the cup is dashed to the ground by Tiridate, who enters just in
time. A nearly identical scene is worked out in *Floridante* (1721)—sufficient testimony to its theatrical appeal. *Rodelinda* (1725) contains
an equally telling prison scene, which has recently been favorably
compared (by Hugo Leichtentritt) to the famous one in Beetho-
ven's *Fidelio,* with which, indeed, it has striking features of resemblance. *Alessandro* itself has a prison scene, though one not so affecting
as the preceding; and, speaking generally, there is hardly an opera in
which someone does not suffer duress for a time, and later make his
escape by force or stratagem.

   Of all the operas mentioned, *Floridante* seems most likely to have
contributed elements to *The Beggar's Opera,* not only in the prison
scene, but also in two noteworthy parting scenes between the hero
and his love. Floridante, meditating in his dungeon, displays fine
courage without any of the fortifying draughts which Macheath found
so necessary under similar circumstances. Chained to a pillar, he sings
defiantly: "These shackles and this horror cause no fear in my breast.
My torment is welcome to me." He greets as his deliverer the cup of
death which his love comes to bring him. "Oh cara soave morte!" he
cries to Elmira: "oh troppo a te crudele, troppo pietoso a me, fiero
tiranno! candida man, lascia ch'io stempri in baci su te il cor mio! tu
dolce puoi far morte." Polly and Lucy only wish that they might suffer
in Macheath's place; but Elmira attempts to exhibit "l'ultima prova
d'un amor fedele" by drinking the poison herself, in this intensely
dramatic and memorable scene.

   The parting between Polly and Macheath at the end of Act I is
obviously patterned on the fervent protestations and lingering fare-
wells of high romance. "Is there any Power, any Force," asks Macheath, "that could tear me from thee?" And they sing together the
well-known duet, "Where I laid on *Greenland's* Coast—Were I sold

on *Indian* Soil." "But oh!" says Polly, "we must part." And she sings the plaintive "O what Pain it is to part!" concluding, with perhaps a little admixture of Juliet: "One Kiss and then—one Kiss—begone—farewell . . . A few Weeks, perhaps, may reconcile us all . . . MAC-HEATH. Must I then go? POLLY. And will not Absence change your Love? . . . O how I fear!—How I tremble." And they sing a final song as they part, "looking back at each other with fondness; he at one Door, she at the other." With all this it is interesting to compare the conclusion of Act I of *Floridante:*

> FLORIDANTE. Ch'io parta? ELMIRA. Ch'io ti perda? Anima mia! In van l'invidia rea lo spera. FL. In vano me'l prefigge il destin, se non m'uccide. Solo partir? ELM. Sola restar? FL. Lasciarti? ELM. Più non vederti? Oh Dei! Non so. FL. Non vo'. ELM. Troppo amo. FL. Troppo adoro. Ahi! che a pensarlo sol, sento che moro.

Elmira then sings an aria, not about Greenland's coast, but to the following similar effect: "I shall sooner see the stars plunge into the sea than abandon my dear love. Thou art my life, my fate." To this, Floridante replies in similarly impassioned style, and a little later both join in a duet which prettily rings the changes on the same theme:

> FL.   Ah mia cara, se tu resti,
>   infelice a morte io vo.
> ELM.   Ah mio caro, se tu parti,
> FL.   se tu resti,
> ELM.   se tu parti,
> {FL.   infelice a morte io vo.
> {ELM.   per l'affanno io morirò.
> ELM.   Altra spene
> FL.   altro bene
> ELM.   senza te, cor mio, non ho.
> FL.   senza te, cor mio, non ho.

If this was not the scene which Gay had in mind, it will, under submission, do well enough.

It does not appear to have been Gay's method to paraphrase the actual songs or scenes of his originals. Rather, he re-created, so that while many of the images reappear so sharply that we cannot doubt a reminiscence, yet it is hard to convince ourselves that a specific passage is the unquestionable original of one in Gay. For example, is or is not Lucy's "I'm like a skiff on the ocean tossed, Now high now low with each billow borne" indebted to the air of Berenice in *Scipione?*—

> Com' onda incalza altr' onda,
> pena sù pena abbonda,
> sommersa al fin è l'alma in mar d'affano.

In general, all Gay's similes except the ones which are obviously ludicrous, like the housewife's rat, may be suspected of operatic parentage.
The following parallel, however, seems to be more than fortuitous.
Polly, toward the end of Act II, has a song—set, it is amusing to note,
to an air by Sandoni, Cuzzoni's own husband—which reads as follows:

> Thus when the Swallow, seeking Prey,
>   Within the Sash is closely pent,
> His Consort, with bemoaning Lay,
>   Without sits pining for th' Event.
> Her chatt'ring Lovers all around her skim;
> She heeds them not (poor Bird!) her Soul's with him.

In the opera *Scipione,* produced a year and a half before *The Beggar's
Opera,* Berenice, a prisoner of war, is followed by her lover, who sings
this aria:

> Lamentando mi corro a volo,
> qual colombo che solo,
> và cercando la sua diletta
> involata dal casciator;
> E poi misero innamorato
> prigionero le resta stato;
> mà la gabbia pur lo alletta,
> perchè restaci col suo amor.

It may be objected that we have been assuming a rather intimate
acquaintance on Gay's part with the particulars of Italian opera. Not
more intimate, in my opinion, than the probabilities warrant. That
Gay was himself musical admits of no dispute. All his life he wrote
ballads and lyrics to be sung, and from first to last his works display a
wide familiarity with popular song. (That Pepusch, as Burney suggests, selected the tunes for *The Beggar's Opera* and *Polly* is pure non-
sense, not worth a moment's consideration. If the internal evidence of
the lyrics did not disprove the suggestion, the list of popular songs at
the end of Gay's *Shepherd's Week,* 1714, would by itself be enough to
resolve any doubts.) He himself is known to have played the flute.
He moved in a fashionable set that would as a matter of course have
interested itself in opera, just as people of fashion today, whether or

not they love music, attend the opera for social reasons. But Gay had a better reason, for he was even professionally connected with it. He wrote the libretto of *Acis and Galatea,* which, in 1719 or 1720, Händel set to music that puts this work among the composer's masterpieces. There is little probability that Gay intended a serious attack upon Italian opera, and he may even have been somewhat appalled at the amount of damage caused by his play. For his ridicule does not go beyond poking affectionate fun at conventions which, like most conventions objectively regarded, have their ludicrous side. Händel had the sense to see this truth, and there is no evidence that *The Beggar's Opera* ever caused a rift between the two men. Years before *Acis and Galatea,* Händel had set a lyric for Gay's early play, *The What D'Ye Call It.* (Gay used the tune again in his opera.) And in 1732, after *The Beggar's Opera* and *Polly* had done their worst, Händel returned to *Acis and Galatea* in order to rework it. Intrinsically, there is nothing in *The Beggar's Opera* which even approaches significant criticism of serious opera; and Professor Dent,[5] in contrast to most who have written on the subject, has sound sense on his side when he declares: "The Italian opera was killed, not so much by the fact that *The Beggar's Opera* made its conventions ridiculous (for its conventions could at that time have been ridiculous only to quite unmusical people), as by the incontestable attraction of the new work itself."[6] Everything considered, *The Beggar's Opera* may more properly be regarded as a testimonial to the strength of opera's appeal to John Gay's imagination than as a deliberate attempt to ridicule it out of existence.

Further evidence of Gay's serious musical taste lies closer at hand. So much has been made of the popular character of the melodies in *The Beggar's Opera* that it will probably surprise most readers to learn that nearly a third of the airs employed are by known composers; for none, I believe, of the editions of the play, nor of its songs, takes the trouble to point out the fact, although students have traced nearly every one of the tunes to earlier sources. We have hardly noticed how amply Gay laid under contribution the most reputable composers of his age. Purcell leads the list, in number as in excellence. But Händel follows him close; and among other composers who make an appearance are Buononcini, Sandoni, Akeroyde, Leveridge, and Eccles. Nevertheless, Gay had a sure ear for a good tune, whether or not it bore the distinction of a famous name; and it cannot be said that the anonymous airs which he selected are noticeably inferior, as a class, to the others.

III

What has neither been forgotten nor ignored is the poet's ability to devise excellent lyrics for his tunes. In approaching this aspect of the play, we move at once from the ephemeral causes of its popularity to grounds which have permanent validity. Gay's easy grace, his power of being witty whilst remaining fluent and singable, have never been touched unless by poets who have written with a tune in mind. Even Burns—who did so write—though his emotional range was much wider and deeper, seldom hit the level of Gay's succinct wit in song, but generally resorted to ampler forms for his most pungent expression. In mere singing quality, few English lyric poets have surpassed Gay at any time since Elizabethan days, and probably none save Burns since his own day. Everyone has his own favorites in *The Beggar's Opera,* and it is almost an impertinence to single out for quotation things so familiar and beloved. But Gay's special flavor, his ironic wit, his perfect sense of how to match a tune with words, are brilliantly displayed in Macheath's sardonic meditation upon experience:

> Man may escape from Rope and Gun;
>   Nay, some have out-liv'd the Doctor's Pill;
> Who takes a Woman must be undone,
>   That Basilisk is sure to kill.
> The Fly that sips Treacle is lost in the Sweets,
>   So he that tastes Woman, Woman, Woman,
> He that tastes Woman, Ruin meets.

More typical, perhaps, of Gay's performance is the Gilbertian verve and speed of the following:

> If you at an Office solicit your Due,
>   And would not have Matters neglected;
> You must quicken the Clerk with the Perquisite too,
>   To do what his Duty directed.
> Or would you the Frowns of a Lady prevent,
>   She too has this palpable Failing,
> The Perquisite softens her into Consent;
>   That Reason with all is prevailing.

In quite another category stand the lines of the cotillion in Act II—a silvery Augustan echo of the golden chime of the Renaissance:

> Let us drink and sport to-day,
>   Ours is not to-morrow.
> Love with Youth flies swift away,
>   Age is nought but Sorrow.
>   Dance and sing,
>   Tíme's on the Wing,
>   Lífe never knóws the return of Spring.
> CHORUS. Let us drink &c.

The note of that stanza, though it exactly expresses the nostalgic quality of much of Purcell's music, is very rare in Gay's work.

The scrupulous ear that so nicely adjusted the phrases of the lyrics has exerted the same felicitous control over the dialogue. Not enough praise has been accorded to Gay's prose. The wit of his epigrams, to be sure, has received applause. But the perspicuous timing of his cadences, even in passages devoid of epigrammatic pointing, is worthy of careful study. He never taxes the ear. The ease and polish of his phrases is perfectly calculated for oral delivery. It is self-conscious, but not insistent; and it has just the right amount of emphasis to gratify the listener. Take for example a passage which eschews the advantages of aphorism, the quarrel of Peachum and Lockit—a delightful and conscious parody[7] of the familiar scene between Brutus and Cassius in *Julius Caesar,* as well as a fling at the differences between the brothers-in-law, Walpole and Townshend:

> PEACHUM. Here's poor *Ned Clincher*'s Name, I see. Sure, Brother *Lockit,* there was a little unfair Proceeding in *Ned*'s case: for he told me in the Condemn'd Hold, that for Value receiv'd, you had promis'd him a Session or two longer without Molestation.
> LOCKIT. Mr. *Peachum*—this is the first time my Honour was ever call'd in Question.
> PEACHUM. Business is at an end—if once we act dishonourably.
> LOCKIT. Who accuses me?
> PEACHUM. You are warm, Brother.
> LOCKIT. He that attacks my Honour, attacks my Livelihood.—And this Usage—Sir—is not to be borne.
> PEACHUM. Since you provoke me to speak—I must tell you too, that Mrs. *Coaxer* charges you with defrauding her of her Information-Money, for the apprehending of curl-pated *Hugh.* Indeed, indeed, Brother, we must

punctually pay our Spies, or we shall have no Information.

LOCKIT. Is this Language to me, Sirrah,—who have sav'd
you from the Gallows, Sirrah!
                                          [*Collaring each other.*

PEACHUM. If I am hang'd, it shall be for ridding the
World of an arrant Rascal.

LOCKIT. This Hand shall do the Office of the Halter you
deserve, and throttle you—you Dog!—

PEACHUM. Brother, Brother—We are both in the Wrong—
We shall be both Losers in the Dispute—for you know
we have it in our Power to hang each other. You
should not be so passionate.

LOCKIT. Nor you so provoking.

PEACHUM. 'Tis our mutual Interest; 'tis for the Interest of
the World we should agree. If I said any thing, Brother,
to the Prejudice of your Character, I ask pardon.

LOCKIT. Brother *Peachum*—I can forgive as well as resent.
—Give me your Hand. Suspicion does not become a
Friend.

PEACHUM. I only meant to give you Occasion to justify
yourself.

When he heightens the dialogue by the addition of epigrammatic
statement, Gay comes very near the level of Congreve himself. What
he lacks of the Congrevean brilliance, he compensates for by never
giving more at a time than ordinary attention will sustain without
conscious effort. He seldom allows himself Congreve's length of phrase.
It is illuminating to compare the pace of the two:

FAINALL. You are a gallant man, Mirabell; and though
you may have cruelty enough not to satisfy a lady's
longing, you have too much generosity not to be tender
of her honour. Yet you speak with an indifference
which seems to be affected, and confesses you are conscious of a negligence.

MIRABELL. You pursue the argument with a distrust that
seems to be unaffected, and confesses you are conscious
of a concern for which the lady is more indebted to
you than is your wife.

Gay's tempo is more rapid: his cadences beach themselves much
sooner, with an impact that is less impressive to watch, but more immediately felt:

PEACHUM. Dear Wife, be a little pacified. Don't let your
Passion run away with your Senses. *Polly,* I grant you
hath done a rash thing.

MRS. PEACHUM. If she had had only an Intrigue with the
Fellow, why the very best Families have excus'd and
huddled up a Frailty of that sort. 'Tis Marriage, Husband, that makes it a blemish.

PEACHUM. But Money, Wife, is the true Fuller's Earth
for Reputations, there is not a Spot or a Stain but
what it can take out. A rich Rogue now-a-days is fit
Company for any Gentleman; and the World, my
Dear, hath not such a Contempt for Roguery as you
imagine.

For the most part, Gay's epigrams do not bear lifting out of their contexts so well as do Congreve's; but Congreve would have found it difficult to better the aphorism of Macheath:

Do all we can, Women will believe us; for they look
upon a Promise as an Excuse for following their own
Inclinations.

IV

Gay has invented for us a vivid group of people, with an appeal that
is hard to resist. They are so delightful, and, in the discrepancy between
their reprehensible ends and the self-righteousness with which they
pursue them, so ludicrous that we may miss the richer significance of
the satire in our mere spontaneous enjoyment. The matter is treated
with so light a hand that we incline to ignore its serious implications.
It is important, therefore, to remind ourselves of the actual weight of
these persons, for without this solid underpinning Gay could hardly
have made his play carry the considerable cargo of its deeper meaning,—could hardly have made it a social commentary which, for all its
surface playfulness, fulfills some of the profoundest ends of comedy.

Each of the leading characters is a positive force. Let us hold in
abeyance for the moment our amused perception of their real worth,
while they parade before us in the favoring light of their own self-
regard. Peachum is a man of responsibility who has constantly to
make decisions affecting the welfare and the lives of many people. He
has to weigh the importance of particular cases, adjudicate conflicting
claims, and issue commands. And his orders are not lightly disobeyed.
His wife has a proper sense of her husband's importance in their

world, and of her own position. She shares his counsels, but respects his authority and does not abuse her privilege. Her solicitude for her family's reputation is keen, her maternal sense is well developed. She does not lightly give way to emotion, but, on a sufficient occasion, her passions are impressive. Polly is neither feather-brained nor impulsive, but basically prudent and steady. She accepts, and respects, her parents' values, and her single point of difference with them is rationally grounded though admittedly in significant accord with her inclinations. Filch, the servant, recognizes that his own interests are identified with his masters', and is accordingly trusted and accepted almost as one of the family. He is a boy of the brightest parts, quick and apt, ready to give his best efforts to the discharge of his varied responsibilities. Lockit is another, but lesser, Peachum, with a philosophy equally well developed though not quite so fully uttered, and with a visible satisfaction in the power he wields. His daughter Lucy is a Salvator Rosa set over against the Claude of Polly. In her tempestuous nature we can trace Ercles' vein:

> The raging rocks
> And shivering shocks
> Shall break the locks
> Of prison gates.

She has a streak of tenderness, but in anger she is terrible and dangerous. She is crafty and determined in pursuit of revenge, and does not flinch from the possible consequences. As for Macheath, his sangfroid, dash, and prodigality of purse and person make him a favorite with both sexes. He is not easily cast down, and he knows that there are things worse than death in the human lot. Hazlitt calls him "one of God Almighty's gentlemen." His gallantry and good breeding rise, declares Hazlitt, "from impulse, not from rule; not from the trammels of education, but from a soul generous, courageous, good-natured, aspiring, amourous. The class of the character is very difficult to hit. It is something between gusto and slang, like port-wine and brandy mixed."[8]

None of these persons appears to be suffering from a sense of inferiority. Their words give proper dignity to their ideas, and their conduct proceeds in accordance with principles to which they have given a good deal of thought. Without in the least minimizing the pleasure of their company, one may assert that, with the possible exception of Polly, they all have a better opinion of themselves than we do. For we are not taken in: we know them for the immoral rogues that they are. They are the most immediate objects of Gay's satire. However loftily they bear themselves, the human reality of their lives is sordid and contemptible. Remembering the dreariness of many of the products of "realism" in later days, we may well be grateful for an occasional example of the mock heroic, which subjects to the purposes of humor the matter generally reserved for "realistic" treatment. The flair for this inverted kind of burlesque has, for reasons which might elsewhere be significantly pursued, been all but lost in our time. It is enough to note here that, in our recognition of Gay's burlesquing of the highflown manners and sentiments of operatic romance, we ought not to lose sight of the fact that he is simultaneously ridiculing a low society by decking them in all this borrowed finery. For burlesque has a two-edged blade, though both edges need not be equally sharp. "Had the Play remain'd, as I at first intended," says Gay in the person of the Beggar, with glancing irony, "it would have carried a most excellent Moral. 'Twould have shown that the lower Sort of People have their Vices in a degree as well as the Rich: And that they are punish'd for them."

The characters in the play are aware of our low opinion of them, and stand on the defensive against us. Offspring of corruption as they are, feeding on sin and death, what are their bulwarks, that so magnificently shore up their self-respect?

It is not by maintaining that the bases of our criticism are unsound that they are able to repel our attack. Truth and falsehood, good and evil, right and wrong are for them fundamentally the same as they are for us. Peachum, for example, accepts the conventional morality, and can even afford to make gestures of kindliness when they do not interfere with more important considerations. He delights "to let Women scape." "Make haste to *Newgate,* Boy," he commands Filch, "and let my Friends know what I intend; for I love to make them easy one way or other." And Filch, in the orotund fashion of sentimental drama, replies, "I'll away, for 'tis a Pleasure to be the Messenger of Comfort to Friends in Affliction." Neither Filch nor Mrs. Peachum is a stranger to feelings of gratitude and good will. Peachum, moreover, is above petty animosities. When Polly recoils from the idea of having Macheath impeached, protesting that her blood freezes at the thought of murdering her husband, Peachum replies:

> Fye, *Polly!* What hath Murder to do in the Affair? Since
> the thing sooner or later must happen, I dare say, the

Captain himself would like that we should get the Reward for his Death sooner than a Stranger. Why, *Polly,*
the Captain knows, that as 'tis his Employment to rob, so
'tis ours to take Robbers, every Man in his Business. So
that there is no Malice in the Case.

Clearly, these are no devils. Evil is not their good.

Rather, they stand us off by admitting the justice of our cause and
then diverting our attack all along the line to their betters. Gay himself is easily deflected and we follow him in full cry. Here we reach
the second degree of his satire, and it is on this level that the main attack is launched. People in the honorable walks of life—men of great
business, ladies of fashion, lawyers, courtiers, statesmen—it is these who
come in for the hottest fire. "Murder," declares Peachum, "is as fashionable a Crime as a Man can be guilty of. . . . No Gentleman is
ever look'd upon the worse for killing a Man in his own Defense." If
Macheath cannot do well at the gaming tables, the fault lies in his
education: "The Man that proposes to get Money by Play should have
the Education of a fine Gentleman, and be train'd up to it from his
Youth." "Really," replies Mrs. Peachum to her husband, "I am sorry
upon *Polly's* Account the Captain had not more Discretion. What
business hath he to keep Company with Lords and Gentlemen? he
should leave them to prey upon one another." Society is a casino. Both
sexes play; and since the only purpose that motivates their play is the
desire of gain, it follows that very few persons are above sharp practice. "Most Ladies take a delight in cheating, when they can do it with
Safety," declares Mrs. Trapes. Gamesters are the vilest of Mechanics,
but "many of the Quality are of the Profession," and they have admittance to the politest circles. "I wonder," remarks Matt of the Mint, "I
wonder *we* are not more respected."

> Thus Gamesters united in Friendship are found,
> Though they know that their Industry all is a Cheat;
> They flock to their Prey at the Dice-Box's Sound,
> And join to promote one another's Deceit.
>   But if by mishap
>   They fail of a Chap,
> To keep in their Hands, they each other entrap.
> Like Pikes, lank with Hunger, who miss of their Ends,
> They bite their Companions, and prey on their Friends.

Money will do anything in this fashionable world. Ladies marry in
hopes of soon being widows with a jointure. When Polly announces

that she has married for love, her mother is horrified: "Love him! I thought the Girl had been better bred." And to marry a highwayman: "Why, thou foolish Jade, thou wilt be as ill us'd, and as much neglected, as if thou hadst married a Lord!" But Polly herself knows—at least in her own opinion—"as well as any of the fine Ladies how to make the most of my self and of my Man too."

No love is lost in those exalted spheres. And even friendship proceeds merely upon the foot of interest. "Those that act otherwise are their own Bubbles." Promises are plentiful, but a court friend was never known to give anything else. Quite the contrary: "In one respect," says Peachum, "our Employment may be reckon'd dishonest, because, like great Statesmen, we encourage those who betray their Friends." But again: "Can it be expected that we should hang our Acquaintance for nothing, when our Betters will hardly save theirs without being paid for it?" And think of the legal profession. Robbery may be common elsewhere, but beside the wholesale robbery of the law it is nothing at all. "Gold from Law can take out the Sting," but, on the other side,

> It ever was decreed, Sir,
> If Lawyer's Hand is fee'd, Sir,
> He steals your whole Estate.

It appears, then, that if the Newgate people are culpable, they are merely imitating their betters, who must be charged with equal blame. But grant so much, and we must grant more. The criminals press their advantage by suggesting that guilt is proportional to the amount of harm done, which in turn depends on the degree of power to execute it. There is no question where the power resides. The statesman may think his "trade" as honest as Peachum's, but logic will say him no. Thinking of our own days, we shall have little heart to contradict logic. Then, sings Macheath unanswerably:

> Since Laws were made for ev'ry Degree,
> To curb Vice in others, as well as me,
> I wonder we han't better Company,
>   Upon *Tyburn* Tree!

> But Gold from Law can take out the Sting;
> And if rich Men like us were to swing,
> 'Twould thin the Land, such Numbers to string
>   Upon *Tyburn* Tree!

Moreover, Macheath and his gang have one more shaft to shoot, for what it is worth. They can set an example of loyalty and generosity and honor among themselves. "Who is there here," cries Nimming Ned, "that would not dye for his Friend?" "Who is there here," adds Harry Padington, "that would betray him for his Interest?" "Show me a Gang of Courtiers," says Matt of the Mint, "that can say as much." Macheath prides himself upon being a man of his word and no court friend. "We, Gentlemen," he declares, "have still Honour enough to break through the Corruptions of the World.—And while I can serve you, you may command me."

Here the defense rests its case. The ground has been occupied before, and will be again. The abuse of power, the chasm between profession and practice in high place, the constant defeat of principles by wealth, the oppression of desert born a beggar, "the spurns that patient merit of the unworthy takes," the immorality and selfishness of privileged society—all these themes are the stock-in-trade of satirists, familiar to our ears as household words. This is the habitual level of Swift, whose way is to show how much more reprehensible those are whom the world admires than those whom the world despises.

But Gay's satire does not stop at this point. There are hints in *The Beggar's Opera* of a more revolutionary doctrine. If we really believe in truth and justice and the general welfare, doubtless we should all be glad to see temporary violations of these principles set right. We should welcome, should we not, a fairer distribution of this world's goods, juster apportionment of the right to life, liberty, and the pursuit of happiness? But do we not, on the contrary, resist by all the means in our power any attempts at readjustment? Are not Macheath and his fellows more active laborers for the general good than we? We adopt the principles but obstruct their realization. The Newgate gentry adopt them and work for the cause:

> BEN BUDGE. We are for a just Partition of the World, for every Man hath a Right to enjoy Life.
> MATT OF THE MINT. We retrench the Superfluities of Mankind. The World is avaritious, and I hate Avarice. A covetous fellow, like a Jack-daw, steals what he was never made to enjoy, for the sake of hiding it. These are the Robbers of Mankind, for Money was made for the Free-hearted and Generous.

Who, then, are the true friends of man? Are they not the so-called enemies of society? Is it possible to be actively a friend of mankind without being a revolutionary? The established order is radically iniq-uitous: how can we defend the *status quo* and remain true to the principles to which we profess allegiance?

Thus it becomes clear that *The Beggar's Opera,* half a century before Figaro burst upon the world, foreshadowed in significant ways the point of view which Beaumarchais was to develop with such devastat-ing results.[9] That the political and social implications of the earlier work did not explode with equal violence is in large measure due, of course, to the different temper of society at the time. But equally it is due to the broader base of Gay's satire. Figaro, besides being the spokesman of democratic defiance against rank and privilege, is basi-cally the wholesome representative of those conventional virtues that popular sentiment judged worthy of perpetuation. He is therefore a revolutionary symbol to which generous souls could pay sympathetic homage.

There is no comparable figure in the earlier play. For the Newgate knaves, however they may color their actions, are only masquerading. When their conduct is scrutinized, it is obvious that self-interest is at the bottom of everything they do. It is shot through with bad faith and disloyalty even to their own class. Jealousy and suspicion are the rule here as elsewhere. In the end, Macheath is forced to draw the inevi-table conclusion from his experience: "That *Jemmy Twitcher* should peach me, I own surpriz'd me!—'Tis a plain Proof that the World is all alike, and that even our Gang can no more trust one another than other People."

The world is all alike! That is the final lesson of Gay's satire. We laughed at the obvious reversal of accepted values which runs through the play. We laughed to hear Black Moll's industry commended, knowing that that industry was actively expended upon thievery and playing the whore. Laziness is a vice, and it was refreshing to see sloth in the performance of crime meet with its due punishment. But, *mutatis mutandis,* were we not laughing at ourselves? As Peachum told his wife, "The World, my Dear, hath not such a Contempt for Roguery as you imagine." We are all cheats, paying lip service to one set of principles and motivated in actual truth by another. Every man pre-sents to the world an idealized dream picture as his authentic and veracious self-portrait. The institutions of society, which we pretend are so solidly established, rest on a fiction that has no external actu-ality. The ideals we profess are impossible to live by in this world, for they are undermined both from within and without. Private interest

seldom coincides with public good, and private interest has the con-
trolling hand, whether in the political, the social, the commercial, or
the sexual sphere. Of this truth we are reminded in the play. "Now,
Peachum," soliloquizes Lockit, "you and I, like honest Tradesmen,
are to have a fair Tryal which of us two can over-reach the other."
"All men," reflects Mrs. Peachum, "are thieves in love, and like a
woman the better for being another's property." "Of all Animals of
Prey," says Lockit, again, "Man is the only sociable one. Every one
of us preys upon his Neighbour, and yet we herd together." "Well,
Polly," sighs Mrs. Peachum, "as far as one Woman can forgive another, I forgive thee." The opposition of class against class, youth
against age, sex against sex, individual against individual, is both inevitable and involuntary. We are predatory by the mere physiological
premisses of our common humanity. Under the conditions of existence, idealism is a merely relative term. "Oh, gentlemen," cried
Hotspur before he died,

> the time of life is short;
> To spend that shortness basely were too long
> If life did ride upon a dial's point,
> Still ending at the arrival of an hour.

The irony is that, paying homage all our lives to these principles, it
would hardly be possible to point to a single hour in which we lived in
entire accordance with them. This is the doom of man, and each of us
postures as if it were reversed for him, condemning others for what he
excuses in himself, and generally playing such fantastic tricks before
high heaven as are enough to make immortals laugh themselves to
death. Fixed in this dance of plastic circumstance, we persist in declaring that we are the captains of our souls. Existence itself is the
ultimate irony.

To go on breathing in the utter vacuum of this realization is impossible, and most of us are able to enter it only at rare moments. Acceptance of the pessimistic view may generate reactions which are dia-
metrical opposites. The picture may be seen as comedy, or it may be
seen as tragedy. To the romantic vision, speaking generally, it will appear tragic; to the classical, comic. The romantic attitude, being
chiefly concerned with the individual ego, finds this spectacle of a
divided self all but intolerable, and, to restore inner consistency, may
take refuge in the Byronic pose. If I cannot be true to the ideals I profess, let me overturn those ideals and set up others that will be valid,

and in accordance with the facts of my existence. "Evil, be thou my good!" Thus, in solitary grandeur, the diabolist may enjoy the luxury of integrity. For man in society, however, such an escape is hardly possible. The eighteenth century was not an age of solitaries; its characteristic orientations concerned man as a social being. It took little pleasure in exploring the orbit of the lonely soul through infinite space; it derived strength and assurance from solidarity. The contradictions of life become once again endurable when shared with one's brother men, and it is possible to be objective in contemplating the universal lot. Thus the age of Gay tended to see the irony of existence as fundamentally comic. For Swift, indeed, who had to watch the comedy through eighteenth-century eyes but with the passionate emotions and gigantic ego of a romantic, the spectacle turned bitter. Gay's good-humored view of it, as seen in *The Beggar's Opera,* is essentially characteristic both of his age and of himself. It was Gay who devised for his own epitaph the well-known lines:

> Life is a jest; and all things show it.
> I thought so once; but now I know it.

NOTES

1. Cf. especially W. E. Schultz, *Gay's Beggar's Opera: Its Contents, History and Influence* (New Haven, 1923) , and E. M. Gagey, *Ballad Opera* (New York, 1937) .
2. Schultz, *op. cit.,* p. 143.
3. London, 1934.
4. Schultz credits Gay with breaking the five-act theatrical tradition. "Gay's three acts," he declares, "among the very first to stand alone, furnished a pleasing contrast to the five acts of the majority of comedies; and . . . exerted a real influence, if we may judge by later work . . . [which took up] the battle for a shorter dramatic scale" (*op. cit.,* p. 281). But Gay was merely following the established operatic tradition in this matter.
5. E. J. Dent, *Händel* (London, 1934) , p. 77) .
6. Neither, though the point is hardly worth defending, does Gay's epigrammatic motto for *Muzio Scævola* sound like the word of a man who despised the class to which this work belonged:
> Who here blames words, or verses, songs, or singers,
> Like *Mutius Scævola* will burn his fingers.
7. Cf. Swift to Gay, March 28, 1728: "I did not understand that the scene of Lockit and Peachum's quarrel was an imitation of one between Brutus and Cassius, till I was told it."
8. *On the English Stage,* July 27, 1816, quoted by Schultz, *op. cit.,* p. 274.

9. "Mais il y a un jour où se remassent dans une explosion unique tous les sentiments de toute nature, moraux, politique, sociaux, que l'œuvre des philosophes avait développés dans les cœurs, joie de vivre, avidité de jouir, intense excitation de l'intelligence, hains et mépris du présent, des abus, des traditions, espoir et besoin d'*autre chose:* ce jour de folie intellectuelle où toute la société de l'ancien régime applaudit aux idées dont elle va périr, c'est la première représentation du *Mariage de Figaro* (27 avril 1784) ."—Lanson, *Hist. de la Litt. Française,* p. 807.

ALAN S. DOWNER

❀

Nature to Advantage Dressed:
Eighteenth-Century Acting

For the student of acting and actors, the eighteenth century is a rich period. Within a century the careers of such players as Betterton, Quin, Macklin, Garrick, and Kemble ran their courses; these were actors of varying techniques, yet they had in common their century's earnest desire to imitate "nature" and they all subscribed to the same basic set of acting conventions. The century is rich too in theorists and critics: Gildon, John and Aaron Hill, Churchill, Lloyd, Hiffernan.

To be natural, to hold the mirror up to nature, is the chief, but not the sole, tenet of the actor's creed. It is this tenet which caused Macklin to revolt against the furious rant of Powell, and probably Powell to revolt against the restraint of Betterton. Each artist is, of course, entitled to his own interpretation of nature. On the other hand, actors for centuries have been automatically gesturing with the up-stage hand, kneeling on the down-stage knee, making turns toward the audience, because the conventions of the theatre so dictate. For acting is an art handed on from generation to generation of players. Shakespeare directed John Lowin in *Henry VIII* at Blackfriar's, and Davenant, with Lowin in mind, directed Betterton's Harry a half-century later.[1] It is not the directors alone who cling to tradition; Betterton himself, as Alexander (in *The Rival Queens*) ,

> when rehearsing his character, was at a loss to recover a
> particular emphasis of Hart, which gave a force to some

From *PMLA*, LVIII (1943) , 1002-37. Reprinted by permission of the Modern Language Association of America.

> interesting situation of the part; he applied for informa-
> tion to the players who stood near him. At last, one of
> the lowest of the company repeated the line exactly in
> Hart's key.[2]

Although Davies intended this anecdote to illustrate the modesty of a
great actor, it also illustrates the actor's trust in tradition. "As I pronounced it to you" is not a covert warning but a tenet of the actor's
creed.

It will be instructive, at the beginning, to compare various actors in
the same scene. This is, fortunately, a simple task since the eighteenth-
century theater was a repertory theater, and critics and audiences were
interested in "points." One of the actor's most telling points is found
in Hamlet's first meeting with the ghost of his father.

Thomas Betterton had inherited the Shakespearian tradition, and
contemporary writers seem to feel that he adhered to it closely. Colley
Cibber thus reports Betterton's action in the scene chosen for comparison:

> This was the light into which Betterton threw this scene;
> which he open'd with a pause of mute amazement! then
> rising slowly to a solemn, trembling voice, he made the
> ghost equally terrible to the spectator as himself! and in
> the descriptive part of the natural emotions which the
> ghastly vision gave him, the boldness of his expostulation
> was still govern'd by decency, manly, but not braving; his
> voice never rising into that seeming outrage, or wild de-
> fiance of what he naturally rever'd.[3]

The key words of the description are *solemn, trembling,* and *manly,*
which Cibber chose with care to contrast Betterton with a later Hamlet whose violence shocked him:

> You have seen a Hamlet perhaps, who, on the first ap-
> pearance of his father's spirit, has thrown himself into all
> the straining vociferation requisite to express rage and
> fury, and the house has thunder'd with applause; tho' the
> mis-guided actor was all the while (as Shakespear terms
> it) tearing a passion into rags.—I am the more bold to
> offer you this particular instance, because the late Mr.
> Addison, while I sate by him, to see this scene acted,
> made the same observation, asking me with some sur-
> prise, if I thought Hamlet should be in so violent a pas-

sion with the Ghost, which tho' it might have astonish'd,
it had not provok'd him?[4]

Davies identifies this later Hamlet as Wilks and records an anecdote
which is perhaps more instructive than is the way of theatrical anecdote generally. Barton Booth played the ghost to Wilks' Hamlet and,
meeting him the next day,

> "I thought," said he, "Bob, that last night you wanted to
> play at fisty-cuffs with me: you bullied that which you
> ought to have revered."[5]

Charles Macklin, revolting against the convention of violent acting,
returned in his own way to the simplicity of Betterton.

> After the short ejaculation of "Angels and ministers of
> grace, defend us!" he endeavoured to conquer that fear
> and terror into which he was naturally thrown by the first
> sight of the vision, and uttered the remainder of the ad-
> dress calmly, but respectfully, and with a firm tone of
> voice, as from one who had subdued his timidity and
> apprehension.[6]

Respect and terror become the accepted emotions to be portrayed in
the scene, as opposed to the bravado of the Wilks school.

> When Mr. Garrick first saw the ghost the terror he
> seemed to be impressed with, was instantaneously com-
> municated to the audience; his expostulations with the
> vision, though warm and importunate, were restrained by
> filial awe. The progress of his impassioned sensation, till
> the ghost beckoned him to retire with him, was accom-
> panied with terror and respect.[7]

A comment of Dr. Johnson's, however, indicates that Garrick had not
thrown overboard all the tricks of his predecessors. Boswell had asked
Johnson if he would not start, "as Mr. Garrick does," if he saw a
ghost. Dr. Johnson replied, "I hope not. If I did, I should frighten
the ghost."[8] The good Doctor was no doubt indulging himself to
amuse Bozzy, but, as later evidence will show, he was not far from
expressing the truth. *Filial awe* was present to satisfy the critics, but
the terror instantaneously communicated to the audience must have
been at variance with the calm and respect of Macklin's interpretation.

John Philip Kemble went a step further:

In that truly celebrated scene, where Hamlet encounters his father's spirit, Mr. Kemble shines with super-eminent lustre. Never was the poet's meaning more strongly marked in the actor's face than in his during the recital of the horrid deed. The performer's reception of the Ghost can only raise one emotion in the minds of his audience, that of silent admiration: surprise and terror, in reality, benumbs all his limbs. When he arrives at that part where he declares,

> "I will speak to thee; I'll call thee Hamlet,
> "King, father, royal Dane—Oh, answer me," &c.

his gradual recovery from a state of the most uncommon amazement and terror to a more calm and composed turn of mind, plainly denotes the command he must necessarily have over the passions; and the succeeding interrogations,

> "But tell me why,
> "Thy cannonized bones, hearsed in death,
> "Have burst their cearments?"

are finely marked by an earnest desire of information, mixed with a natural awe resulting from the fear of giving offense to the spirit. Some critics have objected to his making use of too much action during the succeeding conversation between Hamlet and the Ghost, and, perhaps with reason; yet his countenance is so highly expressive of that proper indignation against the murderer of his father, that we are inclined to make some allowance for the too frequent movement of his arms. . . . His behaviour on the departure of the Ghost presents us with a fine picture of filial reverence.[9]

As much sport was made, by his critics, of Mr. Kemble's use of *too much motion*, as Dr. Johnson made of Garrick's starts, and Booth of Wilks' violence. Yet the actions of each of these players, as well as of Betterton and Macklin, were justified and approved by other critics, and accepted as true by audiences. Throughout the eighteenth century, this strange paradox of the actor persists. The art of acting is traditional, conventional, hereditary, yet the art of the individual actor is a constant revolt against tradition, convention, heredity.

II

There were, then, four "schools" of acting in the eighteenth century. For convenience, they may be called after their most important figures—Betterton, Cibber-Booth-Wilks, Macklin-Garrick, and Kemble. To call them simply Pre-Garrick, Garrick, and Post-Garrick, as is the tendency of stage historians, is to be unfair to a series of great actors. It is impossible, of course, to set exact dates for the flourishing of these schools. Betterton left the stage in 1710, but Bowman, "the last of the Bettertonian school,"[10] was playing in 1731. Nearly half a century after Garrick had made his first appearance, a York paper of 1788 reported, "Mrs. Mills surpass'd our expectations in Lady *Macbeth,* for tho' she represented the part in the *old* style, yet she was nevertheless pleasing, and gave general content."[11] Styles of acting change, but the change is gradual. Not only the actor but the audience must change, for the spectator must be prepared to believe what he sees. This explains the long contest for supremacy between actors of such differing techniques as Quin and Garrick. The eighteenth century, however, recognized the distinctions between the schools and an examination of the practice of the leading actors of each school will establish the distinctions for the twentieth century.

I. *Betterton.* Even in the days of Garrick, critics looked back upon the early years of the century with considerable longing.[12] Betterton, Barry, Mrs. Bracegirdle, Mrs. Oldfield, these were the first immortals of the eighteenth-century stage. Their "school" of acting was a school of nature, insofar as the drama of the time allowed. Contemporary comedy, while mannered, was no more mannered than contemporary life, but the heroic drama would hardly permit naturalism in its actors. It was in the revivals of the earlier romantic plays that serious natural acting was employed, consciously and conscientiously. Betterton's style of acting was restrained and grave, and his gestures were few and controlled. Aston records that the great actor rarely lifted his arms higher than his stomach,[13] which would eliminate at once nearly the entire range of pompous and rhetorical gesture. Aston continues:

> His actions were few, but just. . . . He was better to meet than to follow for his Aspect was serious, venerable, and majestic. . . . His Voice was low and grumbling; yet he could Time it by an artful *Climax,* which enforc'd universal Attention, even from the *Fops* and *Orange-*

> *Girls. . . . Betterton* kept his Passion under, and shew'd
> it most. . . . *Betterton,* from the Time he was dress'd, to
> the End of the Play, kept his Mind in the same Tempera-
> ment and Adaptness, as the present Character required.[14]

For all his restraint, however, Betterton could produce an energetic delineation of a passion when the occasion demanded. *The Laureat,* one of the many publications devoted to the stultification of Colley Cibber, quoted a member of the audience who had *frequently* witnessed Betterton's Hamlet. This gentleman had seen the actor's

> Countenance (which was naturally ruddy and sanguine)
> in this Scene of the fourth Act when his Father's Ghost
> appears, thro' the violent and sudden Emotions of Amaze-
> ment and Horror, turn instantly on the Sight of his
> Father's Spirit, as pale as his Neckcloth, when every
> Article of his Body seem'd to be affected with a Tremor
> inexpressible.[15]

This perhaps refutes, to some extent, Aston's complaint that Betterton "appeared a little too grave for a young Student . . . and his *Repartees* seem'd rather as *Apopthegms* from a *Sage Philosopher,* than the *Sporting Flashes* of a young HAMLET,"[16] although Aston was speaking of Betterton at the age of 63. However, as Aston points out, Betterton maintained his reserve even in such plays as *The Rival Queens* and *Venice Preserved* and succeeded where the ranter Powell failed utterly.[17] It seems a safe conclusion that Betterton's school of acting taught restraint, even in the most exaggerated rôles, a restraint that was made the more possible by the smallness of the theaters and the actor's habit of playing on the apron of the stage.[18]

Facial expression played an important part in the acting technique of the period. Sandford, whom King Charles called the best villain in the world, "acted strongly with his face."[19] Doggett, the comedian, "was the best face-player."[20] Of Mrs. Barry, Aston related, "Her Face somewhat preceded her Action, as the latter did her Words, her Face ever expressing the Passions."[21] Accustomed as the contemporary spectator is to the immobile expressions of modern actors, to *act strongly with the face* clearly suggests overacting. In the light of the general evidence for restraint in other branches of the art, however, it would seem that the actors stopped short of distortion.

II. *Cibber-Booth-Wilks.* Under the triumvirate, the style of acting of the Bettertonian school began to be modified. If the keyword of the older school in serious acting was *restraint*, the keyword of the new is *exaggeration*, although it is exaggeration gradually developed. Betterton and the leading players of his day seem to have devoted the greater part of their attention to the reading of lines and the presentation of action in the round. It was Mrs. Barry's avowed intention "to make herself Mistress of her Part, and leave the *Figure* and *Action* to *Nature*."[22] Such attention as was paid to the details of business was usually devoted to the action of comedy, which demanded the careful elaboration of characteristic gestures and traits.[23] The careful study of the business of a serious play, however, came more and more to be the actor's problem. In the hands of a great actor, a carefully studied part can be most revealing. In the hands of anyone less than great, attention to details becomes finicking, mechanical, and frequently ridiculous.

Barton Booth was generally accepted as the successor, if not the equal, of Betterton. To him fell the great rôles of the standard drama, of Shakespeare, Otway, and Rowe. "He had a Talent," wrote Aaron Hill, of "discovering the Passions, where they lay hid in some celebrated Parts, by the injudicious Practice of other Actors."[24] How this remark is to be interpreted is suggested by a speech from *Othello* (III, 3) as marked for performance by Booth.

> *After the exit of Iago, a long pause, the eye kept looking after Iago . . .*
>> This fellow's of exceeding honesty   *Spoken in a low*
>> And knows all qualities with a learned spirit
>> Of human dealings.   *tone of voice.*
>>> *Pause, the look starting into anger.*
>> If I do prove her haggard,
>> Though that her jesses were my dear heart strings
>> I'ld whistle her off and let her down the wind
>> To prey at fortune.
>>> *A long pause, as to ruminate.*
>> Haply, for I am black
>> And have not those soft parts of conversation
>> That chamberers have, or for I am declined
>> Into the vale of years,—yet that's not much—
>>> *After a pause, the following start of violent passion:*
>> She's gone: I am abus'd and my relief
>> Must be to loathe her. O curse of marriage,
>> That we can call these delicate creatures ours
>> And not their appetites!

*What follows in a quicker, contemptuous
tone:*
I had rather be a toad,
And live upon the vapour of a dungeon,
Than keep a corner of the thing I love
For other's uses. [Cut four lines.]
*A look of amazement, seeing Desdemona
coming.*
Look where she comes!
*A short pause, the countenance and voice
softened.*
If she be false, O, then heaven mocks itself!
I'll not believe 't.[25]

It will be observed that what Booth has done is to divide the soliloquy
into its *emotional* components, the exact antithesis of the declamatory
method of acting and delivery. The frequent pauses to indicate mental
reaction punctuate the speech and prevent its becoming a mere aria.[26]

Barton Booth is not to be taken as typical of the followers of Betterton, since he seems to have adhered more closely to that actor's practice than his contemporaries. *Restraint* was still an article of his creed.
In *Othello,* Theophilus Cibber pointed out, "all his Grief, though most
feelingly expressed, was never beneath the Hero,"[27] observing the
golden rule of not too much. That this was not the general practice is
borne out by Cibber's further lament over the "repeated Examples of
extravagant affected Starts, twitching of Limbs, Jerkings of the Body,
Expansion of the Hands, sprawling of the Fingers, and other uncouth
Violences, the Mockery of Attitude."[28]

It is one thing to seek out the emotion behind a speech and interpret
it through the voice and attitude, and quite another to interpret literally the author's words and the poet's images. Colley Cibber, a comedian of the first rank, was a serious actor of a somewhat lower level. It
is possible that the ridiculous piece of business credited to him by
Davies in a performance of *Henry VIII* may have been based on comic
techniques. At Wolsey's speech:

This candle burns not clear; 'tis I must snuff it;
Then, out it goes (III, 2),

Cibber imitated "with his forefinger and thumb the extinguishing of a
candle with a pair of snuffers." This action, Davies reported, was much
commended by the spectators, but, as he observes, "surely the reader

will laugh at such mimicry, which, if practised, would make a player's action as ridiculous as a monkey's."[29] Once begun, however, over-action (over-attention to detail) became the actor's creed, and not even the reforms of Macklin or Garrick could banish it from the theater. "These mummeries," Cibber's son declared, "on the many, may pass for spirited Action;—yet are, in Reality, but a Set of—Mechanic Motions, as Indistinguishably as frequently used."[30] From this time on, references are frequent to the tragic strut, the exaggerated start.

> THEATRIC Monarchs in their tragic Gait
> Affect to mark the solemn Pace of State.
> One foot put forward in Position strong,
> The other like its Vassal dragg'd along.
> So grave each Motion, so exact and slow,
> Like wooden Monarchs at a Puppet-Show. . . .
>
> However foreign from the Poet's Art,
> No tragic Hero but admires a Start.
> What though unfeeling of the nervous Line
> Who but allows his *Attitude* is fine?
> While a whole Minute equipoiz'd he stands,
> Till Praise dismiss him with her echoing Hands. . . .
> When *Romeo* sorrowing at his *Juliet's* Doom,
> With eager Madness bursts the canvas Tomb,
> The sudden Whirl, stretch'd Leg, and lifted Staff,
> Which please the Vulgar, make the Critic laugh.[31]

A further description of the tragic strut may be gleaned from Churchill's famous *Rosciad*.

> Next Holland came,—with truly tragic stalk,
> He creeps, he flies,—a hero should not walk.
> As if with heaven he warr'd, his eager eyes
> Planted their batteries against the skies;
> Attitude, action, air, pause, start, sigh, groan,
> He borrow'd, and made use of as his own.[32]

The exaggerated start he illustrates from the practice of Spranger Barry, a contemporary of Garrick's.

> Some dozen lines before the ghost is there,
> Behold him for the solemn scene prepare:
> See how he frames his eyes, poises each limb,
> Puts the whole body into proper trim:—

> From whence we learn, with no great stretch of art,
> Five lines hence comes a ghost, and, ha!, a start.[33]

More details of the tragic hero's deportment are to be found in Churchill's description of Thomas Sheridan at work, Sheridan who was not only a successful actor, and manager, but a teacher of actors.

> His action's always strong, but sometimes such
> That candour must declare he acts too much.
> Why must impatience fall three paces back?
> Why paces three return to the attack?
> Why is the right leg, too, forbid to stir,
> Unless in motion semi-circular?
> Why must the hero with the Nailor vie,
> And hurl the close-clench'd fist at nose or eye?[34]

It is unfortunate that in considering the descriptions of actors by their contemporaries so much allowance must be made for prejudice and puffing. Churchill intended to exalt Garrick and his methods, and his strictures on the other actors can hardly have been unbiased. The observations, however, seem to be accurate when placed beside prints of the period, and once the bias is noted it is harmless enough.

Occasionally it is possible to balance two prejudices against each other. James Quin aroused the anger of several critics and won praise from several others. Churchill thus describes him as Zanga in Young's *Revenge:*

> His words bore sterling weight; nervous and strong,
> In manly tides of sense they roll'd along:
> Happy in art, he chiefly had pretence,
> To keep up numbers, yet not forfeit sense. . . .[35]

> His eyes in gloomy socket taught to roll,
> Proclaim'd the sullen "habit of his soul:"
> Heavy and phlegmatic he trod the stage,
> Too proud for tenderness, too dull for rage.[36]

Against such a description, which suggests declamation and an excess of gravity, may be placed a description of Quin in the same rôle as observed by Tobias Smollett. It should be noted at the outset that the following passage is tinged with malice, for Smollett had an intense dislike of actors and of Quin in particular, but it suggests the lengths to which an actor—if not Quin—might go in the over-interpretation of a poet's lines.

> He took it up;
> But scarce was it unfolded to his sight,
> When he, as if an arrow pierced his eye,
> Started and trembling dropt it on the ground.

In pronouncing the first two words this egregious actor stoops down, and seems to take up something from the stage; then proceeding to repeat what follows, mimicks the manner of unfolding the letter; when he mentions the simile of the arrow piercing his eye, he darts his fore-finger towards that organ, then recoils with great violence when the word *started* is expressed; and when he comes to *trembling dropt it on the ground,* he throws all his limbs into a tremulous motion, and shakes the imaginary paper from his hand.

The latter part of the description is carried on with the same minute gesticulation while he says,

> Pale and aghast a while my victim stood,
> Disguised a sigh or two and puffed them from him;
> Then rubb'd his brow and took it up again.

The player's countenance assumes a wild stare, he sighs twice most piteously, as if he were on the point of suffocation, scrubs his brow, and bending his body, apes the action of snatching an object from the floor.

Nor is this dexterity of dumb show omitted, when he concludes his intimation in these three lines:

> At first he look'd as if he meant to read it,
> But, check'd by rising fears, he crush'd it, thus,
> And thrust it like an adder in his bosom.

Here the judicious performer imitates the confusion and concern of Alonzo, seems to cast his eyes upon something from which they are immediately withdrawn, with horror and precipitation, then shutting his fist with a violent squeeze, as if he intended to make immediate application to Isabella's nose, he rams it in his own bosom, with all the horror and agitation of a thief taken in the manner. . . . Nothing can be more trivial, forced, unnatural, and antic than this superfluous mummery.[37]

The general impression of Quin as recorded by his contemporaries hardly agrees with Smollett's. Cumberland, in his *Memoirs,* recalls him thus:

Quin presented himself upon the rising of the curtain in a green velvet cloak, embroidered down the seams, an enormous, full-bottomed wig, rolled stockings, and high-heeled square-toed shoes. With very little variation of cadence, and in a deep full tone, accompanied by a saw-ing kind of action, which had more of the senate than the stage in it, he rolled out his heroics with an air of dignified indifference.[38]

Against these, in Quin's favor, may be set John Hill's observation that, "No man ever arriv'd at an equal perfection in speaking the sublime with Mr. *Quin.*"[39]

III. *Macklin-Garrick.* This was the style of acting which Garrick set himself to reform, the style which he once declared would never go down with an audience. "How do you know?" asked Colley Cibber, "you never tried it."[40] Garrick, however, had tried it, or at least a burlesque of it, in his famous revival of *The Rehearsal.* In the course of his performance, he seized an opportunity to mimic certain actors of the old school, among them one Delane. Garrick "retired to the upper part of the stage, and drawing his left arm across his breast rested his right elbow upon it; raising a finger to his nose, he then came forward at a staitly gait, nodding his head as he advanced."[41] Burlesque it as he might, and declare it dead, Garrick was never able to drive this type of acting from the stage. Exaggeration clings to the second rate actor in all periods, the exaggeration of violence, or of solemnity, and no shining example can wholly reform him.

It is possible that Garrick has been given credit for more natural acting than he actually practised. But that Charles Macklin was ever anything but a naturalistic performer cannot be questioned. When he first attempted to get into a London company, he was fond of recalling, "I spoke so familiar . . . , and so little in the hoity-toity-tone of the tragedy of that day, that the manager told me I had better go to grass for another year or two."[42] Back to grass he went, but to speak *familiar* was his style and he clung to it. It was a style which had its roots in an earlier day, in the days before exaggeration, for he "will honestly tell us, that he owed no small part of his knowledge in acting to the lessons he gained from Mr. Chetwood, prompter of Drury-lane theatre."[43] Macklin, of course, made his great hit, and his great reform, in his interpretation of Shylock. It was one reformation that took. Of his performance, *The Dramatic Censor* said,

> Macklin looks the part as much better than any other
> person as he plays it. In the level scenes his voice is most
> happily suited to that sententious gloominess of expres-
> sion the author intended, which with a sullen solemnity
> of manner marks the character strongly. In his malevo-
> lence there is a forcible and terrifying ferocity. In the
> third act scene, where alternate passions reign, he breaks
> the tones of utterance, and varies his countenance ad-
> mirably, and in the dumb action of the trial scene he is
> amazing beyond description.[44]

Macklin's chief contribution, aside from a general toning down of
bombastic declamation, was the *broken tones of utterance* of which
The Dramatic Censor speaks. It was his reform, although it was the
source of most of the acclaim visited upon Garrick. That he may have
carried his reform to an extreme is suggested by Churchill's comment,
that he "largely deals in half-form'd sounds,"[45] but that may be
Churchill the champion of Garrick speaking.

Naturalism, or restraint, was not accepted without a struggle. John
Hill, a solemn critic of acting, was particularly distressed that Macklin, "that great enemy to unnecessary vehemence," was not able to
teach his pupils to distinguish "between a judicious and unnatural sup-
pression of the signs of rage. . . . Let us not always take the exclamations, or the contortions [of an exaggerated actor] for fire, nor the ice
[of the 'underplayer'] for prudence."[46] Garrick himself seems to have
taken a middle course, erring on the side of too much, rather than too
little, fire.

David Garrick in fact was more of a refiner than a reformer of previous acting techniques. From Macklin he took the natural speech and
the broken tones of utterance, from the older school he took the fire of
romantic acting and the careful attention to grace in posture and gesture,[47] and a certain method of delivery which even his most loyal
supporters decried. Davies was pleased to report that after his trip
abroad Garrick "utterly dropt that anxious exertion at the close of a
speech, both in look and behaviour, which is called by the comedians,
a claptrap."[48] But even the broken tones were used by the actor to
extort applause. As Samuel Foote wrote,

> The Transition from one Passion to another by the sud-
> denness of the Contrast, throws a stronger Light on the
> Execution of the Actor; and thus the Groundlings, who
> are caught more by the Harmony and Power of the Voice

than Propriety, are easily drawn in to applaud what must grieve the Judicious. I have been the longer on the last Particular, because it is not in this Place alone [*Lear*, 1. 4], that Mr. G traps the Unwary by the same Bait.[49]

To correct the possible prejudice of a rival actor and manager there is this report of Garrick's performance of Lear:

> [he] was transformed into a weak old man, still retaining an air of royalty; in the mad scenes his genius was remarkably distinguished; he had no sudden starts, no violent gesticulation; his movements were slow and feeble; misery was depicted in his countenance; he moved his head in the most deliberate manner; his eyes were fixed; or if they turned to anyone near him, he made a pause, and fixed his look on the person after much delay; his features at the same time telling what he was going to say before he uttered a word.[50]

John Hill mentions that Garrick as Lear sometimes so far forgot his regal character "that in this whole part of the play, he looks as like a mad any thing else, as a mad king," and suggests that he should join his life, spirit, and vivacity to the dignity of Quin.[51] Too natural, not too restrained but too common, too undignified, Garrick may have been in this rôle. But that his must have been a moving performance is indicated by Thomas Wilkes:

> I never see him coming down from one corner of the stage, with his old grey hair standing, as it were, erect on his head, his face filled with horror and attention, his hands expanded, and his whole frame actuated by a dreadful solemnity, but I am astounded, and share in all his distresses. . . . Methinks I share in his calamities, I feel the dark drifting rain, and the sharp tempest. . . . [In the fifth act] His leaning against the side of the scene, panting for want of breath, as if exhausted, and his recollecting the feat, and replying to the fellow who observes, that the good old King has slain two of them, *Did I not, fellow?* have more force, more strength, and more propriety of character, than I ever saw in any other actor.[52]

Both descriptions of Garrick as Lear emphasize the fact that his facial expressions acted as much as his body, or his voice. He had reverted to

some extent to the earlier tradition mentioned in connection with
Sandford and Doggett and Mrs. Barry of playing with the face. His
first appearance as Richard announced this principle.

> The moment he entered on the stage, the character he as-
> sumed was visible in his countenance; the power of his
> imagination was such, that he transformed himself into
> the very man; the passions rose in rapid succession, and
> before he uttered a word, were legible in every feature
> of that various face—his look, his voice, his attitude,
> changed with every sentiment.

How Garrick broke the tones of utterance is well illustrated from the
same play. Richard

> started from his dream; he was a spectacle of horror—he
> called out in a manly tone
> > Give me another horse;
> he paused, and with a countenance of dismay, advanced,
> crying out in a tone of distress
> > Bind up my wounds,
> then, falling on his knees, said in a most piteous accent
> > Have mercy, heaven![53]

In an attempt to forestall criticism at the time of his first performance of Macbeth, Garrick published a curious burlesque attack on himself called *An Essay on Acting in which will be considered the Mimical
Behaviour of a certain Fashionable Faulty Actor*.[54] In this pamphlet
he discusses his approach to the characters of the Scots king, and Ben
Jonson's Abel Drugger, one of his most famous comic performances.
Most illuminating is his description of the action—and the motivation
for the action—of Macbeth in the Dagger Scene:

> Macbeth as a preparation for this vision is so prepossessed
> from his humanity, with the horror of the deed which by
> his more prevailing ambition he is incited to, and for the
> perpetration of which he lies under a promissory injunc-
> tion to his lady, that his mind being torn by these dif-
> ferent and conflicting ideas, his senses fail and present
> that fatal agent of his cruelty—the dagger, to him—Now
> in this visionary horror, he should not rivet his eyes to an
> imaginary object, as if it really was there, but should shew
> an unsettled motion in his eye, like one not quite awak-
> ened from some disordering dream; his hands and fingers

> should not be immovable but restless, and endeavouring to disperse the cloud that over-shadows his optic ray, and bedims his intellects; here should be confusion, disorder, and agony! "Come let me clutch thee," is not to be done by one motion only, but by several successive catches at it, first with one hand and then with the other, preserving the same motion, at the same time, with his feet, like a man who out of his depth and half drowned in his struggles catches at air for substance.[55]

If this business sounds suspiciously like a claptrap, one should recall that Garrick was not above it. Even Churchill is forced to admit that sometimes "The start may be too frequent, pause too long."[56] The actor was particularly fond of starts and pauses in his dying scenes, of which Foote wrote that he was "for once pleased with *Tate's* Alteration of *Shakespear*, because it has prevented my commenting on Mr. *G's* manner of Dying, about which, I am afraid, we should have some Disputes."[57] Foote was not so reluctant in one of his performances when he burlesqued Lothario's death in the manner of Garrick:

> Adorns my fall
> And chea-chea-chea-chea-chea-chears
> My heart in dy-dy-dying.[58]

The sum of the technique of the Macklin-Garrick school seems to be that what Macklin taught, Garrick tricked up for popular consumption. Beside the trumpeting and contortion of most of his contemporaries he must have seemed a natural actor indeed, but beside the extreme restraint of Macklin his subscription to the command *Be not too tame neither* must have been evident. As far as the eighteenth-century audience was concerned, John Hill was justified in declaring that it would not mistake ice for prudence.

   IV. *Kemble-Siddons.* Mrs. Siddons, leader of the fourth school, played an unfortunate season with Garrick in 1765. They did not make a good acting team. She had a native stiffness of gesture which ill suited his graceful and fluent style,[59] and it was a stiffness which she later utilized to good advantage. Her acting was in the manner of Quin and Barton Booth, somewhat modified by the naturalism of Garrick. "The quality of abstraction," she said, "has always appeared to me to be so necessary in the art of acting."[60] Her brother, John Philip Kemble, is usually described as an actor of classic dignity and little else,[61] and Macready remembered the "grand deportment" of Mrs. Siddons.[62]

But this was the period when melodrama and romantic drama were once more coming into popularity, and the manners of Cato could not very convincingly be adopted by Rolla. Naturalistic the school may not have been; that it was also some distance removed from the neo-classic there are instances to show.

An ill-tempered pseudonymous writer, Theatricus Automaton, attacking Mrs. Siddons, Kemble, Lewes, and Mrs. Jordan in a series of papers in *The Attic Miscellany,* affords revealing glimpses of these actors at work. Addressing Kemble on his performance of Henry V, Theatricus writes,

> I COMMEND your choice of attitude in the beginning
> of a turbulent speech; it summonses all the muscles to
> their duty; . . . besides the representation of a *windmill*
> occupies the stage more compleatly than any other fig-
> ure . . . , as the attitude has the peculiar effect (par-
> ticularly in a tall man) of keeping/ the secondaries at
> their proper distances: moreover, it prepares the au-
> dience for something to be admired, and gives them time
> to adjust their canes, and dispose of their gloves, prefa-
> tory to a clap, which never fails to fill up the punctuation
> of a long speech uttered by a leading performer.[63]

Accompanying this criticism is an amusing cartoon of Kemble in his regal robes acting like a *windmill,* flailing his arms, distorting his features, and twisting his body. It is perhaps significant that the cartoon was reprinted elsewhere,[64] without reference to Kemble, and titled "The Theatrical Ranter." It suggests, at any rate, that Kemble's style of acting was better fitted to the high-sounding melodramatics of *Pizarro,* than the tall, preternaturally solemn character studies of Sir Thomas Lawrence would indicate.

Playing to the audience, employing claptraps, of which Theatricus speaks in the above quotation, is not limited to the classical actor, as Foote's strictures on Garrick show. By the nature of his style, however, the classical actor shows less regard for what is going on on the stage and speaks, almost as from a rostrum, to the spectators. Here again Theatricus objects, this time to Kemble as Othello.

> Now I am on the subject of this play, give me leave to
> express my warm approbation of your conduct, in deliver-
> ing that part of Othello's speech to the senate which re-
> lates to the "Anthropophagi . . . ," to the gallery, as a

matter below the notice of the "most potent, grave, and reverend signiors," upon the stage. Moreover, I applaud *addressing the audience* on every occasion.[65]

Such critical remarks, obviously biased, can be taken to correct the enthusiasm of critics who are guilty of overpraising their favorites. Even an enthusiastic supporter of Kemble, the anonymous author of the description of his performance of Hamlet quoted above, was forced to apologize for his idol's use of too much action. This action seems to have concerned itself mainly with unnecessary, or at least unmotivated, gestures with the arms. The rest of his "business" was marked by dignity, if not grace, and his manner of speaking was attacked by one critic who wrote that the actor's

> aim
> By cold correctness is to rise to fame
> With such precision all his steps advance,
> As prove, if not to act, he's learned to dance.
> While his vast form with conscious pride appears,
> And his dark eye-brows piteously he rears,
> I wait the coming speech; but wait in vain,
> For, ah! he speaks in such an under strain,
> As tho' a cold distress'd him, or he fear'd
> The critick's fiat should his voice be heard . . .
> While his spread arms in graceless circles move,
> Whether the author meant his pow'rs should prove
> The tyrant's anger, or the hero's love.[66]

The same poetical critic attacks Mrs. Siddons for her employment of claptraps. After paying some respect to her "natural manners," he continues:

> Yet less by these she gains her hearer's hearts,
> Than stage-trick pauses, attitudes, and starts.
> By arts thus mean the public she commands,
> And gains the tumult of applauding hands.[67]

One of her starts, and a very terrifying one indeed, occurred in her celebrated personation of Mrs. Beverly in *The Gamester*.

> The climax to her sorrows and sufferings was in the dungeon, when on her knees, holding her dying husband, he dropped lifeless from her arms. Her glaring eyes were fixed in stony blankness on his face; the powers of life seemed suspended in her; her sister and Lewson gently

raised her, and slowly led her unresisting from the body, her gaze never for an instance averted from it; when they reach [*sic*] the prison door she stopped, as if awakened from a trance, uttered a shriek of agony that would have pierced the hardest heart, and, rushing from them, flung herself, as if for union in death, on the prostrate form before her.[68]

As Lady Randolph in *Douglas,* having watched the slaying of her son, "The anguish of her soul seemed at length to have struck her brain. The silence of her fixed and vacant stare was terrible, broken at last by a loud and frantic laugh that made the hearers shudder."[69] Theatricus Automaton objects to these starts, not because they are claptraps, but because they seem not to proceed from nature. In his letter to her he incidentally reveals the careful planning which went into one of her portrayals.

In short, madam, I am convinced that the profession of acting may be reduced to a mere mechanic art, as much so, as that of making shoes. I would always have by me a set of starts, attitudes, and *shakes of the chin,* ready cut and dried for every occasion that could occur; and when I had hit upon a mode of performing a part to my mind . . . , I would never after alter in the smallest degree; but have a look and an attitude for every word, and a particular place on the stage where to set my foot ever after, with an exactness that might be written down in the Prompter's book.[70]

Lesser players of the Kemble-Siddons school illustrate its practises equally well. There is a print of Holman as Chamont in *The Orphan* as he recites:

curse on thy scandalous age;
Which hinders me to rush upon thy throat,
And tear the root up, of that cursed bramble.[71]

This is certainly a ranting speech, but the print does not suggest ranting action. Holman stands with his feet gracefully apart, stern face turned left, and sword half drawn. As Alexander in an undated print,[72] his feet are again gracefully planted, his left hand clutches his robe while his right is raised above his head with the index finger pointing. Other prints seem also to indicate that Holman was given to statuesque poses, to gestures with the whole arm. Yet these prints must be balanced by this description in verse:

> To hear him speak, and bellow, rant and rage,
> Like some vile stroller on a country stage,
> And view each attitude, each stage grimace,
> And all the sad contortions of his face.
> Then when he starts, or stamps the harmless ground,
> To see him look with confidence around,
> And hint *'tis now I justly claim your hands,*
> While the bold look the ready clap commands.[73]

From such contradictory statements it would appear that the practice of the fourth "school" was a careful adaptation of those that had gone before. It was neo-classical in its accent on dignity, on carefully planned and minimum action, on rhetorical speech, on claptraps and addresses to the audience. But the drama of the period demanded certain lapses from the dignity of the neo-classical, the rants of Rolla and the starts of the Stranger, with which the actors of the period were sufficiently able to cope.

III

If it is difficult to recapture the actions of actors long dead, how much more difficult is it to hear their voices across the centuries. Yet speech and action are inseparable in the actor's art, and it is impossible to understand one without some knowledge of the other. Nor is it safe to infer the manner of the actor's speech from the style of the author's writing, for it has been pointed out above that the rants of heroic drama were restrained in Betterton's delivery, that the curse of *The Orphan*—for all the slurs of the satirist—could hardly have been ranted by Holman. Throughout the eighteenth century, however, rant was the commonest method of delivery for tragic verse, the most unvarying subject of attack by theatrical critics.

Rant, of which there are two types, should be distinguished from cadence, a form of delivery more or less peculiar to the first decade of the century. Due to a confusion of terms it is difficult to form a definite idea of cadence, contemporary writers using the word *tone* with gay inconsistency to describe both cadenced speech and monotone. Speaking of Mrs. Horton, Genest writes, "she had in all probability acquired that unnatural mode of speaking which was in fashion at the time when she came on the stage, but which was exploded before she left it."[74] The actress's career began at Drury Lane in the 1714-15 season and extended to the season of 1750 at Covent Garden. Aaron Hill, in the dedication to *The Fatal Vision* in 1716, inveighs against the affected, vicious, and unnatural tone of voice then common on the stage.[75] Aston mentions that "Mrs. *Barry* had a manner of drawing out her Words, which became her, but not Mrs. *Braidshaw,* and Mrs. *Porter,*"[76] her successors. This statement is enlarged upon by the author of Betterton's *History of the English Stage:*

> It was certain Mrs. *Barry* was Mistress of a very good Understanding, yet she having little, or no Ear for Music, which caused her to be thought dull when she was taught by the Actors, because she could not readily catch the Manner of their sounding Words, but run into a Tone, the Fault of most young Players.[77]

"Old Colley," as teacher of Peg Woffington in tragedy, is criticized by Davies for insisting upon a "particular *tone,* as he called it,"[78] which may mean either cadence or the monotone of declamation. "In tragedy," Cibber declared, "the manner of speaking varies as little as the blank verse it is written in,"[79] which certainly suggests the monotone of declamation, yet in his *Apology* he writes:

> In the just delivery of poetical numbers, particularly where the sentiments are pathetick, it is scarce credible upon how minute an article of sound depends their greatest beauty or inaffection. The voice of a singer is not more strictly ty'd to time and tune, than that of an actor in theatrical elocution: the least syllable too long, or too slightly dwelt upon in a period, depreciates it to nothing; which very syllable, if rightly touch'd, shall, like the heightening stroke of light from a master's pencil, give life and spirit to the whole.[80]

Cibber's comparison of the actor with the singer recalls the statement that Mrs. Barry had no ear for Music. "He must be a very ignorant player," wrote a critic in 1692, "who knows not there is a musical cadence in speaking; and that a man may as well speak out of tune, as sing out of time."[81] Betterton, quoting "an eminent writer," observes:

> The Operation of Speech is strong, not only for the Reason or Wit therein contained, but by its Sound. For in all

> good Speech there is a sort of Music, with respect to its
> Measure, Time and Tune. . . . Nor are the Words with-
> out their Tune or Notes even in common Talk, which to-
> gether compose that Tune, which is proper to every Sen-
> tence, and may be pricked down as well as any musical
> Tune. With respect also to Time and Measure, the
> Poetic is less various . . . being like that of a short Coun-
> try Song repeated to the End of the Poem.[82]

It is perhaps difficult to conceive what speaking in cadence may have
consisted in. The comments of contemporary writers and critics suggest that it was closely parallel to the "modulation" practised by Garrick. Theophilus Cibber wrote of Booth:

> The Tones of his Voice were all musical, and he had so
> excellent an Ear, no one ever heard a dissonant Note
> come from him. He was not only harmonious, but prop-
> erly so; while he filled the Ear, he spoke to the Heart;
> avoiding a Monotone, which had been too frequently per-
> ceived in some other Actors of Merit. His Voice was
> raised or sunk, extended or contracted, swelled or sof-
> tened, rapid or slow, as the Sense and Spirit of the
> Author, or the several Tempers and Emotions of Mind,
> in different Characters, required. . . . In *Speaking*, as
> in *Writing*, to aim only at being musical, will tire the
> Ear.—[83]

That this cadenced speech existed, however, there seems to be no
doubt. To what source it may be traced, when it first arose, and precisely how it sounded, are questions which, for the present, must be
left unanswered. But from at least 1692 until the retirement of Booth
and Cibber a musical ear and the ability to tone words was a necessary part of the actor's equipment.[84] Booth retired in 1728, Cibber in
1732, and Mrs. Horton in 1750. In the two decades between Cibber's
exit and Mrs. Horton's, a change took place in theatrical speech. In
the earlier period, cadence was preferred to rant. In the later, cadence
was supplanted by "natural speaking."

Rant, of course, continued to be practised. Eighteenth-century critics
complained of two types of rant, the declamatory monotone, and the
vocal claptrap. Certain rants proceed out of the nature of the writing;
only a great actor can rise above these. But there are other ranting
tricks which are a substitute for genuine ability, and it is necessary to

make a distinction if a proper judgement is to be passed upon the merits and, indeed, upon the style of the actors.

A famous essay in *The Spectator* discusses the literary rant, and its performance by an actor who was himself given to exaggeration and bombast.

> There is also another particular which may be reckoned among the blemishes, or rather the false beauties of our English tragedy: I mean those particular speeches which are commonly known as rants. The warm and passionate parts of a tragedy are always the most taking with an audience; for which reason we often see the players pronouncing, in the violence of action, several parts of the tragedy which the author writ in great temper, and designed that they should have been so acted. I have seen Powell very often raise himself a loud clap by this artifice; . . . by adding vehemence to words where there was no passion, or inflaming a real passion into fustian . . . he has given them such sentiments as proceed rather from a swelling than a greatness of mind. Unnatural exclamations, curses, vows, blasphemies, a defiance of mankind, and all outraging of the gods, frequently pass upon the audience for towering thoughts.[85]

"*POWELL*," according to Aston, "attempted several of *Betterton's* Parts, as *Alexander, Jaffier, &c.* but lost his Credit; as, in *Alexander*, he maintain'd not the Diginty [*sic*] of a King, but *Out-Heroded* HEROD; and in his poison'd mad Scene, out *rav'd all Probability*."[86] Powell was not alone in his out-Heroding. Milward "could not often distinguish noise from passion, and ranting from sensibility."[87] Nor apparently could the audiences, for Robert Wilkes complained in 1730, "the Taste in general is so depraved, that there is little or no applause to be gained in Tragedy, but at the expence of lungs."[88]

Dr. Johnson defined the declamatory style as "a kind of rant, with which the players run on, without regard either to accent or emphasis."[89] Davies speaks of the strong emphasis which Quin stamped on almost every word in a line, and again, of his manner of "heaving up his words."[90] And John Hill describes it as "that unmeaning recitation, that unnatural and monotonous delivery which too many of our second rate players have fallen into."[91] The tender passions were designated by "turgid vociferation or effeminate whine," the heroic by "outra-

geous and unnatural rants.''[92] Nor was any distinction made by the
ranter as to the nature of the part he was playing.

> How oft a *buskin* doth a message bring,
> Stalking along as tho' himself were king; . . .
> In the same scene, see *kings* debase the stage,
> With speech and action that might suit a *page*.
>   THO' some there are, adorn'd with regal vest,
> Scorn to be less than that for which they're drest,
> So speak full three times louder than the rest; . . .
>   YET these are fav'rites of the thoughtless croud,
> Who wisely judge they're great, because they're loud.[93]

The poet is echoed by John Hill: "There was a time indeed when
every thing in tragedy, if it was but the delivering a common message,
was spoken in high heroics."[94] This false and unnatural style of delivery was so intrenched in the actors of the interregnum between Betterton and Garrick that as late as 1744, the retired Cibber was attempting to persuade Mrs. Pritchard to *"tone* her words," as Lady Constance
in *Papal Tyranny*.[95]

He had, however, chosen the wrong pupil, for Mrs. Pritchard was
already taking over, because of her "natural and easy dialogue," the
characters formerly in the possession of Mrs. Horton—who stood for
everything Cibber was attempting to teach.[96] Rant never left the stage,
but a reformation had taken place sometime after the retirement of
Cibber which affected the acting style and the manner of delivery of
the top-ranking actors, if it had little effect on their subordinates.
Davies claims that the reformation dates from Garrick's initial appearance.

> Mr. Garrick's easy and familiar, yet forcible style in
> speaking and acting, at first threw the critics into some
> hesitation concerning the novelty as well as the propriety
> of his manner. They had long been accustomed to an ele-
> vation of the voice, with a sudden mechanical depression
> of its tones, calculated to excite admiration, and to intrap
> applause. To the just modulation of the words, and con-
> curring expression of the features from the genuine work-
> ings of nature, they had been strangers, at least for some
> time.[97]

It is probable that this reformation of Garrick's, like his reformation
of the acting style, should be credited in part to Macklin, who, as early

as 1730, had been criticized by the managers for speaking too familiarly. Macklin conducted one of the first schools for actors in London and his manner of teaching was observed by Aaron Hill who himself intended to establish a dramatic academy.

> It was his manner to check all the cant and cadence of tragedy; he would bid his pupils first speak the passage as they would in common life, if they had any occasion to pronounce the same words; and then giving them more force, but preserving the same accent, to deliver them on the stage.[98]

Breaking the tones of utterance, or modulation, now became the favored method of delivery, declamation was completely out of critical favor.

> 'TIS not enough the *Voice* be sound and clear,
> 'Tis Modulation that must charm the Ear.
> When desperate Heroines grieve with tedious Moan,
> And whine their Sorrows in a see-saw Tone;
> The same soft Sounds of unimpassioned Woes
> Can only make the yawning Hearers doze.[99]

It is not to be supposed that even the most "easy and familiar" speaker permitted himself to become inaudible. On the contrary, John Hill found it necessary to caution not only the minor actor—Walker, Delane, Ryan—against overstraining his voice "when the circumstances of his part make it necessary that he should be vehement," but also David Garrick himself. "When in *Richard* he cry'd out to *Richmond, Richard is hoarse with calling thee to battle,* the audience was so sensible of the truth of the expression, that they cou'd scarce distinguish the sounds that conveyed it to them."[100]

It is probably safe to conclude, in the light of the available evidence, that at no time was theatrical speech in the eighteenth century wholly natural. Natural speech was demanded neither by the plays nor the spectators. From Betterton to Kemble a certain amount of exaggeration, whether it be cadence, rant, modulation, or vocal claptraps, was countenanced and even demanded not only by the audience but by the critics. Rant alone the critics decried, yet Macklin himself admitted that it had its uses.

> It is certain that the players ought very carefully to avoid a too lofty and sonorous delivery when a sentiment only,

not a passion, is to be express'd: it ought also, as the
excellent instructor just mention'd us'd eternally to be in-
culcating into his pupils, to be always avoided when a
simple recital of facts was the substance of what was to
be spoken, or when pure and cool reasoning was the sole
meaning of the scene: but tho' he banish'd noise and
vehemence on these occassions, he allow'd that on many
others, the pompous and sounding delivery were just,
nay were necessary in this species of playing, and that no
other manner of pronouncing the words was fit to ac-
company the thought the author expressed by them, or
able to convey it to the audience in its intended and
proper dignity.[101]

Cato and Comus are the particular examples cited in which swelling
delivery is required, but in actual practice even a "domestic" tragedy
like The Gamester was able to provide Mrs. Siddons with opportunities
for effects which a critic with fine restraint has declared might be somewhat overpowering for a modern audience.[102]

IV

During the period of the Restoration and for many years thereafter
actor were trained as they had been in the days of Shakespeare, by their
elders in the profession. Occasionally the company manager or some
theatrical amateur would undertake the direction of the tyro. Betterton and Cibber were most particular about the instruction of begin-
ners and Macklin established a school for the propagation of his
principles.

As the century progressed toward Garrick, however, the amateur
became more and more vocal, expressing his views about actors and
their art not only in the playhouses but in the public prints. Mr.
Bickerstaffe frequently called his reader's attention to the technical
side of the actors' performance as well as to the critical aspects of the
play, and The Gentleman's Magazine reprints with increasing frequency instructive notes on the art from other periodicals.[103] It was
not long before the first of a long series of actor's handbooks made its
appearance, credited, significantly enough, to a great actor, but actually ghost-written. In the fifty years from 1741 to 1790 nearly twenty
of these (for the most part small) volumes were published.

A good deal is to be learned from these handbooks not only of the

philosophy of acting and of the principles which the authors were
attempting to graft onto the practical theater, but of the practical
theater itself. The same caution must be observed in reading them that
is observed in reading the critics and historians. Ample allowance must
be made for prejudices, for over-zealous devotion to a "philosophy,"
for too close adherence to the ancient writers. In very few instances
are the authors connected with the professional stage. With these limitations in mind, an examination of the precepts of the theatrical
teachers of this half century will possibly help to clarify for present
day students the eighteenth-century attitude toward acting and, by
defining the actor's approach, enable them to understand his practice.

A consensus of the handbooks reveals considerable unanimity about
most of the fundamental requirements of the actor. John Hill lists the
qualities of a stage player as Understanding (which "governs the
helm, . . . directs the whole fabric, and calculates and marks out its
course") ,[104] Sensibility ("a disposition to be affected by the passions,
which are the subjects of dramatic writing") ,[105] Fire, Distinguished
Figure ("We have had very few instances in *England,* in which an actor has been able to make his way to applause in the higher characters
without personal charms") ,[106] Gaiety of Temper in Comedians (" 'Tis
only by thoroughly relishing the comedy in their own breasts that they
can ever represent it feelingly to us, or acquire our applause by it") ,[107]
Elevated Souls in Heroes, Natural Amorousness in Lovers (for imitated passions may deceive audiences, but not the passion of love) .[108]

About the subjects of the actor's preliminary study, also, there is
fundamental agreement. He should be familiar with "the ancient Poets
for the true characters of ancient heroes."[109] the tragedies and epics to

> Learn thence the passions—learn from ev'ry page
> The action, speech, that dignifie the stage.[110]

He should study the ancient orations,[111] and moral philosophy to learn
manners and passions.[112] "A knowledge of grammar, beside detecting
the ignorance and mistakes of transcribers, will likewise teach an actor
to detect the lapses of authors themselves, who, from being too warmly
engaged in the main design, will sometimes commit the greatest in-
accuracies."[113] In addition, Wilkes declares the necessity of an acquaintance with the languages of all nations ancient and modern.[114] A
knowledge of the manners and customs of all nations should be part
of the actor's equipment,[115] including polite life in his own coun-

try,[116] religious ceremonies, triumphs, processions, and costume.[117] This knowledge the actor is to acquire from a study of history-painting and sculpture. "I cannot conclude this Article," wrote Pickering, "without recommending to those who attempt to succeed *Capitally* upon the Stage, the Study of the best *Painting, Statues,* and *Prints,* many of which may be inspected upon easy Terms."[118] Betterton pointed out that "The studying History-Painting would be very useful . . . , because the knowledge of the Figure and Lineaments of the Persons represented will teach the Actor to vary and change his Figure."[119] Cooke recommends specific statues as of especial value. Male aspirants should study the two Antinouses, Hercules Farnese, Apollos Belvidere and de Medici, Caracalla, Fighting and Dying Gladiators. Female tyros should study Venus de Medici, Venus de Calipaedia, Diana, Flora, and The Graces.[120] It is somewhat difficult for the student of today to appreciate the fact that the proper study of mankind is Greek statuary; yet the eighteenth-century teachers could point to an actor of the highest rank who practised what they taught.

> Mr. *Booth's* Attitudes were all picturesque.—He had a good Taste for Statuary and Painting, and where he could not come at original Pictures, he spared no Pains or Expence to get the best Drawings and Prints: These he frequently studied, and sometimes borrowed Attitudes from, which he so judiciously introduced, so finely executed, and fell into them with so easy a Transition, that these Masterpieces of his Art seemed but the Effect of Nature.[121]

Cibber's report of Booth suggests that the dignified stance and graceful posing so frequent in portraits of eighteenth-century actors may be as much due to the actor's study of ancient sculpture as to the artist's natural tendency to paint in that style. At any rate, the modern reader is hardly surprised at Wilkes' statement that the English stage has produced but ten first rank actors in fifty years. Considering the equipment which the teachers felt necessary, it is a wonder that there was more than one, inasmuch as dancing, fencing, and an intimate knowledge of nature are also required.[122] Perhaps Hiffernan, although farther from the ideal, approaches the real when he declares

> Although learning cannot hurt, but rather assist; yet no more is to be insisted upon than a tolerable share of instruction at some of our reputable schools, or by private

study under a judicious guide. An undeniable proof in
support of this assertion are the many celebrated actresses
in this and all other countries, and ages, wherein dramatic exhibitions have flourished.[123]

Since the passions are the subjects of dramatic writing, it is not surprising that large sections of the guidebooks are devoted to their delineation. Occasionally the approach to the delineation of a passion is
"scientific," including a theory of origin and a table of relationship and
relative intensities, but more often it consists of a simple recipe which
any amateur, provided with a mirror (as actually recommended by
Betterton), could follow.

The most "scientific" approach was that of Aaron Hill. In *The
Prompter* he analyzed the passions into six "primaries," Joy, Sorrow,
Fear, Scorn, Anger, Amazement. The "secondaries" formed on these
were Jealousy, Revenge, Love, and Pity.[124] Upon mature consideration,
however, he admitted the secondaries to primary rank. "At first, it
should be noted, that there are only *ten* dramatic passions; that is, passions which can be distinguished by their outward marks, in action; all
others being relative to, and but varied degrees of, the foregoing."[125]
To accomplish the portrayal of any passion Hill presents the following
formula:

> *First,* the imagination must conceive a *strong idea* of the
> passion.
> *Secondly,* But the idea cannot *strongly* be conceived,
> without impressing its own form upon the muscles of
> the *face.*
> *Thirdly,* Nor *can* the look be muscularly stamped, with-
> out communicating, instantly, the same impressions to
> the muscles of the *body.*
> *Fourthly,* The muscles of the body (braced or slack, as
> the idea was an active or passive one), must, in their
> natural, and not-to-be-avoided consequence, by im-
> pelling or retarding the flow of animal spirits, trans-
> mit their own conceived sensation to the sound of the
> *voice,* and the disposition of the *gesture.*[126]

Simple as the formula is, however, Hill cautions the would-be actor
that, "the happiest Qualification which a *Player* should desire to be
Master of, is a *plastic Imagination.*"[127]

The application of the formula to the several passions is fully developed in *An Essay on the Art of Acting,* a restatement of Hill's theories earlier laid down in *The Prompter.* A passion chosen from the basic ten will illustrate the author's treatment.

> When the actor has discovered, that the passion in this place is *joy,* he must not, upon any account, attempt the utterance of one single word, till he has first compelled his fancy to conceive an idea of joy. And it would be his natural, though most difficult way, to endeavour the effacement of all note, or image of himself, and forcibly bind down his fancy to suppose, that he is, really, *Torrismond*—that he is in love with *Leonora,* and has been blessed, beyond his hope, by her kind declaration in his favor.
>
> But there is a shorter road to the same end. . . . When he believes himself possessed of such an idea of joy, . . . let him not imagine the impression rightly hit, till he has examined both his face and air, in a long, upright, looking glass. . . . If . . . he has hit the conception exactly, he will have the pleasure, in that case, to observe, in the glass, that his forehead appears open, and raised, his eye smiling, and sparkling, his neck will be stretched and erect, without stiffness, as if it would add new height to his stature; his breast will be inflated, and majestically backened; his back-bone erect, and all the joints of his arm, wrist, fingers, hip, knee, and ancle, will be highstrung and braced boldly.[128]

Other teachers were equally explicit. Wilkes gives a long list of passions though without attempting to systematize them. His treatment of admiration (wonder) and its "superlative" degree is typical.

> Simple admiration occasions no very remarkable alteration in the countenance; the eye fixes upon the object; the right-hand naturally extends itself with the palm turned outwards; and the left-hand will share in the action, though so as scarcely to be perceived, not venturing far from the body; but when this surprise reaches the superlative degree, which I take to be astonishment, the whole body is actuated: it is thrown back, with one leg set before the other, both hands elevated, the eyes larger than usual, the brows drawn up, and the mouth not quite shut.[129]

Pickering emphasizes the importance of the leg, or stance, in delineating certain passions.

> In *Astonishment and Surprize,* arising from *Terror,* the *left Leg* is drawn back to some Distance from the other; under the same Affection of the Mind, but resulting from an *unhop'd-for Meeting* with a beloved Object, the *right leg* is advanced to some Distance before the *Left.*
> But *Anger and Threatening* may be strongly supplied with Grand Expressions from these limbs.[130]

Samuel Foote, having systematized the passions into painful and pleasurable ("and in this Sense, all the Passions may be reduced to Love and Hatred, nay perhaps to one, Love; and even that may be altogether resolved into Self-Love, and this into a Principle of Self-Preservation, or necessary invincible Desire of Pleasure or Happiness"),[131] removes his tongue from his cheek and illustrates, as one actor to his fellows, the delineation of Rage:

> the Expression of the Voice and Eyes are quick, and less violent Rage is different from the Extravagance of that Passion; in the first Circumstance, their [*sic*] is a Loudness in the Tone of the Voice, a Rapidity in the Utterance, and a lively Quickness in the Eye; in the last, the Violence and Force of the Passion are curbs to our natural Powers, the Voice is low, but forcible, the Utterance slower, and an extravagant Wildness in the Eye. But in every Degree of this Passion, the Muscles are contracted.[132]

The general rules for the use of gesture on the stage, apart from its use to delineate passions, confirm the evidence of prints and paintings that grace was the essence of the eighteenth-century actor's style, grace even in the midst of the trend toward naturalism. Pickering, whose concern with the use of the legs has been noted above, decries the lack of grace in the average actor's gait:

> The frequent Traverses, and sudden Turnings upon the Stage, make the Management of the *Feet* and *Legs,* no trivial Concern of the Actor. The bombast *Strut,* the diminutive *Trip,* the *unweildy* and *awkward* Movement of the *Feet* in Turnings; the Toes turn'd in, or placed in a strait Line with the Bone of the Leg; will lessen all

the Dignity and Gracefulness of the other Parts of Attitude.[133]

Betterton's concern is with the hands and arms:

> It were to be wished that this Art [of using the hands]
> were a little revived in our own Age, when such useful
> Members, which of old contributed so much to the Ex-
> pression of Words, should now puzzle our Players what
> to do with them, when they seldom or never add any
> Grace to the Action of the Body, and never almost any
> thing to the Explanation or fuller Expression of the
> Words and Passions.[134]

John Hill points out the necessity for decorative, as well as interpre-
tive, gesture:

> In many scenes of tragedy . . . the actor is . . . ex-
> pected not only to use every proper gesture in its utmost
> force, that can mark to the audience any passion, any
> affection of the soul; but he must even have recourse to
> many others which have no regular significance in their
> own nature, and yet serve to keep up the life and spirit
> of the action.[135]

This general insistence upon grace is emphasized in the detailed rules
of gesture laid down by Hiffernan:

> The entire body is to bear firmly on the floor, and not
> to shift its place, or change its attitude every moment,
> which would incur the charge of an unballasted restless-
> ness.
>   There must be a meaning of necessity, or of grace, for
> every diversified direction of the head. . . .
>   The countenance is always to be turned toward the
> speaker, and from the eyes through an escaping look no
> consciousness is to be gathered of any spectators being
> present, even in soliloquies, which are but thinking
> aloud; or in side speaking. . . .
>   Wherefore it follows that the direction of the eyes must
> always illustrate the sense of the words. . . .
>   The duty of the eyebrows is to be neither too sluggishly
> quiescent, nor too wantonly active, but to observe a free,
> easy, and well-timed obsequiousness to the sentimental
> expression of the eyes, which may poetically be called the
> soul of the countenance.[136]

Particular accent upon grace is found in Hiffernan's directions for the
use of the hands and arms.

> The hands are never to be raised above the head, un-
> less upon some very extraordinary occasion, nor veil the
> face, unless when unlucky in expressing grief.
> The arms should . . . enjoy a modulation of move-
> ment, which would banish from our sight all crude be-
> ginnings and abrupt endings of different gestures.[137]

A similar insistence upon grace of delivery is visible in the handbooks. Understanding, and realistic delivery are not enough; "let our
conception of what we are to speak be ever so just, and the ear ever
so true, yet, when we are to deliver it to an audience . . . , there must
go along with the whole, a natural freedom, and becoming grace, which
it is easier to conceive than describe."[138] Cibber illustrates this point by
referring to Eastcourt, an actor of the second rank, who was an amazing mimic off stage, and a thorough student of character in the library,
but was ineffective on stage because he lacked the detachment from his
studied character which would have permitted him to read his lines
with grace and "natural freedom." Hill declares monotony to be the
actor's downfall, monotony stemming not only from lack of modulation in the voice, but from frequent repetition of the same inflexions,
and closing flourishes.[139] In this he is supported by the anonymous poet
of the *Essay on the Stage*, who writes:

> HARD is the task in fetter'd rhime to teach
> The grace of attitude, the art of speech; . . .
> NO affectation can with justice please;
> Your speech be freedom, and your action ease.
> Avoid the habits, and conceit of those,
> Whose constant flourishes each sentence close;
> Nor join with those, who keep still drudging on,
> All parts alike in one continu'd tone:
> Tho' fear should startle, or tho' rage inflame,
> Their periods rise and fall and close the same.
> SOME to do right are ever in the wrong,
> And change their tones as oft as in a song.[140]

To avoid monotony, as Hiffernan points out, a good ear is absolutely
essential,[141] although more than that is required in the rhyming tragedies. Here common sense will lessen the jingling monotony of the
couplets. "Whoever has seen *Hannibal's Overthrow* has found that

some, tho' very good players, and particularly excellent in their characters there, have not the address to keep the unnatural jingle of the
rhyme out of their ears, even in some of the most passionate scenes;
but the subalterns never fail to give it us strong at every tenth syllable,
let the sense fare as it can."[142]

Another word appears side by side with *grace* in most of the acting
textbooks, and with increasing frequency. Wilkes goes so far as to make
it almost synonymous with grace. "The beauty of all action consists in
its ease and freedom; that is, making it appear to be the natural consequence of that passion, humour, or sentiment, with which the Actor is
supposed to be animated at that juncture."[143] The phrase, "appear to
be," is worth noting for it is soon to disappear from the books. When
Aston, writing of Mrs. Verbruggen, could say approvingly, "She was all
art, and her acting all acquired, but she dressed it so nice, it looked
like nature; there was not a look, a motion, but what were all designed; and these at the same word, period, incident, were every night
in the same character alike, and yet all sat charmingly upon the ear,"[144]
Wilkes speaks of one, not an "actor of genius," who "in lifting, holding
up his hand, standing still, &c. always to a second of time, observes the
same movements."[145] Theatricus Automaton, as quoted above, was
later in the century to attack Mrs. Siddons violently for her studied
business and movement on the stage. Indeed, in 1788, a verse writer
flings caution, rules, and his predecessors in actor-training to the winds
and advocates nature as the sole guide for the player.

> Think not, by rules, I would a pow'r impart
> Which scorns the trammels of fastidious Art,
> Direct thee when to clasp thy hands with grace,
> To beat thy bosom, and avert thy face,
> To gaze with love, with sternness frown severe,
> To shake with mirth, or drop the artful tear.
> Rules heap'd on rules too oft our play'rs confess,
> Rules heap'd on rules their native pow'rs oppress.
> Thou scorn them all;—yet would'st thou wish to find
> One leading precept to direct thy mind,
> This maxim keep, forsaking all beside,
> *Tho' Art may curb, let* NATURE *be thy guide:*
> So shalt thou rise superior to controul,
> While Passion's tumults agitate thy soul.[146]

Thus smooth was the way prepared for Edmund Kean.

It is of some interest to observe how closely the eighteenth-century actor followed nature. To what extent, for example, did he lose himself in the character he was portraying? Hart, the older contemporary of the rising Betterton, observed that "it is impossible to act with grace except that the actor has forgot that he is before an audience."[147] Betterton is dogmatic: "An Actor . . . must transform himself into every person he represents, since he is to act all sorts of Actions and Passions."[148] According to Davies, Ben Johnson the player, was "of all comedians, the chastest, and closest observer of nature. Johnson never seemed to know that he was before an audience."[149] Milward, although not a player of first rank, declared, "in several of his Parts, a careful attention to the Speeches that were address'd to him, hardly ever failed of bringing him to feel Emotion altogether as strong and affecting as those of Nature on the same Occasions; and that sometimes *real Tears* made the Application of an Handkerchief absolutely necessary to him."[150]

The teachers, too, were of the common opinion that the first rank actor loses himself in his character. "A Man who suffers himself to remember that he is a *Player* upon the *Stage,* must in that Instant be *out,* and the Audience will *see it,* whether he *perceives it* or not."[151] "The player," says Hill, "is never to lose sight of this great point, that his private sentiments and character are to be hid behind those of the character he portrays."[152] With one accord the teachers imitate the famous Horatian pronouncement (*si vis me flere*), and there is little variation in their words. Wilkes: "Unless he [the Actor] himself be affected with what he says and does, he cannot hope to inspire the beholders with sympathetic feelings."[153] Hill: "To feel the passions we are to point out to others, is certainly a necessary first step to perfection in playing."[154] And Riccoboni: "Declaiming in the *Language of the Soul,* on which the good or bad Success of a Speaker depends . . . is no other than *one's feeling the thing he pronounces.*"[155] Robert Lloyd sums up the attitude of the preceptors after paying tribute to Knowledge of Nature as the actor's sole art:

> To this one Standard make your just Appeal
> Here lies the golden Secret; learn to FEEL.
> Or Fool or Monarch, happy or distrest,
> No Actor pleases that is not *possess'd.*[156]

To be possess'd—to forget that he was before an audience—was the actor's ideal. Actually, however, the relationship between actor and audience was more intimate than this oft repeated principle would suggest.

> THERE is a Fault which stirs the Critic's Rage,
> A Want of due Attention on the Stage.
> There have been Actors, and admir'd ones too,
> Whose tongues wound up set forward from their cue.
> In their own Speech who whine, or roar away,
> Yet unconcern'd at what the rest may say.
> Whose Eyes and Thoughts on diff'rent Objects roam
> Until the Prompter's Voice recall them home.[157]

Betterton points out that it was not merely the supernumeraries who were "regardless of the great Concern of the *Scene*," and who whispered to one another, saluted friends in the pit, or simply gazed about,[158] or, as Wilkes puts it, remained "a mere expletive on the Stage."[159] Some of the actors attempted to screen their inattention to the business of the scene from the audience. Hiffernan exclaims, "how improper in our theatric ladies is all screening of the eyes and countenance behind a fan, in order to take a sly peep around the boxes, to descry if any friends or admirers be there; and learn from their approving looks, if the dear creatures be enraptured with one's acting that night."[160] And some had not the interest to be even so subtle. On Easter Monday, 1763, Mrs. Cibber (chosen by John Hill as the model for all aspiring actors)[161] appeared in *Hamlet*. "During the third act she rose up three several times and made as many courtesies, and those very low ones, to some ladies in the boxes."[162] Hill mentions Ann Barry and Peg Woffington as other actresses who allowed themselves to be distracted,[163] and cautions the beginner that nothing is more difficult than standing for a long time before an audience with nothing to do.[164] Milward's rather naïve acknowledgement that by paying attention to the other speakers in a scene he has been able to experience emotions has been quoted above, and it is significant that a critic thus praises Yates:

> in his silence, happily employ'd
> He looks continual meaning on the void.[165]

From such observations and warnings, covering the entire period, it is safe to conclude that the typical actor of the eighteenth century was not too conscientious about being the thing he represented. At least one actor was frank to admit this to Dr. Johnson, as Boswell reports:

Johnson indeed had thought more on the subject of acting than might generally be supposed. Talking of it one
day to Mr. Kemble, he said, "Are you, sir, one of those
enthusiasts who believe yourself transformed into the
very character you represent?" Upon Mr. Kemble's answering that he never felt so strong a persuasion himself; "To be sure not, sir, (said Johnson) the thing is
impossible. And if Garrick really believed himself to be
that monster, Richard III, he deserved to be hung every
time he performed it."[166]

NOTES

1. John Downes, *Roscius Anglicanus*, ed. M. Summers (London, n.d.) , p. 21.
2. Thomas Davies, *Dramatic Miscellanies* (London, 1785) , III, 288-289.
3. Colley Cibber, *An Apology for his Life* (London: Everyman's Library, n.d.), p. 57.
4. *Ibid.*
5. *Dramatic Miscellanies*, III, 32. A more complete picture of Wilks' style may be made from Davies' observation: "His greatest fault in deport-ment came from his aptness to move or shift his ground. It was said of him by some critic, that he could never stand still" (*Dramatic Miscel-lanies*, III, 41) , and Wilks' own observation (see below) , "that there is little or no applause to be gained in Tragedy, but at the expence of lungs."
6. Davies, *Dramatic Miscellanies*, III, 30.
7. Thomas Davies, *Memoirs of the Life of David Garrick, esq.* (London, 1780) , I, 56.
8. *Boswell's Life of Johnson,* ed. G. B. Hill (Oxford, 1887) , v, 38.
9. Anon., *A Short Criticism on the Performance of Hamlet by Mr. Kemble* (London, 1789) , pp. 12-14.
10. Davies, *Dramatic Miscellanies*, II, 100.
11. *The Theatrical Register* (York, 1788) , p. 52.
12. Although John Hill concludes his treatise with this statement: "Let us acknowledge that among the capital parts of the modern theatre, some ought to be play'd with more truth, others with more spirit, and some with more graces: But let us not deceive ourselves so far as to suppose that there were not grounds for wishes of the same kind in the days of *Wilks,* of *Booth,* and *Betterton.*"—*The Actor* (London, 1750), p. 326.
13. Anthony Aston, *A Brief Supplement to Colley Cibber, esq.* in Watson Nicholson, *Anthony Aston* (South Haven, Mich., 1920) , p. 75.
14. *Ibid.*, pp. 75-77.
15. Robert W. Lowe, *Thomas Betterton* (London, 1891) , p. 86.
16. Aston, *Brief Supplement*, p. 76.
17. *Ibid.,* p. 77.
18. Colley Cibber, *Apology*, p. 212.

19. Aston, *Brief Supplement*, p. 83.

20. *Ibid.*, p. 88.

21. *Ibid.*, p. 79.

22. Thomas Betterton, *The History of the English Stage* (London, 1741), p. 62. There is some question about the authorship of this volume. It is certainly not by Betterton although the section entitled "The Duty of a Player" could have been taken as stated, from his papers. Certain passages are literally quoted from Gildon's *Life of Thomas Betterton* (London, 1710). Lowe (*Thomas Betterton*, p. 125) assigns the authorship to Edmund Curll, the publisher.

23. Colley Cibber, *Apology*, p. 90; John Genest, *Some Account of the English Stage* (Bath, 1832), II, 277.

24. Theophilus Cibber, *The Lives and Characters of the most Eminent Actors and Actresses of Great Britain and Ireland, from Shakespear to the Present Time. Interspersed with a General History of the Stage* (London, 1753), p. 42. In spite of his impressive title page, Cibber never got beyond an epistle to Warburton and a life of Booth.

25. Benjamin Victor, *The History of the Theaters in London and Dublin from the Year 1730 to the Present Time* (London, 1761), II, 12.

26. There are other instances of the employment of the dramatic pause in this period. "Wilks who above fifty years since acted Mark Antony, as soon as he entered the stage, without taking any notice of the conspirators walked swiftly up to the dead body of Caesar and knelt down; he paused some time before he spoke; and, after surveying the corpse with manifest tokens of the greatest sorrow, he addressed it in the most affecting and pathetic manner."—Davies, *Dramatic Miscellanies*, II, 241.

27. *Lives and Characters*, p. 50.

28. *Ibid.*, pp. 50-51. Theophilus Cibber was a fine one to talk!

29. *Dramatic Miscellanies*, I, 397.

30. *Lives and Characters*, pp. 50-51.

31. Robert Lloyd, *The Actor. A Poetical Epistle* (London, 1760), pp. 6-7.

32. *The Poetical Works of Charles Churchill* (London, 1844), I, 37.

33. *Ibid.*, I, 92. *Cf.* the description of Garrick in the same scene (of *Hamlet*) as quoted above.

34. *Ibid.*, I, 103.

35. *Ibid.*, I, 95.

36. *Ibid.*, I, 99-100.

37. *Peregrine Pickle*, Chap. xciv (Everyman's Library ed., 1930, II, 241-242).

38. *Memoirs of Richard Cumberland* (London, 1807), I, 80.

39. *The Actor*, p. 99.

40. Davies, *Dramatic Miscellanies*, III, 502.

41. Genest, *Some Account of the English Stage*, IV, 21. A contemporary estimate of Delane compares him with Quinn: "*D-l-ne* is also esteemed a just Player; and though he has often a more loud Violence of Voice, yet, either from an Imitation of *Q . . . n*, or his own natural Manner, he has a Sameness of Tone and Expression, and drawls out his Lines to a displeasing Length: But that loud Violence of Voice is useful to him when Anger, Indignation, or such enrag'd Passions are to be express'd; for

the shrill Loudness marks the Passion, which the sweet Cadence of
Q . . . n's natural Voice is unequal to."—*An Apology for the Life of
Mr. T . . . . C . . . . , Comedian*, London, 1740, p. 139.
42. Edward Abbott Parry, *Charles Macklin* (London, 1891), p. 21.
43. Davies, *Dramatic Miscellanies*, III, 470. Chetwood presumably joined the
staff of Drury Lane in the season 1722-1723, early enough to become well
acquainted with the older style of acting.
44. Parry, *Charles Macklin*, p. 67.
45. *Poetical Works*, I, 64.
46. *The Actor*, pp. 32-33.
47. Macklin, according to John Taylor, at least in *Macbeth* was not notable
for "studied grace of deportment, but he seemed to be more in earnest
in the character than any actor I have consequently seen." (Parry,
Charles Macklin, p. 161). On the other hand, contemporary prints show
Garrick always in an artistic pose employing a graceful gesture. In an
engraving after Isaac Taylor, by T. Lowndes, published 3 August, 1776,
Garrick is seen as Tancred in *Tancred and Sigismunda* as he cries:

Earl Osmond's wife
Heavens! and did I hear thee right? marry'd? marry'd!
Lost to thy faithful Tancred! Lost for ever!   (4.2)

The actor's countenance is grieving but not writhing. From the position
of his cloak he must have turned suddenly towards the lady. Both arms
are extended, the hands out, the left above the right, and the fingers of
the right hand are spread, with the palm down; the knees are slightly
bent, feet carefully apart, the right foot somewhat advanced.

Another engraving, published by J. Wenman, 1 August, 1778, shows
Garrick as Demetrius in *The Brothers* reading the lines:

I prefer
Death at your feet, before the world without you.   (2.1)

The actor faces stage right. His face is set, his feet arranged as in the
scene from *Tancred*. His right hand is raised head high, his left extended
before his waistline, both palms out. A later line in the same play,

Necessity, for Gods themselves too strong, is weaker than thy charms
(5.3)

shows Garrick with his left hand on his breast, his right flung out dropping a dagger, and his head averted from a female on his left; his face
is pained but there is no exaggeration in the pose. (Published by T.
Lowndes, 11 October, 1777.)

As Benedict crying,
Ha the Prince and Mons. Beau! I will hide me in the arbor.   (2.2)

Garrick is depicted leaning slightly to stage right, both knees somwhat
bent, legs and feet gracefully apart; his left arm, crooked at the elbow,
is raised shoulder high; the forefinger of his left hand rests at his nose.
His right hand stretches forward, with the palm down, to balance the
pose. (Published by J. Wenman, 1 July, 1778).

Perhaps the most revealing of all the prints is undated and to be
identified only by its title, "Mr. Garrick in Four of his Principal Tragic
Characters." Here is easily observed in such widely differing roles as Lear,

Macbeth, Richard III, and Hamlet, the emphasis upon grace of attitude, stance, and gesture. (In the Harvard College Theater Collection.) The difference between an actor of the Garrick school and Macklin is readily observed in an illustration chosen by G. C. O'Dell (*Shakespeare from Betterton to Irving*, New York, 1920, I, 370). Macklin, as Shylock, is surrounded by the other members of the cast in various statuesque poses, but he himself is quite devoid of "studied grace."

48. *David Garrick*, II, 99-100.

49. Samuel Foote, *A Treatise on the Passions, so far as they regard the stage, with a critical Enquiry into the Theatrical Merit of Mr. G——K, Mr. Q——N, and Mr. B——Y* (London, n.d.), p. 18. There is a curious attempt to take down Garrick's manner of reading Hamlet's famous soliloquy in Joshua Steele's *Prosodia Rationalis: or an Essay towards establishing the measure and melody of speech* (London, 1779), pp. 39-48. The reading of an older actor (Mossop?) is first given. It would be pleasant to be able to report that the modern reader can at last reproduce exactly Garrick's way with a soliloquy but the system of recording is intolerably complicated, and too many of the qualities of an actor are impossible of transcription. Steele's notation tells us little that we could not gather from the contemporary critics cited above.

50. Genest, *Some Account*, IV, 468.

51. *The Actor*, pp. 171-172.

52. Thomas Wilkes, *A General View of the Stage* (London, 1759), pp. 234-235.

53. Genest, *Some Account*, IV, 14.

54. (London, 1744). For proof of authorship see Davies, *David Garrick*, I, 163-164.

55. P. 17.

56. *Poetical Works*, I, 106.

57. *A Treatise on the Passions*, p. 24.

58. Churchill, *Poetical Works*, I, 13 n.

59. It is possible that she was somewhat overawed by Roscius. Thomas Campbell, in his *Life of Mrs. Siddons* (London, 1839), relates the story of their appearance in *Richard the Third*, concluding, "Garrick's acting that night must have been startling. From what his contemporaries have said of it, we may guess that his impressiveness bordered upon excess. He made the galleries often laugh when he intended that they should shudder" (p. 41).

60. Campbell, *Mrs. Siddons*, p. 117.

61. See, among others, Helen Ormsbee, *Backstage with Actors* (New York, 1938), p. 102.

62. *Macready's Reminiscences, and Selections from his Diaries and Letters*, ed. by Sir Frederick Pollock (London, 1875), I, 5.

63. *The Attic Miscellany; or Characteristic Mirror of Men and Things* (London, 1789), I, 88. Cf. Mrs. Siddon's declaration that applauses in the midst of scenes "are really necessary, in order to give one breath and voice to carry one on through some violent exertions."—Campbell, *Mrs. Siddons*, p. 142.

64. A copy in The Harvard College Library is identified as from *The Carleton House Magazine*.
65. *Attic Miscellany*, I, 156.
66. Anon., *The Modern Stage Exemplified* (London, 1788), p. 10.
67. *Ibid.*
68. *Macready's Reminiscences*, I, 55-56.
69. *Ibid.*, I. 57. Young, an actor who admired Mrs. Siddons as genuinely as Macready did and who was more nearly her contemporary, declared that "She never sought by unworthy means to entrap her audience. She disdained to apply to any of the petty resources of trickish minds, in order to startle or surprise her hearers. There was no habitual abruptness, no harshness about her. You never caught her slumbering through some scenes, in order to produce, by contrast, an exaggerated effect in others." (Campbell, p. 371). It is interesting to compare this statement with Young's description of the actress in *Coriolanus* (Campbell, p. 250), or Bartley's in *The Earl of Warwick* (Campbell, p. 158). When Bartley speaks of her entrance ("the giantess burst upon the view"), and of her "fine smile of appalling triumph," and confesses that he was struck breathless, the modern reader may be permitted to wonder whether there may not have been some small application to the resources of trickery to startle and surprise the audience.
70. *The Attic Miscellany*, I, 407.
71. Published in J. Bell's *British Library*, 1 June, 1792.
72. In the Harvard College Library.
73. *Modern Stage Exemplified*, p. 23.
74. *Some Account*, IV, 311.
75. London, 1716, p. vi.
76. *Brief Supplement*, p. 79.
77. P. 16.
78. *David Garrick*, I, 310.
79. *The Provok'd Husband* (London, 1727), Dedication.
80. *Ed. cit.*, p. 62.
81. *The Fairy Queen: an Opera* (London, 1692), Preface, sig. A 4.
82. *History of the English Stage*, p. 46.
83. *Lives and Characters*, p. 44.
84. Mrs. Cibber, the unfortunate wife of Theophilus, clung to the older tradition of cadenced speech in the heyday of Garrick. "As *Calista*, Mrs. Cibber sang, or at least recitatived, Rowe's harmonious strain in a key high-pitched, yet sweet withal, something in the manner of the *Improvisatore*." (Campbell, *Mrs. Siddons*, p. 75.) According to Boucicault, who was perhaps wiser in theatrical tradition than in theatrical history, this was the common style of the day: "the great English tragedians before Kean used their treble voice—the teapot style. They did it as if they played on the flute."—*The Art of Acting* (New York, 1926), p. 29.
85. No. 40 (16 April, 1711).
86. *Brief Supplement*, p. 77.
87. Davies, *David Garrick*, I, 26.
88. Wilkes, *General View of the Stage*, p. 108, *n*.

89. *Boswell's Life of Johnson,* ed. cit., I, 168.
90. *David Garrick,* I, 98; I, 40.
91. *The Actor,* p. 193.
92. Wilkes, *General View of the Stage,* p. 107.
93. Anon., *An Essay on the Stage, or the Art of Acting. A Poem* (Edinburgh, 1754) , pp. 7-8.
94. *The Actor,* p. 194.
95. Davies, *Dramatic Miscellanies,* I, 41.
96. *Ibid.,* I, 186.
97. *David Garrick,* I, 40.
98. Genest, *Some Account,* IV, 76.
99. Lloyd, *The Actor,* pp. 9-10.
100. *The Actor,* pp. 46-49.
101. *Ibid.,* pp. 194-195.
102. A. W. Ward in *The Encyclopedia Britannica* (eleventh ed., Cambridge, 1910) , VIII, 532.
103. See, for ex., III, 6, 67; IV, 593; V, 197, 314, 315, 730, etc.
104. *The Actor,* p. 7.
105. *Ibid.,* p. 14.
106. *Ibid.,* p. 53.
107. *Ibid.,* p. 93.
108. *Ibid.,* p. 122.
109. Betterton, *op. cit.,* p. 49.
110. *An Essay on the Stage,* p. 5.
111. William Cooke, *The Elements of Dramatic Criticism* (London, 1775) , p. 188.
112. Betterton, *op. cit.,* p. 50.
113. Cooke, *op. cit.,* p. 183.
114. *General View of the Stage,* p. 83.
115. *Ibid.*
116. Roger Pickering, *Reflections upon Theatrical Expression in Tragedy* (London, 1760) , p. 20.
117. Cooke, *op. cit.,* p. 188.
118. *Op. cit.,* p. 38.
119. *Op. cit.,* pp. 87-88.
120. *Op. cit.,* pp. 200-201.
121. T. Cibber, *Lives and Characters,* p. 51. Mrs. Siddons was also a student of the art of the sculptor to improve her "taste in drapery and attitude."—Campbell, *Mrs. Siddons,* p. 254.
122. *An Essay on the Stage,* p. 5; Wilkes, p. 92; Hiffernan, p. 118; Pickering, pp. 19-20; Cooke, pp. 179, 190.
123. Paul Hiffernan, M.D., *Dramatic Genius, in Five Books* (London, 1770) , p. 73.
124. *The Gentleman's Magazine,* V, (1735) , 314.
125. Aaron Hill, *An Essay on the Art of Acting; in which the Dramatic Passions are Properly Defined and Described, with Applications of the Rules peculiar to each and Selected Passages for Practice* (London, 1779) , p. 11.

126. *Ibid.*, p. 10.
127. *The Gentleman's Magazine, loc. cit.*
128. Pp. 12-15.
129. *General View of the Stage*, p. 118.
130. *Reflections on Theatrical Expression*, p. 31. In the first instance he is referring to Hamlet and the Ghost; in the second to Oroonoko and Imoinda.
131. *Treatise on the Passions*, pp. 11-12.
132. *Ibid.*, p. 12.
133. *Reflections on Theatrical Expression*, p. 31.
134. *History of the English Stage*, p. 69. "You must never," he cautions, "let either of your Hands hang down, as if lame or dead. . . . Your arms you should not stretch out side-ways, above half a Foot from the Trunk of your Body," since the hands must always be in "View of your Eyes." *(Ibid.*, p. 103) . It is worth noting that much of the material of Betterton's *History* including these instructions is taken from Charles Gildon's *Life of Betterton* (London, 1710) . Since the instructions as to the use of the arms and hands coincide with Aston's report of Betterton's actual practice, quoted above, it seems entirely possible that they may have been, as *The History* declares, found among the actor's papers.
135. *The Actor*, p. 177.
136. *Dramatic Genius*, p. 79.
137. *Ibid.*, p. 118.
138. Colley Cibber, *Apology*, p. 64.
139. *The Actor*, p. 197.
140. Pp. 9-10.
141. *Dramatic Genius*, p. 78.
142. Hill, *The Actor*, p. 191. Hill quotes this *Tag* from *The Orphan*,
    To his temptation lewdly she inclin'd
    Her soul, and for an apple damn'd mankind.
This tag was "for a long time deliver'd, by successive players, with such a religious observance of the rhyme, that there was almost as absolute a stop at the end of one of the lines, as at that of the other"—p. 192.
143. *General View of the Stage*, p. 114. "However, the general criteria of the *truly beautiful* of acting in *comedy*, as well as the *truly sublime* of acting in *tragedy*, consists in the performers appearing to be the very characters they represent."—Hiffernan, *Dramatic Genius*, p. 99.
144. Genest, *Some Account*, II, 277.
145. *General View of the Stage*, p. 152.
146. *The Modern Stage Exemplified*, p. 2.
147. *The Tatler*, no. 138.
148. *History of the English Stage*, p. 48.
149. *David Garrick*, I, 30.
150. Pickering, *Reflections on Theatrical Expression*, p. 54. Actors have always disputed the virtue of the ability to produce Real Tears during a performance. Betterton remembered Mrs. Barry's declaration that "she never spoke these Words in the *Orphan—Ah! poor* CASTALIO!— without weeping." (*History of the English Stage*, p. 55) . John Hill, on

the other hand, felt that Spranger Barry's real tears in Sciolto did not make his performance any more convincing. According to Hill, an actor needs not only to *feel*, but to know the *tricks* to express that feeling. (*The Actor*, pp. 41 *ff*.)

151. *The Gentleman's Magazine*, XIII (1743), 254, quoting from *The Champion*.
152. *The Actor*, p. 95.
153. *General View of the Stage*, p. 83.
154. *The Actor*, p. 40.
155. Lewis Riccoboni, *An Historical and Critical Account of the Theatres in Europe* (London, 1741), p. 25. Diderot, whose work falls outside the scope of this essay, would of course have made short labor of Riccoboni, Hill, *et al*. As a matter of fact, the work to which he replied in his famous *Paradoxe* was a French translation (*Garrick: ou les acteurs anglais*) of John Hill's *The Actor*. I do not believe that it has been previously noted that Hill's work was in turn in part a translation of Remond de Sainte-Albine, *Le Comédien*. Hill makes only a middling kind of acknowledgement to Ste.-Albine in his Preface.
156. *The Actor*, p. 4.
157. *Ibid.*, pp. 13-14.
158. *History of the English Stage*, p. 51.
159. *General View of the Stage*, p. 155.
160. *Dramatic Genius*, p. 81.
161. *The Actor*, pp. 183-184.
162. *The Theatrical Review, or Annals of the Drama* (London, 1763), p. 213.
163. *The Actor*, pp. 26-27.
164. *Ibid.*, p. 255.
165. Hugh Kelly, *Thespis: or a Critical Examination into the Merit of the Principal Performers belonging to Drury-Lane Theatre* (London, 1766), p. 15.
166. *E.l. cit.*, IV, 243-244.